D0058689

THE FEDERAL RESERVE SYSTEM

THE FEDERAL RESERVE SYSTEM

★ ★ ★ ★ ★ ★——————————————————————

Herbert V. Prochnow, EDITOR

*Vice President, The First National Bank of
Chicago*

HARPER & BROTHERS, PUBLISHERS, NEW YORK

*HG
2563
.P7*

THE FEDERAL RESERVE SYSTEM

Copyright © 1960, by Herbert V. Prochnow
Printed in the United States of America
All rights in this book are reserved.
No part of the book may be used or reproduced
in any manner whatsoever without written permission except in the case of brief quotations
embodied in critical articles and reviews. For
information address Harper & Brothers
49 East 33rd Street, New York 16, N. Y.
C-K

Library of Congress catalog card number: 60-6767

CONTENTS

v

80093

List of Contributors

E. Sherman Adams, Deputy Manager, Department of Monetary Policy, The American Bankers Association, New York City; former Assistant Vice Chancellor and Lecturer in Finance, New York University

Clay J. Anderson, Economic Adviser and Officer, Federal Reserve Bank of Philadelphia; Lecturer in Finance, Wharton School of Commerce, University of Pennsylvania

Jules I. Bogen, Professor of Finance, Graduate School of Business Administration, New York University

George W. Coleman, Economist, Mercantile Trust Company, St. Louis

David C. Elliott, Vice President, The Cleveland Trust Company, Cleveland

Peter G. Fousek, Research Department, Federal Reserve Bank of New York

J. Herbert Furth, Associate Adviser, Division of International Finance, Board of Governors of the Federal Reserve System; Adjunct Professor of Economics, American University, Washington, D.C.

David L. Grove, Vice President and Economist, Bank of America National Trust and Savings Association, San Francisco

Herman E. Krooss, Professor of Economics, Graduate School of Business Administration, New York University

James N. Land, Senior Vice President, Mellon National Bank and Trust Company, Pittsburgh

David H. McKinley, Associate Dean, College of Business Administration, Pennsylvania State University

Gordon W. McKinley, Executive Director of Economic and Investment Research, Prudential Insurance Company of America

THOMAS O. WAAGE, Assistant Vice President, Federal Reserve Bank of New York

CHARLS E. WALKER, Vice President and Economic Adviser, Federal Reserve Bank of Dallas (presently on leave as Assistant to the Secretary of the Treasury)

MABLE T. WALLICH and HENRY T. WALLICH, Professor of Economics, Yale University (presently on leave as a member of the President's Council of Economic Advisers); former Assistant to the Secretary of the Treasury

CHRISTOPHER W. WILSON, Vice President and General Counsel, The First National Bank of Chicago

C. RICHARD YOUNGDAHL, Vice President, Aubrey G. Lanston & Co., Inc.; former Assistant Director, Division of Research and Statistics, Board of Governors of the Federal Reserve System

PREFACE

WITH each succeeding year the Federal Reserve System has occupied an increasingly significant role in the American economy. Today a knowledge of the major functions and methods of operation of the System is almost imperative for businessmen, bankers, and students of the nation's economic life.

An understanding of the Federal Reserve System—the central bank of the United States—necessarily requires some familiarity with the reasons for its establishment and the history of its development. With this background of knowledge one can understand better the instruments of general and selective credit control which play so large a part not only in the operations of the System but also in the American economy.

Among the subjects of this book are the history of the Federal Reserve System, a description of the System's functions and methods of operation, and evaluation of its place in our financial and business structure, and an analysis of its impact on banks and other types of financial institutions, as well as its relation to the American economy generally. The book also includes a discussion of the international aspects of the System's operations.

In addition, there may be readers who would like at least a basic knowledge of how the central banking systems of other nations function. To make the book reasonably comprehensive in this respect also, the final chapter analyzes the essential characteristics of the central banking systems of other nations and compares them to the Federal Reserve System.

The contributing authors bring a thorough understanding of the System. In addition, many of them have a special competency in specific aspects of the System's operations. In order to bring broad experience and knowledge to the book, the authors were chosen from the universities, the Federal Reserve System, and private banks and financial institutions.

Each author has been given complete freedom of expression, and the views he presents are his own and not necessarily those of the institution with which he may be associated. Each assumes responsibility only for the chapter he has written. In any instances where some of the authors may have opposing points of view, these views are retained in the book with the thought that they may be of interest to the reader. Furthermore, where there may be differences of opinion on a subject, each author has been encouraged to present the different sides of the discussion so the reader will understand the problem fully.

If the book is helpful to businessmen, bankers, attorneys, accountants, university students, and others who would like to understand the Federal Reserve System and the vital role it plays in the American economy, it will have served its purpose.

HERBERT V. PROCHNOW

Chicago, Illinois
July 19, 1959

INTRODUCTION

THE Federal Reserve Act of 1913 is one of the most significant legislative acts dealing with finance and banking in the history of the nation. The central banking system which it established has now been in operation for approximately one-half century, and its impact has been felt in almost every important segment of American economic life. The operations of the Federal Reserve System have expanded substantially over the years, and the System has come to have a far greater influence in the economy than perhaps even the most far-sighted bankers, businessmen, government officials, and economists had originally anticipated.

However, despite the large role which the System now plays in our economy, its organization, functions, powers, and operations are not well understood by most of the American people. Even in those fields of economic activity most directly affected by the operations of the System, there is not infrequently evidence of a lack of understanding of the purpose of the System, its proper functions, and its precise workings. A widespread lack of public knowledge of the operations of the System may reflect the mistaken belief that this subject is far too complex and technical for most laymen.

This inadequate public understanding of the Federal Reserve System is unfortunate. It undoubtedly leads some persons to look hopefully to the System to correct weaknesses in our economy over which actually it may have little or no control. The failure to appreciate the vast achievements of the System since its establishment also leads to underestimating the role that it may play in the growth and stability of the nation's economic life. In addition, the absence of widespread knowledge of at least the fundamental functions of the System, and of what may properly be expected from it, sometimes results in uninformed criticism and in unwise demands being made upon it. The System provides no magic formulas or monetary panaceas for the painless correction of maladjustments resulting from the economic excesses of individuals and governments or from unwise fiscal policy.

The System sometimes must make decisions without being able to make a precise evaluation of the magnitude and strength of all the countless and complex forces that determine the trend of the nation's economy. The information at hand may be incomplete or there may be a considerable lag before the statistics relating to important economic events are available for the record. Timeliness in recognizing changing trends when statistical information may lag makes decisions of monetary policy exceedingly difficult. Federal Reserve authorities are engaged in an endless search for all the economic forces which have a bearing on current trends and for the most accurate evaluation of these forces.

Psychological considerations also invariably help to determine the decisions of millions of individual consumers, and these decisions may be determinative factors in the direction the economy is to move. They are certain to have an impact upon monetary policy. However, measurements of anticipated consumer decisions are still relatively hazardous economic undertakings. There are likewise other major domains of our economic life where there is a need for far more statistical information and for a refinement of the figures presently available.

There has unquestionably been a vast expansion and a commendable improvement in accuracy in the statistical information which is at the disposal of the Federal Reserve authorities as the basis for making decisions. However, public psychology, political activities, inadequate information, and international instability are only a few of the many factors that may make decisions on monetary policy difficult to arrive at with assurance. At what point has a business boom gone too far? Which instruments of credit control should be used, and to what extent? When is the money market too tight, too easy? At what precise point should the Federal Reserve authorities seek to prevent or moderate a possible decline in business? How reliable at any given time are each of the economic indices by which these decisions are made? These are only a small number of the many perplexing questions which confront those who have the responsibility for monetary policy.

The officials of the System are also confronted with pressures from both the private and government sectors of the economy. These officials must objectively analyze these pressures to determine whether any of them have merit, and they must refuse to yield to those which seek to benefit some segments of the economy at the expense of others. These are not easy assignments. They require a high degree of intellectual competency, a thorough understanding of central banking, and not infrequently the courage to act decisively in the face of criticism. In times of an inflationary business boom, for example, there are always those who plead for easy money and low interest rates, although sound monetary policy and the best interests of the nation may require a tighter money market and higher interest rates. To yield to such pleas results only in greater maladjustments in the economy and finally in the necessity for more drastic monetary action.

Those who have managed the Federal Reserve System in the course of its history have unquestionably made some policy decisions which would have been made better today. When one considers all the perplexing and bewildering monetary and fiscal problems that resulted from two world wars, the depression of the 1930's, the Korean hostilities, and a cold war crowded into the years since the System was established, the record of accomplishment has much to commend it. Moreover, during this period, the United States became the leading economic and financial power of the world. The United States did not seek this power and in many ways was not prepared for it. Our private banks were concerned almost exclusively with the banking problems of a domestic economy that was moving forward by vast strides. The Federal Reserve System during at least its early years was engaged to a great extent in correcting those weaknesses which had been revealed in our monetary system before 1913. Facilitating the smooth flow of funds from section to section of the country as the need arose, providing for the rapid negotiation of checks at par, receiving and disbursing funds for the United States Treasury, rediscounting commercial paper, and assuring a more elastic currency were responsibilities which received major attention.

However, it gradually became apparent that while the foregoing activities were not only necessary but also highly important functions of the System, new responsibilities were developing. Today the Federal Reserve System is expected to play an influential role in preventing marked inflationary or deflationary trends in the economy, encouraging economic growth, and also assuring greater economic stability by helping to level out even the lesser upward and downward swings of an historically restless business cycle. It should be emphasized again that regardless of the competency of its management, the System should not be held responsible for the results of unsound economic and fiscal policies which may be pursued in private and public sectors of the economy and over which the System may have little or no control.

As noted earlier, the over-all record of the System's achievements since its establishment has been good. With the growth of its responsibilities and the expansion of its instruments of monetary policy, the System seems destined to have an increasing role in the American economy.

THE FEDERAL RESERVE SYSTEM

Chapter 1

THE HISTORICAL BACKGROUND
OF THE AMERICAN BANKING SYSTEM

THE intricate and sophisticated banking system that we have in the United States today is the result of a long process of historical evolution and transformation, going back not only far into the colonial period, but deep into European history as well. In western Europe, where commerce was relatively far advanced, commercial banks were already old by the fifteenth century, and central banks of issue, like the Bank of Barcelona and the Bank of Genoa, had come into existence around the time that Columbus discovered America. Like modern commercial banks, these early European banks accepted deposits, made loans and discounts, and dealt in commercial paper. They were organized to serve an already thriving business class, and their operations were designed more to facilitate exchange than to supply capital funds. It can be said, therefore, that they resulted more from a plentitude than from a shortage of capital funds.

COLONIAL BANKS

Unlike their European predecessors, banks in the colonies rose from an acute shortage rather than from an oversupply of capital. The colonists had not brought any appreciable amount of wealth with them, and they therefore had to rely for capital on what they could borrow from England or on what they could save from current production. But they could not borrow much from England, and to accumulate capital by saving was a time-consuming process much too slow to satisfy a people impatient to raise their standard of living.

The colonists were well aware that the shortage of capital was the

1

chief obstacle in the way of increasing their standard of living. They
were also of the opinion that money was the same as capital. They
therefore constantly experimented with ways of increasing the money
supply in the belief that this would automatically increase their capital
supply. Eventually, they hit upon a plan for turning their most plentiful resource—land—into money. This they did by the simple expedient of creating banks which printed paper money and loaned it
against mortgages on land. Beginning in 1686, colony after colony
formed such institutions. Although they were called banks, they were
really nothing but "batches of paper money." They were land banks
and little resembled modern commercial banks. Modern banks deal
in bank credit or, in other words, in bank deposits, or what may be
called "checkbook money." They make loans and discounts, thereby
creating deposits. Colonial banks, on the other hand, did no discounting business, nor did they create deposits. Their functions were confined to printing paper money and lending it to landowners on a
long-term basis. What little commercial banking business existed in
the colonies was carried on by merchants like Thomas Hancock, John
Hancock's uncle. They accepted deposits and made loans by discounting thier customers' promissory notes as an incident to their regular
trading business.

THE FIRST COMMERCIAL BANK—THE BANK OF NORTH AMERICA

The first real commercial bank to be formed in the colonies was
the Bank of North America, which opened in Philadelphia in 1782
with a nominal capital of $400,000 and a paid-in capital of $254,000.
Like most of the early commercial banks in the larger cities, it had a
long and successful career until it was absorbed in 1923 by the Pennsylvania Company for Insurance on Lives and Granting Annuities.
The Bank of North America acted in every sense like a modern commercial bank. It made short-term loans, accepted deposits, and dealt
in bills of exchange. In addition, it issued paper money. For a while,
it also acted as a central bank, lending money to the government,
holding its deposits, and otherwise acting as its fiscal agent. But it
lost this status after the formation of the Federal Government following the signing of the Constitution. At that time, Secretary of the
Treasury Alexander Hamilton urged Congress to grant a charter
creating a Bank of the United States.

Hamilton wanted the United States to become a rich and powerful nation through industrial and commercial growth. He favored a bank because he thought it would facilitate the industrial growth that he was so eager to encourage. He argued that a national bank would make a threefold contribution to the economy. First, it would create money and thereby increase the country's active and productive capital. Hamilton pointed out that under the principle of a fractional reserve, a bank could issue two or three dollars in paper money for every dollar it had in gold and silver. Second, a bank would help the Government in borrowing, because it would increase the money supply and, therefore, the supply of capital. Third, it would for the same reasons facilitate the payment and collection of taxes. "It is evident," Hamilton wrote, "that whatever enhances the quantity of circulating money, adds to the ease with which every industrious member of the community may acquire that portion of it of which he stands in need."

Hamilton's Report on the Bank immediately aroused vigorous opposition and set in motion a debate that anticipated most of the issues that were to crop up over and over again in subsequent controversies over the complicated problems of money and banking. The Jeffersonians, who favored agrarianism rather than industrialism, opposed Hamilton's recommended bank for both political and economic reasons. They argued that such a bank would be unconstitutional and would dangerously extend Federal power. Economically, they were suspicious of banks and of paper money, the commodity in which early banks dealt. They recognized that banks created money, but they did not think that money was the same as capital. They therefore did not believe, as Hamilton did, that banks created capital. They insisted, moreover, that banks encouraged usury, diverted funds from agriculture, and by issuing paper money increased speculation and drove specie out of the country.

Although conceding that these charges were true in certain cases, Hamilton insisted that a national bank would promote lower interest rates by increasing the supply of money. Nor would it diminish the funds available for agriculture, because there would always be lenders who, "from a spirit of caution, will incline to vest their funds in mortgages on real estate rather than in the stock of a bank, which they are apt to consider as a more precarious security." In answering the criticism that paper money would drive specie out of circulation, Hamilton pointed out that the abundance of a country's precious metals was not so important as the "quantity of the productions of its labor and industry." To the charge that banks encourage speculation—a charge that was to be made again and again in the future—Hamilton merely questioned whether it would be wise to root out the advantages of credit because it now and then ran to excess.

THE FIRST BANK OF THE UNITED STATES

Despite the objections of the Jeffersonians, Congress, in 1791, granted a charter to the First Bank of the United States, but limited it to twenty years. The Bank was capitalized at $10 million. It was empowered to discount notes and make loans, but at an interest rate not to exceed 6 per cent. It could accept deposits and issue bank notes, but all its debts—including notes, but not deposits—were not to exceed its capital. It was not permitted to buy or sell goods or real estate or to purchase stock (i.e., bonds) from the Federal Government.

It is highly unlikely that any more than $400,000 in real money out of the nominal capital of $10 million was ever paid into the Bank, for, as we have noted, capital funds were extremely scarce in early America. Even the Federal Government, which owned one-fifth of the Bank stock, did not pay its subscription in cash. Yet, despite the relatively small amount of real money with which it opened, the Bank was remarkably successful, especially in its operations as fiscal agent for the Government. Nevertheless, it was not popular, and its charter was not renewed when it expired in 1811. Albert Gallatin, Jefferson's Secretary of the Treasury, had come to favor the Bank because it was so helpful to the Treasury in its fiscal affairs. But most of the Jeffersonians, who now controlled the Government, had never become reconciled to the Bank, and it went out of existence.

STATE COMMERCIAL BANKS

Meanwhile, the state governments had also begun to charter commercial banks by special acts of legislation. There were at least twenty-nine such institutions in existence in 1800, including the oldest existing commercial bank, the Bank of New York (1784). These first banks were soundly operated, although occasionally, it is true, they did get into difficulties because of runs by depositors or note-holders. In these instances, however, banks averted disaster by getting financial help from the United States Treasury and from the Bank of the United States. Often, when a bank was short of cash and beset by creditors' demands, the Treasury or the Bank came to its rescue with cash deposits. Thus the Bank and the Treasury acted together as a central bank, and as long as the Bank was in existence, it was of immeasurable importance in helping to keep the other banks in a solvent position. There were apparently no bank failures in the United States until 1809, when the Farmers Exchange Bank of Glocester, Rhode Island, an extremely badly operated bank, collapsed. Thereafter, and until the 1930's, commercial banks in the United States experienced harrowing difficulties periodically.

The principal reasons for the waves of bank failures that occurred regularly in the United States were the establishment of banks in areas where the population was too small and industry and commerce were too limited to permit banks to succeed, a deficient understanding of the nature of commercial banking, a general lack of able bank management, and the absence of a central bank. Commercial banks could succeed in the big cities where industry and commerce were sufficiently developed to enable banks to make commercial loans. So long as these banks were conservatively conducted, the chance of failure was relatively small; for if creditors insisted upon drawing down their deposits, loans could be called and enough assets could be liquidated quickly to pay off depositors' demands. This, of course, would result in extreme hardship for some debtors, but painful though the operation was, at least it avoided many of the failures that might otherwise have occurred.

Failures could be averted by conservative management even more easily when a central bank was in existence, for then banks could obtain help in time of crisis by borrowing from the central bank, i.e., by shifting part of their assets to the central bank. All this, however, was true much more for the cities than for the country. Country banks could not liquidate their loans as quickly as city banks could, nor could they shift them as easily. The reason for this is not difficult to understand. Country banks often existed in areas where commerce and industry were either totally absent or meagerly developed. Consequently, they could not make short-term loans. If they wished to do any volume of business, they were forced to make long-term loans to land speculators or farmers. In times of crisis, they could not liquidate or shift these loans fast enough to satisfy the demands of their creditors. For the most part, these creditors were noteholders, for country banks usually made loans by giving the borrower their own printed bank notes (pocketbook or folding money), rather than by giving him a bank deposit (checkbook money). City banks (and modern commercial banks), on the other hand, made loans by creating bank deposits, or bank credit, rather than by actual creation of paper money.

Commercial banks, in other words, exchanged their own promises to pay for the borrower's promise to pay. Ordinarily, the city bank's promise to pay was evidenced in the form of a bank deposit. The country bank's promise was its own bank note, the so-called "state-bank note." This note bore, upon its face, a promise to pay the value of the note, presumably in specie, on demand. Often, however, this announcement was nothing more than a legend, for bankers were tempted to issue large quantities of notes, and when the holders of these notes brought them to the bank for redemption, the banker could not raise enough specie to redeem them. The tendency to overissue, always alluring, was most attractive in periods of war and prosperity, when the demand for money was much greater than it normally was. Thus the first experience with overissue occurred during the War of 1812, when the Government borrowed heavily from the state banks, selling them securities in exchange for bank notes. State banks were formed all over the country, and by the end of the war there were 250 of them. They issued paper money far in excess of what could reasonably be redeemed with available specie, and the whole system of redemption broke down. Under the pressure of a huge flood of money, moreover, prices rose rapidly, and by the end of the war they had doubled.

THE SECOND BANK OF THE UNITED STATES

The Federal Government, which had done much to create the inflation, now attempted to alleviate it by trying to tighten the money supply. At first, it tried to persuade the state banks to resume specie payments voluntarily. This, of course, would have forced the state banks to contract their currency issues, which they were not willing to do. The effort at "moral suasion" failed, and when it failed, the Government switched its emphasis. It reluctantly abandoned its constitutional hostility to a national bank and recommended that Congress issue a charter for a Second Bank of the United States. Thus, in 1816, the Second Bank came into existence. Again the charter was limited to twenty years. But this bank was much larger than its predecessor.

Its capital was $35 million, of which the Federal Government again subscribed one-fifth.

The Second Bank was not only a mammoth institution, but it was a central bank in every sense of the word. It acted as the Federal Government's fiscal agent, issued notes, and dealt in bills of exchange. Its power to issue notes gave the Bank some control over the money supply, for it could increase or reduce the amount of money it issued. But the Bank was also at all times in a position to exercise a powerful control over the state banks and thereby over the money market in general. Through its activities in collecting taxes, in receiving money in payment of loans, and in settling foreign and intersectional balances, the Bank was constantly receiving a stream of state-bank notes. It was, therefore, a creditor of the state banks and could exercise its creditor function to encourage expansion or contraction of the money market. By sending state-bank notes back for redemption in coin, the Bank could contract the money supply. By following a lenient policy in demanding redemption, it could encourage state banks to expand their circulation. It could also affect the money market by lending money to the state banks or by buying securities from them. The president of the Second Bank did not exaggerate when he rashly boasted that the Bank had the power of life and death over the state banks.

Although the Second Bank had extraordinary powers, it did not at first exercise these powers, preferring to take a hands-off attitude, but this almost resulted in disaster. Money inflation continued almost without abatement, for the state banks did not contract their issues once they became aware of the Bank's hands-off policy. The Bank, on the other hand, was continuously redeeming paper money in specie and its reserves eventually ran out. Then the Bank found itself close to bankruptcy. In order to survive, it began a ruthless policy of deflation. Few new loans were granted, and those that were due were not renewed. Paper-money issues were sharply curtailed, and the money market in general was rigorously tightened. Partly as a result of this, the United States, in 1819, experienced its first business depression. Although it could be argued that this depression was inevitable, the Bank was held responsible and its prestige and public relations suffered a blow from which it never recovered. With the depression, its days were numbered. For a while, however, it continued to prosper. Under the able leadership of Nicholas Biddle, who succeeded as president in 1823, it grew rather than faltered. Exercising its powers as a central bank, it kept a tight rein over the money market and prevented the state banks from expanding. But it was constantly assailed by a whole host of enemies: the hard-money agrarians who disliked all banks; the state banks outside of the big cities; a new class of businessmen who, being long on ideas and short of capital, were seeking places to raise funds and did not find a receptive audience in the Bank; the debtor groups who wanted easier money than the Bank was willing to provide; a group of New York financiers who wanted to move the financial center from Philadelphia to New York; and finally those who thought that the Bank was dangerous to democratic institutions because of its enormous size. All these groups found a spokesman in Andrew Jackson, who, after his election in 1828, moved against the Bank and Biddle in the first battle of the Bank war, one of the most colorful and publicized episodes in American history.

In a sense the struggle over the Bank was a contest between strong central banking and loose state banking. In another sense, it was a contest between big business and small business. It was also a contest between the conservative businessmen of the old school and the entrepreneurs of the new school. It was also a fight between creditors and debtors. But, however interpreted, the Bank had no chance to survive, for its enemies far outnumbered its friends. Its charter, it will be recalled, was to expire in 1836, but Biddle did not wait for that date. In a misguided moment, he asked for recharter in 1832. Congress passed the recharter bill, but Jackson vetoed it, and Congress was not able to repass it over his veto.

The matter became an issue in the presidential election of 1832, when Jackson soundly defeated Henry Clay, the Bank's champion. Jackson now took the offensive. He ceased depositing Government funds in the Bank and placed them instead in various state banks, called "pet banks." This action nullified most of the Bank's powers; for once it had lost its position as the Government's fiscal agency, it could no longer control the state banks, and they entered upon a period of spectacular growth. Ironically enough, the hard-money agrarians, like Jackson and Senator Thomas Hart Benton, who heartily disliked all banks, had given the state banks their greatest encouragement. Now, when the state banks and the money supply multiplied overnight, they were dismayed by what they had done; but because of their interpretation of the Constitution, they thought they were powerless to act, and money expansion kept right on through a period of booming prosperity to its ultimate end in the panic and depression of 1837.

THE INDEPENDENT TREASURY SYSTEM

With the panic, the public enthusiasm for banks turned to revulsion against them. Two courses of action were followed in an endeavor to correct the weaknesses in commercial banking. The Federal Government attempted to separate itself from the banking system. The state governments engaged in zealous attempts at reform. Neither effort, however, was very successful. The Federal Government adopted the Independent Treasury system, under which all Government dues were payable in specie and all Government moneys were held in its own vaults, known as subtreasuries. The Independent Treasury system was an avowed attempt on the part of the National Government to divorce itself from the banking system; but although it continued in existence with some modifications until 1914, it could not succeed in its chief objective. The Treasury could separate but not divorce itself from the banking system, for whatever it did affected the commercial banks. Thus when the Treasury collected money from the public, it drew specie out of the economy and thus reduced bank reserves, tending to contract the money market. On the other hand, when the Treasury paid out money, it fed gold back into the economy and increased bank reserves. The banks, therefore, had to be attentive continuously to what the Treasury was doing, and had to cut their loan policies to fit the cloth that was being woven by the Government's activities.

STATE BANKING REFORM

The activities of the state governments were even less successful in accomplishing effective banking reform. Of course, these efforts to make state banking safe and sound did not begin with the panic of 1837. Early in the century the government of Massachusetts and the Boston banks had instituted some banking reforms. Indeed, one of the most famous landmarks in American banking history, the Suffolk Banking System, appeared in 1824. For some time before then, the weak country banks of New England had been circulating their notes in Boston and driving the strong Boston bank notes out of circulation. Naturally, the Boston banks did not take kindly to this, and they finally grouped together to put a brake on country-bank-note circulation. They proposed that the country banks deposit specific sums in Boston for purposes of redemption. If this were done, the Boston banks agreed to redeem the country-bank notes at par. But if a bank refused to join the system, the Boston banks refused to redeem its notes at par and sent them back for redemption as fast as they were received. Grumble as they would about the ruthlessness of "the money power," the country banks had no choice but to join the system. Thus, in essence, the Suffolk System constituted a New England central bank.

Shortly after the Suffolk System, New York adopted the Safety Fund System. Based on the practices of the Chinese merchants, under which the strong protected the weak, this system was similar to the present Federal Deposit Insurance Corporation. Each bank in New York State deposited a percentage of its capital in a fund to be used to assist insolvent banks. Never popular with the strongest banks, the Safety Fund was abandoned and replaced during the depression of 1837 by the New York free banking system.

Free banking, the most common type of banking reform instituted by the states during the depression, had four main features. First of all, under free banking, a special act of legislation to obtain a bank charter was no longer required. Second, the system provided for bank notes secured by government bonds. Third, reserves were required against deposits; and fourth, banks were periodically examined by the state.

Free banking was first adopted in Michigan in 1837, but it was a complete fiasco there because the territory did not have sufficient industry and commerce to be able to sustain sound commercial banking. The free banking system adopted by New York in 1838 was, on the other hand, quite successful and it served as a model for many other states and eventually for the Federal Government when it passed the National Bank Act in 1863.

The state banking laws undoubtedly strengthened the banking system. Nevertheless, bank failures continued at a high rate, and as more and more state banks came into existence, a vast variety of state-bank notes appeared. By the Civil War, there were 1,600 different state banks issuing 7,000 different currencies. With so many notes in circulation, it became impossible for most people to differentiate between those that were good and those that were bad. Counterfeiters, therefore, had a field day. All in all, noteholders and depositors in the state banks continued to suffer huge losses, some estimates putting the amount as high as $50 million a year.

THE NATIONAL BANKING SYSTEM

The state banking system or lack of system horrified conservatives, especially the hard-money group that traced its ancestry back to Jacksonian Democracy. Among the members of this group was Salmon P. Chase, Secretary of the Treasury during the Civil War. At his first opportunity, Chase recommended that something be done to produce order in the banking system, especially in its currency issues.

Acting on Chase's recommendations, Congress passed the National Bank Act in 1863. The Act, together with its amendments in 1864, provided for free banking on a national scale. It required every national bank to maintain a reserve in lawful money against its deposits. Reserve city and city banks required 25 per cent and country banks 15 per cent, but part of these reserves (half for city banks and three-fifths for country banks) could be deposited in New York City banks. In addition, every national bank was required to purchase and deposit with the Comptroller of the Currency in Washington United States bonds equal to one-third of its capital, but not less than $30,000. The banks received interest on these bonds, and in addition they could issue national bank notes (paper money) equal to 90 per cent of the par or market value (whichever was lower) of the deposited bonds. These notes would circulate, and it was hoped that they would become the most important currency in the country. In addition to the bonds, each bank was required to maintain a 25 per cent reserve against note circulation. The notes, moreover, were taxed at a rate of one-half of 1 per cent semiannually.

At first, the state banks were reluctant to shift to national bank charters because national regulation was much more stringent than state regulation. But then in 1866 a tax of 10 per cent was imposed on state-bank notes and it became manifestly unprofitable to issue them. Immediately, state banks shifted to the national banking system. Thus by 1866, state-bank notes, by far the most prominent currency in the prewar period, had practically disappeared. On the other hand, national bank notes circulated to the extent of about $276 million. But they were not the most important type of money in circulation. Over $400 million of United States notes, or "greenbacks," were in circulation at the end of the Civil War. These greenbacks had been issued by the United States Government during the Civil War to help defray the costs of the war. They were fiat money; that is, they were backed only by the Government's promise to pay.

In addition to the national bank notes and the greenbacks, the currency of the United States at the end of the war included some subsidiary silver coin. Paradoxically, gold, considered the best of all moneys, circulated only to a small extent. It was the only legal tender in payment of customs duties and of interest and principal on the Government debt. But aside from these payments, it did not circulate. One of the most important reasons for this was that the heavy paper-money issues during the war had forced the United States to abandon the practice of redeeming paper money for gold. Consequently, paper money could not now be redeemed at its par value in gold. Gold could, however, be purchased in the free market at a premium in terms of paper money. Because gold was worth more than paper money, holders hoarded it. Thus the United States at the end of the Civil War was on an irredeemable paper-money standard. In 1875, however, the gold standard was restored, effective in 1879, and it remained in effect from then until 1933.

THE WEAKNESSES OF THE NATIONAL BANKING SYSTEM

As has been noted, it was expected that the national bank currency would provide an adequate and satisfactory money supply, but these expectations never materialized. The national bank notes were based on Federal debt, and in the years following the Civil War, the Government continuously ran a surplus and continuously repaid its debt. Thus it reduced the base against which bank notes could be issued. Much of the Federal debt, moreover, was noncallable and bore an interest rate much higher than the prevailing market rate. It therefore sold at a premium, making it unattractive for banks to use for purposes of issuing bank notes. Bankers could not be expected to be widely enthusiastic about buying bonds for $1,250 against which they could issue only $900 in currency, especially since they had to pay a tax and maintain an extra reserve against this currency. Consequently, after about 1875, national bank note circulation declined almost steadily, sinking to a little bit more than $100 million in 1890.

National bank currency not only declined alarmingly over the long run, but it was inelastic in the short run. That is, its volume tended to expand in depression and contract in prosperity. In prosperity periods, bankers found private loans more profitable than government bonds, and they therefore tended to sell their bonds. In depression periods, on the other hand, there were few borrowers, and bankers bought government bonds with their idle funds.

The inelasticity of the national bank currency has always been considered the system's greatest weakness, but its evils can be exaggerated. A far greater weakness in the Act was that it encouraged bank reserves to be sent to New York and thereby led to currency immobility. Under the terms of the Act, it may be recalled, country banks could deposit part of their reserves in New York. They availed themselves freely of this privilege, for New York had a thriving call-money market, and New York banks were willing to pay interest on interbank deposits which they loaned out in the call-money market to security buyers. Country-bank money piled up in the nation's financial center with great disadvantages to the money market. In the spring and in the fall, when agricultural activity was at its height, country banks drew down their deposits, depleting the city banks of their reserves. This created a semiannual tightness in the money market which periodically developed into a severe crisis. Thus if the New York banks were heavily extended, the country-bank demands would so diminish their reserves as to cause a reserve deficiency. Then the New York banks would have to call in loans, and if money was tight the effects of this attempted liquidation would snowball with almost universally disastrous results. When the banks, for example, called on a borrower to repay his loan, and he did not have ready cash, he put pressure on his debtors, and they in turn put pressure on their debtors, and so on all through the whole economy. What made matters worse, there was no central bank or similar institution to which the banks could go for help in time of difficulty. Indeed, the individual banks, instead of helping each other, actually put pressure on each other in times of crisis, aggravating the already intense money-market difficulties. National banks were therefore in much the same situation as a horse on a tether. Within the limits of their reserves, they could expand at a furious rate, but once they had reached the limit of their reserves, they could no longer expand and were brought to an abrupt halt. In periods of economic recovery banks expanded at a rapid rate, but at the height of the boom, they were unable to expand the money supply any further. Then a crisis occurred. Thus the national banking system, although not responsible for causing panics, such as occurred in 1873, 1893, and 1907, was responsible for greatly aggravating them. If a central bank had been in existence, these panics would not have been so severe, for the banks would have been able to obtain cash in times of great demand.

Unquestionably, the National Bank Act made banking safer than the state commercial banks had been, but it is questionable whether it was as conducive to economic growth, for it had grave and provoking weaknesses. We may sum up these weaknesses as follows: it produced an inelastic currency, it immobilized the money supply, and it aggravated panics. To be sure, it produced a safer currency than had existed under the old state banking system, but it was a far cry from a perfect system. It was, moreover, crude, clumsy, and discriminatory, for it provided no system for interregional check clearance; it had no central head; and, because national banks could not make long-term loans, it favored industry and commerce over agriculture. It was a system better fitted for a dog-eat-dog economy than for the complicated and intricately intermeshed structure that the United States had become by the late nineteenth century.

THE CONTEST OVER EASY MONEY—GREENBACKS AND SILVER

Many Americans intuitively disliked the national banking system. This was especially true of the farmers in the West and in the South. They regarded it as a creature of Wall Street, which to them epitomized the "money power." To the debtors of the agrarian West and South, the money power was an oppressive force which was directly responsible for all their economic misfortunes. It was especially responsible, the farmers thought, for the decline in farm prices that went on intermittently all through the last thirty-five years of the nineteenth century. The farmer believed that falling prices were caused by an insufficient amount of money. Or, to put it more positively, he believed that if the money supply were increased, prices would automatically rise. But how could the money supply be expanded? At first, greenbacks offered a way, and the debtor classes and others who regarded falling prices as an evil called upon the Federal Government to print more paper money. Greenbacks, however, quickly proved to be a lost cause. But just about the time that this was realized, another panacea offered itself, this time in the form of silver.

To understand how this came about, we must for a moment backtrack in financial history. Originally, in 1792, the United States had adopted a bimetallic monetary standard. That is to say, it made both gold and silver the basis for coinage. Anyone could take gold or silver to the mint and have it coined into gold or silver coins. In exchange for 247½ grains of gold, one could obtain at the mint a $10 gold piece; for 371¼ grains of silver, the mint would give a silver dollar. This meant that the mint ratio between silver and gold was 15 to 1. Later, in Andrew Jackson's administration, the gold dollar was devalued; that is, the content of a $10 gold piece was reduced to 232.2 grains, while the content of the silver dollar remained the same. Because of this devaluation, the mint ratio was now 16 to 1. We may express this in another way. Silver was worth at the mint $1.292 an ounce and gold was worth $20.67 an ounce.[1]

In the open market, however, silver was worth considerably more than $1.292 an ounce. Holders of silver sold their bullion in the market rather than to the mint, and silver dollars, therefore, disappeared from circulation. Indeed, so few were coined that in 1873 the United States eliminated them from its coinage. In the same year, however, the great Comstock lode was opened in Nevada and a literal Eldorado of silver flowed forth. As the supply of silver increased, its market price declined; and by 1874, it was worth $1.238 an ounce. If bimetallism had still been in existence, silver producers would have been able to sell their silver to the mint for $1.292 an ounce instead of in the market at $1.238. This would have meant not only a greater profit for silver miners but also a vast increase in the quantity of money, for silver was by now plentiful enough to satisfy the most rabid of easy-money enthusiasts. Immediately, those who wanted more money in order to increase prices began to work toward a restoration of bimetallism at 16 to 1. It was, of course, realized that if the bimetallists were successful, gold would disappear from circulation[2] and would cease to be a real monetary standard. To some the very thought of such a development was revolting. They therefore immediately entered the lists against the champions of silver, and the battle over the monetary standard was drawn.

On balance, the advocates of the gold standard were successful in thwarting the efforts of the silverites. The latter never succeeded in restoring bimetallism, although they did win two relatively small victories. In 1878, Congress passed the Bland-Allison Act, under which

[1] These prices are derived as follows: 371.25 grains of silver was equal to $1. Since there are 480 grains in an ounce, an ounce of silver was worth 480 divided by 371.25, or $1.292. Similarly, an ounce of gold was worth 480 divided by 23.22, or $20.67.

[2] It will be remembered that at this time gold did not circulate, but it was the *de facto* standard.

the Treasury was to buy between $2 and $4 million of silver a month and coin it into standard silver dollars. Then in 1890, the Sherman Act replaced the Bland-Allison Act and the Treasury began to buy 4½ million ounces of silver a month. Neither of these measures fully satisfied the demand for free silver. They did obviously increase the money supply, but it is questionable whether they had any effect on the price level.

THE DEFEAT OF EASY MONEY—THE GOLD STANDARD ACT

The silverites continued to battle for the cause, and the gold standard adherents continued to resist them. Then in the election of 1896 the Republican party, supporting the gold standard, defeated the Democrats, who supported bimetallism. Viewing this as a mandate from the people, the new administration passed the Gold Standard Act of 1900, which legally established gold as the sole monetary standard. But the Act did more than that. It tackled the complex problems of the national bank currency and eliminated many of the obstacles that were preventing the expansion of national bank circulation. It lowered the minimum capital required by national banks, it reduced the tax on national bank notes, it permitted national banks to issue notes up to the full par value of government bonds, and it eliminated the premium on government bonds by replacing the existing noncallable, high-interest-bearing bonds with long-term, low-interest bonds.

But the Act could not repair the basic weaknesses of the national banking system. That required a complete overhauling of the banking law, and at the moment the administration was not willing to take such drastic action. It required a major panic to persuade the lawmakers to undertake a major reform of the banking system. Such a panic occurred in 1907, and when it was over Congress moved toward a complete and radical overhauling of the banking law. In May 1908, it passed the Aldrich-Vreeland Act, a piece of stopgap legislation designed to prevent the kind of thing that had occurred in the panic. At that time currency had almost completely disappeared into hoards; banks had lost a large part of their reserves and had no place to go to replenish them. To prevent a recurrence of such a currency famine, the Aldrich-Vreeland Act created a National Currency Association with the power to issue emergency currency to banks that were in difficulties as a result of a general money stringency. The Act also created a Monetary Commission to make a study of necessary and desirable changes in the money and banking system.

THE ALDRICH BILL—FORERUNNER OF THE FEDERAL RESERVE ACT

Out of the Monetary Commission's study came the first attempt to establish a central bank along the lines of the Federal Reserve. This was the Aldrich bill, introduced in 1912. It would have created a central bank called the National Reserve Association. Membership in the Association was to be voluntary. Bank notes were to be issued against general assets and Government bonds. There were also provisions for central rediscounting of commercial paper, reserves against deposits, and reserves against bank note issues.

Under the Aldrich bill, control over the Association was to be vested in the nation's bankers, rather than in the Government. This was enough to doom the bill, for it threatened to bolster the power of the so-called "money trust." Then too, the Aldrich bill was politically impossible, for it was a Republican measure introduced in a Democratic Congress. In addition to these formidable disadvantages, the bill aroused the deep-seated distrust of central banking which agrarians had nurtured ever since the days of Andrew Jackson's war against "the Bank." Faced with these obstacles, the bill could not succeed. It did, however, accomplish the most important spadework. Now it was only a question of time before some variety of central banking would be adopted, for the weaknesses in the American money and banking structure had come to be widely recognized. After almost 300 years of trial-and-error experimenting, the United States found itself with a national banking system infected by the weaknesses of currency inelasticity and immobility; a variety of state banks operating under the laws of forty-eight different states; and a hodgepodge currency system that included gold and silver, bond-secured national bank notes, and a supply of greenbacks whose volume was fixed at about $350 million. It had no central bank, but a central bank seemed to be the only vehicle whereby some rationality could be injected into the banking system so that it would conform to the requirements of a well-developed economy. A central bank was, therefore, inevitable, and 1913 was a most propitious moment to create one.

SUGGESTED READINGS

CATTERALL, RALPH C. H., *The Second Bank of the United States,* Chicago, University of Chicago Press, 1903.

HAMMOND, BRAY, *Banks and Politics in America: From the Revolution to the Civil War,* Princeton, Princeton University Press, 1957.

HELDERMAN, LEONARD C., *National and State Banks: A Study of Their Origins,* Boston, Houghton Mifflin Company, 1931.

SMITH, WALTER BUCKINGHAM, *Economic Aspects of the Second Bank of the United States,* Cambridge, Harvard University Press, 1953.

SPRAGUE, OLIVER M. W., *History of Crises Under the National Banking System,* Publications of the National Monetary Commission, Vol. V, No. 3, Washington, Government Printing Office, 1911.

STUDENSKI, PAUL, and KROOSS, HERMAN E., *Financial History of the United States,* New York, McGraw-Hill Book Company, 1952.

Chapter 2

THE FEDERAL RESERVE ACT

GENERAL OBJECTIVE OF THE ACT

THE Federal Reserve Act, passed in 1913, was the result of prolonged Congressional study of the history of central banking in other countries and of our own banking experience. In enacting this legislation, the Congress sought to avoid either political or private domination of the monetary system. To that end, it created an institution, known as the Federal Reserve System, which is a blending of public and private participation under the coordination of a public body called the Board of Governors. Decentralization is an important characteristic of the System.

The intent of the Congress, reaffirmed on various occasions since 1913, was that the Federal Reserve System should be independent— not independent of Government, but independent within the general structure of the Government. This does not mean that the System can or should pursue a course that is contrary to the objectives of national economic policies; but it does mean that in deciding upon and carrying out monetary and credit policy within the framework of those general objectives it is to have freedom to exercise its best collective judgment independently. The Federal Reserve System has been likened broadly to a trusteeship created by the Congress to administer the nation's credit and monetary policies—a trusteeship dedicated to helping safeguard the integrity of money. The processes of policy determination within the System have been surrounded with carefully devised safeguards against domination by any special interest group.

THE BOARD OF GOVERNORS

The Federal Reserve Act provided for the establishment of twelve Federal Reserve Banks rather than the single central bank that had been contended for by some. With twelve Banks, it was essential to provide a mechanism for coordinating their activities and welding them into a system. The Board of Governors is this central coordinating and policy-making body. It exercises broad supervisory powers over the operation of the entire Federal Reserve System, but engages in virtually no operations itself.

The Board is composed of seven members appointed by the President and confirmed by the Senate, each for a term of fourteen years (except when an appointment is made to fill out an unexpired term). The terms are so staggered that one expires every two years. No member is eligible for reappointment after he has served a full term of fourteen years. The long terms, their staggered expirations, and the provision against reappointment after a full term has been served tend to minimize political and popular pressures on the Board and create conditions conducive to its independence.

In selecting members of the Board, the President is specifically charged in the Federal Reserve Act with giving "due regard to a fair representation of the financial, agricultural, industrial, and commercial interests, and geographical divisions of the country." Not more than one member may be selected from any one of the twelve Federal Reserve districts. No member may be an officer, director, or stockholder in any banking institution or trust company.

The Federal Reserve Act indicates that a member may be removed by the President "for cause."

Members of the Board are required to devote their entire time to its business. The Board's offices are located in Washington, D.C.

The President designates one of the members of the Board as chairman and another as vice chairman, each to serve as such for a term of four years. The chairman of the Board, subject to its supervision, is the Board's active executive officer.

Some of the functions of the Board are:

1. To fix, within statutory limits, the reserves which member banks in the Federal Reserve System are required to maintain against their deposit liabilities.

2. To review and determine the discount rates which are established biweekly at Federal Reserve Banks subject to the approval of the Board of Governors.

3. To participate, as members of the Federal Open Market Committee (described in a later section of this chapter), in determining the policies whereby the System influences the availability of credit

primarily through the purchase or sale of U.S. Government securities in the open market.

4. To fix margin requirements on loans on stock exchange collateral.

5. To exercise supervision over the Federal Reserve Banks, including special supervision over their foreign contacts and international operations.

6. To perform various supervisory functions with respect to commercial banks that are members of the System and to administer Federal Reserve, bank holding company, and other legislation.

The statutory limits within which the Board may fix reserve requirements with respect to deposit liabilities of member banks, as above stated, and the requirements actually in effect on August 31, 1959, are shown in the table below:

	Statutory Limits[1]		In Effect on Aug. 31, 1959
	Minimum	Maximum	
On net demand deposits of:			
Member banks in the two Central Reserve cities of New York and Chicago[2]	10%	22%	18%
Member banks in a large number of smaller cities classified as Reserve cities	10	22	16½
Member banks located elsewhere (commonly called "country banks")	7	14	11
On time deposits of all member banks	3	6	5

[1] The Board of Governors is authorized to place individual Central Reserve or Reserve city member banks in a lower reserve classification when deemed reasonable and appropriate in view of the character of their business.

[2] Amendments to the Federal Reserve Act which were enacted in July 1959 provide that after three years New York and Chicago shall be classified as Reserve cities and the Central Reserve city classification shall cease to exist.

For a long period of years, member banks have been able to treat as reserves only balances standing to their credit on the books of Federal Reserve Banks. In July 1959, however, amendments to the Federal Reserve Act authorized the Board of Governors to permit member banks to count also as reserves all or part of their currency and coin on hand. As of August 31, 1959, it was not known when the Board would begin to put this change into effect.

In authorizing the Board to make changes in reserve requirements within the statutory limits, the Federal Reserve Act specifies that the changes are to be made "to prevent injurious credit expansion or contraction." A change in requirements can have a pronounced effect in tending to expand or contract credit and the volume of money in existence. Such changes are therefore not an appropriate instrument for frequent use.

Language in the Federal Reserve Act to the effect that the decisions of Federal Reserve Banks in regard to discount rates are subject to "review and determination" by the Board of Governors has been construed by the Attorney General to mean not only that the Board must pass on rates proposed by Federal Reserve Banks but also has power to establish discount rates on its own initiative.

The power to fix margin requirements on loans on stock market collateral is the only selective or special-purpose credit control that the Board is now authorized to administer and apply. In various periods prior to 1954, it also had the power to apply controls to consumer installment credit and residential mortgage loans.

Outside the area of major credit policies, the Board discharges many of its statutory duties through the issuance of written regulations.

In discharging its supervisory responsibilities with respect to Federal Reserve Banks, the Board through its staff examines each Federal Reserve Bank and branch at least once a year.

The Board handles most of the relations of the Federal Reserve System with the legislative and executive branches of the Federal Government. As part of its miscellaneous activities, the Board assembles and maintains various monetary and financial records and issues publications in which many of these statistics are made available to the public.

Funds to defray the Board's expenses are obtained by assessments on the twelve Federal Reserve Banks.

FEDERAL RESERVE BANKS

In contrast to the Board of Governors, the Federal Reserve Banks are engaged primarily in operations.

As previously stated, there are twelve of the Banks. The map on

BOUNDARIES OF FEDERAL RESERVE DISTRICTS AND THEIR BRANCH TERRITORIES

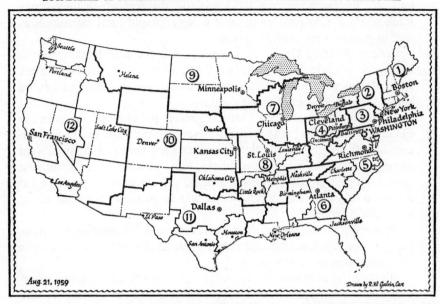

THE FEDERAL RESERVE SYSTEM

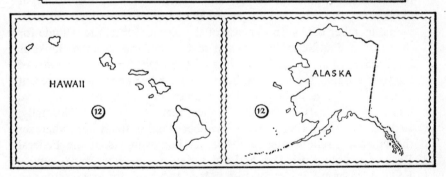

Legend
— Boundaries of Federal Reserve Districts — Boundaries of Federal Reserve Branch Territories
✪ Board of Governors of the Federal Reserve System
◉ Federal Reserve Bank Cities   • Federal Reserve Branch Cities

page 23 shows the location of these Banks and their branches and indicates the boundaries of the respective districts which they serve. Each of the Banks and branches is a regional and local institution as well as part of a nationwide system.

Federal Reserve Banks deal mainly with member banks and the United States Treasury. Some of them, particularly the New York Federal Reserve Bank, also have transactions with foreign central banks and monetary authorities.

Operating in accordance with the general policies laid down in the Federal Reserve Act, the Federal Reserve Banks are primarily concerned with serving the public interest, and not with making profits for themselves. Unlike commercial banks, they are not primarily business undertakings. As will be outlined later, private citizens share in the direction of Federal Reserve Banks, but in so doing they are acting in a public capacity.

In handling business relations with commercial banks that are members of the System, the individual Federal Reserve banks have a maximum degree of autonomy.

Most of the activities of the Federal Reserve Banks in terms of actual volume of transactions are of a clerical and routine nature. Important policy decisions are largely confined to (1) proposing changes in the discount rate for review and determination of the Board of Governors, and (2) deciding whether or not to make loans to individual member banks. In the case of the discount rate, the latitude for diversity of final action among the several Federal Reserve Banks is in practice relatively limited. Most of the time the discount rates of the twelve Banks are uniform, but there have been occasions in recent years when for a short period of months one or more Banks have maintained a rate somewhat higher than the others. Normally, Federal Reserve Banks lend member banks freely at whatever the current discount rate may be, but borrowing from the Federal Reserve is only a privilege and not a right for member banks, and a Federal Reserve Bank can refuse to lend to a bank for any reason that the Federal Reserve Bank deems adequate, such as previous excessive or long-continued borrowing by the bank.

The Federal Reserve Act provides that Federal Reserve Banks may, subject to the provisions of law and the orders of the Board of Governors, extend to member banks "such discounts, advancements and accommodations as may be safely and reasonably made with due regard for the claims and demands of other member banks, the maintenance of sound credit conditions, and the accommodation of commerce, industry and agriculture"; and requires Federal Reserve Banks, "in determining whether to grant or refuse advances, rediscounts and other credit accommodations," to give consideration to whether or not "undue use is being made of bank credit for the speculative carrying of or trading in securities, real estate, or commodities, or for any other purpose inconsistent with the maintenance of sound credit conditions."

Federal Reserve Banks are required to carry certificates representing beneficial ownership of gold held by the U.S. Treasury equal to at least 25 per cent of their own liabilities in the form of Federal Reserve notes, reserve balances of member banks, and other deposits. Present holdings of such certificates are greatly in excess of the required amount.

A substantial part of the routine work of Federal Reserve Banks relates to member-bank reserve accounts. As previously stated, member banks are required to carry reserves equal to a specified percentage of their net-demand deposit liabilities, plus a specified lower percentage of their time deposit liabilities. Reserve requirements are computed for individual member banks by averaging the daily deposit liabilities over a weekly period for banks in Central Reserve and Reserve cities and over a semimonthly period for banks located elsewhere. A member bank's deposit liabilities are constantly changing and so is its reserve account balance with its Federal Reserve Bank. The Federal Reserve Banks operate as a huge agency for the collection of checks and other items such as drafts, promissory notes, and bond coupons. Each member bank's reserve account balance is increased by the checks and other items which it deposits with Federal Reserve Banks and is reduced by the checks and other items drawn on it which come in clearances against it through Federal Reserve Banks. If it deposits paper money or coin with, or requisitions such currency from, its Federal Reserve Bank, this also changes its reserve account balance at the Reserve Bank. When a member bank's reserves fall below the required amount, the bank, at least for a time, may borrow the deficiency from its Reserve Bank, in preference to making some other adjustment in its position.

Checks collected and cleared through Federal Reserve Banks must be paid in full by the banks on which they are drawn, without deduction of any charge.

The twelve Federal Reserve Banks maintain a fund in Washington through which money is transferred, on telegraphic instructions, from the account of one Federal Reserve Bank to that of another. Such transfers consist mostly of settlements for checks collected, transfers for the account of member banks and their customers, and transfers for the United States Treasury.

The Federal Reserve Banks keep a large stock of paper money and coin on hand to meet the fluctuating demands for currency as a circulating medium. The paper money consists mainly of Federal Reserve notes, but includes also Treasury currency, principally in the form of silver certificates and United States notes.

The cost of clearing and collecting checks and other items and of supplying and shipping paper money and coin is borne entirely by the Federal Reserve Banks. These and other services are provided for member banks free of charge.

The Federal Reserve Banks act as fiscal agents for the United States Treasury and in that capacity carry the principal checking accounts of the Treasury, handle much of the work entailed in issuing and redeeming United States Government obligations, and perform numerous other important fiscal duties for the Government.

The stock of each Federal Reserve Bank is held by the member banks of its district. Each member bank is required to subscribe for and hold such stock in an amount determined in accordance with a formula based on the member bank's own capital and surplus. Stock of Federal Reserve Banks does not have the normal attributes of common stock. The dividends on it are fixed by law at 6 per cent per annum. The residual interest in the surplus of the Federal Reserve Banks belongs to the United States Government and not to the Banks' stockholders.

At the end of June 1959, total outstanding stock of all twelve Federal Reserve Banks amounted to $379,882,000 and their total capital accounts, including surplus and other items, were $1,430,-707,000.

Each Federal Reserve Bank has a board of nine directors, of whom six are chosen by member banks. Of these six, three are bankers and the other three must be engaged in commerce, agriculture, or some other industrial pursuit and not connected with any bank as an officer, director, or employee. In voting for the directors, the member banks in a district are divided into three groups of similar capitalization, and no officer or director of a member bank is eligible to serve as one of the three banker directors of the district's Federal Reserve Bank unless he is nominated and elected by the group which includes the bank of which he is an officer or director. This results in one of the three banker directors being from a large bank, another from a medium-sized bank, and the third from a small bank.

The three directors of a Federal Reserve Bank who are not elected by member banks are appointed by the Board of Governors. None of the three so appointed may be an officer, director, employee, or stockholder of any bank. Of the three, the Board of Governors designates one as chairman and another as deputy chairman of the board of directors of the Federal Reserve Bank. It is required that the chairman shall be a person of "tested banking experience." The chairman also acts as Federal Reserve Agent and in that capacity discharges certain routine statutory responsibilities.

All members of the board of a Federal Reserve Bank are elected or appointed for three-year terms (except when election or appointment is to fill out an unexpired term). Terms are so staggered that the term of one director in each of three categories expires each year.

The directors of a Federal Reserve Bank supervise its affairs. Subject to the approval of the Board of Governors, they appoint the President and First Vice President of the Bank, each for a five-year term (except when an appointment is made to fill out an unexpired term).

Salaries of all officers and employees of Federal Reserve Banks are subject to the approval of the Board of Governors.

While Federal Reserve Banks earn income, their operations are not carried on for this purpose but are determined by Federal Reserve credit policies.

The income which the Banks earn is derived mainly from interest on U.S. Government securities owned, and to a much lesser extent from interest on loans to member banks and miscellaneous sources.

Most of the Banks' expenses are incurred in handling clerical work. Net expenses in 1958, however, were less than one-fifth of current earnings, and dividends, fixed at 6 per cent on capital stock, are relatively small in relation to income. By far the greatest part of income is paid over to the United States Treasury as interest on Federal Reserve notes. Such payments amount to 90 per cent of earnings remaining after deduction of expenses and dividends. The practice of making such payments was started in 1947 as a consequence of the large increases in earnings which Federal Reserve Banks had realized from the acquisition of U.S. Government securities in connection with the financing of World War II. By making these payments the Federal Reserve seeks to avoid the criticism that it is profiting at the Treasury's expense. The authority it relies upon in making the payments is a section of the Federal Reserve Act which provides for the charging of interest on Federal Reserve notes.

As may be seen from the map on page 23, all of the Federal Reserve Banks except those located in Boston and Philadelphia have one or more branches, the maximum number being four. The branches have been established primarily for the greater convenience of member banks and to expedite collections. Subject to such rules and regulations as the Board of Governors may prescribe, each branch is operated under the supervision of a board of directors which is required to consist of not more than seven or less than three directors, of whom a majority shall be appointed by the Federal Reserve Bank of the district and the remaining directors by the Board of Governors. All of the directors hold office during the pleasure of the Board of Governors.

FEDERAL OPEN MARKET COMMITTEE

The Federal Reserve Act created a Federal Open Market Committee consisting of the members of the Board of Governors and five representatives of Federal Reserve Banks. Such representatives are required to be presidents or first vice presidents of Federal Reserve Banks and are elected annually by the boards of directors of Federal Reserve Banks as follows: one by the Bank in New York; one by the Banks in Boston, Philadelphia, and Richmond; one by the Banks in Cleveland and Chicago; one by the Banks in Atlanta, Dallas, and St. Louis; and one by the Banks in Minneapolis, Kansas City, and San Francisco. In actual practice, the last four memberships on the Committee are rotated among the Federal Reserve Banks in the respective groups. Also, in actual practice, representatives of all twelve Federal Reserve Banks attend meetings of the Open Market Committee and participate freely in the discussion, although only those who are members of the Committee vote.

Alternates to the five representatives of Federal Reserve Banks on the Open Market Committee are required to be chosen in the same manner as the representatives, and such alternates must also be presidents or first vice presidents of Federal Reserve Banks.

The Federal Reserve Act requires the Open Market Committee to meet at least four times a year, in Washington. Since June 1955, when its Executive Committee was abolished, it has usually met at three-week intervals.

The Open Market Committee is the policy-forming agency that directs the purchase and sale of U.S. Government securities in the open market. Execution of policies so established is under the direction of the Manager of the System Open Market Account, who is also Vice President in charge of the securities function at the New York Federal Reserve Bank there and has his office at that Bank.

Open-market operations derive their importance from the fact that they increase or reduce the total amount of reserves available to member banks. When Federal Reserve Banks buy U.S. Government securities in the market, the checks which they issue in payment eventually come into the possession of member banks in customers' deposits and then are redeposited by the member banks in their reserve accounts at Federal Reserve Banks, increasing the balances in the accounts. By a reverse process, sales of securities by Federal Reserve Banks reduce the reserves of member banks.

By buying or selling securities, the Federal Reserve can quickly create easier or tighter money conditions, as from time to time it may deem appropriate. Open market operations are a much more flexible instrument of control than are changes in reserve requirements.

FEDERAL ADVISORY COUNCIL

The Federal Reserve Act also established a Federal Advisory Council of twelve members, one from each Federal Reserve district. The member for each district is elected annually by the board of directors of the Federal Reserve Bank for that district. The Federal Reserve Act requires that the Council shall meet at least four times a year and specifies that at least those required meetings shall be held in Washington. All members of the Council are private commercial bankers.

The Federal Reserve Act empowers the Council, either directly or through its officers, to confer with the Board of Governors on general business conditions, to make representations regarding matters within the jurisdiction of the Board, to call for information, and to make recommendations in regard to discount rates, rediscount business, note issues, reserve conditions in the various districts, open-market operations, and the general affairs of the Federal Reserve System. The Council's function is entirely advisory.

MEMBER BANKS

All banks with national charters are required to be members of the Federal Reserve System. Banks with state charters may voluntarily join the System if qualified for membership and accepted by the Board of Governors. In passing on applications for membership, the Board of Governors is required to consider the financial condition of the applying bank, the general character of its management, and whether or not the corporate powers exercised are consistent with the purposes of the Federal Reserve Act. Certain minimum requirements as to capital must be met by an applying bank as a condition for admission to membership.

Every member bank is required to subscribe to the capital stock of the Federal Reserve Bank in its district. Its maximum subscription is an amount equal to 6 per cent of its capital and surplus, but only half this amount must be paid in, the other half being subject to call.

As a member of the Federal Reserve System, a bank assumes a number of important obligations: to comply with the reserve requirements of the Federal Reserve and to keep its required reserves on deposit without interest at the Federal Reserve Bank in its district (or, to the extent eventually permitted by the Board of Governors, in the form of currency and coin on hand); to be subject to various requirements of Federal law with respect to branch banking, holding-company regulation, interlocking directorates, certain loan and investment limitations, and other matters; and, if the member is a state-chartered bank, to be subject to general supervision and examination by the Federal Reserve System. (Pursuant to legislation antedating the establishment of the Federal Reserve System, banks with national charters are examined by the office of the Comptroller of the Currency, a division of the Treasury Department.)

Perhaps the most burdensome obligation of Federal Reserve membership for many state-chartered banks is that of complying with reserve requirements. In many cases, a state-chartered bank, if it were not a member of the Federal Reserve System, would be permitted by the laws of its state to keep lower reserves and to maintain part of them in interest-bearing form, such as U.S. Government securities and other governmental obligations.

In return for the obligations which they assume, member banks are entitled, among other things, to borrow from their respective Federal Reserve Banks (subject to tests for borrowing set by statute and regulation) when temporarily in need of additional reserves; to use Federal Reserve facilities for collecting checks, settling clearing balances, and transferring funds to other cities; to obtain currency whenever required; to share in the informational facilities provided by the Federal Reserve System; to participate, as previously stated, in the election of six of the nine directors of their respective Federal Reserve Banks; and to receive a cumulative statutory dividend of 6 per cent on their respective holdings of paid-in capital stock of Federal Reserve Banks.

At the end of 1958, the Federal Reserve System had 6,312 member banks. Of these, 4,578 were national banks and 1,734 were state-chartered banks.

In number the member banks comprise somewhat less than half of all the banks in the country, but they hold about 85 per cent of all demand deposits and approximately one-half of all time deposits.

DEFECTS IN THE BANKING SYSTEM WHICH THE FEDERAL RESERVE SYSTEM WAS DESIGNED TO REMEDY

The principal defects of the American banking system, as it existed prior to the enactment of the Federal Reserve Act, were decentralization, inelasticity of credit, cumbersome transfer facilities, and an inadequate government depositary system.[1]

The most serious feature of the decentralization was the wide scattering of reserves. Individual banks carried higher reserves than they would have needed if there had been some central institution to which they could have turned for support, and such reserves were so jealously guarded in times of stress that they were comparatively ineffective in preventing trouble. There was no effective way of assembling them at the points where danger threatened. The Federal Reserve Act altered this condition greatly, not only by requiring member banks to keep reserves with Federal Reserve Banks, but also by empowering the Federal Reserve, within certain limits based on gold holdings, to create additional reserves for the commercial banking system by making loans to or discounting paper for individual member banks when the accommodation is deemed appropriate, and by purchasing U.S. Government securities in the open market.

Even when prices are stable and the general economy is showing only normal growth, there are seasonal fluctuations in the amount of

[1] E. W. Kemmerer, *The ABC of the Federal Reserve System,* Princeton, Princeton University Press, 1938, Chapters II–V.

money required to transact the country's business. Also, changes in economic conditions cause variations in the requirements for money. The banking system as it existed prior to the advent of the Federal Reserve was ill equipped to provide elasticity in the money supply to meet these needs. By contrast, the Federal Reserve, through its power to vary the quantity of reserves available to its member banks, is in position to permit, if not actually to stimulate, seasonal and other desirable fluctuations in the volume of money.

The collection and money-transfer system which the Federal Reserve Banks operate is a great improvement over the facilities which previously existed. As stated above, checks collected and cleared through Federal Reserve Banks must be paid in full by the banks on which they are drawn, without deduction of any charge. Prior to the advent of the Federal Reserve, there was a wide variation of practice with respect to levying of collection charges.

The services which Federal Reserve Banks perform for the U.S. Treasury in their capacity of fiscal agents have facilitated the Treasury's operations and made the Treasury a less disruptive influence in the money market. Under existing practices, Treasury funds are drawn into Federal Reserve Banks from commercial bank depositaries at frequent intervals and then disbursed relatively promptly, so that the fluctuations in total member bank reserves due to the Treasury's operations are now relatively moderate and not often a major disturbing influence in the money market.

SUGGESTED READINGS

BACH, G. L., *Federal Reserve Policy Making,* New York, Alfred A. Knopf, 1950, Chapters II, VIII, and XIV.

BOARD OF GOVERNORS OF THE FEDRAL RESERVE SYSTEM, *The Federal Reserve System—Purposes and Functions,* Washington, 1954, Chapters V, XI, and XII.

BURGESS, W. RANDOLPH, *The Reserve Banks and the Money Market,* New York, Harper & Brothers, 1946, Chapters I–II.

GOLDENWEISER, E. A., *American Monetary Policy,* New York, McGraw-Hill Book Company, Inc., 1951, Chapters V and XV.

KEMMERER, E. W., *The ABC of the Federal Reserve System,* Princeton, Princeton University Press, 1938, Chapters II–IX.

JOINT COMMITTEE ON THE ECONOMIC REPORT, *Monetary Policy and the Management of the Public Debt,* Washington, Government Printing Office, 1952, Part 1, pp. 207–337.

MEMBERS OF THE STAFF OF THE BOARD OF GOVERNORS OF THE FEDERAL RESERVE SYSTEM, *Banking Studies,* Washington, 1941, pp. 229–292.

Chapter 3

FEDERAL RESERVE BANK STATEMENTS AND THEIR INTERPRETATION

THIS chapter deals with the statements of condition and earnings and expenses of the Federal Reserve Banks. Before going into the items on these statements, however, it will be helpful briefly to summarize what the Federal Reserve Banks do.[1] The functions of an institution largely determine the character of its assets and liabilities, and the nature of its income and expenses.

The Federal Reserve Banks perform the functions of a central bank. These functions are different from those performed by commercial banks, other financial institutions, and business firms. The work of the Reserve Banks falls into two main categories: routine services performed principally for the commercial banks and the Federal Government, and regulation of credit and the money supply.

The Reserve Banks render a variety of services which enable commercial banks and the Federal Government better to serve the public. Notes issued by the Federal Reserve Banks constitute about 85 per cent of the total amount of currency in circulation. Each Reserve Bank serves as a paying and receiving center for currency and coin, and a clearing center for checks drawn on commercial-bank deposits. Much handling is required in order that upwards of $30 billion of currency and coin, and over $100 billion of demand deposits, will serve efficiently as means of payment. As fiscal agent of the Federal Government, the Reserve Banks hold deposits of the Treasury, pay checks drawn on these deposits, and issue and redeem savings bonds and other Government securities. The Reserve Banks also make loans to member banks.

[1] For a more complete description, see Chapter 2.

The primary responsibility of the Federal Reserve System is to use its authority to regulate credit and the money supply in such a way as to keep total spending in line with the total supply of goods and services available for purchase. More specifically, the objectives are to keep the price level stable, help maintain a reasonably full use of resources, and promote stable economic growth. System actions to achieve these objectives operate primarily through their effect on bank reserves and the lending capacity of member banks.

STATEMENT OF CONDITION

Any financial or business firm acquires assets and incurs liabilities in the normal course of its operations. The nature of its assets and liabilities is determined by the character of its operations; hence it is well to keep in mind the functions of the Reserve Banks when interpreting the statement of condition.

The Board of Governors issues a weekly statement of condition, showing the consolidated assets and liabilities of the twelve Reserve Banks and the assets and liabilities of each Reserve Bank at the close of business each Wednesday. The weekly statement (H.4.1) consists of three major parts: (a) a list of the items affecting reserves; (b) the consolidated assets, liabilities, and capital of the twelve Federal Reserve Banks; and (c) the assets, liabilities, and capital of each Reserve Bank. To interpret the statement properly requires an understanding of what each asset and liability represents.

Explanation of Assets

The asset section of the statement of condition of the twelve Federal Reserve Banks combined for the week ending March 26, 1958, is reproduced in Table 1, p. 35.

An explanation of these assets in the order in which they appear on the statement follows:

Gold certificate account. The total amount of gold certificates on hand and due from the Treasury. Actually, only a small amount of the gold certificates are held on the premises of the Reserve Banks. This item consists largely of a credit in an account maintained by the Treasury, which is payable in gold certificates. Gold certificates and the gold certificate account are backed 100 per cent by gold held by the Treasury.

Redemption fund for Federal Reserve notes. The law requires that

TABLE 1. STATEMENT OF CONDITION
OF THE TWELVE FEDERAL RESERVE BANKS COMBINED
(In thousands of dollars)

Assets	March 26, 1958	Change Since March 19, 1958	March 27, 1957
Gold certificate account	21,048,391	− 12,001	+ 273,999
Redemption fund for F.R. notes	855,732	− 1,966	+ 3,585
Total gold certificate reserves	21,904,123	− 13,967	+ 277,584
F.R. notes of other Banks	503,076	+ 12,044	+ 95,449
Other cash	488,048	− 2,021	+ 40,681
Discounts and advances	117,914	− 112,926	− 498,670
Industrial loans	507	+ 33	− 288
Acceptances—bought outright	39,430	+ 1,005	+ 16,755
U.S. Government securities:			
Bought outright—			
Bills	789,260	+ 87,500	+ 484,555
Certificates	19,946,105	—	+8,583,906
Notes	—	—	−8,571,413
Bonds	2,789,257	—	− 12,493
Total bought outright	23,524,622	+ 87,500	+ 484,555
Held under repurchase agreement	—	—	− 25,500
Total U.S. Government securities	23,524,622	+ 87,500	+ 459,055
Total loans and securities	23,682,473	− 24,388	− 23,148
Due from foreign banks	15	—	− 7
Uncollected cash items	4,529,611	−1,983,135	− 81,500
Bank premises	85,636	+ 198	+ 9,985
Other assets	173,400	+ 12,507	+ 27,970
TOTAL ASSETS	51,366,382	−1,998,762	+ 347,014

a fund be maintained with the Treasury for the payment of Federal Reserve notes turned into the Treasury for redemption. The redemption fund consists of gold certificates or credits payable in gold certificates. It should be noted, however, that since the nationalization of gold in 1934, Federal Reserve notes have been redeemable in lawful money instead of gold.[2]

Total gold certificate reserves. Represents the sum of the gold certificate account and the redemption fund for Federal Reserve notes. The Federal Reserve Banks are required by law to maintain a minimum gold certificate reserve equal to 25 per cent of their combined Federal Reserve note and deposit liabilities.

Federal Reserve notes of other Banks. Combined holdings of Federal Reserve notes issued by other Reserve Banks.

Other cash. Currency, other than Federal Reserve notes, and coin held by the Reserve Banks.

Discounts and advances. This amount represents primarily short-term loans outstanding to member banks, with Government securities as collateral. At times it may include small amounts of eligible commercial paper discounted for member banks, and loans to foreign central banks.

Industrial loans. The total amount of Reserve Bank loans outstanding to industrial borrowers. An amendment to the Federal Reserve Act (Section 13b) authorized the Federal Reserve Banks to make loans to business firms unable to get credit from other financial institutions on reasonable terms. Section 13b was repealed effective August 21, 1959.

Acceptances. The face amount of prime bankers' acceptances owned by the Reserve Banks. This item is divided into two parts: the amount of acceptances held as a result of outright purchases in the market, and the amount held under repurchase agreement, i.e., under an agreement whereby dealers are to repurchase the acceptances within a specified time.

U.S. Government securities. The total amount of Government obligations bought outright and held, as of the reporting date, in the System Open Market Account, classified by type of security. The participation of each Reserve Bank in the ownership of these securities is on the basis of a formula adopted by the Federal Open Market Committee.

The amount of Government securities held under repurchase agree-

2 See Federal Reserve Act as amended, Section 16, Article 1, p. 58.

ment represents short-term issues purchased from Government securities dealers under an agreement whereby the dealers are obligated to repurchase the securities within a specified period (not to exceed fifteen days) at the same price at which the securities were sold to the System.

Total holdings of Government securities include both those bought outright and those held under repurchase agreement.

Due from foreign banks. Funds of the Reserve Banks held on deposit in foreign banks.

Uncollected cash items. Total amount of checks in process of collection through the Reserve Banks for which payment has not yet been received.

Bank premises. The book value of building and equipment.

Other assets. A miscellany of assets not listed above.

Explanation of Liabilities and Net Worth

There are two types of claims against the assets of any business—claims of creditors and those of the owners. The owners' claim is a residual representing the excess of total assets over total liabilities. The liabilities and capital account sections of the weekly statement for March 26, 1958, are reproduced in Table 2, p. 38.

The nature of each liability is explained below:

Federal Reserve notes. The total amount of Federal Reserve notes issued by the twelve Reserve Banks less the amount of its own notes held by each Bank. Federal Reserve notes, in addition to being a first claim on the assets of the issuing Reserve Banks, are an obligation of the Government of the United States. They must be backed by a minimum reserve of 25 per cent in gold certificates. The amount not covered by gold certificates must be backed by collateral consisting of eligible commercial paper or Government securities.

Deposits. Represents the total deposit balances held in the Reserve Banks classified according to ownership. The largest item—member-bank reserves—is the total amount of deposits of member banks in the Reserve Banks. These deposits count as legal reserve which member banks are required to hold against their customers' deposits. The Reserve Banks also hold deposits of the United States Treasury. Foreign deposits in the Reserve Banks consist mainly of balances of foreign governments and central banks.

Other deposits than those classified above consist of balances of nonmember banks held in the Reserve Banks for check-clearing pur-

TABLE 2

| | | Change Since | |
LIABILITIES (In thousands of dollars)	March 26, 1958	March 19, 1958	March 27, 1957
Federal Reserve notes	26,472,927	− 77,558	+ 101,260
Deposits:			
Member-bank reserves	18,426,390	− 545,350	+ 76,868
U.S. Treasurer—general			
account	622,859	+ 522,705	+ 132,986
Foreign	255,628	+ 12,667	− 89,215
Other	393,478	− 17,033	+ 94,003
Total deposits	19,698,355	− 27,011	+ 214,642
Deferred-availability cash items	3,825,671	−1,863,424	+ 21,754
Other liabilities and accrued			
dividends	18,232	+ 1,843	− 516
TOTAL LIABILITIES	50,015,185	−1,966,150	+ 337,140
CAPITAL ACCOUNTS			
Capital paid in	349,799	+ 114	+ 19,034
Surplus (Section 7)	809,198	—	+ 61,605
Surplus (Section 13b)	27,543	—	—
Other capital accounts	164,657	− 32,726	− 70,765
TOTAL LIABILITIES			
AND CAPITAL ACCOUNTS	51,366,382	−1,998,762	+ 347,014
Ratio of gold certificate re- serves to deposit and F.R. note liabilities combined	47.4%	—	+ .2%
Contingent liability on accept- ances purchased for for- eign correspondents	127,625	+ 353	+ 68,690
Industrial loan commitments	997	− 32	− 977

poses, Reserve Bank checks outstanding, and a miscellany of other balances payable on demand.

Deferred availability cash items. The total face value of checks received by the Reserve Banks for collection for which the sending bank has not yet been given credit. The Reserve Banks give the sending banks credit for checks according to a time schedule, the maximum deferment being two days.

Float is the difference between uncollected cash items and deferred availability cash items. The difference represents the amount for which credit has been given but for which payment has not yet been received.

Other liabilities and accrued dividends. Miscellaneous obligations such as accrued expenses and dividends accrued but yet unpaid on Reserve Bank stock owned by member banks.

Capital paid in. The total amount actually paid in by member banks for the capital stock of the Reserve Banks. Each member bank is required by law to subscribe to the capital stock of the Reserve Bank of its district a sum equal to 6 per cent of its own paid-up capital stock and surplus, but only one-half of this amount has actually been paid in.

Surplus (Section 7). Total accumulated earnings transferred to surplus under Section 7 of the Federal Reserve Act, which authorized that net earnings after payment of dividends should be paid in to the surplus of the Reserve Bank.

Surplus (Section 13b). The amount received from the Treasury to make industrial loans as authorized by Section 13b of the Federal Reserve Act together with the retained earnings on such loans. The Act repealing Section 13b also provided that each Reserve Bank should pay to the United States the total amount received from the Treasury under Section 13b.

Other capital accounts. This item consists mainly of contingency reserves, and net earnings which as yet have not been allocated.

Federal Reserve Bank indebtedness is primarily to holders of Federal Reserve notes and to member banks with deposit balances in the Reserve Banks to meet reserve requirements. It should be noted that these two liabilities do not represent the same potential drain on assets as do the liabilities of most financial and business institutions. Federal Reserve notes, which constitute over one-half of total liabilities, are redeemable on demand in any lawful money. It is hard to visualize a situation in which holders would redeem a substantial volume of Federal Reserve notes in other kinds of lawful money. Neither do the reserve deposits of member banks represent a potential drain similar to customers' deposits in a commercial bank. In the first place, they are "captive" deposits in the sense that member banks are required by law to hold a minimum percentage of their customers' deposits in the form of a deposit balance in a Reserve Bank. Although a member bank can draw down its reserve balance below the minimum for any one day, it must pay a penalty if the average for the reserve period drops below the legal minimum. Furthermore, a reduction in member-bank deposits, such as occurs when there is an outflow of currency into circulation, is usually offset by an increase in another Federal Reserve Bank liability, namely, Federal Reserve notes.

A final point which should be noted is that in case of dissolution or liquidation of a Reserve Bank, the Federal Reserve Act provides that any surplus remaining after the payment of debts, dividend requirements, and the par value of stock outstanding shall be paid to the United States, not the stockholding member banks.

Interpreting the Statement of Condition

The statement of condition of a business—assets, liabilities, and net worth—shows its financial position as of a given date. The trained analyst uses the statement for a number of purposes, such as determining whether total assets are sufficient to meet total liabilities, whether current assets will provide enough cash to pay short-term liabilities, and whether capital provides a sufficient cushion to protect the claims of creditors. Because of the nature of their liabilities, however, such types of analyses are of little significance in the case of the Federal Reserve Banks.

The most useful information that can be derived from the weekly statement of condition is what is happening to bank reserves and why. Federal Reserve actions to influence credit and the money supply, and thus to influence prices, business activity, and employment, operate directly on member-bank reserves. An increase in the volume of reserves enlarges and a decrease contracts the capacity of member banks to make loans and investments. The first page of the weekly report (H.4.1) gives the sources and uses of reserve funds, and whether member-bank reserves are increasing or decreasing and why.

Sources and Uses of Reserves[3]

Data on the first page of the weekly report show the factors influencing bank reserves—Reserve Bank credit and related items. Data are weekly averages of daily figures, including changes from the preceding week and from the corresponding week in the previous year. In view of the large day-to-day fluctuations in some of these items,

[3] For a more detailed explanation of sources and uses of reserves, see Board of Governors of the Federal Reserve System, *Banking and Monetary Statistics,* Washington, D.C., 1943, pp. 360-66; and *Federal Reserve System—Purposes and Functions,* Washington, D.C., 1954, Chapter VIII.

daily averages are more representative and meaningful than amounts on a specific date and changes between specific dates. This part of the weekly report shows the two main groups of factors which affect member-bank reserves: primary sources of reserves and uses other than member-bank reserves themselves.

TABLE 3

Member Bank Reserves, Reserve Bank Credit, and Related Items	Averages of Daily Figures		
	For Week Ending March 26, 1958	Change from March 19, 1958	Week Ending March 27, 1957
	(In millions of dollars)		
Reserve Bank credit:			
U. S. Government securities—			
Bought outright—System account	23,518	+ 88	+467
Special certificates	—	− 50	—
Held under repurchase agreement	34	+ 14	− 9
Acceptances—bought outright	40	—	+ 17
Loans, discounts, and advances—			
Member-bank borrowings	164	+ 39	−655
Other	3	+ 2	− 23
Float	983	+ 10	+ 16
Total Reserve Bank credit	24,742	+104	−188
Gold stock	22,498	− 43	+193
Treasury currency outstanding	5,180	+ 2	+ 97
	52,420	+ 63	+102
Money in circulation	30,524	− 68	+ 22
Treasury cash holdings	790	− 14	− 23
Treasury deposits with F.R. Banks	580	+323	+227
Foreign deposits with F.R. Banks	258	+ 1	− 76
Other deposits with F.R. Banks	1,143	+ 32	+195
Other F.R. accounts (net)	400	− 7	+ 4
	33,695	+267	+348
Member bank reserves—	18,725	−205	−246
Required reserves (estimated)	18,041	−282	−321
Excess reserves (estimated)	684	+ 77	+ 75

The three primary sources which may add to reserve balances of member banks are Federal Reserve Bank credit, gold holdings of the Government, and Treasury currency outstanding. Increases in Federal Reserve Bank credit make additional reserves available to member banks. When a Reserve Bank makes a loan to a member bank, the proceeds are credited to the latter's deposit or reserve account. When the System buys Government securities it pays for them by credits to member bank reserve accounts, reserve accounts of dealer banks, and the New York bank which clears securities transactions for non-bank dealers. As explained previously, float represents credit given to member banks for checks sent in for collection but for which payment has not been received. On the other hand, a decrease in Federal Reserve Bank credit tends to reduce the supply of reserves.

An increase in the monetary gold stock also tends to increase member-bank reserves. Imported gold is purchased by the Treasury and paid for by check drawn on its balance in a Federal Reserve Bank. The seller deposits the check in his own bank, which in turn sends the check to a Reserve Bank for collection, thus receiving credit for a corresponding amount to its reserve account. The Treasury usually replenishes its balance by issuing gold certificates to the Reserve Banks. An increase in the amount of Treasury currency, such as silver certificates, also adds to the supply of reserves. Summarizing, increases in the three principal sources of reserves tend to increase member-bank reserve balances, and decreases tend to reduce them.

Only a part of the funds made available from these primary sources, however, is held at any one time in the form of reserve balances of member banks. Other uses absorb some of these funds, the principal use being money in circulation. An increase of money in circulation tends to reduce reserves because member banks draw on their deposits in the Reserve Banks to pay for the currency needed in meeting their customers' demands. The shifting of Treasury, foreign, and other deposits from commercial banks to the Federal Reserve Banks tends to reduce member-bank reserves because, directly or indirectly, payment is made by charging member-bank reserve accounts. Increases in uses —money in circulation, Treasury cash holdings, Treasury deposits, foreign deposits, other deposits, and other Federal Reserve accounts —absorb reserves and tend to reduce member-bank reserve balances. On the other hand, decreases in uses tend to increase member-bank reserves.

Using these principles as a guide, the major factors affecting member-bank reserves for the week and year ending March 26, 1958, can be readily determined. For the week, a net increase in Reserve Bank credit, primarily in holdings of Government securities and in member-bank borrowing, supplied $104 million of reserves. An item which shows up infrequently around a tax payment date is the special certificate. Occasionally, the Treasury borrows directly from the Reserve Banks, by issuing a special certificate, to meet expenditures pending an inflow of tax receipts. This borrowing is for only a few days. During the week ending March 26, the Treasury repaid borrowing totaling $50 million, the effect of the repayment being to reduce Reserve Bank credit. Among the other sources of reserves, the only significant change was a reduction in the gold stock. Thus the three principal sources supplied net $63 million of reserves. Uses, however, absorbed on balance $267 million for the week, the primary factor being an increase of over $300 million in Treasury deposits in the Reserve Banks. The net effect of the changes in sources and uses was an average reduction of $205 million in member-bank reserves.[4]

For the year ending March 26, total Reserve Bank credit declined $188 million, the increase in holdings of Governments being more than offset by a reduction in member-bank borrowing. Increases in gold stock and Treasury currency more than offset the decline in Reserve Bank credit, the net result being an increase of $102 million in reserves supplied. Uses, primarily increases in Treasury and other deposits in the Reserve Banks, absorbed $348 million of reserves. Member-bank reserve balances thus declined $246 million.

Importance of Trends

What does the weekly statement of condition tell us about current Federal Reserve policy? Can it be used to determine whether the System is pursuing a tight- or an easy-money policy, or whether it is moving toward more or less restraint or ease? There are no simple rules which will give the right answer to such questions. There are certain guides, however, which can be helpful.

The weekly statement should be interpreted with great care in seeking clues for Federal Reserve policy intentions. In the first place, sharp and erratic changes frequently occur in some of the items affecting member-bank reserves. Bad weather delaying the transportation

---

[4] Uses of $267 million minus additional reserves supplied of $63 million, as shown in the statement, give $204 million, the discrepancy representing the rounding of the detailed figures.

of checks may cause float to rise several hundred million dollars in one day. Treasury deposits in the Reserve Banks may rise or fall considerably more than expected, thus tending to absorb or increase member-bank reserves. There is a pronounced seasonal movement in money in circulation. The seasonal increase in money in circulation in the latter part of the year is a substantial drain on member-bank reserves. On the other hand, the return flow of money from circulation following Christmas may add over a billion dollars to member-bank reserves within a few weeks. Typically, there is a significant outflow of currency preceding a holiday and a return flow following it.

Secondly, because of the impact on reserves of factors such as those enumerated above, changes in Reserve Bank credit and in member-bank reserve balances are not in themselves an accurate indicator of what the Federal Reserve is trying to do. For example, a decline in float or an increase in Treasury deposits at the Reserve Banks may absorb more reserves than is considered desirable. Under such circumstances, the Federal Reserve may offset the absorption of reserves by buying Government securities. If factors not subject to System control are adding too much to reserves, the Federal Reserve may sell Government securities or allow them to run off to absorb the excess. Thus the Federal Reserve may act to supply or withdraw reserves, not because it is attempting to ease or tighten credit, but to offset the impact of other factors. Unexpected and unpredictable changes in factors such as float and Treasury balances in the Reserve Banks may result in unintended changes in the total volume of bank reserves. For reasons such as these the weekly statement may show a change in Reserve Bank credit and in member-bank reserve balances, even though there has been no change in Federal Reserve policy with respect to ease or restraint.

A much clearer indication of Federal Reserve intentions with respect to tightening or easing credit is the trend in selected items over a period of time. Inasmuch as Federal Reserve actions impinge directly on reserve positions, two key items to follow are excess reserves and member-bank borrowing from the Reserve Banks. In recent years, free and net borrowed reserves have come into common usage. Free reserves refer to the amount by which the total excess reserves of member banks are greater than their total borrowings from the Reserve Banks. This net excess over borrowings represents the amount of reserves available to member banks to support an expansion in loans and deposits. Net borrowed reserves represent the total amount by which total borrowings from the Reserve Banks exceed total excess reserves. Inasmuch as member banks are reluctant to be in debt to the Reserve Banks, a net borrowed reserve position tends to discourage credit expansion.

The following chart shows the monthly averages of excess reserves and borrowings of member banks, and net free or net borrowed reserves for the period 1952-57. Monthly averages, by smoothing out some of the week-to-week changes, show the trend more clearly than weekly data.

From about mid-1952 to mid-1953, total member-bank borrowing was considerably larger than total excess reserves. The net borrowed reserve position which prevailed during this period reflected the restrictive credit policy pursued by the Federal Reserve. Shortly after mid-1953, total borrowings dropped below excess reserves, resulting in net free reserves. As it became clear in the latter part of 1953 that a business recession was under way, the Federal Reserve moved to a policy of "active ease." The objective was to keep member banks supplied with ample reserves to meet all sound credit needs. This policy of active ease is reflected in the sharp decline in member-bank borrowing and, to a lesser extent, in the rise in excess reserves. During the latter part of 1953, and in 1954, member banks had a substantial volume of free reserves, which encouraged investments and credit expansion.

Another shift in credit policy began to emerge in the fall of 1954. The sharp upturn in business activity in late 1954 was accompanied by an unusually rapid expansion in bank loans and other forms of credit. In view of the rapid rise in business activity and expansion of credit, the Federal Reserve began to move away from its previous policy of active ease. The gradual shift toward less ease is indicated by the shrinkage in free reserves brought about by an increase in member-bank borrowing and a decline in excess reserves.

By mid-1955 there was little slack left in the economy, but credit expansion was continuing unabated. The Federal Reserve moved toward a restrictive policy. Total borrowings rose above excess reserves, with the result that member banks were operating on net borrowed reserves. The tight-money policy pursued by the Federal Reserve from about mid-1955 to the latter part of 1957 was reflected in a relatively high level of member-bank borrowing and a low level of excess reserves, except for temporary changes brought about mainly by seasonal factors at the end of the year.

In summary, a policy of credit restraint is reflected in pressure on member-bank reserve positions. Member-bank borrowing rises

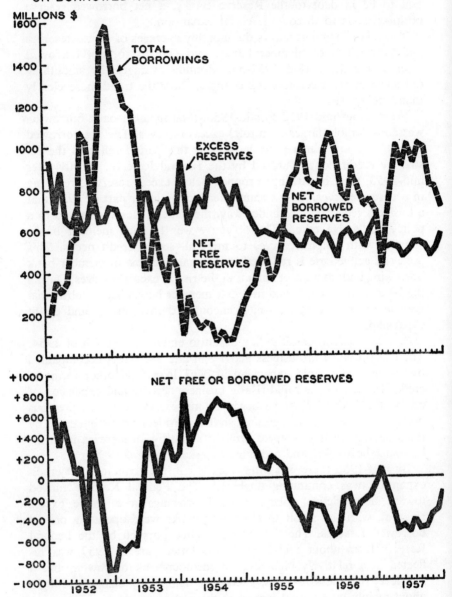

EXCESS RESERVES, BORROWINGS AND NET FREE
OR BORROWED RESERVES OF MEMBER BANKS 1952-1957

and, if long continued, moves above excess reserves. A credit policy of increasing restraint is likely to be accompanied by a growing volume of net borrowed reserves. On the other hand, when the objective is one of ease, the Federal Reserve increases the supply of reserves available to the banks. Funds so supplied are used to repay indebtedness to the Reserve Banks, and member-bank borrowing declines. An easy-money policy, therefore, is reflected in a declining or low level of member-bank borrowing and a rising or relatively high level of excess reserves.

EARNINGS AND EXPENSES

A statement of the earnings and expenses of the twelve Federal Reserve Banks combined, of each Federal Reserve Bank, and of the Board of Governors is given in the Annual Report of the Board of Governors of the Federal Reserve System.[5] Like the statement of condition, the significance of earnings and expenses of the Federal Reserve Banks differs from that of an ordinary corporation. The Federal Reserve Banks, although privately owned, are not operated for profit. Quite properly, the Federal Reserve Act limits the dividends to stockholding member banks to 6 per cent annually. Federal Reserve policies and operations are not determined by the profit motive; instead, they are directed toward best serving the public interest.

The statement of earnings and expenses of the twelve Federal Reserve Banks combined for 1956 is reproduced below.

TABLE 4. EARNINGS AND EXPENSES OF FEDERAL RESERVE BANKS
DURING 1956

Current Earnings and Expenses	
Discounts and advances	$ 23,024,697
Industrial loans	35,621
Commitments to make industrial loans	14,972
Acceptances	547,170
U.S. Government securities	571,788,486
All other	238,146
Total current earnings	$595,649,092
Salaries	
Officers	5,449,677
Employees	72,810,052

[5] For example, see the Annual Report for 1956, pp. 63-65, 69-70, 80-83.

Directors and other fees	348,008
Retirement contributions	6,920,835
Traveling expenses	1,464,312
Postage and expressage	15,586,655
Telephone and telegraph	1,190,712
Printing, stationery, and supplies	5,574,919
Insurance	1,128,429
Taxes on real estate	3,138,279
Depreciation (building)	3,229,455
Light, heat, power, and water	1,278,129
Repairs and alterations	1,380,489
Rent	458,354
Furniture and equipment	
Purchases	2,343,523
Rentals	4,582,017
Assessment for expenses of Board of Governors	5,339,800
Federal Reserve currency	5,603,176
All other	1,712,081[1]
Total	139,538,902[1]
Less reimbursement for certain fiscal agency and other expenses	18,356,406[1]
Net expenses	121,182,496

Profit and Loss

Current net earnings	$474,466,596
Additions to current net earnings:	
Profits on sales of U.S. Government securities (net)	268,090
All other	91,025
Total additions	359,115
Deductions from current net earnings:	
Charge-offs on bank premises	20,147
Reserve for contingencies	340,270
All other	22,135
Total deductions	382,551
Net deductions	23,436
Net earnings before payments to U.S. Treasury	474,443,160
Paid U.S. Treasury (interest on F.R. notes)	401,555,581
Dividends paid	18,904,897
Transferred to surplus (Sec. 7)	53,982,682
Surplus (Sec. 7) Jan. 1	693,611,316
Surplus (Sec. 7) Dec. 31	747,593,998

[1] After deducting $415,326 of prorated inter-Bank expenses to avoid duplication in combined totals.

Sources of Earnings

The Federal Reserve Banks combined had total earnings of nearly $600 million in 1956. Two sources provided practically all of the earnings.

Interest on Government securities supplied 96 per cent of total earnings in 1956. This has been much the largest source of earnings since the sharp increase in Federal Reserve holdings of Government securities in the early thirties. The next largest source of income is interest on loans and discounts to member banks. Other minor sources of earnings are interest on holdings of bankers' acceptances, on loans to business firms, and on profits on the sale of Government securities. Although thus far it has occurred infrequently, the Federal Reserve System sometimes incurs a net loss on the sale of Government securities during the year.

With these two primary sources of earnings, it is apparent that earnings fluctuate with changes in interest rates and in the volume of Reserve Bank earning assets, namely, loans to member banks and holdings of Government securities. In a period of recession, earnings tend to decline. An easy-money policy, as we have seen, results in a substantial decrease in member-bank borrowing from the Reserve Banks. Although holdings of Government securities may rise as purchases are made in supplying additional reserves, market rates of interest decline during a period of recession. Because most of the Government securities owned by the Federal Reserve System are short-term, the decline in interest rates soon begins to reduce income from the Government portfolio. Total current earnings dropped from $513 million in 1953 to $438 million in 1954, and then to $412 million in 1955.[6] The small decline in earnings in 1955, despite the recovery in business activity which began in late 1954, reflected the low coupon rate on Governments acquired earlier and somewhat lower average holdings of Governments than in 1954. Reduced earnings on Government securities more than offset the effects of the rising level of member-bank borrowing and increases in the discount rate which were more pronounced in the latter part of the year.

In periods of prosperity and credit restraint, a larger volume of member-bank borrowing, a higher discount rate, and a higher yield on Government securities combine to increase Reserve Bank earnings, but only with some time lag. For example, total earnings,

[6] See Annual Report for 1956, pp. 82-83.

which had declined to $412 million in 1955, rose to $596 million in
1956.[7]

Expenses

The items of expenditure listed in the earnings and expense statement are largely self-explanatory. Salaries of officers and employees
is the largest item, accounting for 56 per cent of total expenses in
1956. The next largest item, postage and expressage, consists mainly
of transportation charges on currency shipments and check collection.
Federal Reserve currency expense includes the cost of printing and
issuing Federal Reserve notes. There is also an annual assessment
on the Reserve Banks to cover the expenses of the Board of Governors and its staff. In 1956 the assessment was $5.3 million.

A functional distribution of Reserve Bank expenses for the period
1946-50 was prepared by the Chairman of the Board of Governors
in reply to questions submitted by the Subcommittee on General
Credit Control and Debt Management of the Joint Committee on the
Economic Report.[8] This classification is of interest because it shows
the cost of performing the major functions of the Reserve Banks.

Three of the functions accounted for over four-fifths of Reserve
Bank expenses during the five-year period. Approximately one-third
of total expenses was incurred in handling check collection, currency,
and securities. The principal costs involved in this function are in
check collection; receiving, sorting, and paying out currency; the
issue, redemption, and retirement of Federal Reserve notes; the purchase and sale of Government securities for the System Open Market
Account; and holding securities in custody for member banks.

Operations as fiscal agent for the Treasury and Government agencies accounted for nearly one-fourth of total expenses. Among the
more important operations included in this function are the issue,
exchange, and redemption of United States Government securities,
including savings bonds; handling Government checks and maintenance of the Treasury's general account in the Reserve Banks;
and handling withheld taxes, currency reports, and miscellaneous
foreign activities. The Reserve Banks also act as fiscal agent for Government agencies such as the Commodity Credit Corporation. The cost

[7] *Ibid.*, pp. 82-83.
[8] See *Monetary Policy and Management of the Public Debt—Their Role in
Achieving Price Stability and High Level Employment,* Joint Committee on the
Economic Report, 82nd Congress, 2nd Session, Washington, D.C., Government
Printing Office, 1952, Part 1, pp. 315-320.

of fiscal agency operations varies widely, depending on the volume of financial activities of the Federal Government.

The general function of providing space, equipment, and personnel and administrative services absorbed about one-fourth of total expenses. A variety of expenditures is included in this function, the more important expenses being maintenance of banking premises, purchase and repair of furniture and equipment, telephone and telegraph facilities, operation and maintenance of the vault, maintenance of the guard force, personnel services, general postage and expressage, and insurance, such as fire insurance on furniture and equipment, and workmen's compensation insurance.

The four other principal functions accounted for less than one-fourth of total expenses. General administration and policy formulation, including such expenses as salaries of senior officers, travel expenses, research and statistical work, directors' fees, operations of the library, and the assessment for expenses of the Board of Governors absorbed about 10 per cent of total expenses. Credit operations, including the handling of advances to member banks and bank supervision, accounted for 5 per cent; and accounting and auditing took about the same percentage of the total. Expenses incurred in handling foreign operations amounted to less than 1 per cent of total expenditures.

Net earnings after expenses and deductions are distributed in three ways. As pointed out earlier, a 6 per cent dividend is paid on paid-in capital stock owned by member banks. Approximately 90 per cent of net earnings after dividends are paid to the Treasury. Under Section 16 of the Federal Reserve Act, the Board of Governors has authority to charge the Federal Reserve Banks interest on Federal Reserve notes outstanding not covered by gold certificates. In recent years the Board of Governors has fixed a rate of interest on uncovered Federal Reserve notes outstanding that will result in the payment of approximately 90 per cent of net earnings after dividends to the Treasury. This procedure achieves the objective of the franchise tax formerly levied on net earnings of the Federal Reserve Banks but repealed when the Reserve Banks were required by legislation to use approximately $139 million of their accumulated surplus to purchase stock in the newly formed Federal Deposit Insurance Corporation. In 1956 the Federal Reserve Banks paid over $400 million to the United States Treasury. The remainder of net earnings, amounting to over $50 million in 1956, was transferred to surplus.

Control of Expenses

It is pertinent at this point to describe briefly the procedures that have been established for auditing Reserve Bank operations and controlling expenditures. Each Reserve Bank has a resident auditor who is an officer of the Bank and is directly responsible to the board of directors. The Reserve Bank auditor and his staff make a comprehensive and thorough audit of all phases of the Bank's operations throughout the year. Reports of the audit are submitted to the board of directors and a copy is furnished to and reviewed by the Board of Governors. All expenditures are carefully audited to determine whether they are properly authorized and whether they fall within the restrictions prescribed by the board of directors.

Each Federal Reserve Bank and branch, as required by the Federal Reserve Act, is examined at least once a year by the staff of examiners of the Board of Governors. This examination is thorough and covers all phases of the Bank's operations—whether the program of the resident auditor is adequate and effective, and whether the Bank's expenditures are in conformity with the rules and regulations prescribed by the Board of Governors.

In addition to constant supervision by the board of directors and the senior officers of a Reserve Bank, budgetary procedures have been prescribed as a further step in keeping expenditures under close control. Each Reserve Bank and branch is required to prepare an annual budget which is submitted to the Board of Governors for analysis and review. The budget, which is initially prepared by the staff of a Reserve Bank, is reviewed by the senior management, by the board of directors, and then by the Board of Governors of the Federal Reserve System.

The accounts of the Board of Governors are audited at least once a year by a well-qualified outside auditing firm. The Board's staff also prepares an annual budget which is submitted to the Board of Governors for review. Once approved by the Board, the budget officer has the responsibility of seeing that expenditures are in accordance with the budget.

SUGGESTED READINGS

Bank Reserves—Some Major Factors Affecting Them, New York, Federal Reserve Bank of New York, 1951 (pamphlet).

BOARD OF GOVERNORS OF THE FEDERAL RESERVE SYSTEM, *The Federal Reserve System—Purposes and Functions,* Washington, D.C., 1954, Chapter XIII.

BOARD OF GOVERNORS OF THE FEDERAL RESERVE SYSTEM, "Member Bank Reserves, Reserve Bank Credit, and Related Items," *Banking and Monetary Statistics,* Washington, D.C., 1943, pp. 360-67.

CHANDLER, LESTER V., *The Economics of Money and Banking,* New York, Harper & Brothers, 1948, Chapter XIII.

General Credit Control, Debt Management and Economic Mobilization, materials prepared for the Joint Committee on the Economic Report, 82nd Congress, 1st Session, Washington, D.C., Government Printing Office, 1951, pp. 304-320.

"Supply and Use of Member Bank Reserve Funds," *Federal Reserve Bulletin,* Vol. 21, 1935, pp. 419-29.

Utilizing the Weekly Federal Reserve Statement, New York, American Institute of Banking, 1938, pp. 47-85.

Chapter 4

MONETARY POLICY
AND ECONOMIC STABILITY

IN THE United States, economic stability has been accepted as a major goal of public policy for some years. The Great Depression of the 1930's, with its huge loss of economic output as represented by idle man power and other resources, impressed upon the American people the importance of national efforts to avoid large-scale unemployment. In the post-World War II period, persistent inflationary pressures have emphasized the importance of policies to protect the purchasing power of the dollar.

THE EMPLOYMENT ACT OF 1946

Congress, in 1946, explicitly recognized the Government's responsibility for promoting economic stability. The Employment Act of 1946 directs the Federal Government

to coordinate and utilize all its plans, functions, and resources for the purpose of creating and maintaining, in a manner calculated to foster and promote free competitive enterprise and the general welfare, conditions under which there will be afforded useful employment opportunities, including self-employment, for those able, willing, and seeking to work, and to promote maximum employment, production, and purchasing power.

This excerpt from the declaration of policy of the Employment Act deserves careful study. Although most public discussion has been directed toward the final clause—the promotion of "maximum employment, production, and purchasing power"—the earlier portions of the declaration are in some respects more important in that they in effect set forth the means by which the objectives of the Act are to be achieved. For example, Government action must be undertaken "in a manner calculated to foster and promote free competitive enterprise"; this stricture rules out extreme approaches that would involve undue resort to direct intervention in the economy. Moreover, the Government is charged with the responsibility of "creating and maintaining . . . conditions under which there will be afforded useful employment opportunities," not with a responsibility for actually providing employment through Government projects. Finally, the declaration of policy clearly aims at fostering long-run sustainable growth, and this goal rules out policies that would result in secular inflation.[1] The objectives of the Employment Act might be summarized as follows: the promotion of relatively full and efficient use of the nation's economic resources and reasonable stability of the price level, in a manner consistent with our system of free competitive enterprise.

In view of these considerations, fiscal and monetary policies are generally regarded as the primary public instruments for promoting the ends of the Employment Act. These measures operate indirectly, within the framework of a free enterprise system, but nevertheless powerfully affect the flow of spending relative to the flow of goods and services. In 1950, a highly regarded subcommittee of the Congressional Joint Committee on the Economic Report stated unanimously: "We recommend not only that appropriate, vigorous, and coordinated monetary, credit, and fiscal policies be employed to promote the purposes of the Employment Act, but also that such policies constitute the Government's primary and principal method of promoting those purposes."[2]

[1] The conviction on the part of Federal Reserve authorities that the Employment Act includes an implicit mandate with respect to price stability is illustrated by the reply of the Chairman of the Board of Governors of the Federal Reserve System, William McChesney Martin, to a question submitted by a Congressional committee in the summer of 1957. Mr. Martin said: ". . . it would be impossible 'to foster and promote . . . the general welfare' and 'to maintain maximum employment, production, and purchasing power' if prices were highly unstable and credit use were unrestricted. The achievement of these objectives requires the maintenance of reasonable stability in the value of the dollar as well as the avoidance of credit liquidation that would inevitably follow excessive credit expansion." See *Investigation of the Financial Condition of the United States, Hearings before the Committee on Finance, United States Senate,* 85th Congress, 1st Session, Washington, Government Printing Office, 1957, Part 3, p. 1256.

[2] *Report of the Subcommittee on Monetary, Credit, and Fiscal Policies of the Joint Committee on the Economic Report,* 81st Congress, 2nd Session, Washington, Government Printing Office, 1950, p. 1.

Spending, Output, and Prices

Both fiscal and monetary policies affect economic activity primarily through their influence on the flow of spending relative to the flow of goods and services. Experience has demonstrated that the flow of spending, consisting of money and credit, may be subject to wide fluctuations. Thus the problem of promoting economic stability is primarily one of keeping the flow of spending in reasonable balance with the stream of goods and services. If the flow of spending expands relative to the flow of goods and services, any existing slack in the economy, in the form of idle human and material resources, will tend to be eliminated. Producers will attempt to step up output in order to meet the increase in demand, and economic resources will be used more fully. Once these resources are in relatively full use— once "full employment" has been attained—strong pressures on prices will tend to emerge. On the other hand, a contraction in the stream of spending relative to the goods stream will tend to have an opposite effect. Resources will be idled, prices may tend to decline, and recession and depression may result.

The role of fiscal policy in influencing the flow of spending is beyond the scope of this book. Suffice it to say that the Federal Government, through use of its taxing, spending, and borrowing powers, can exert substantial influence on the willingness and ability of individuals and businesses to purchase goods and services. While the significance of such influence is beyond question, the use of fiscal policy as an effective stabilization device involves complex difficulties of timing that severely hamper its flexible use. In this chapter, and throughout this book, our attention is devoted primarily to monetary policy.

The importance of monetary policy as a stabilization device is readily apparent when it is recognized that perhaps nine-tenths or more of the dollar volume of transactions are effected through transfer of demand deposits in commercial banks. It is through affecting the cost, availability, and volume of bank credit that monetary policy exerts its most important influence.

EXPANSION AND CONTRACTION OF BANK DEPOSITS

How do demand deposits in commercial banks come into existence? How are they extinguished? A clear understanding of the process of demand-deposit expansion and contraction is essential to an understanding of the mechanics of monetary policy.

Expansion of Demand Deposits

Four rigid but not unrealistic assumptions must be made if the process of deposit expansion is to be fully explained.

1. Assume that commercial banks, because of either law or custom, maintain a 20 per cent cash reserve in relation to their demand deposits. If the banks involved were members of the Federal Reserve System, they would (as is explained in Chapter 5) have to hold these reserves as deposits in the Federal Reserve banks of their respective districts. However, the theory of deposit expansion is equally applicable to nonmember banks, which are usually permitted to hold their reserves in the form of cash in vault and deposits in other commercial banks. The theory is also applicable to banks, such as those in England, that are not subject to legal reserve requirements, but which customarily hold a portion of their assets in the form of cash and deposits in other banks. This first assumption is necessary because it places an ultimate limit on the amount of deposit expansion possible on the basis of a given volume of available reserves.

2. Assume that individual bankers consider any new primary deposits to be stable, in that the funds will not be withdrawn from the individual bank for a reasonable period of time. (Primary deposits are those which increase the cash reserves of a bank, resulting from customer deposit of currency or checks drawn on other banks.) The importance of this assumption is apparent; an individual banker can ill afford to expand loans and investments on the basis of funds that may shortly be withdrawn from the bank.

3. Assume that the demand for loans on the part of customers of the banks, or that the availability of suitable investments such as Government securities, is sufficient to absorb all of the funds that the banks can safely lend and invest. *Maximum* deposit expansion can occur only if the outlets for bank lending and investing are adequate.

4. Assume, finally, that the full proceeds of each individual loan will be withdrawn from the lending bank within a short period of time—a few days at the most—but will be redeposited in one or more other banks. While this assumption is somewhat unrealistic, in that banks commonly require business borrowers to maintain minimum deposit balances equal to a certain percentage of their lines of credit or loans, the departure from reality is only a matter of degree and in

no way affects the principles to be illustrated. Moreover, it is probable that some of the funds created in the process of deposit expansion would not be redeposited in other banks but would be withdrawn in the form of currency. Again, the assumption that the full proceeds of each loan will be redeposited in other banks greatly simplifies' the illustration and in no way nullifies the principles to be set forth.

The preceding assumptions provide a basis for determining the maximum possible deposit expansion within the banking system on the basis of a given volume of excess cash reserves. Suppose, for example, that Bank A receives $100,000 in new primary deposits, perhaps resulting from a net reserve-creating event such as a gold import or a net inflow of currency from circulation. This transaction would be reflected on the books of Bank A as follows:

Assets	Liabilities
(1) Cash reserves + $100,000	Demand deposits + $100,000

How much can Bank A safely expand its loans, on the basis of the $100,000 of new reserves it has obtained? The answer, on the basis of the assumptions stated above, is $80,000. In arriving at this figure, the two critical assumptions are that Bank A maintains a 20 per cent reserve in relation to its demand deposits, and that the full proceeds of the loan will be withdrawn from Bank A within a relatively short period of time. Following the withdrawal of the loan proceeds, the transactions involved in the example can be summarized as follows:

Assets			Liabilities		
(1) Cash reserves	+	$100,000	Demand deposits	+	$100,000
(2) Loans	+	80,000	Demand deposits	+	80,000
(3) Cash reserves	−	80,000	Demand deposits	−	80,000
So					
Cash reserves	+	$ 20,000	Demand deposits	+	$100,000
Loans	+	80,000			

Transaction (1) reflects the acquisition by the bank of the $100,000 in cash reserves and an equivalent increase in demand deposits. Transaction (2) represents the loan extension, which is almost invariably in the form of deposit credit to the borrower. And transaction (3) reflects the subsequent withdrawal of the loan proceeds by the borrower (probably by transferring his deposit to another party by drawing a check on the bank). At the end of the chain of transactions, the books of the bank balance, and its cash reserve position (20 per cent) is just sufficient to support its expanded volume of deposits. Any lesser expansion of loans would have left excess cash reserves on hand; any greater expansion would have caused the bank to be short of reserves relative to deposits.

Before continuing with an explanation of the process of multiple deposit expansion in the banking system, three observations concerning the preceding example are in order. First, the expansion on the part of an individual bank, which is much less than is possible in the banking system as a whole, nevertheless represents deposit creation. It therefore tends to expand the flow of expenditures. Study of the example indicates that the volume of demand deposits, as a result of the transactions, has increased by $80,000: the original $100,000 deposit remains in Bank A, and someone possesses the $80,000 claim that grew out of Bank A's lending transaction. In essence, Bank A created $80,000 through the lending operation.

Second, the general rule to be remembered is that an individual bank can safely expand its earning assets (loans and investments) by an amount approximately equal to its excess cash reserves. Excess cash reserves represent the amount of cash on hand over and above legal requirements or the amount the bank desires to hold because of custom or habit. The individual bank is limited to this amount of expansion because of the probability that the proceeds of the loan will be withdrawn. Consequently, expansion greater in amount than the available volume of excess reserves would subject the bank to a reserve deficiency.

Third, although the process of expansion is illustrated by means of a bank loan, the same comments apply to investments in the form of purchases of Government and other securities. In our example, Bank A could just as well have purchased $80,000 of Government securities instead of granting a loan for that amount. In so far as Bank A is concerned, the only difference as reflected on its books would be an $80,000 rise in holdings of Government securities instead of an $80,000 increase in loans. Moreover, the cashier's check drawn by Bank A in payment for the securities would, under the assumptions, have been redeposited in one or more other banks, and the money supply would have increased by $80,000.

Multiple Expansion in the Banking System

The expansion process on the basis of new reserves does not end with the individual bank. The last of the four assumptions should be recalled; namely, that the full proceeds of the loan would be withdrawn from the lending bank and redeposited in one or more other banks. If the $80,000 of loan proceeds are redeposited in Bank B, this latter bank finds itself with excess cash reserves and is in a position to expand its earning assets by an amount equal to the excess funds. In this instance, however, the maximum expansion is only $64,000, inasmuch as $16,000 of the new reserves obtained by Bank B (or 20 per cent of $80,000) would be immobilized to support the new deposit. Thus, the transactions at Bank B, following the completion of the loan transaction and the withdrawal of the loan proceeds by the borrower, can be summarized as follows:

	Assets			*Liabilities*	
(1) Cash reserves	+	$80,000	Demand deposits	+	$80,000
(2) Loans	+	64,000	Demand deposits	+	64,000
(3) Cash reserves	−	64,000	Demand deposits	−	64,000
So					
Cash reserves	+	$16,000	Demand deposits	+	$80,000
Loans	+	64,000			

Again, as in the case of Bank A, the books of Bank B are in balance, and it has retained just enough of the new cash reserves— no more, no less—to support the $80,000 increase in demand deposits. Given the four basic assumptions, Bank B has expanded its earning assets by the maximum possible amount.

The process of multiple expansion should now be reasonably clear. When the loan proceeds are withdrawn from Bank B, they will in turn be redeposited in one or more other banks, and so on. The entire process is summarized in the following table:

	Increase in Deposits	Increase in Required Reserves	Increase in Loans (or Investments)
Bank A	$100,000	$ 20,000	$ 80,000
Bank B	80,000	16,000	64,000
Bank C	64,000	12,800	51,200
Bank D	51,200	10,240	40,960
Bank E	40,960	8,192	32,768
Additional banks	163,840	32,768	131,072
Total	$500,000	$100,000	$400,000

The maximum amount of deposits that a given volume of reserves will support can be easily computed, once the required or customary reserve ratio is known. The multiplier for computing the amount of potential expansion is the reciprocal of the reserve ratio requirement (that is, the reserve ratio requirement, as a decimal, divided into one). Thus, as in the example presented above, $100,000 of reserves will support an ultimate deposit total of $500,000 inasmuch as the reciprocal of the reserve ratio requirement is 5 (that is, $1 \div .20$). On the other hand, $100,000 in reserves would support $1,000,000 in deposits if the requirement were only 10 per cent; $300,000, if the requirement were 33⅓ per cent; and so on.

Multiple expansion is possible in the banking system, as opposed to an expansion of approximately one-for-one in the individual bank, because the withdrawal of funds that constitutes a drain on the individual bank is not necessarily a drain on the banking system as a whole. Under the fourth assumption set up for the example, the reserves move from bank to bank but never leave the banking system. In actual practice, a portion of the reserves would no doubt move out of the banking system in the form of an increase in currency in circulation. Such a drain would, of course, reduce the amount of the maximum potential expansion. While it is impossible to predict in advance the portion of a given volume of new reserves that will be absorbed by an increase in currency in circulation, it is probable that the resultant expansion in the money supply would in general reflect the ratio between demand deposits and currency that generally prevails. In late 1959 this ratio was approximately 4 to 1. It should be noted, however, that growth in certain types of bank loans, such as those to finance payrolls, is likely to be accompanied by a larger drain of currency into circulation than other types of credit extension.

The preceding example is highly formalized for purposes of exposition. Actually, the cash reserves that permit expansion would not flow in the precise amounts described above from one bank to the next, but would be separated into units of varying size and, one might say, move almost helter-skelter through the banking system. As a general rule, small banks might be expected to end up with a relatively small portion of a given volume of new reserves obtained by the banking system, large banks with a somewhat larger share.

Contraction of Bank Deposits

It is apparent that withdrawal of the original primary deposits that provided the basis for the multiple expansion would result in a reserve deficiency in Bank A, which in turn would be forced either to obtain new reserves from some source or to reduce its deposits. If it is assumed that no new reserves are available to the banking system as a whole, the total of bank deposits would have to be contracted by an amount equal to five times the reserve loss (assuming still a 20 per cent reserve requirement). While the initial impact of the reserve deficiency would fall on Bank A, secondary effects would be transmitted throughout the banking system as Bank A attempted to increase its reserves and/or reduce its deposits (by curtailing its lending operations and liquidating investments). For example, Bank A, in attempting to build up its reserves, might sell some Government securities to a customer of Bank B; this action would shift pressure to the latter bank, as the check drawn by the customer in payment for the securities cleared. Bank B would have to take steps to strengthen its reserve position, and pressure might in turn be shifted to Bank C; and so on. Again, the pressures would not be transferred from bank to bank in a precise and predictable manner, but would flow through the banking system in a manner determined primarily by market forces. The essential point is that the net loss of reserves would destroy the basis for a given volume of deposits, forcing the banking system to engage in operations that would restore an appropriate relation between reserves and deposits.

Legal and Institutional Basis of Multiple Expansion

The ability of commercial banks in the United States to create demand deposits, which for all practical purposes are money, through their lending and investing activities rests upon one legal and two institutional factors. First, the expansion is possible only because the United States has a fractional-reserve banking system, in that banks are permitted to hold fractional cash reserves behind their deposit liabilities. If banks were required by law to hold 100 per cent reserves behind deposits, multiple expansion would be impossible.

Second, an important institutional factor that enables banks to engage in multiple expansion of deposits is the "banking habit," or the preference on the part of individuals and institutions to hold balances in the form of claims on banks (deposits) rather than in the form of currency and coin. Most individuals and institutions prefer to hold their currency and coin to the minimum consistent with everyday needs. Moreover, the widespread and growing acceptability of bank checks in ordinary exchange has furthered the banking habit. A preference for currency and coin over bank deposits would reduce or, at the extreme, even eliminate the potential for multiple deposit expansion.

Finally, the process of multiple expansion is, in essence, a process of money creation because demand deposits are generally acceptable in exchange. Bank demand deposits account for about 80 per cent of the money supply and, as already noted, an estimated 90 per cent or more of the dollar volume of transactions. With their liabilities circulating as money, and with the ability to expand those liabilities greatly on the basis of a given volume of reserves, commercial banks occupy a strategic position in the financial system and, indeed, in the economy as a whole. It is obvious that an efficient and workable system of monetary control must include some mechanism for influencing bank deposit creation.

BANK RESERVES, INTEREST RATES, AND MONETARY POLICY

Bank deposit creation and extinction are influenced significantly by Federal Reserve policy, and this policy in turn operates mainly through affecting the reserve position of the banking system. It should be clear, from the example presented in this chapter, that the availability of reserves is a critical factor in the willingness and ability of individual banks and, therefore, the banking system to expand deposits by lending and investing. Inasmuch as the instruments of Federal Reserve policy are described in detail in subsequent chapters, it is sufficient here merely to list the three general instruments, along with a few words about how their use affects bank reserve positions.

1. *Discount policy* refers to the actions of Federal Reserve authorities in establishing the interest rates (discount rates) applicable to member-bank borrowing from Reserve banks and in administering the discounting operation. Decisions with respect to the level of the discount rate and the terms upon which Federal Reserve credit is available through discounting significantly affect the cost and availability of reserves and, as a consequence, the willingness and ability of banks to expand earning assets. Discount policy is discussed in detail in Chapter 6.

2. By raising or lowering *reserve requirements* of member banks, the Board of Governors of the Federal Reserve System directly reduces or expands the volume of excess reserve funds that can be used to support additional deposit expansion. These actions directly affect bank reserve positions and, indirectly, the cost of reserves throughout

the banking system. The origin, nature, and use of reserve requirements are discussed further in Chapter 5.

3. *Open-market operations* involve the purchase and sale of Government securities and bankers' acceptances for the System by the Federal Reserve Bank of New York, as agent for and subject to the directives of the Federal Open Market Committee. As will be explained in Chapter 7, open-market purchases increase the volume and availability of reserves, and also tend to lower their cost through their effect on interest rates. Open-market sales absorb reserves and thus tend to have an opposite effect on reserve availability and cost.

Monetary Policy and Interest Rates

Interest rates, viewed as the cost of borrowing money, are affected by the central bank in its credit control actions. Generally speaking a restrictive monetary policy tends to push interest rates on all types of credit instruments higher; an expansive policy tends to induce lower rates. The level of interest rates is determined by the forces operating through demand for and supply of bank loans and other types of credit extension, including purchases and sales of Government and other securities. Monetary policy affects particularly the supply of funds available for bank lending, through its affect on bank reserve positions. In addition, open-market operations also exert a direct effect on the yields of the types of securities in which the central bank deals. In recent years, the direct effect on interest rates of Federal open-market operations has been limited by confining dealings to short-term Government securities (usually Treasury bills); prices and yields of short-term instruments respond in only small degree to changes in demand and supply. Nevertheless, experience has demonstrated that the level of interest rates on all maturities of Government and other securities, and on credit extensions by banks and other financial institutions, is markedly responsive to shifts in the direction and degree of Federal Reserve policy.

While the responsiveness of interest rates to central bank actions is a matter of little debate, the precise significance of such changes is an unsettled issue among monetary economists. One group argues that the level of interest rates has little effect on the demand for funds and the level of saving, and, consequently, that actions of the central bank operating through interest rates are of little use in our efforts to promote economic stability. A second group questions this view, maintaining that demand for funds on the part of marginal borrowers (borrowers who are relatively indifferent whether they obtain loan funds or not, or borrowers who intend to finance projects that are marginal with respect to their potential profitability) is affected significantly by the level of interest rates. It is this marginal demand, they maintain, that is particularly important with respect to the flow of spending relative to the flow of goods and services. The second group argues further that the level of interest rates at a given time, and particularly expectations of potential borrowers about the probable trend in interest rates in the future, exert important influences on the *timing* of borrowing operations. This view has been supported during recent periods of high interest rates and limited availability of credit in which prospective borrowers have temporarily and, in some instances, indefinitely postponed financing operations in order to await lower interest rates and more favorable borrowing conditions.

In some credit markets, the availability of credit may be much more important than its cost as a device for rationing a limited supply of funds among borrowers. Some lenders, for a variety of reasons, prefer to vary their lending rates only at relatively infrequent intervals. Consequently, changes in pressures operating through demand and supply, including the effects of monetary policy, are often manifested in changes in the degree of "credit rationing" (lenders' actions in varying the amount of credit they will extend at a given interest rate) and other variations in credit terms, rather than in changes in interest rates. The availability of credit, as contrasted with its price, appears to be most significant in those credit markets in which the terms are negotiated between the borrower and the lender (e.g., the market for bank loans), as opposed to an open market in which there are a large number of participants and in which borrowers are confronted with a large number of alternatives in obtaining credit.

While the precise significance of the level of interest rates as contrasted with the availability of credit is still an unsettled issue, it must be remembered that the purpose of a restrictive monetary policy is simply to dampen spending, and the purpose of an expansive policy is simply to stimulate spending. It is of little significance for this discussion, which presents the mechanics of monetary policy primarily by describing its effects on the quantity of money, whether the influence of monetary policy stems primarily from its effects on interest rates, the availability of credit, or, as seems likely, a combination of the two.

LIMITATIONS OF MONETARY POLICY

There seems little question but that Federal Reserve authorities can exert considerable influence over changes in the money supply. The larger and more volatile portion of the money supply consists of demand deposits in commercial banks, and the volume of demand deposits is especially sensitive to Federal Reserve actions affecting bank reserve positions and interest rates.

The ability of Reserve authorities to influence significantly the quantity of money has been clearly demonstrated in recent years. For example, restrictive monetary policies during the boom of 1955-57 limited growth in the money supply to a relatively small amount. On the other hand, expansive policies during the recessions of 1953-54 and 1957-58 contributed to growth in the money supply. Under present-day conditions, growth is likely to occur when bank reserve positions ease even though demand for bank loans subsides, as it usually does during a business recession. Confronted with declining loan demand, banks use the additional reserves made available through an expansive monetary policy to purchase Government and other securities from market holders, and to subscribe to new issues offered by the Treasury. Consequently, growth in bank investments may well offset any decline in loans, with the result that total loans and investments increase. Under such conditions, deposits also tend to expand. Adequate influence on the volume of money is, it would seem, well within the powers of the Federal Reserve authorities.

Unfortunately, however, the quantity of money is not the only factor in the spending equation. The rate of use of money—or its "velocity"—is a second important factor in the spending stream. During a period in which demand for goods and services is strong and monetary policy is restrictive, a rising velocity of money may offset the dampening effects on total spending stemming from a diminished rate of growth (or a decline) in the money supply. Conversely, during a business recession, when monetary policy is expansive, a declining velocity of money may more than offset the stimulative effects of a rising money supply.

With respect to efforts to control inflation, some economists argue that the velocity of money is largely beyond the influence of the monetary authorities and that, consequently, the effectiveness of monetary policy as an instrument of economic control is seriously impaired.

Other economists dispute this view. Perhaps the issues can be sharpened if we examine briefly three types of increase in velocity that may occur during a period of inflationary pressures.

1. Velocity may rise gradually over time, or sharply within a short period of time, as individuals and businesses utilize their existing cash balances more intensively. If the rise is gradual and not very pronounced over an extended period, it is probable that a restrictive monetary policy can easily offset the effect of the rise on total spending. However, if the rise in velocity is relatively sharp—perhaps stemming from a sudden jolt to expectations as a result of the outbreak of war—the effectiveness of traditional monetary controls may be limited. It is not so much that the monetary authorities would be powerless to take actions that would offset the effect of the increase in velocity, but that such actions might have to be so severe as to contribute to extreme disorder in financial markets. An example of a sharp rise in velocity and an accompanying surge in total spending, resulting from expectations of shortages of goods and future price rises, was the situation following the outbreak of fighting in Korea in June 1950. Consumers utilized idle balances to purchase homes, automobiles, and other durable goods in large volume. Businesses sharply stepped up their rate of inventory accumulation. The flow of spending expanded rapidly and prices rose.

2. A rise in velocity may also be facilitated by a shift of existing cash balances from more or less inactive to active users of the funds. For example, an individual may utilize part of his idle cash balance to purchase securities from a holder that in turn spends the money for goods and services. In addition, this type of shift may often occur with respect to activities of nonbank financial institutions. Suppose that an individual, attracted by a relatively high rate of return offered on savings and loan shares, transfers what was previously an idle demand deposit in his commercial bank to a savings and loan association through purchase of shares in the association, and that the association in turn uses the newly acquired funds to finance residential construction through mortgage lending. This series of transactions has little effect on the quantity of money, inasmuch as the recipient of the mortgage loan will probably deposit all or most of the funds in his bank, as will the contractor who builds the new house, the suppliers of materials, and so on.

The velocity of money has risen, however, and the increase in velocity is reflected in an increase in total spending. What was previously an idle demand deposit has been activated because it has been transferred to individuals and businesses that seek credit to support additional spending. On balance, the shift of the funds, and the concomitant increase in velocity, are inflationary.

Evidence whether the activation of idle balances through lending activities of nonbank financial institutions seriously complicates the task of monetary control is not conclusive. While most economists readily admit that the activities of these institutions may facilitate increases in the rate of use of money, and therefore total spending, the quantitative significance of such transfers, and the consequent impairment of the effectiveness of monetary control, is a subject about which relatively little is known. One group of economists argues, without much empirical support, that monetary controls should be extended to the nonbank financial institutions, on the ground that their activities seriously reduce the effectiveness of monetary control. They also maintain that traditional monetary actions result in undue hardship on the commercial banking system, inasmuch as effective monetary restraint during a period of inflation requires greater and greater pressure on the quantity of money, and therefore the banking system, to offset the effects of rising velocity.

Also lacking empirical verification is the argument that facilitation of increases in velocity by the activities of the nonbank financial institutions is of little quantitative significance and that traditional monetary actions can cope adequately and easily with such trends. Clearly, these arguments can be resolved only by intensive study of the financial structure and the impact of the flow of funds among various financial institutions.[3]

[3] In the writer's opinion, the argument that the activities of nonbank financial institutions seriously impair the effectiveness of general monetary policy has been overstated. The writer subscribes to the view expressed by Dr. Karl R. Bopp, President of the Federal Reserve Bank of Philadelphia, as reflected in Dr. Bopp's reply to a question submitted by the Senate Finance Committee in 1958. He said: "As far as financial intermediaries are concerned, it should be remembered that they do not operate in a vacuum. They operate in organized and customers' money and capital markets which are influenced by monetary policy. In fact, one consequence of the institutional developments of recent decades is that both borrowers and lenders have more options. A man who wishes to finance the purchase of a house or of an automobile can apply at several different types of institutions. Alternatively, one who wishes to save in liquid forms has numerous options. Banks and other institutional lenders in turn may lend to consumers, to homeowners, to business firms, and others. Is it not reasonable to suppose that as the number of options increases—as the network of credit contacts becomes more elaborate—the influence of the monetary authorities permeates the economy more thoroughly and more quickly?

3. The third type of rise in velocity is the most complicated and, at times, perhaps the most important of the three discussed in this chapter. Whereas the first type relates to more active use of idle balances by their owners, and the second pertains to a shift of idle balances from inactive to active users, the third type involves a concurrent destruction and creation of commercial bank deposits, but with the newly created deposits moving into the hands of active users, as contrasted with destruction of inactive balances. For example, commercial banks as a group may sell Government securities to nonbank investors, such as business corporations. Both earning assets and deposits of banks tend to decline, inasmuch as deposits are, in effect, canceled in payment for the securities. However, the banking system will experience a slight rise in its excess reserves; deposits have declined, but reserves are unchanged; consequently, required reserves have decreased and excess reserves have risen. This increases the lending ability of the banking system by approximately the same amount as the decline in investments.

Now, if commercial banks are confronted with a strong loan demand on the part of businesses and consumers, as is likely during a period of inflationary pressures, the banks will tend to use the additional excess reserves for lending. In the process, new deposits about

---

Incidentally, doesn't the widespread ownership of the Federal debt operate in the same direction? Doesn't the credit market become more fluid and doesn't the burden of distributing credit fall more on price and less on administration or rationing?" See *Investigation of the Financial Condition of the United States, Joint and Supplemental Comments of the Presidents of the Federal Reserve Banks in Response to the Questionnaire of the Committee on Finance, United States Senate,* 85th Congress, 2nd Session, Washington, Government Printing Office, 1958, Chapter 1, pp. 77-78.

Moreover, it may be noted in passing that higher interest rates during a period of inflationary pressures do not operate solely, or perhaps even primarily, in the direction of pulling idle balances into active use. To the extent that increases in rates stem from pressures of demand for funds to finance spending on goods and services, this contention may be true. But to the extent such increases result from the effects of a restrictive monetary policy on the supply of funds, the higher rates are indicative of a shortage of funds to finance spending plans. Whether the net result of the interaction of demand forces, representing attempts of individuals and businesses to obtain funds for spending for goods and services, and the supply forces, representing in part the restrictive effects of monetary policy, is to activate idle balances and thus support additional spending would seem to depend on the relative level of demand as opposed to the severity of the monetary policy of restraint. At any rate, there is support for the view that a sufficiently restrictive policy can partly or perhaps fully offset the inflationary impact of activation of previously idle balances during a period of inflationary pressures.

equal in amount to those destroyed as the Government securities were liquidated will be created. The new deposits, however, flow into the hands of active spenders, individuals and businesses that borrow from banks for the express purpose of buying goods and services. On the other hand, the deposits destroyed in the securities transactions can be assumed to have been relatively idle, or funds seeking attractive investment opportunities, such as those afforded by the desire of banks to sell Government securities.

The net result of the series of transactions is that the money supply does not change; the original decline in deposits accompanying the securities sales is roughly offset by the increase stemming from bank lending operations; but the velocity of money tends to rise, inasmuch as the new deposits flow into the hands of businesses and consumers that desire to purchase goods and services.

This type of shift, and an accompanying expansion in velocity and spending, was undoubtedly an important factor in the upsurge in total spending in 1955-56. The money supply rose by a relatively small amount during that period, but velocity, and with it total spending, expanded markedly. Total bank loans advanced $19.7 billion, as contrasted with a $10.5 billion decline in bank holdings of Government and other securities. This shift, and the accompanying expansion in velocity, was a practical example of the type of situation described in principle above.

This third type of increase in velocity, facilitated as it is by bank deposit destruction and creation, would seem to be subject to considerable influence by monetary policy. It would be a relatively simple matter for the central bank to absorb the additional excess reserves that the banking system obtains by selling securities to nonbank investors. This could be done either by raising reserve requirements or by net sales of Government securities in the open market. Consequently, creation of new deposits for individual and business borrowers would be minimized and the resulting increase in spending (rise in velocity) would also be limited.

Monetary Policy in Economic Recession

Much has been written about the alleged ineffectiveness of monetary policy in combating economic recession. Unfortunately, many of the recent statements on the matter are still colored by experiences in the Great Depression; there is a disturbing tendency to assume that the ineffectiveness of the expansive monetary policy of the mid-1930's in restoring full prosperity in turn proves that monetary policy can make little or no contribution in combating the types of economic recession that have occurred since the end of the Second World War.

It is a mistake to draw close parallels between postwar recessions and the Great Depression of the 1930's. The monetary policies that were followed during the early stages of the recession of 1929-31, and particularly the policies of 1931-33, were not nearly so expansive as those adopted in the postwar recessions. Admittedly, there were in the earlier period a number of legal and institutional factors that hampered the execution of a truly expansive policy; but the fact remains that monetary developments helped in only small measure to cushion the downturn and, at certain times, actually tended to increase deflationary pressures.

Once the economy had fallen to the depths of depression reached in 1932-33, one could hardly expect monetary policy alone to restore the economy to high levels of production and employment. Deep pessimism prevailed. Productive capacity, relative to current and prospective market demand, was very large; consequently, few attractive investment opportunities existed. Large quantities of financial assets had become frozen as a result of the unprecedented number of bank suspensions. Of particular significance from the standpoint of our discussion was the sharp contraction in the money supply in 1931-33. Under such conditions, it was little wonder that the expansive monetary policies of 1934-36 appeared to have little effect in stimulating recovery.

The legal impediments to implementing a truly expansive policy during a recession have either been eliminated or, for one reason or another, are much less significant. Moreover, the abandonment of the international gold coin standard of the type prevailing in the early 1930's has provided the monetary authorities with greater freedom of action in combating recession. It is to be hoped, in addition, that we have learned from experience, and that both public and official attitudes about the proper role of monetary policy in fighting recession reflect the advances in economic understanding that have occurred during the past thirty years. The rapid adjustment of policy to changes in the business situation since 1951 supports this view.

It should be clear that experience in the 1930's cannot be viewed as indicative of the effectiveness of monetary policy in combating recessions in the postwar period. It must be admitted, however, that monetary policy is probably more effective in limiting inflation than in stimulating recovery from a business decline. This is because access to money is a prime requisite for inflationary increases in spending; but access to money during a slump is not alone sufficient to assure spending. To admit this is not to admit, however, that monetary policy is of little or no use as an antirecessionary instrument. The three major means by which an expansive policy cushions a downturn and promotes recovery are discussed briefly below.

1. An expansive monetary policy cushions a downturn and mitigates recessionary pressures by assuring adequate liquidity in the liquidation phase of the recession. This function is especially important in the event that inventory liquidation, as has been the case in each of the postwar recessions, is a major factor in the downturn. In pre-World War II recessions, inventory liquidation often became disorderly, partly because of inadequate availability of credit on reasonable terms. Businesses, confronted with topheavy stocks of goods and a need for liquidity, sometimes were forced to offer goods at sacrifice prices. Such actions tended to reinforce recessionary pressures and to deepen the downward spiral. In postwar recessions, however, inventory adjustments have proceeded in a smooth and orderly fashion, partly as a result of the liquidity promoted by an expansive monetary policy.

2. By channeling reserves into the banking system, an expansive monetary policy places banks in a position to meet all worthy demands for funds. During a period of business expansion and rising loan demand, banks commonly reduce their liquidity by selling Government and other securities and lending to businesses and individuals. During a business recession, as loan demand subsides, banks will quickly rebuild their liquidity positions—by reducing indebtedness to the Federal Reserve banks, enlarging cash assets, and accumulating Government and other securities—as an expansive monetary policy provides them with additional reserves. This rebuilding of liquidity puts banks into a position to meet worthy loan demands of businesses and individuals. Consequently, a credit atmosphere conducive to recovery is established.

3. Finally, an expansive monetary policy makes a positive contribution in combating recession by promoting growth in the money supply. As noted earlier, banks, confronted with declining loan demand, use the additional reserves made available through an expansive monetary policy to purchase Government and other securities from nonbank investors, and to subscribe to new Treasury issues.

Consequently, growth in bank investments is likely to outpace the decline in bank loans; total bank credit, and thus bank deposits, tend to expand.

The tendency for money supply to grow—and sometimes at a rapid rate—stands in sharp contrast to trends in pre-World War II recessions. The money supply declined during those periods; at times, the decline became so pronounced as to become a major positive force in the downward spiral. As already noted, the sharp contraction in the money supply was a prime factor tending to push the economy further into the depths of depression in 1932-33. The present-day tendency for the money supply to rise during recessions, because of the combination of an expansive monetary policy and the availability of a large volume of high-grade investments for bank purchase, is one of the major factors tending to prevent cumulative, self-feeding deflationary spirals. Monetary policy, by promoting growth in the money supply, both cushions a business downturn and provides a financial atmosphere essential to and conducive to recovery.

SUMMARY

Monetary policy, along with fiscal policy, is one of the primary means for promoting the goals of the Employment Act of 1946. In this chapter, an attempt has been made to describe the process of expansion and contraction of demand deposits in the banking system, and to evaluate the role of monetary policy as a stabilization device. We can conclude by stating that monetary policy significantly influences the flow of spending relative to the flow of goods and services through its effect on interest rates and the availability of credit. Inasmuch as monetary policy is probably more effective in curtailing spending in a boom than in promoting spending during a business recession, it would seem that every effort must be made to prevent undue expansion and speculation in periods of expanding business activity. It is by avoiding such excesses that the resulting adjustments can be limited in severity.

SUGGESTED READINGS

BOARD OF GOVERNORS OF THE FEDERAL RESERVE SYSTEM, *The Federal Reserve System—Purposes and Functions,* Washington, D.C., 1954, Chapters I-III, IX-X.

"Federal Financial Measures for Economic Stability," *Federal Reserve Bulletin*, May 1953, pp. 456-62.

"Influence of Credit and Monetary Measures on Economic Stability," *Federal Reserve Bulletin*, March 1953, pp. 219-34.

"The Monetary System of the United States," *Federal Reserve Bulletin*, February 1953, pp. 98-106.

Chapter 5

LEGAL RESERVE REQUIREMENTS

IN THE preceding chapters the effect of changes in reserve requirements on the power of the commercial banking system to expand and contract credit was explained and illustrated. It is important to realize that the method of determining the reserve which must be held against deposits exercises great influence upon the power to expand and contract credit. The realization that this was the principal function performed by reserves is of relatively recent origin. Historically, the function of reserves had been to provide the liquidity of the banking system, and the reserve requirements were related to that function. Only after a clearer understanding of the monetary system emerged was it realized that the function of the reserve was not primarily to provide liquidity but to limit expansion. It is the purpose of this chapter to examine the various forms in which reserve requirements can be expressed, the meaning and significance of the various methods, and a brief history of American reserve requirements.

The reserve requirement does not need legal force in order to perform the function of limiting the expansion of credit. If a rigidly held tradition developed that a certain percentage of deposits must be held as reserves, the limit to the expansion of credit would be just as effective as if it had been enacted into law. In countries that have a small number of commercial banks and a long-established tradition of reserve requirements, it is not always necessary to establish legal reserve requirements. Custom, for example, is sufficient in England; but in a country where there are many thousands of banks, legal regulations are undoubtedly necessary. Reserve requirements established by legislative action are administratively simple and more efficient where there are large numbers of banks. This undoubtedly goes far toward explaining the existence of reserve requirements enforced by legislation in the United States.

HISTORY OF RESERVE REQUIREMENTS

It is necessary to trace briefly the history of legal reserve requirements in this country. The fractional reserve system of banking is
almost as old as banking itself, but in the early period there were
no fixed reserve requirements. They developed only by custom as
banks found it necessary through experience to hold a certain portion
of their assets in cash and other funds immediately available. Legal
reserve requirements now exist in other countries, as will be seen in
Chapter 17, but the most significant development has taken place in
the United States.

In the early history of the United States there was no requirement
for the maintenance of reserves against either deposits or notes, and
the first legal reserve requirement was established to insure that banknotes could be converted into specie. Two states—Virginia in 1837
and New York in 1838—made provisions for specie reserve against
banknotes. The development of reserve requirements against bank
deposits came at about the same time. In 1838 the banks in New
Orleans agreed on a voluntary basis to carry a specie reserve equivalent to one-third of their combined deposit and note liability. Five
years later that voluntary agreement was made compulsory by the
Louisiana state legislature. These arrangements, it will be noted, followed closely upon the heels of the panic of 1837, in which a large
number of banks failed. The practice of requiring the maintenance of
reserves spread slowly in the following years.

It was not, however, until the period following the panic of 1857
that there was renewed emphasis on reserve requirements. The banks
in the New York Clearing House agreed in 1858 to maintain at all
times an amount in coin equivalent to not less than 20 per cent of their
net deposits. This rule influenced the formulation of reserve requirements of the National Bank Act, which was passed five years later.

In the same year, Massachusetts enacted legislation requiring
banks to maintain specie reserve against their note and deposit liabilities. This law permitted a bank to count, as a part of its reserve,
the noninterest-bearing deposits which it held in other banks. The
New York legislature considered similar legislation in the same year,
but did not enact any legislation until 1882. In the years following the
passage of the National Bank Act of 1863, state legislatures adopted
laws regulating reserve requirements. The acts passed by Maine and

New Hampshire made a distinction in the reserve requirements between time deposits and demand deposits. These features were further supplemented by a law enacted by Nebraska which provided for different reserve requirements for banks acting as the reserve banks for other banks.

The National Bank Act, which established the national banking system, was passed in 1863. Originally, it provided for the same reserve to be held against both notes and deposits. In 1874, however, the reserve requirement against notes was abolished and a 5 per cent gold redemption fund was required to be maintained in the Treasury in Washington. The original National Bank Act provided that the banks in New York must maintain a reserve of 25 per cent in their own vaults. Banks in sixteen other cities were required also to maintain 25 per cent reserve, half of which could be held in their own vaults in lawful money and the other half on deposit with banks in New York City. The remaining national banks were required to maintain a reserve of 15 per cent, but three-fifths of this reserve could be deposited in national banks in the cities mentioned earlier. New York was always a central reserve city, but Chicago and St. Louis were made reserve cities in 1887. The law with regard to the reserve requirement against deposits was revised in 1887 and again in 1903.

The New York banks made strenuous efforts to secure the deposit of the reserves of the banks outside the central reserve cities, and after a considerable period of trial and error they settled upon an interest rate of 2 per cent, which was paid on the deposits of this type.

With the passage of the Federal Reserve Act in 1913 there was a general revision of the laws governing legal reserve requirements. On June 21, 1917, the Act was amended to provide some further changes in the reserve requirements of the member banks of the Federal Reserve System. The framers of the Federal Reserve Act provided for a gradual transfer of bank reserves from the reserve city and central reserve city banks to the Federal Reserve Banks, and after a period of time reserves consisted solely of balances with the Federal Reserve banks and cash in the vaults of the member banks. The law governing reserves furthermore provided for a reduction in reserve requirements. They were established at 13 per cent on the net demand deposits of central reserve city banks, 10 per cent on the net demand deposits of reserve city banks, and 7 per cent on the net demand deposits of country banks. The reserve against time deposits was fixed at 3 per cent. In the case of the reserve requirements against de-

mand deposits, the 1917 law resulted in the reduction of five percentage points for each class of member banks and a two-percentage-
point reduction in the reserve requirements against time deposits. The
law furthermore provided that only realized balances held with the
Federal Reserve Bank could be counted as reserves. This provision
of the Act operated to eliminate correspondent bank balances as
reserves and also vault cash.

Before the 1917 amendment, whatever portion of its required reserves
each bank carried in its own vault had to be gold or other lawful money;
consequently it drew a material distinction between lawful money (gold,
gold certificates, silver certificates, Treasury notes of 1890, greenbacks,
and silver coin) which could be counted as reserve and other forms of
money (national banknotes and Federal Reserve notes) which could not
be counted as reserve; and, in practice, it requested shipments only of
lawful money and shipped to the Federal Reserve Bank or paid out over
its counter those forms which could not be counted as legal reserve. The
effect was that lawful money (particularly gold and gold certificates)
tended to concentrate in the members' vaults and to be circulated to the
exclusion of national banknotes and Federal Reserve notes. All reason
for this discrimination was removed by the 1917 amendment and the
members no longer clung so tenaciously to their gold.[1]

These reserve requirements remained unchanged for almost two
decades. While there were some minor changes in the methods of
calculating reserves, the actual percentage requirements were not
changed by law until the passage of the Banking Act of 1935. This
change, however, was made as the result of several factors. The
devaluation of the dollar and the rapid inflow of gold resulted in the
accumulation of vast excess reserves in the hands of member banks.
This threatened to lead to a period of rapid inflation; consequently,
legislation was believed to be necessary to mop up the excess reserves.
The Federal Reserve System could not take direct action by means of
open-market operations to reduce reserve balances because its portfolio of U.S. Government securities was not large enough. Even if the
portfolio had been large enough, changes of this magnitude might
have been injurious to efforts to stimulate industrial activity.

No significant change occurred in reserve requirements during the
early part of the depression of the 1930's, but that was not true as
the depression deepened. As might be expected, there were many

[1] Ray B. Westerfield, *Money, Credit, Banking,* New York, The Ronald Press
Company, 1938, pp. 609-11.

requests for monetary measures to reduce the severity of the financial strain on the economy. One of the results of this pressure was the passage of the Thomas Amendment. The objective of the amendment was essentially inflationary, but it included clauses designed to give the Federal Reserve System power to restrain inflation if it got out of control. It was genuinely feared that some of the monetary measures would lead to ruinous inflation, and the American Bankers Association urged that the monetary authorities be given powers to restrain it. The Act provided that in periods of emergencies the Board of Governors of the Federal Reserve System could, with the approval of the President, change the reserve balances which were required to be maintained against demand or time deposits. It is significant to note that this amendment established no limits upon the power to change the requirements.

This provision upon further study was felt to be unsatisfactory, but the problem of excess reserves became even greater. The fear of a ruinous inflation was increased by the steady inflow of refugee gold which was building up balances which could not be dealt with by traditional monetary measures. This problem led to a revision of the permissive legislation. The consent of the President to change reserve requirements was no longer required. The new Act provided that the Board could not lower reserve requirements below the existing levels, but it had the power to double them. The original legislation provided that the reserve requirements of the central reserve city and the reserve city banks could be changed simultaneously. The reserve requirements of the country banks could be changed independently. By 1942, it was found necessary to amend the Act to permit the reserve requirements of the central reserve city banks to be changed without regard to the reserve requirements of other classes of banks.

The Board lost little time in exercising its authority to raise reserve requirements. The first change came in August 1936. The increase did not, however, represent a change in monetary policy. It was an attempt to gain control over a large volume of excess reserves which accumulated as the result of gold imports.

The power to vary reserve requirements was originally designed to cope with an unusual inflow of gold, but it was not long before the Federal Reserve System attempted to use it as a means of influencing the level of the money supply and thus indirectly the level of business activity. Business had risen almost steadily during 1936-37, but in the latter year it fell sharply. Early in 1938 the Board reduced reserve requirements in the hope that easy money would lessen the strain on the banking system and would encourage further expansion of business. The move was only moderately successful. Gold from abroad continued to pour in, and there were recommendations that the power to change reserve requirements should be increased, although legislation was never passed authorizing these changes. In November 1941, the reserve requirements were raised to the maximum. These requirements prevailed throughout the war with one exception. Taking advantage of the legislation passed in 1942, the reserve requirements on the demand deposits of the central reserve city banks were reduced to 20 per cent, the same level as the reserve city banks.

The period after the end of the war was an extremely difficult one. The Federal Reserve System was attempting to maintain almost the same structure of interest rates which had prevailed during the war. Both individuals and businesses which held U.S. Government securities attempted to turn them into cash in order to finance capital expenditures and the purchase of consumer goods. The Federal Reserve System became, therefore, the residual buyer of government securities. In effect, it monetized the public debt. These purchases brought about inflationary pressures, and the discussion of the desirability of anti-inflationary measures which would not change the interest rate structure resulted in many proposals to change reserve requirements and to impose new requirements of one kind or another.

The efforts to curb inflation resulted in the passage of special legislation which permitted the Federal Reserve System to raise reserve requirements. This power was contained in an Act passed by Congress in 1948, but it terminated on June 30, 1949. The law gave the Board power to raise maximum reserve requirements for demand deposits by four percentage points and one and one-half percentage points on time deposits. The Board utilized these powers almost immediately. The reserve requirements on time deposits were brought to the maximum and the requirements on reserve city and country bank demand deposits were raised to 22 and 16 per cent, respectively. The Board had already utilized its existing authority to raise the reserve requirements on the demand deposits of central city banks to 26 per cent, and the special provisions of the law were never employed against its demand deposits.

The year 1949 was one of declining industrial activity, and the Federal Reserve System reduced reserve requirements at various times during that year in order to stimulate industry and trade. No further change was made until the Board raised reserve requirements in 1951 in order to curb some of the inflationary pressures resulting from the outbreak of hostilities in Korea.

There was no change in reserve requirements until 1953, when they were lowered again in an effort to stimulate industrial activity. A further reduction occurred in 1954. In 1958—a year of declining activity—the Federal Reserve Board reduced reserve requirements further. In a series of half-point steps, reserve requirements against the demand deposits of central reserve city banks were lowered from 20 per cent to 18 per cent, reserve city banks from 18 per cent to 16.5 per cent, and country banks from 12 per cent to 11 per cent. This was the second time in which fractional changes were employed as a method of supplying reserves. Table 1 traces the history of reserve requirements since the Board of Governors was granted the power to vary them.

In 1959, there was another change in the legislation governing the reserve requirements of member banks of the Federal Reserve System. The Board was authorized to permit the member banks to treat cash as reserves. The minimum reserve requirement against the demand deposits of Central Reserve city banks was lowered from 13 per cent to 10 per cent, and 22 per cent was fixed as the minimum reserve requirement against the demand deposits of Central Reserve city and Reserve City banks. The law also specifies that the Central Reserve city classification terminates July 28, 1962. The Board also was given power to permit banks located in Central Reserve and Reserve cities to maintain lower reserve requirements based upon the nature of the bank's business rather than geographical location.

The United States is not alone in maintaining legal requirements concerning demand and time deposits. Indeed, most countries of the world now have reserve requirements of some kind against commercial bank liabilities, but they differ in many respects from those of the United States. According to the studies of the New Fork Federal Reserve Bank, only a few countries had reserve requirements twenty years ago; but after the mid 1930's, legislation of this type became more common. Many countries now have legal provisions permitting the central bank to vary the reserve requirements in the same manner that the Federal Reserve System can vary member-bank reserve requirements in the United States. In some countries the law establishes special types of reserve requirements in which government securities

TABLE 1. MEMBER BANK RESERVE REQUIREMENTS*
(Per cent of deposits)

Effective Date of Change	Net Demand Deposits[1]			Time Deposits	
	Central Reserve City Banks	Reserve City Banks	Country Banks	Central Reserve and Reserve City Banks	Country Banks
1917—June 21	13	10	7	3	3
1936—Aug. 16	19½	15	10½	4½	4½
1937—Mar. 1	22¾	17½	12¼	5¼	5¼
May 1	26	20	14	6	6
1938—April 16	22¾	17½	12	5	5
1941—Nov. 1	26	20	14	6	6
1942—Aug. 20	24				
Sept. 14	22				
Oct. 3	20				
1948—Feb. 27	22				
June 11	24				
Sept. 16, 24[2]	26	22	16	7½	7½
1949—May 1, 5[2]	24	21	15	7	7
June 30, July 1[2]		20	14	6	6
Aug. 1, 11[2]	23½	19½	13	5	
Aug. 16, 18[2]	23	19	12		5
Aug. 25	22½	18½			
Sept. 1	22	18			
1951—Jan. 11, 16[2]	23	19	13	6	6
Jan. 25, Feb. 1[2]	24	20	14		
1953—July 1, 9[2]	22	19	13		
1954—June 16, 24[2]	21			5	5
July 29, Aug. 1[2]	20	18	12		
1958—Feb. 27, Mar. 1[2]	19½	17½	11½		
Mar. 20, Apr. 1[2]	19	17	11		
Apr. 17	18½				
Apr. 24	18	16½			
In effect Aug. 1, 1959	18	16½	11	5	5
Present legal requirements:					
Minimum	10	10	7	3	3
Maximum	22	22	14	6	6

and other bank assets can be counted as a part of the reserves.

An extended treatment of the reserve requirements of foreign banks is not necessary, but a few peculiarities might be pointed out. In some countries reserve requirements against the increases in demand deposits are greater than the reserve against the basic amount. These supplementary reserves are frequently invested in government securities. Likewise it is possible for vault cash to be counted as reserve. The methods of calculating reserve requirements differ from country to country.[2]

As the philosophy of the function of a central bank reserve has changed, there have been a great many proposals for the revision of existing bank reserve requirements. For the most part, these revisions have sought to accomplish specific objectives which have become important from time to time. It must be remembered that the realization that the function of the bank reserve requirements is to enable the central monetary authorities to regulate the maximum expansion of the money supply is a concept which has been recognized only recently. Likewise, the emphasis on the liquidity aspect of bank reserve requirements has been minimized.

As was shown earlier, the liquidity aspect was emphasized at the time when the existing reserve requirement legislation became effective. It was believed desirable that the central reserve city banks should maintain a larger portion of their deposits in cash because they served as the depositories of other banks. The reserve city banks were allowed a lower rate of reserve requirements because a smaller portion of their deposits were deposits of other banks. With the establishment of the Federal Reserve System, this requirement probably became less important, but it is still in effect.

One proposal has been made to revise reserve requirements in such a manner that objectives of the program will be maintained, but the inequities of the existing program will be eliminated. One of the major inequities is that many country banks that do a correspondent bank

---

[2] "Commercial Bank Reserve Requirements Abroad," *Monthly Review*, Federal Reserve Bank of New York, October 1955, pp. 130-135.

[1] Demand deposits subject to reserve requirements which, beginning August 23, 1935, have been total demand deposits minus cash items in process of collection and demand balances due from domestic banks (also minus war loan and Series E bond accounts during the period April 13, 1943 to June 30, 1947).

[2] First-of-month of mid-month dates are changes at country banks, and other dates (usually Thursday) are at central reserve or reserve city banks.

* From *Federal Reserve Bulletin*, August 1959.

business equal to or greater than some reserve city banks are required to maintain a smaller reserve than the reserve city banks. Many banks that by accident are located within the geographical area of central reserve or reserve cities are required to maintain higher reserve requirements although they do no correspondent bank business. Logically, therefore, it has been suggested that reserve requirements be fixed on the basis of the various classes of deposits. This has been described as the Uniform Reserve Plan.

Under this proposal, it is advocated that a higher reserve requirement be imposed for interbank balances, a smaller reserve requirement for other demand deposits, and a nominal reserve requirement for time deposits. This proposal was criticized on the ground that it maintains an outmoded system. It is felt that there is no reason why interbank deposits should carry a higher reserve requirement. It is believed to be unnecessary because control over the expansion of the money supply is asserted to be the basic objective of reserve requirements. Any discriminating treatment of special classes is believed under these circumstances to be unjustified. In short, if the function of reserve requirements is to control the money supply, there is no reason for making one class of deposits bear a greater burden than another.

There may be some merit, however, in the suggestion that a higher reserve requirement should be maintained against interbank balances. A major argument that can be made for a higher reserve requirement against interbank balances is that it requires the banking system to hold a larger portion of volatile deposits in a readily transferable form. It is said that banks which rely for their deposits upon member bank balances probably should not invest in the same manner as other banks. This lesson was learned in the nineteenth century, and a repetition of those experiences is not necessary. The correspondent banking system is based upon the principle that outlying banks can either invest their funds or maintain them on deposit with other banks. The banks receiving the deposits of other banks stand ready to release the deposits upon demand; consequently, it is desirable for bankers' banks to maintain a higher portion of such deposits in liquid form in their own interests.

Banks with volatile deposits have discovered through experience that it is more desirable to maintain a larger proportion of their deposits in liquid form. Reserve requirements have given some legal force to this principle, and the management of the secondary reserve position by the banks themselves tends to reinforce it. By the same token, it is not necessary to maintain such a high percentage of other demand deposits or time deposits in the form of reserve balances with the central bank. These deposits are less volatile.

Banks are also able to invest a larger portion of their secondary reserves in assets that are not readily salable in the money market. This practice, in effect, maintains a slightly less liquid reserve against the deposits that are less subject to fluctuation. This brief description of the Uniform Reserve Plan cannot cover all the facts, but it is probably the most logical derivation of the earlier plans which is consistent with banking experience. No analysis of this plan would be complete without emphasizing the practical difficulties of its administration and the problems of the transition period. It would, of course, be possible to argue that some deposits are more volatile than bank deposits and that, if reserves are to be based upon volatility, other procedures would be desirable. The Federal Reserve System developed a reserve plan based upon velocity turnover, but further examination of such a scheme did not indicate promising results and it was abandoned.

Another suggestion which has been advanced for regulating reserve requirements has been the imposition of a supplementary reserve requirement with the funds to be invested in United States Government securities. It was originally believed by some writers that this would limit the power to expand credit. Unless a special type of government security is created in which to invest supplementary reserves, it would not have much effect on controlling the total power of expansion. This can be made clear best by way of an illustration.

If it is assumed that the reserve requirement is 10 per cent, obviously an addition of $1 million to reserves would permit an expansion in the money supply of $10 million. If the central bank supplies $1 million of excess reserves and if the supplementary reserve requirement is 25 per cent on demand deposits, it means only that $2.5 million of the increase in the money supply would result from purchase of government securities and the other $7.5 million would result from the expansion in other loans and investments. The supplementary reserve requirement would serve only to direct a certain portion of the money expansion into certain types of government securities. It is to be emphasized that it would not necessarily limit the expansion of the money supply.

The preceding illustration presumes that any government securities could be counted as a part of the supplementary reserve. This method of reasoning is not applicable if a special type of security is created, the quantity of which is limited. This can be made clear best by revising the preceding illustration. If it is assumed that the central bank creates $1 million in reserves and the reserve requirement is 10 per cent, it would be possible for the banking system to expand the money supply by $10 million. If, however, there is a requirement that in addition to the primary reserve requirement, 25 per cent of the deposits must be invested in a special government security, it would be possible to limit monetary expansion. If, for example, the government would by regulation make only $1 million of this special security available to the banks, it would be impossible to expand credit by more than $4 million regardless of the primary regulation.

This method could be made to work and it might have some advantages in insuring a market for certain types of government securities or for limiting expansion under temporary circumstances where a change in reserve requirements is undesirable. However, the same objective could be accomplished by raising reserve requirements to a figure which would limit total expansion. This would accomplish the same result in a less complicated manner.

Another version of the supplementary reserve plan would provide for the maintenance of a special reserve against expansions in deposits above a certain figure. If the monetary authorities decided that the existing level of expansion was satisfactory, but that they wished to maintain control over additional increments, it could be done by providing a special reserve against such increments. In either method, expansion could be controlled and a case might be made for the use of the special reserve requirement against additional deposits in the national defense or a wartime economy. Over the longer run, however, it probably would be undesirable to rely upon a supplementary reserve requirement of this nature. It would tend to penalize banks in areas that are growing rapidly, because the reserve requirement would bear more heavily upon them. On the other hand, it would present some administrative difficulties which can best be overcome by adopting a uniform system. It would be much better over the long run to adopt some form of reserve requirement applicable to total deposits rather than to attempt to distinguish reserve requirements against certain requirements which are different than those on an earlier amount.

A third method of controlling the expansion of money has been advocated in the form of a suggestion that different reserve requirements be maintained against different classes of assets. It has been suggested that this is a technique by which the central bank could control the flow of credit into certain types of assets. The commercial banks would tend to hold those assets for which reserve requirements were lowered. This would result in a more direct control of credit extension than any other method. In a sense, it substitutes direct control of credit for indirect control via the money supply.

This plan could, of course, influence the direction of bank investment or lending policies. More specifically, it could be used to channel funds to specific types of industries. It would, of course, permit a greater degree of control over bank lending by the central monetary authorities. The plan is probably administratively unworkable.

One of the best-known suggestions for the revision of reserve requirements was proposed by the Economic Policy Commission of the American Bankers Association and was strongly recommended by the Association in 1958. This proposal was designed to reduce the reserve against demand deposits to 10 per cent for all banks and 2 per cent on time deposits. It was proposed to eliminate all geographical differences in reserve requirements and to permit the counting of vault cash as a part of the reserve. Finally, the reserve authorities were to be given the right to vary the reserve against demand deposits from 8 to 12 per cent. This was an attempt to provide both for a reduction in existing reserve requirements and for a substantial reform as well.

The American Bankers Association formulated an elaborate plan for introducing these reserve requirements. Their proposal for its introduction can best be explained in terms of their projection of economic growth. The Economic Policy Commission stated that if its proposal had been in effect at the time it was being most strongly urged, reserve requirements would have been $8.6 billion rather than $18.4 billion. The Commission also calculated that within five years the commercial banks would require $7.4 billion of additional reserves under present reserve requirements in order to finance the projected rate of growth in the economy. This would mean an increase of $3.4 billion in the reserve against net demand deposits, and the same amount to finance the increased volume of currency in circulation. It was calculated that currency in circulation and total deposits adjusted rise on the average of about 6 per cent per year. This actually was the case over the seventy-nine-year period from 1875 to 1954, according to the National Bureau of Economic Research. Similar data have been compiled by the National Industrial Conference Board. Other studies give figures ranging from 4 to 6 per cent.

The American Bankers Association, however, based its argument upon the projected rate of growth of the real gross national product. Over the past decades it has grown at a rate of about 3 per cent per year. It was calculated that the needed reserves could be provided by reducing reserve requirements over a five-year period. The proposal had many obvious merits. It would be equitable in the approximate amount of relief it gave to various classes of banks. Once adopted, it would be relatively simple to administer. One criticism that was made of the plan was that the reserve ratios were set so low that the multiple by which credit could be expanded would vary between 8 and 12 approximately. However, the plan had commendable features which in the opinion of many bankers outweighed any disadvantages.

The discussion of these reserve plans has emphasized that current reserve requirements are too high. The Federal Reserve Board has taken advantage of opportunities to lower them whenever possible. In 1958 the Board submitted a recommendation to Congress to revise reserve requirements. The Board accepted the suggestions that the member banks be permitted to count vault cash as a part of their required reserves. It has long been argued that failure to count vault cash works a hardship on the country banks. It also requested permission to make more flexible the Board's authority to grant individual member banks in central reserve and reserve cities permission to carry lower reserve requirements than other banks in the area are required to carry. The third important revision recommended by the Board would lower the reserve requirements of the central reserve city banks to the same range as the reserve city banks. It would, however, continue the central reserve city classification. The Board believes that a maximum reserve requirement of 20 per cent against demand deposits would be sufficient for all present and prospective possibilities. This provision would tend to narrow the differential between various classes of banks. Obviously, these changes would have to be made slowly, and the Board has made recommendations covering the transition period. These recommendations formed the basis of the changes (described earlier) made by Congress in 1959.

There is finally a suggestion that a 100 per cent reserve should be required against deposits. This proposal was made initially by Irving Fisher, and it is more properly described as a method of controlling the expansion of credit. The basic objectives of this plan would be to take from the commercial banks entirely the power to expand and contract credit, and it would lodge that power in the hands of the central government. It would in effect nationalize the commercial bank function even if it did not nationalize the commercial banks. According to this plan, the commercial bank, in order to make loans in excess of its capital, would have to apply to the central banks for the authority as well as the funds to make the loans. This proposal has received some support especially from those who believe that monetary policy is a tremendously powerful weapon for the achievement of certain objectives.

SUGGESTED READINGS

Bank Reserves, Some Major Factors Affecting Them, New York, Federal Reserve Bank of New York, March 1951.

Member Bank Reserve Requirements, New York, Economic Policy Committee, American Bankers Association, 1957.

PHILLIPS, CHESTER ARTHUR, *Bank Credit, A Study of Principles and Factors Underlying Advances Made by Banks to Borrowers,* New York, The Macmillan Company, 1920.

The Federal Reserve Re-examined, New York, The New York Clearing House Association, 1953.

WILLIS, H. P., *The Federal Reserve System,* New York, The Ronald Press Company, 1923.

Chapter 6

THE DISCOUNT RATE
AND REDISCOUNT POLICY

1. SOME INTRODUCTORY COMMENTS ABOUT TERMINOLOGY

THERE is difficulty in distinguishing between various meanings of the word "discount." Thus, a consumer interested in the purchase of an automobile finds that his bank may lend to him on an interest-added-at-maturity basis, or on a "discount" basis in which interest is deducted at the time the loan is made. The same consumer may read in the financial section of the *Times* that the bank rate in England has moved up; and, upon studying the article, notes that this is a rate charged to discount houses which handle bills of exchange arising out of the vast import-export transactions of British traders.[1] A few days later the same consumer may hear a radio announcement that the Board of Governors of the Federal Reserve System has raised the rediscount rate by one-half of 1 per cent.

It is in the sense of the last two illustrations, involving the Bank of England and the Federal Reserve System, that the words "discount rate and rediscount policy" are used in this chapter. The words "discount" (British) and "rediscount" (American) relate to a central bank, and describe the process whereby the central bank accommodates its institutional clients. In England these clients are the discount houses that find their loans being called by the joint-stock banks, in all probability because the latter banks find their cash ratios dropping below the desired figures. In the United States the clients are the member banks of the Federal Reserve System and, indirectly through correspondent banking relationships, all the commercial banks of the country.

[1] R. S. Sayers, *Modern Banking*, 2nd ed., London, Oxford University Press, 1947, has a good sketch of the discount work of the Bank of England.

2. THE PROCESS ILLUSTRATED

Teachers of money and banking, equipped with chalk in hand, are prone to explain the discounting process by some such chart as the following:

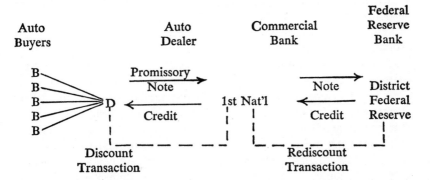

Assuming that these auto buyers are not equipped with cash, the customary transaction involves an installment note, signed by the buyer and his wife, endorsed (with or without recourse) by the automobile sales agency, and discounted by the auto dealer at his commercial bank so that the proceeds of the loan may be remitted to the manufacturer of the autos. If this process reduces the liquidity position of the First National Bank below the desired level, the bank may in turn borrow from the Federal Reserve Bank of the district. This chapter relates to the commercial bank-central bank transaction; and the reader may properly assume that whatever rate of interest is charged by the Federal Reserve is probably going to "back up" on the First National and its rates to customers. Commercial banks operate on small interest markup, and any profit margin in the discount part of the process will soon be wiped out if the Federal Reserve sets a penalty rate and the First National feels compelled to borrow. In fact, the rate is seldom a real penalty rate; it merely tends in that direction.

3. BORROWING AT THE "FED"

In 1956-57 Professor J. S. G. Wilson of the London School of Economics visited various Federal Reserve Banks and also consulted with commercial bankers about the borrowing inclinations of the member banks—that is, whether they look upon borrowing from the Federal Reserve as a normal event, or as a last-resort type of action. Professor Wilson commented thus: "By most banks, this is regarded as the last resort. Only in the Sixth Federal Reserve District (Atlanta) is there any tendency among the banks to regard such borrowing as a primary means of adjustment and this can be explained by the particular philosophy of the Federal Reserve Bank concerned."[2]

Yet, as he found in interviews with ninety commercial banks, the prejudice or tradition against borrowing tends to break down fairly quickly in a tight money situation such as 1957; and, as banks become more sophisticated, they become less concerned about borrowing and even begin to borrow deliberately over statement dates (June 30 or December 31, for example) to get the public accustomed to the idea that borrowing from the "Fed" is a normal way of living.[3] Such a philosophy naturally flies in the face of countless statements by the Federal Reserve that continuous borrowing is anathema. Obviously, then, this chapter deals with a dynamic, rather than a cut-and-dried process in which the ground rules have all been neatly worked out.

There is no more respected authority on the Federal Reserve than W. Randolph Burgess, who has, in effect, enjoyed three banking careers: one with the Federal Reserve of New York as a statistician and Deputy Governor in the 1920's and 1930's; a second as a top executive with the National City Bank of New York in the 1940's, and a third with the U.S. Treasury in the 1950's. Burgess expressed the borrowing ground rules thus: "Member banks are generally unwilling to remain in debt to a Reserve Bank for long periods. This tradition against continued borrowing, inherited from pre-Federal Reserve practices, is a powerful restraint."[4] Granting that some boom-time divergencies may be developing in the legacy from the past, the

[2] J. S. G. Wilson, "A Survey of American Banking," a rough draft of a proposed new book; and published in part in *The Banker* for March, May, June, and July 1957. The quotation is from Part II, p. 39.

[3] Clay Anderson, economic adviser of the Federal Reserve Bank of Philadelphia and chairman of a study group on *The Federal Funds Market*, found varying degrees of reluctance to borrow. Interviews with over 150 banks showed marked reluctance on the part of country banks; less hesitation if the bank was an aggressive big-city (or so-called Reserve City) bank. Dr. Anderson's study was published in May 1959 by the Board of Governors of the Federal Reserve System.

[4] W. Randolph Burgess, *The Reserve Banks and the Money Market*, rev. ed. New York, Harper & Brothers, 1946, p. 231.

reader should assume that the tradition against borrowing goes back to the nineteenth century, when continuous borrowing from correspondents was looked upon with suspicion; that the Federal Reserve discourages such borrowing and encourages only temporary assistance to member banks; and that the tradition is ingrained and persistent. This, then, is a chapter about something you do only part of the time. Like the man who came to dinner, a banker can get pretty unpopular with the Federal Reserve if he overstays his visit.

4. THE MECHANICS OF BORROWING

This is a good point to introduce the thought that borrowing at the Federal Reserve isn't one neat package, but is a complex of various types of borrowing. Note, for example, the rate schedule in effect beginning October 24, 1958, as announced by one of the Federal Reserve district banks.[5] In reading quickly through it (you won't understand it unless you know the statutes involved) you will find *six* different rates. The first one is really the effective rate which appears in financial headlines; the other rates apply to types of borrowing which are rarely used today.

	Per Cent per Annum
Advances to and rediscounts for member banks:	
a. On advances under Section 13 of the Federal Reserve Act as amended, secured by direct or fully guaranteed obligations of the United States	2½
b. Other advances and discounts under Section 13 and 13a of the Federal Reserve Act as amended	2½
c. Advances under Section 10b of the Federal Reserve Act as amended	3
Advances to individuals, partnerships, and corporations other than member banks:	
Advances under the last paragraph of Section 13 of the Federal Reserve Act as amended, secured by direct obligations of the United States	4

[5] *Operating Circular 11A*, Federal Reserve Bank of Philadelphia, September 19, 1958. Subsequently, Congress terminated Section 13b.

Industrial advances and commitments under Section 13b of the Federal Reserve Act as amended:	*Per Cent per Annum*
Advances direct to industrial or commercial organizations, including advances made in participation with other financing institutions	4–6
Commitments to make advances and commitments made to financing institutions to discount or purchase industrial advances	½–1½

It is evident that Federal Reserve Banks extend credit directly to member banks in the form of *advances* and *discounts,* the distinction between the two types of borrowing being that in the advance the member bank borrows on its own collateral note, while in the discount the member bank submits some instrument of a more remote borrower (so-called "eligible paper").

Frequently, the securities which are to be used for collateral are already at the Federal Reserve in a safekeeping status; a telegram or phone call will start the process of shifting them from safekeeping to collateral status. The discount process is more complicated (one of the reasons why it is so little used today) because the instruments signed by customers of the member bank have to be accounted for in detail; and must be returned to the member bank, with other collateral substituted, just prior to the various due dates.

Certain legal documents are involved in the borrowing process, including a resolution authorizing the bank officers to borrow; the bank's promissory note secured as prescribed; or, in case of discounting, an application for discount to due date of commercial, industrial, or agricultural paper, and recent financial statements covering paper of any one borrower which is greater than $1,000. The discount is computed on the basis of actual days; and the Federal Reserve Bank will accept payments, either partially or in full, in advance of maturity, with an appropriate adjustment for unearned discount.

The mechanics illustrate the cliché that the "Fed" is a banker's bank. The banker has to go through certain minimum red tape to get a loan, just as he expects his customers to do in borrowing from him. Working relationships with Federal Reserve are naturally less formal, more friendly, and hardly inclined to end up in a lawsuit. One doesn't make a scene in one's own club.

5. ADVANCES TO MEMBER BANKS

Here the member bank submits its own note, collateraled in any of the following ways:

a. Up to fifteen days against direct obligations of the United States (bonds, Treasury notes, certificates, and the short-term bills issued by the Treasury); or by certain instruments of the Federal Intermediate Credit Banks or Federal Farm Mortgage Corporation. The collateral here is a portion of the national debt.

b. Up to ninety days against eligible paper, including notes, drafts, bills of exchange, and bankers' acceptances. The collateral here is the debt of businesses.

c. Up to four months against any collateral acceptable to the Federal Reserve Bank. This is under the authority of Section 10b of the Federal Reserve Act (more later on this).

6. DISCOUNTS OF ELIGIBLE PAPER FOR MEMBER BANKS

Here the main classes are:

a. Commercial paper maturing within ninety days of the date of the advance or discount, subdivided into
 1. Time paper in the form of negotiable notes, drafts, bills of exchange which are issued or drawn to produce, purchase, carry, or market goods; or to meet current business operating expenses; or to provide for factors' advances to producers of staple agricultural products; or to carry or trade in United States bonds, notes, certificates, or Treasury bills.
 2. Negotiable drafts arising out of domestic shipments or the export of nonperishable, readily marketable staples and secured by shipping documents.

b. Agricultural paper maturing within nine months of date of advance or discount, subdivided into
 1. Negotiable paper issued or drawn for the production of agricultural products; the marketing of such products; and the breeding, raising, fattening, and marketing of livestock.
 2. Similar paper drawn by a cooperative marketing association, if the proceeds are used for advances to members for an agricultural purpose.

3. Certain bankers' acceptances, as defined in Section 13 of the Federal Reserve Act, arising out of actual commercial transactions.
4. Construction loans with original maturities not in excess of six months, and maturing within ninety days of the advance or discount, arising out of financing transactions covering residential or farm buildings.

In addition to such affirmative statements as to the type of collateral which may be pledged for advances or discounts, there are statements throughout the regulations as to what is *not* acceptable collateral, including:[6]

a. Instruments used for any fixed capital purpose; or for financing transactions of a purely speculative character; or for carrying or trading of stocks, bonds, or other investment securities. However, speculation in U. S. Government securities is not proscribed, and in the summer of 1958 such speculation was a problem.
b. Non-negotiable paper; or paper not properly endorsed; or paper in an amount which exceeds the loan limit to any one borrower. (A frequent limitation is 10 per cent of capital and surplus.)

7. ECONOMIC RATIONALE OF ELIGIBLE PAPER

From Civil War days to 1914 the United States operated with a curious assortment of currencies in circulation, notably a fixed sum of United States notes or "greenbacks," which we still see today in the form of $2 bills; a block of political money, known as silver certificates, which was forced into circulation in the long depression of the 1870's (our $1 and many $5 bills are still of this type); and currency printed at the Treasury but issued by the commercial banks under the title of national bank notes. Secretary Chase of President Lincoln's cabinet had envisioned these national bank notes as aiding the financing of the war, in that a national bank first had to acquire government securities and to deposit such collateral with the Treasury *before* the currency could be issued by the bank and circulated.

The idea of currency collateraled by government securities was acceptable from the standpoint of "parking" a portion of the national debt in the banking system; however, the banks were given some discretion over how much currency would be issued (and therefore

[6] The basic regulation is Regulation *A—Advances and Discounts* (latest revision at this writing is dated February 15, 1955), issued by the Board of Governors in Washington. Each of the district banks issues operating circulars and interpretive letters concerning *Regulation A*.

how much collateral would be on deposit) and soon found it advantageous to adjust collateral as prices varied on government securities. Naturally, when a decision was reached to recall securities and sell them in the markets, the concomitant was the disappearance of currency (national bank notes) from circulation. The economic effect might then be just the opposite of what was desirable, with currency being taken out of circulation as a recovery period set in, and vice versa. Secretary Chase had by accident set up a system of *reverse* elasticity, in that the currency tended to disappear at just the wrong time.

Senator Aldrich, Carter Glass, and others who debated the establishment of the Federal Reserve System in 1914 envisioned a new currency to be known as the Federal Reserve note (which is in fact roughly 85 per cent of all our coin/currency in circulation) and which would rise and fall with business needs. This desirable elasticity was to be built into our monetary system by having the member banks discount business instruments at the Federal Reserve Banks, and by issuing a new paper money which would be largely backed by discounted business paper. Again the idea was logical, but subsequent events were to disarrange the plan.

By the Great Depression of the 1930's the member banks had so little eligible paper, or were so reluctant to discount what they had, that Carter Glass (now a Senator) had to plead tearfully before the Congress that the 1914 concept of eligible paper had gone awry and expediency dictated new types of collateral. The emergency legislation of 1932-35 created various other types of advances and discounts listed earlier in this chapter. For example, Section 10b, first passed in 1932 and made permanent in 1935, provided for advances secured "to the satisfaction of" the Reserve Banks, which, as cynics pointed out, meant that any "cat and dog" could now be brought to the central bank and used as collateral. The bitter tears of Senator Glass are understandable in terms of so great a departure from his concept of eligible paper.

8. HOW THE DISCOUNT RATE IS SET BY FEDERAL RESERVE

Having looked at the making of advances and discounts, it is time to investigate the question of who sets the rate and why. The answer begins in the Federal Reserve Act itself, which in sections 4(8), 12m, 13, and 14d states that the Board of Governors of the System has the responsibility to regulate the advance and rediscount policies, and to set the rates charged on such borrowing by the member banks and other specially authorized borrowers.[7] Section 14d says that "subject to review and determination of the Board of Governors" each Federal Reserve Bank "shall establish such rates every fourteen days, or oftener if deemed necessary by the Board."

The language of the Act implied some joint type of action by a district bank of the Federal Reserve, subject to review and determination by the Board in Washington; and it was assumed in the passage of the Act in 1913 that each Reserve Bank might fix its own rate and that the rate might differ from rates in other districts because of the economic development and credit situation prevailing in particular districts. Trouble naturally developed over the words "review and determination," and in 1919 the Attorney General was asked to rule on a situation in which the Board desired a continuance of current rates and a district bank voted to increase its rate. The Attorney General noted that the words "and determination" were added as the bill was considered by Congress, and concluded that the Board could determine the rate and even "require such rates to be put into effect."[8] It is curious that the then Secretary of the Treasury, Carter Glass, agreed with the Attorney General; while in a subsequent reopening of the issue in 1927, the same Carter Glass violently disagreed with the action of the board in forcing a rate reduction on the Federal Reserve Bank of Chicago. If the distinguished author of the Reserve Act couldn't straighten out the intent of the words "and determination," it is clear that ordinary financial folk may justifiably be confused over who really sets the rate.

The actual procedure in the 1930's is summarized thus in one dissertation: at regular weekly meetings, the boards of directors of the Reserve Banks decide whether to continue the rate; if the decision is to continue the rate, the Board is notified immediately; if the decision is to change the rate, the district bank "communicates with the Federal Reserve Board by telephone and receives notice of the confirmation or otherwise"; if the action is not confirmed, there is no announcement; but if the action is confirmed, the press is immediately notified.[9]

[7] Professor G. L. Bach of the Carnegie Institute of Technology has a handy compilation of the various statutes in Appendix I of his *Federal Reserve Policy Making*, New York, Alfred A. Knopf, 1950, p. 264.

[8] 32 *Op. Atty. Genl.* 81, at 84.

[9] Caroline Whitney, *Experiments in Credit Control, The Federal Reserve System*, New York, Columbia University Press, 1934, p. 28.

In 1952, the twelve Presidents of the district banks indicated some reservations over the existing procedure and suggested to the Patman Committee that approval of discount rates be placed in the hands of the twelve-man Open Market Committee. Regardless of any grumbling in the ranks, the official position of the Board of Governors remained unchanged; and we find the Chairman, William McChesney Martin, Jr., speaking before a Congressional subcommittee on June 12, 1956, as follows:

The initiative as to discount rates rests with the directors at each of the twelve banks. They meet regularly, different Reserve Banks having different days, in some instances, for directors' meetings; but each bank acts every fourteen days, either to re-establish or to change its existing discount rate. The action taken, whether to continue the same or to change the rates, is immediately reported to the Board of Governors, and acted upon at a regular or special Board meeting.

Discount rates are a joint responsibility of the Reserve Board and the Reserve Bank directors.

Although the discount rate is fixed periodically by each bank subject to the Board of Governors' approval, in the actual granting of discount accommodation to individual member banks, the Federal Reserve Bank directors act on their own initiative and responsibility, free from intervention or pressures by the Board of Governors or by other Reserve Banks. These directors are always in close touch with conditions in their districts, and the discount operations, including the rates, take account of local conditions and trends. . . .

As discount policy is closely interwoven with open market policy, it is among the important subjects discussed at the frequent meetings of the Federal Open Market Committee, and the Presidents of the Reserve Banks generally express their individual views as to whether they feel they should recommend to their boards of directors changes in discount rates. A consensus may emerge . . . but . . . there is no effort . . . to dictate to any individual Reserve Bank, its president or directors what those rates should be.[10]

9. DISCOUNT RATE HISTORY

During the early years of the Federal Reserve, prior to 1921, a multiplicity of discount rates applied, depending upon the class of paper and maturity. In fact, during the 1920-21 period some of the

[10] Statement of June 12, 1956, by William McChesney Martin, Jr., before the Subcommittee on Economic Stabilization of the Joint Committee on the Economic Report. Mimeographed reprints are on file in the libraries of the district banks.

LEWIS AND CLARK COLLEGE LIBRARY
PORTLAND 19, OREGON

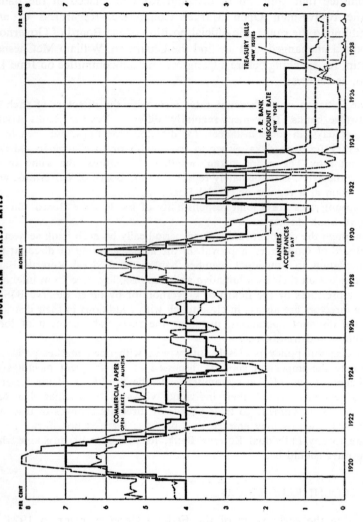

SHORT-TERM INTEREST RATES

PER CENT

MONTHLY

COMMERCIAL PAPER
OPEN MARKET, 4-6 MONTHS

BANKERS' ACCEPTANCES
90 DAY

F. R. BANK
DISCOUNT RATE
NEW YORK

TREASURY BILLS
NEW ISSUES

1920 1922 1924 1926 1928 1930 1932 1934 1936 1938

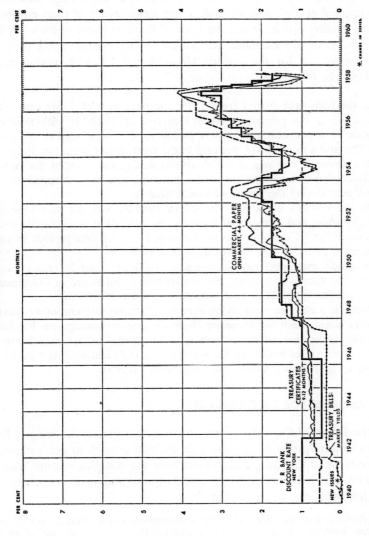

SHORT-TERM INTEREST RATES

PER CENT

MONTHLY

PER CENT

COMMERCIAL PAPER
OPEN MARKET, 4-6 MONTHS

TREASURY
CERTIFICATES
9-12 MONTHS

F R BANK
DISCOUNT RATE
NEW YORK

TREASURY BILLS:
MARKET YIELDS

NEW ISSUES
*

1940 1942 1944 1946 1948 1950 1952 1954 1956 1958 1960

*% CHANGE IN SERIES.

BOARD OF GOVERNORS OF THE FEDERAL RESERVE SYSTEM

Reserve Banks experimented with, and soon abandoned, a progressive rate based upon the amount of accommodation extended to the borrowing bank. Beginning with various dates in 1921, a single discount rate applied at each district bank.[11] For an overview of rates charged by the leading district bank, the Federal Reserve Bank of New York, the reader should examine the accompanying charts issued by the Reserve System for the periods 1919-39 and 1940-58, noting particularly the following:

a. In the forty-year period from 1919, the peak rate of 7 per cent was reached in the primary postwar recession of 1920-21; with another peak of 6 per cent for a short period in the stock market crisis of 1929, and a third of 3½ per cent in the tight-money period of 1957.
b. The discount rate was in the doldrums during the years of the Great Depression at levels of 1½ and 1 per cent, and even dropped to ½ per cent during the period of World War II.
c. As the nation's economy slumped in 1929-31 the rate was lowered *eight* times, and in the brief recession of 1957-58 it was lowered four times. Clearly, the rate moves downward in recession periods to encourage member bank borrowing and easy money.
d. In credit expansion periods, such as 1927-29 (four increases) and 1955-57 (seven increases), the district banks and Board of Governors moved the rate higher to discourage excessive borrowing.
e. There is a close correlation between the discount rate and other short-term rates, such as those on four-six month instruments handled through commercial paper houses, or ninety-day acceptances bearing the approval of banks, or the shorter-term debt instruments issued by the U. S. Treasury during and since World War II.

10. REASONS FOR RATE CHANGES

The Board of Governors never formally announces the reasons for rate changes, probably because it is difficult enough to get a change without attempting to get agreement over the complex reasons which may be involved. In responses to a 1931 questionnaire on rate changes, the following reasons stand out:[12]

[11] *Banking and Monetary Statistics,* Washington, Board of Governors of the Federal Reserve System, pp. 422-442, tabulates the history of the period up to Pearl Harbor. Subsequent rates appear in monthly issues of the *Federal Reserve Bulletin.*
[12] *Hearings before a Sub-Committee of the Committee on Banking and Currency of the United States Senate, 71st Congress, 3rd Session, 1931, Pursuant to S.Res. 71,* Appendix, Part 6, pp. 748-93.

a. To bring the rate into line with open market rates of interest. (Here the Reserve Banks follow the money market rather than lead it.)
b. To bring the rate of one district bank into line with rates charged in other districts. (Differential rates occur between districts, but usually only for short periods of adjustments.)
c. To influence member-bank borrowings—i.e., to check increases or decreases in credit throughout the banking system.
d. To influence credit supplies in the nation as a whole.
e. In the case of *plus* changes in the rate, to check security speculation, or to force seasonal liquidation of credit.
f. In the case of *minus* changes, to attract member bank borrowings away from commercial banks in larger centers, or to check a decline in general business activity, or to repel gold imports.

The list is still a good one for the current period, if one adds the important thought that the United States now has two monetary controllers—the Board of Governors *and* the Treasurer of the United States—and the exigencies of floating and refloating our national debt require the Board of Governors to keep a close tab on what the U.S. Treasurer is doing, and vice versa. In another section of this book the interrelationship between the "monetary twins" is explored in some detail; and the reader will read about a period of Federal Reserve subservience during World War II, another period of controversy culminating in the Accord of March 1951 as the System tried to recover control of credit, and, finally, the uneasy armistice existing between the two controllers since 1951.

Any generalization about factors influencing changes in rates is a hazardous one, at best. One Federal Reserve economist has expressed it thus: "Traditionally, the discount rate has been maintained above the rate on Treasury bills and other prime short-term paper but below the rates on less than prime market paper and rates charged by banks to their customers."[13]

Or take a typical news story accompanying a rate change:

DISCOUNT RATE BOOSTED TO 2½% FROM 2%
IN 5 FEDERAL RESERVE DISTRICTS

A Federal Reserve spokesman in Washington said the increase in the discount rate was a technical correction aimed at bringing it more in line with interest rates in the money market generally.

For the past several weeks, the average yield paid by the Treasury in

[13] Thomas R. Atkinson, "The Discount Rate and Bank Lending," *Monthly Business Review*, Federal Reserve Bank of Atlanta, February 1953, pp. 9-10.

its weekly sales of three-month bills has been nearly a percentage point above the discount rate. The Reserve Board usually does not like to see such a spread in rates because commercial banks presumably could borbor from the Federal Reserve at the lower rate to invest in Treasury bills.[14]

The Board makes the change without explanations; outsiders do the interpreting.

11. THEORIES OF MEMBER BANK BORROWING

In 1954 the Reserve System handled 10,000 advances and discounts totaling $22.8 billion.[15] What can be said about the motivations for this vast activity?

Any theory about member-bank borrowing must center around the role of the legal reserve account of the member bank—the account which earns the banker no interest; gives him liquidity; fluctuates up and down with the flow of checks and other items back and forth to his district bank; and which is set by the Board of Governors as a percentage of his demand and time deposits. Bankers don't have to keep this legal reserve account at Fed equal to the specified percentage each and every day; they are merely expected to do so over an average of a week or two, depending upon the location of the member bank. But the banker does know that if the average balance for the reporting period drops *below* the specified percentages (after certain deductions for balances due from correspondent banks and cash items in process of collection), the district bank is required by law to assess a penalty interest rate for the deficiency consisting of 2 per cent plus the then-existing Reserve discount rate.[16] If the deficiencies continue, other penalties come into effect and the position of the member bank becomes more embarrassing (warning letter to the directors of the member bank, special inspection, and so on). Any theory of member-bank borrowing must, therefore, fit the complexity of the borrowing psychology; the alternatives open to the member banker; and the credit-control mission of the Federal Reserve System.

In general, the theories of borrowing divide into those emphasizing

[14] *Wall Street Journal*, October 24, 1958. Just before the announcement of the change, the longest issue of regular bills was quoted at 2.75-2.72 per cent, leaving a spread of ¾ per cent.

[15] *Money: Master or Servant*, Federal Reserve Bank of New York, May 1955. See the tabulation on Federal Reserve operations at end of the booklet.

[16] *Regulation D—Reserves of Member Banks*, issued by the Board of Governors of the Federal Reserve System, Washington.

need, or those stressing *profit.* The need theory says that banks are always reluctant to borrow, and do so only when this is the only way in which customer demands can be met. The cost of borrowing is relatively incidental. The predominant factor is the need by the member bank to preserve and build its customer relation.[17]

The profit theory states that when member banks are faced with a legal reserve problem (i.e., a deficiency in their account at the district bank), they adjust by borrowings or by open-market loans, and the decision about which choice is made will rest on the relative costliness of the two alternatives. The volume of borrowing thus becomes a function of the profitability of open-market loans relative to the discount rate; that is, when open-market rates run *above* the discount rate, member banks borrow from the "Fed" rather than contract loans. Robert C. Turner[18] explored this theory at some length in his dissertation at Ohio State and concluded that:

a. The profit theory is certainly a partial explanation of changes in volume of borrowing by member banks.
b. Borrowings only occur up to a limit. (The tradition against borrowing comes into play.)
c. When the profit spread is negative, as in the depressed 1930's, borrowings tend to be low.
d. The theory seems to work only when a substantial volume of open-market holdings exist. (Alternative course must be present.)
e. The theory is most applicable to districts of the Federal Reserve having the larger banks.

The natural conclusion of the reader is that both theories, and probably a lot of others, are at work simultaneously. Dr. Riefler wrestled with the world of interest rates over many years, and noted in 1930 that money rates "respond to a common pull that affects the market as a whole." This moving together stems mainly from Reserve Bank credit, with the member-bank borrowing constituting a "marginal supply of lending power [which] is decisive in the money market."[19] The significance for the Board of Governors is that when a decision is made to restrict member-bank borrowings, the rate should be raised quickly to the level of open-market rates; or, con-

---

[17] See W. W. Riefler, *Money Rates and Money Markets,* New York, Harper & Brothers, 1930; or W. R. Burgess, *The Reserve Banks and the Money Market,* New York, Harper & Brothers, 1946.
[18] *Member Bank Borrowing,* Columbus, Ohio University Press, 1938, p. 96.
[19] Riefler, *op. cit.,* pp. 16-18.

versely, when the opposite effect is desired, the rate should be dropped *quickly* and *heavily*.

12. EFFECTIVENESS OF DISCOUNT RATE POLICY

In the 1930's the huge excess reserves of member banks precluded any effective use of the rediscount as a monetary control device; and when peacetime demand for commercial loans returned in 1946, the Federal Reserve found itself enmeshed in moral commitment to Secretary of the Treasury Snyder to support the flotation of the national debt by keeping interest rates low. Not until 1951 was it possible for the Board of Governors to revive the sleeping control (last used in the 1920's and early 1930's). Almost immediately, economists began to "rediscover" a traditional weapon of credit control. As the rediscovery proceeded, delighted writers noted that the effectiveness of rediscounting hinges upon (1) the *cost* of borrowing in relation to alternative ways of meeting the legal reserve specified by the Board; (2) the extent to which member banks get "pushed" by commitment on lines of credit, by realtors, and by durable-goods sellers and thus *need* to borrow; and (3) the attitude of the particular banker and his board toward the long-standing *tradition* that borrowing constitutes an admission of financial weakness. Cost, need, old habits, and many other factors are obviously involved in the post-1951 renascence of the rediscount as a control device.

A good summary of where we stand at present is contained in a 1953 study of the Federal Reserve by the New York Clearing House Association, as follows:

Discount rate increases will have no immediate effect in tightening credit, apart from their psychological significance, if banks are in possession of excess reserves or acquire reserves as a result of open-market purchases of Government securities by the Reserve System. Similarly, rate decreases will have no immediate effect in easing credit if member banks are out of debt and have no need for additional reserves.

If Federal Reserve credit is not being supplied through the open market, individual member banks needing reserves will be forced to obtain them by borrowing or through the sale of Government securities (or other assets). . . . To discourage excessive borrowing, the discount rate must be higher than the rates for securities used in the adjustment of reserve positions. The proper relationship of the discount rate to the market will depend upon the strength of credit demands and upon the strength of the traditional reluctance of banks to incur indebtedness.[20]

Member-bank borrowings in the first fifteen years of the Federal Reserve System were often quite large (around or above the billion-dollar mark), with a $2.8 billion peak in the money-market crisis of November 1920. After 1933 and for almost twenty years the borrowing privilege was little used because of depression, wartime, and postwar conditions. Beginning in 1951, borrowings returned to the kit bag of monetary tools and in 1952-53 and 1955-57 the member banks used extensively their privilege of visiting the advance/discount window at the Fed. The evidence suggests that the discount rate has more usefulness as a credit control in a normal or boomtime economy; while in a protracted depression it tends to be of little significance. More than one commentator on the discount rate speaks of its importance as a "brake" but not as an "accelerator." The member banks can be invited, but not compelled, to borrow; and when, as in the 1930's, the member bank is amply supplied with legal reserves, it sees no reason to go to the discount window. In tight credit conditions the initiative (to make or not to make a loan with the central bank) still rests with the member bank; however, the "Fed" now finds the rate to be a sensitive one because so many banks present themselves at the window.

13. SUGGESTIONS FOR REFORM OF THE BORROWING PROCESS

A quite obvious recommendation is to clarify the jurisdictional problems in connection with the discount rate. Since the Open Market Committee by day-to-day purchases or sales of Government securities sits in the most advantageous position for the control of member-bank reserves, it seems questionable to have another agency, the Board of Governors, setting the jolting changes in the percentages required to be maintained by member banks, and also in the borrowing rate. The three credit controls are inextricably related and it would seem more appropriate for a single agency of the Federal Reserve to assess and determine all three. Evidently, the System itself is concerned about this problem because in recent years the practice has developed of bringing the district bank presidents more

[20] *The Federal Reserve Re-Examined,* New York, New York Clearing House Association, 1953, p. 88.

closely into the decisions of the Open Market Committee (which is, of course, the Board plus five president).[21]

The most novel suggestion over the years in connection with the discount rate is that of Dr. Lauchlin Currie, who was a long-time staff member of the Division of Research and Statistics of the Board. Dr. Currie recommended the abolition of discounting on the thesis that when member banks borrow from the "Fed," they are thwarting the operation of other credit controls (open-market operations and legal-reserve percentage changes) which have placed the banks under pressure.[22] Under Currie's reform the banks outside New York would rely on their New York balances to adjust their reserve positions; the Reserve Banks outside of New York would be sort of branches of the sensitive New York bank; and the American central bank would resemble the English system.

Another area which needs "reading up" is probably that of the emergency legislation of the 1930's which ordered the Federal Reserve to undertake direct bank loans to business borrowers (Section 13b of the Act);[23] or provided for advances to individuals, partnerships, and corporations collateraled by U.S. Government securities (Section 13-13); or advances to the member banks secured to the satisfaction of the Reserve bank (Section 10b); or the never-used provision covering group loans to member banks (Section 10a). The New York Clearing House Association studied all of these so-called temporary/emergency provisions and concluded in 1953 that only Section 10b seemed to be desirable. The over-all criticism of the various sections was that they were outside the main mission of the American central bank and were so little used or needed that they should be repealed.

14. A NEW MONEY MARKET—"FEDERAL FUNDS"

When W. Randolph Burgess wrote the Number 1 text on the money market in 1936, he noted the emergence of an informal money market dealing in "Federal funds," as follows:

[21] All of the District Bank presidents now attend meetings of the Open Market Committee and personally discuss all of the Reserve tools. The Federal Reserve Act should be amended to recognize this wider participation by the presidents.

[22] Lauchlin Currie, *The Supply and Control of Money in the United States,* Cambridge, Harvard University Press, 1934, p. 182.

[23] Subsequent to drafting of this chapter, Congress terminated Section 13b of the Act. Section 601 of the Small Business Investment Act, approved August 21, 1958, repealed Section 13b, effective one year after the date of enactment.

A bank which finds itself with surplus reserve deposits at the Federal Reserve Bank frequently sells these funds to some other bank which is deficient in its reserves. The balances at the Reserve Banks thus purchased, which are known as "Federal funds," are different from other funds because they represent immediate cash that day at the Reserve Bank, whereas an ordinary bank check is not cash until it has gone through the clearings the following morning. . . . The transaction amounts to buying today's money with tomorrow's money and paying interest for a day.[24]

This interest-for-a-day market developed out of the individual negotiations between New York banks and has since spread throughout the country. Inasmuch as it is a form of borrowing by the member banks, it is here discussed as an appendix to the discount process.

The rate on Federal funds hops about a great deal because of the one-day character of the market; the volatility of changes in supply and demand of reserves; the activities of dealers in Government securities (they also need Federal funds to make payment on the day securities are delivered); and the time differences. The rate can vary from hour to hour. Its upper limit is, of course, the discount rate at the "Fed" because it would be unusual for a member bank to pay more for Federal funds than the going discount rate; the lower limit would be the bookkeeping and wire transfer and related cost.[25]

Professor J. S. G. Wilson of the London School of Economics made a coast-to-coast tour of commercial banks and the Federal Reserve during the 1956-57 period, and noted the following characteristics of the Federal funds market:[26]

a. The market dates back to 1921 but has only become a national market in the 1950's.
b. When reserves are short the banks adjust their Government securities portfolio or borrow at Federal Reserve; but when reserves are plentiful the surplus goes begging. ("You can have millions dying on you.")
c. The focal point of the New York section of the market is a stock exchange firm (Garvin, Bantel & Co.) which acts as a clearinghouse.[27] Commissions are seldom charged.
d. In effect, lines of credit for Federal funds have come into existence between dealer banks in the money centers and their bank borrowers.

[24] Burgess, op. cit., p. 152n.
[25] Hobart C. Carr, "Federal Funds," Money Market Essays, New York, Federal Reserve Bank of New York, March 1952, p. 13.
[26] Wilson, op. cit., Part II, pp. 26-31.
[27] Irving Trust Company (New York) has also entered this field. Some correspondent banks also buy and sell Federal funds as a service to their correspondents.

These limits are not disclosed and are subject to revision as circumstances change.

e. Lending limits (based on capital and surplus) are no problem for the larger banks; but smaller banks often use Garvin, Bantel & Co. to be placed in touch with several potential buyers.

f. Time zones are important. In the mid-section of the country, the banker has to make up his mind early in the morning and then get on the bank wires; otherwise, he "misses the boat" and has to borrow at "Fed." The West Coast banks interested in the New York market must sell by 11 A.M. and buy in New York by 11:45 A.M.

g. Rates in the Chicago, Texas, and San Francisco markets tend to follow the earlier New York rate. Even after New York closes, the closing rate often continues to be the basic rate for West Coast transactions.

During the tight-money period of 1956-57, Federal funds were loaned frequently at rates of 3 per cent, so that a $10 million one-day loan by a large bank would produce a gross interest of $833. In the 1955-57 period the New York stock exchange firm which specializes in Federal funds placed some $300 million to $700 million daily, and on occasions even as much as $1 billion.[28]

The informal arrangements noted by Burgess have clearly grown into something substantial in the money market. Robert V. Roosa of the Federal Reserve Bank of New York summarizes the position of Federal funds as "binding all parts of the financial mechanism together and keeping it marginally sensitive."[29] For single days the dollar total now exceeds the borrowings of member banks from the Federal Reserve—partly out of convenience but mostly out of the reluctance of member banks to be indebted to the central bank. Already, the Federal-funds device fills a real need in the adjustment of member-bank legal reserves. The larger banks estimate today's need and borrow for one day. Alternative methods of borrowing involve greater interest cost because the transactions extend over two or more days. Thus, the Federal-funds rate appears to be supplanting the Treasury-bill rate as the best indicator of short-term money rates; and we may expect that this new national market will be quite an adult when it grows up.

[28] Leif H. Olsen, "From Bank to Bank," *The New York Times*, September 23, 1956.

[29] *Ibid.* See also Robert V. Roosa, *Federal Reserve Operations in the Money and Government Securities Markets*, New York, Federal Reserve Bank of New York, July 1956, pp. 30-31.

15. THE BORROWING PROCESS SUMMARIZED

A review of the writings of the Federal Reserve "founding fathers" shows that they visualized the granting of credit through loans to the member banks as the main credit control of the System.[30] It hasn't worked out that way. By the 1920's the open-market control had evolved, and in 1935 the Board of Governors was granted an entirely new control in the form of variable legal reserve percentages. The borrowing process ceased to be significant from the early 1930's to the return of tight money in the 1950's; and when it did return it was largely in a form (advances) quite opposite to the expectations (rediscounts) of the framers of the Act in 1913.

The shift from rediscounts to advances was quite logical. Business borrowers from banks are never impressed by a rediscount of their paper at the regional Federal Reserve; member banks dislike the red tape of compiling the financial statements and other information required for a rediscount; and, most important, member banks believe that they will need to borrow for only a few days or weeks. The banks customarily keep a batch of securities in safekeeping at Federal Reserve, and the mechanism of an advance is more convenient, less costly, more flexible, and less noticed by the commercial bank's own customers. No one really should have been surprised that advances superseded rediscounts; it was no contest.

The economist views the forty years in another way. Whether rediscounts or advances are used by the borrowing bank, the credit effect is the same: new reserves are immediately created and the familiar multiplication process of additional demand deposits (money) is set to occur *if the member banks are willing to extend credit to their customers.* In the case of Federal funds, however, the economist notes that this is a mere swapping among the member banks of already-in-existence legal reserves; and the temporary assuaging of a bank's legal reserve problem through the use of Federal funds has no real effect on the nation's money. Federal funds are an interesting illustration of the ingenuity of financial folk, but they do not alter the fundamental credit-granting power of the central bank to bring into existence, or to extinguish, legal reserves of member banks.

[30] J. Laurence Laughlin, *The Federal Reserve Act: Its Origin and Problems,* New York, The Macmillan Company, 1933, pp. 250 *et. seq.*

SUGGESTED READINGS

ANDERSON, CLAY J., *The Federal Funds Market,* Board of Governors of the Federal Reserve System, Washington, D.C., May 1959.

BOPP, KARL R., "Borrowing from the Federal Reserve Bank," *Business Review,* Federal Reserve Bank of Philadelphia, June 1958, pp. 3-9.

BURGESS, W. RANDOLPH, *The Reserve Banks and the Money Market,* New York, Harper & Brothers, 1946, Chapter XIV.

CARR, HOBART C., "Federal Funds," *Money Market Essays,* Federal Reserve Bank of New York, March 1952, pp. 13-16.

"Discount Policy: 1940-1957," *Monthly Review,* Federal Reserve Bank of Minneapolis, July 31, 1957, pp. 6-10.

"Discount Rate and the Discount Policy," *Business Review,* Federal Reserve Bank of Philadelphia, January 1959, pp. 16-26.

"40 Years of the Federal Reserve Act," *Annual Report of the Federal Reserve Bank of Philadelphia,* March 15, 1954 (tabulation at center pages).

FOUSEK, PETER G., *Foreign Central Banking: The Instruments of Monetary Policy,* Federal Reserve Bank of New York, November 1957, pp. 13-30.

Regulation A—Advances and Discounts by Federal Reserve Banks, Board of Governors of the Federal Reserve System, Washington, D.C.

SMITH, WARREN L., "Discount Rate as a Credit Control Weapon," *Journal of Political Economy,* University of Chicago Press, April 1958, pp. 171-77.

"The Discount Rate and Rediscount Policy," *The Effects of Federal Reserve Policies—Monetary Study No. 4,* Economic Policy Commission of American Bankers Association, New York, 1954, pp. 8-10.

Chapter 7

OPEN-MARKET OPERATIONS

THROUGH open-market operations the Federal Reserve System is able to develop whatever condition of tightness or ease in the money and credit markets it may consider appropriate to the prevailing economic situation. By means of open-market operations the System can continuously modify that ease or tightness, on a day-to-day and week-to-week basis, as changing circumstances may require.

Whether there is a tone of tightness in the money and credit markets, or a tone of ease, or a tone something between these extremes depends to a considerable extent on the volume of funds which member banks need to borrow at the Federal Reserve Banks in order to meet their reserve requirements. In this country there is a reluctance on the part of member banks to remain indebted to the Reserve Banks. Credit at commercial banks tends to be more difficult to obtain and to be somewhat higher in price whenever total member-bank borrowing at the Federal Reserve Banks is large. Conversely, bank credit tends to be more readily available and less expensive when borrowing is small.

By open-market operations the System can control within narrow limits the aggregate volume of member-bank borrowing. The Federal Reserve can allow a large volume of such borrowing to develop with a growth in credit demands, it can bring such a condition about on its own initiative should that become desirable, or it can relieve member banks of the need for borrowing should that be appropriate to the developing business and credit situation.

Purchases of Government securities by the Federal Reserve Banks supply member banks with reserve balances; open-market sales absorb these balances. Purchases or sales may be made merely to offset the effects of a number of factors that are constantly tending to increase or decrease balances. If the factors were not offset, large changes would occur in the volume of member-bank borrowing, many of which would be undesirable from the standpoint of proper monetary management. By purchasing securities, for example, the System may compensate for various factors tending to drain away reserves, such as outflows of gold, increases in currency in circulation, transfers of funds into Treasury or other accounts held at the Federal Reserve Banks, or decreases in "float," i.e., uncollected checks held by Reserve Banks for which credit has been given to the depositing bank. On the other hand, sales of securities by the Federal Reserve may be undertaken to offset the effects on member-bank reserve balances of the opposite movements in these items. By open-market action, therefore, the System may prevent these movements from affecting the average over-all reserve position of member banks and thus from interfering with the maintenance of the desired degree of tightness or of ease in the money market.

Open-market purchases or sales may also be made in order to ease or tighten member-bank reserve positions and thereby to change deliberately the tone of the credit market. Unless member banks are already largely out of debt to the Reserve Banks, purchases of securities by the Federal Reserve will tend in the first instance to be reflected in a correspondingly smaller volume of member-bank borrowing at the discount windows of the Reserve Banks. This development will operate to create an easier tone in the money market, to lower money-market rates, and to enlarge the availability of bank credit. Sales of securities by the System (made to tighten bank credit rather than merely to offset the effects of other factors affecting reserves) will be reflected initially in an enlarged need for borrowing by member banks from the Reserve Banks. This development will tend to reduce the availability of bank credit, increase its cost, and engender a more cautious attitude on the part of lenders throughout the money and capital markets.

A particular level of member-bank borrowing does not, of course, always produce the same response in the money and capital markets. That response will vary depending on such factors as the direction in which credit policy is shifting, the liquidity of the secondary reserve position of the banks, special tax laws, and the demand for and availability of nonbank credit in the various sectors of the market. The Federal Reserve System must work through open-market purchases and sales to find the level of borrowing (or of free reserves) that produces the desired atmosphere in the credit markets, in large part by trial and observation; and to maintain that atmosphere, or one of more or of less restraint, the System must continuously watch the results being achieved and modify constantly its "target" of borrowing.

Most banks in this country are reluctant to remain indebted to the Federal Reserve for large amounts and for protracted periods, partly because of the experience of bankers over many periods of financial crises in the past and partly because some depositors dislike seeing their banks assume large liabilities that take precedence over those to the depositors. The reluctance of member banks to borrow at the Reserve Banks has also been carefully cultivated by the Federal Reserve System, however, both in Regulation A of the Federal Reserve Board and in the daily contacts between member banks and officers of the Federal Reserve Banks.

Because most member banks are not willing to remain indebted to the Reserve Banks, it is possible for the Federal Reserve System to ease or tighten the tone of the money and capital markets with open-market operations. It can ease the tone of the market by supplying reserve funds and relieving the volume of member-bank borrowing, and it can tighten the tone by absorbing reserve funds and forcing member banks as a group further into debt at the discount windows of the Federal Reserve Banks. As long as member banks are reluctant borrowers at the discount window, the response in the credit markets to such changes tends to be, to a certain extent, independent of the level of the discount rate. That is, with a large volume of member-bank borrowing, there can be a certain restrictive tone in the money markets even with a relatively low discount rate. Conversely, a small volume of borrowing will create a certain tone of ease in the money markets even when the discount rate is high. Without reluctance by member banks to borrow at the Reserve Banks there would not be much of an independent response in our credit markets to open-market operations. Changes in the credit climate would depend to a far greater degree than at present on large and rapid changes in the discount rate.

By enlarging or reducing the volume of member-bank borrowing through appropriate open-market operations, the Federal Reserve can prepare the credit market for changes in the discount rate. When the tone of the money market is tightened due to an increase in member-bank borrowing, banks are under pressure to get out of debt by selling short or intermediate-term Government securities and curtailing their positions in other money-market assets. Market rates will tend to rise in relation to the prevailing discount rate as member banks cut back their holdings of money-market paper and tighten lending practices in an effort to get out of debt and remain out of debt to the Reserve Banks. It may then become desirable for the Federal Reserve to raise the discount rate so as to bring it into line with higher market rates and thereby to reinforce the more restrictive climate throughout the credit markets. In the same way, open-market operations are used to ease credit pressures and to prepare the way for a reduction in the discount rate. Open-market operations and the discount rate are thus companion pieces in the Federal Reserve's credit control arsenal.

EARLY OPEN-MARKET DEVELOPMENTS

Authority to engage in open-market operations was granted to the Federal Reserve Banks in the original Federal Reserve Act. Under Section 14, the Federal Reserve Banks were empowered to buy or sell (1) cable transfers and bankers' acceptance and bills of exchange eligible for rediscount, (2) United States Government securities, and (3) municipal warrants maturing within six months.

The legislative history of the Act suggests that there was, from the first, some awareness of the potential role that open-market operations might play as an instrument of credit policy. While the discount rate was regarded by the legislative framers of the System as the principal measure by which the Federal Reserve was to exert its influence over the credit situation, open-market operations were recognized as having a function in making the discount rate effective in the market, particularly when rediscounts were small and when banks held excess funds at the Reserve Banks.[1]

However, despite evidence of some legislative appreciation of the potential importance of open-market operations, there is no indication that they were used prior to 1922 to effectuate credit policy. Open-market operations of the Federal Reserve Banks were by law made subject to such rules and regulations as the Federal Reserve Board might prescribe. In December 1914, the Board gave "the banks authority to purchase Government bonds within the limits of prudence

[1] U.S. House of Representatives, *Report No. 69*, 63rd Congress, 1st Session, 1913, p. 32.

as they might see fit."[2] At this time, of course, the total Federal debt was small and the availability of Government issues in the market was limited. Prior to the entry of the United States into World War I the Reserve Banks made some small purchases of Government securities, in part to obtain income and in part in anticipation of the issuance of Federal Reserve bank notes in substitution for national bank notes as provided by law. During the war period, Treasury financing was not supported by open-market action but rather by increases in member-bank discounts at the Federal Reserve Banks. Holding of Government securities by the Reserve Banks remained small and reflected temporary accommodations to the Treasury and the use of Government securities as collateral for Federal Reserve bank notes.

In the two years immediately following World War I the System applied a considerable restraint on credit and monetary expansion by means of sharply increasing discount rates and a highly restrictive policy at the discount windows. Holdings of Government securities remained largely unchanged in 1919 and 1920 at around $300 million. Almost all of these holdings were held as collateral for outstanding Federal Reserve bank notes.

OPERATIONS IN BANKERS' ACCEPTANCES

Purchases by the Federal Reserve Banks of bankers' acceptances are made under the open-market authority, and beginning in 1916 this paper was held in substantial amounts by the System. These purchases, however, are not regarded here as coming within the scope of open-market operations, since until 1955 they were not conducted at the initiative of the System.

From the first it became a policy of the System to promote the use of bankers' acceptances by attempting to foster the kind of market for them that existed abroad. System purchases of bankers' acceptances were so conducted that these operations were actually more similar to the discount function than to the open-market function. Within established limits approved by the Federal Reserve Board, the Reserve Banks fixed rates at which they stood ready to buy acceptances. Acceptances were sold to the System at the initiative of the market, in such amounts as the market might choose to dispose of at these buying rates.

Buying rates were reduced when the Federal Reserve Banks wished

[2] Federal Reserve Board, Annual Report, 1914, p. 16.

to attract acceptances and they were raised to cut down on the volume of offerings, depending on the credit objectives of the System at the time.[3] Buying rates were intended, normally, to be somewhat above the market, so as to make the System a buyer only as required by the special peaks of credit pressures. As a practical matter, however, purchases of bankers' bills tended to enlarge during phases of credit restraint, thus running counter to basic credit policy objectives. This reflected the fact that, since the System desired to promote the market for this particular credit instrument, it was not in a position to raise its buying rates as ruthlessly as would have been necessary in order to avoid increasing its holdings during periods of credit restraint.

With the collapse of short-term interest rates in 1933, market rates on bankers' acceptances moved well below the posted buying rate of the Reserve Banks. The System's portfolio of bankers' acceptances ran off and, except for a brief period in 1946, the Federal Reserve Banks held no acceptances from 1933 until 1955.

The practice of posting a buying rate on bankers' acceptances was discontinued in March 1955, and open-market operations in them were begun on the same basis as with Government securities. Purchases are now made at the market on the initiative of the Federal Reserve System. A well-spaced maturity schedule is maintained so that holdings can be reduced, should that be desirable, by not replacing maturing bills. Repurchase agreements are also made with dealers in bankers' acceptances when circumstances are such that the System wishes to supply funds to the market for temporary periods. Since 1955 the System has maintained a portfolio which has ranged in size from about $10 million to $40 million, depending on over-all credit policy.

DEVELOPMENT OF COORDINATION IN THE OPEN-MARKET FUNCTION

Use of open-market operations in Government securities as an instrument of Federal Reserve credit policy began in 1922 and 1923 with the development of a System organization for coordinating the operations of the several Reserve Banks and for directing these in accordance with credit policy objectives. In 1921 the drop in discounts that accompanied the business readjustment of that period cut

[3] The Reserve Banks, under this practice, did not sell any acceptances in the market, but held them to maturity.

heavily into the earnings of the Reserve Banks. To rebuild their earnings the Reserve Banks began to buy United States Government securities. These purchases, however, were made by each individual Reserve Bank in accordance with decisions taken by its board of directors, and the transactions were executed by each Reserve Bank where and as it saw fit.

Such uncoordinated operations caused several problems. One of these had to do with the effect on the functioning of the market for Government securities. By competing among each other to buy, usually in New York, the Reserve Banks tended to bid up unduly the prices of Government securities. This served to create, on occasion, an artificial situation in the market for Government securities that complicated the financing problems of the Treasury. Another problem arose from the reserve funds which were thereby injected into the banking system. It soon became evident that purchases of securities by the Reserve Banks were not adding to the total earning assets of the System; instead, under the conditions then prevailing, the reserve funds created by these purchases were being used to reduce total discounts at the Reserve Banks. Thus, although an individual Reserve Bank might add to its total assets by such purchases, the initial effect, at least, was to bring about a compensating reduction in member-bank discounts somewhere in the System.

When the Federal Reserve authorities came to see the relation between open-market operations and changes in the pressures being exerted at the discount window, they found the key to the effective use of open-market operations as a major policy instrument. In May 1922, at the request of the Federal Reserve Board, the Conference of Governors of the Federal Reserve Banks considered the problems raised by uncoordinated open-market actions and established the Committee on Centralized Execution of Purchases and Sales of Government Securities. This committee, which was made up of the Governors of the Federal Reserve Banks of Boston, New York, Philadelphia, and Chicago, was given the responsibility for executing Government security transactions of the several Reserve Banks in an orderly manner so as to avoid disrupting effects on the market. The committee had no authority to make policy recommendations to the Reserve Banks or to interfere in their decisions. Later that year, however, when the membership of the committee was expanded to include the Governor of the Federal Reserve Bank of Cleveland, the functions of the committee were enlarged to allow it to make recommendations regarding the advisability of open-market purchases and sales, although these recommendations were in no way binding on the directors of the individual Reserve Banks.

With the growth in understanding of the relation of open-market operations to the credit climate, it became apparent that there was a need for a common set of purposes and objectives to govern the open-market operations of the various Reserve Banks. In the spring of 1923, the Federal Reserve Board adopted a resolution which created the Federal Open Market Investment Committee and which provided that open-market purchases and sales should be made "with primary regard for the accommodation of commerce and business and to the effect of such purchases and sales on the general credit situation."[4] The Committee, which had the same membership as the earlier Committee on Centralized Execution of Purchases and Sales, was placed under the general supervision of the Federal Reserve Board and given the "duty . . . to devise and recommend plans for the purchase, sale, and distribution of open market purchases of the Federal Reserve banks in accordance with the above principles. . . ."[5]

In the fall of 1923, in a further attempt to unify the open-market policy of the System, the Federal Reserve Banks and the Board agreed to establish an open-market investment account, to be prorated among the Reserve Banks on the basis of an agreed formula. The investment account could be increased or decreased by the Committee with the approval of the Board. Each Federal Reserve Bank, however, could refuse to participate in any proposed action, and each retained the right to engage in open-market purchases and sales for its own account should it choose to do so.

The arrangement requiring approval of open-market transactions by the individual banks was cumbersome and potentially unwieldy. Being so involved, it may have caused delays which affected the basic decisions of the Committee and the Board. It was made to work reasonably well most of the time, however, primarily because each important policy change was thoroughly discussed at joint conferences (usually semiannual) attended by the Board and by the Governors and Chairmen of all the Federal Reserve Banks.

Further changes in the organization of the open-market function were made in 1930, when the committee was enlarged to include all

[4] U.S. House of Representatives, Committee on Banking and Currency, *Stabilization Hearings* . . . , 69th Congress, 1st Session on H.R. 7895, 1926, p. 865.
[5] *Ibid.*

of the Governors of the Reserve Banks and redesignated as the Open Market Policy Conference. An executive committee of five was established to act in the execution of Conference policies. Specific legal status was later given to this general arrangement in the Banking Act of 1933, which provided in addition that open-market operations by an individual bank for its own account must be restricted to emergencies unless approved by the Federal Reserve Board.

In the discussions in Congress leading up to the Banking Act of 1935, a great deal of consideration was given to the open-market powers of the Federal Reserve System, and many suggestions were made to change the organizational arrangements for the formulation of open-market policy. Arguments were advanced for placing the entire authority in the Federal Reserve Board in order to eliminate the division of authority and responsibility for open-market operations and to place this authority along with that for other instruments of credit control in one body. Others held that the existing organization, or at least a committee containing some members from the Reserve Banks, should be continued in order to avoid placing open-market policy entirely in the hands of a "politically controlled" group and to keep a regional character in the System.

These views were compromised, and the Banking Act of 1935 provides for a Federal Open Market Committee composed of the members of the Board and five representatives from the Federal Reserve Banks, each to be selected annually by the boards of directors of stipulated groups of Reserve Banks. Authority and responsibility for determination of open-market policy was for the first time fully centralized. Each Reserve Bank was required to participate in the operations undertaken by the Committee and was forbidden to engage in open-market transactions without its approval. The law also instructed the Committee, in formulating its policies, to consider the needs of commerce, industry, and agriculture and the general credit situation of the country.

The Federal Open Market Committee is required by law to meet at least four times a year at the call of the Chairman of the Board of Governors or at the request of any three members of the Committee. For more than twenty years after its establishment the Committee also selected from its members an executive committee of five which met frequently and which supervised the execution of open-market activities within a broad framework of policy laid down by the full committee. In 1957 the executive committee was abolished and since then the full Committee has been meeting about every three weeks. Transactions for the System Account continue to be executed by the Federal Reserve Bank of New York as agent, as they have been from the time the Account was first established in 1923.

REPURCHASE TRANSACTIONS

In addition to outright purchases and sales of Government securities, the Federal Open Market Committee engages in transactions called repurchases with nonbank dealers in Government securities and bankers' acceptances. Under a repurchase transaction the System buys securities with an agreement to resell them to the dealer within a specified short time, and the dealer in turn agrees to repurchase them. From the standpoint of the Federal Reserve, such transactions provide a means of injecting temporary funds into the money market to relieve pressures caused by fluctuations in factors affecting bank reserves that are expected to be short-lived, or by "a temporary knot in the money market which could not at the moment be untangled."[6] From the standpoint of the dealer, the repurchase instrument serves to lighten the burden of his inventory, without decreasing the variety of securities he may offer his customers.

The repurchase facility is available only when it serves the purposes of the Federal Reserve, although dealers keep the Manager of the Account informed about their potential interest in such transactions. Under present practices, the agreements cover only securities maturing in less than fifteen months and are made for periods ranging up to a maximum of fifteen days. The repurchase rate has usually been the same as the discount rate of the Federal Reserve Bank of New York, although the Manager of the Account has a limited discretion to depart from that rate and he has on occasion done so.

Repurchase transactions are used by the System to smooth out the bumps in the money market. They make it possible for those operating the Account to respond to a special squeeze in the availability of money in the market by supplying reserve funds even before the reason for that squeeze may be understood. On the other hand, by the nature of these transactions those funds will be automatically withdrawn from the market as the need for them disappears.

[6] Robert V. Roosa, *Federal Reserve Operations in the Money Market and Government Securities Markets,* New York, Federal Reserve Bank of New York, 1956, p. 85.

The repurchase facility was frequently used by the System in the 1920's. Usually the transactions involved bankers' acceptances, but sometimes Government securities were used. After World War II the practice was revived as a technique of open-market operations, but it became particularly important in the administration of the Account with the return to a flexible monetary policy in 1951.

DIRECT DEALINGS WITH THE TREASURY

Prior to the Banking Act of 1935 there were no restrictions on the authority of the Federal Reserve banks to buy Government securities directly from the Treasury. As a practical matter these transactions had been confined before that time to temporary purchases of one-day certificates over tax payment dates, made with the objective of smoothing out the effect of tax collections on the money market.[7] There was an uneasiness, however, that by centralizing the open-market function in the new Federal Open Market Committee the way might be opened for inflationary use of the Federal Reserve for the convenience of the Treasury. Accordingly, in the 1955 Act, provision was made that purchases must be made "in the open market," i.e., not directly from the Treasury.

With the entry of this country into World War II, Congress granted the Federal Reserve a temporary authority to purchase up to $5 billion of Government securities directly from the Treasury. This authority has never lapsed, having been renewed time and again on a temporary basis. The legislative history of the authority makes it quite clear, however, that it is intended to be used only temporarily in cases of emergency or to mitigate the impact on the money market of large shifts of funds in and out of the Treasury's account at the Reserve Banks in connection with quarterly tax payments.

The special authority has been used only once since March 1954. With the development in recent years of improved methods of administering the Treasury's cash balances, quarterly tax payments do not produce the sharp fluctuations in bank reserve positions that they formerly did. There is, therefore, no longer much need for the special authority for direct purchases. On the other hand, neither is there a good basis for objecting to the authority on the grounds that it will make possible the misuse of Federal Reserve powers for the Treasury's benefit. This authority was not needed, nor was it used, when the

[7] An exception was a three-month loan of $50 million made in April 1917.

Federal Open Market Committee, in the past, held down the cost of Treasury financing at the expense of an inflationary expansion of credit and money. Prohibition of direct dealings between the System and the Treasury has been called "a pious wish enacted into law, an attempt to meet a real problem by an imaginary remedy. . . ."[8] Our ultimate protection against the debasement of the open-market instrument for the benefit of cheap Treasury financing must be an informed public.

CLASSICAL USE OF OPEN-MARKET OPERATIONS—1923-1929

Although open-market operations had not been used and had probably not been well understood as an instrument of credit policy prior to 1922, they were quickly embraced thereafter as a major tool of credit policy. Over the years from 1922 through 1929 the open-market instrument was used continuously to vary the climate of the credit market in accordance with the swings in the business cycle. In periods of boom, open-market operations were used to tighten the availability of credit and money by putting banks more heavily into debt to the Federal Reserve Banks. In periods of business decline, purchases were made to relieve the volume of that borrowing and thereby to relieve pressures on the money market.

In practice, during this period comparatively small changes in the volume of member-bank discounts and advances carried with them important shifts in the tone of the money markets. As discounts and advances rose up to and above $500 million, the money market tended to become a lenders' market. Credit became less readily avaliable, and market yields tended to be high relative to the discount rate. As discounts and advances fell below $500 million, the tendencies were the opposite. These effects were in a large measure independent of the absolute level of the discount rate, although of course that instrument was used as a companion piece to open-market operations, each supporting and strengthening the effects of the other.

In 1922 the volume of business activity was rising, and over that year and the next open-market operations were used to put member banks under the pressure of increased borrowing at the Federal Reserve Banks. Interest rates rose through the latter part of 1923.

Open-market policy was reversed in 1924 in recognition of the

[8] E. A. Goldenweiser, *American Monetary Policy,* New York, McGraw-Hill Book Company, Inc., 1951, p. 90.

receding volume of business activity. Member-bank discounts and advances at the Federal Reserve were pulled down sharply, averaging only about $250 million in the last few months of that year. Money-market yields dropped equally sharply, a move that was supported by a quick succession of cuts in the discount rates of the Reserve Banks.

The business recovery of 1925 and the prosperity of 1926 were accompanied by restrictive action by the Federal Reserve, and open-market operations were again used to put banks under pressure at the discount window. Beginning in late 1924, the volume of member-bank borrowing increased, reflecting sales by the open-market Account, and from mid-1925 through 1926 discounts and advances of member banks remained above $500 million. Money-market yields rose generally during these two years.

Open-market purchases were undertaken in 1927 to pull down somewhat the volume of member-bank borrowings. Since business activity softened slightly during that year, it is reasonable to assume that the easing open-market actions were related at least in part to that development. There was also at that time, however, a desire to ease money rates in this country in order to help promote the restoration and maintenance of sound currencies abroad. Whatever the basic reasons the System had for taking the action, there was a reduction in the volume of member-bank borrowing brought about by open-market operations, and interest rates declined until the fall of 1927.

Early in 1928, open-market operations were used to bring about a sharp increase in the volume of member-bank borrowing at the Reserve Banks, from around $400 million in the fall of 1927 to about $1 billion by May 1928. Thereafter, through most of 1929, member-bank borrowings were maintained at around that level. This pressure on member-bank reserve positions brought about an increasingly restrictive tone in the money markets.[9] A strong demand for bank credit was also developing largely as a result of speculative activity in stocks. The result was a sharp upsweep in interest rates on money-market securities and on bank loans to businesses. The Federal Reserve discount rates were raised several times in 1928 and 1929 to a high of

[9] Although purchases of bankers' acceptances are not included as open-market operations within the meaning of the term as defined here, it is worth noting that the practice of establishing a buying rate on acceptances brought about results that ran counter to the general objectives of credit policy, particularly in 1928. During that year the System added to its acceptance holdings in what now seems to have been an attempt to support the acceptance market in order to assist agriculture in the crop-moving season.

6 per cent, but these changes were made as an adjustment to market rates and were not used to lead the market. Long-term yields also turned up rather sharply, interrupting a declining trend that had persisted since 1920.

MASSIVE EASING—1929-33

After the crash in the stock market in the fall of 1929, the System moved promptly to engage in large purchases of Government securities in order to cut down the necessity for banks to borrow at the discount window. By the spring of 1930, discounts and advances to member banks were only about $250 million, down from the level of over $1 billion prevailing before the easing action was begun and lower than at any time since the recession of 1924. Over the next year and a half, additional open-market purchases were made so as to reduce further the dependence of member banks at the discount window. By mid-1931, member-bank borrowing was less than $200 million.

Money-market yields dropped sharply from late 1929 to mid-1931 under the impact of this open-market action and of the associated reductions in the discount rates of the Reserve Banks. Rates on bankers' acceptances declined from over 5 per cent to under 1 per cent, and commercial paper rates fell from 6 per cent to 2 per cent during this period. Rates charged on loans to businesses by banks in major northern and eastern cities declined from about 6 per cent to around 4 per cent. Yields on long-term Government and high-grade corporate bonds also reflected the massive easing in bank reserve positions, declining about one-half of one percentage point.

In mid-1931, with the collapse of the banking system in Germany and the abandonment of the gold standard by England, there began a tragic episode in Federal Reserve credit policy. The shock to confidence from these developments, together with the large number of bank failures in this country, resulted in a heavy drain on bank reserves due to an outflow of gold and an increase in the public's demand for currency. Over the fall of 1931 some open-market purchases were made by the System, but not in large enough amounts to offset these factors and to take care of usual seasonal needs. As a consequence member banks were obliged to increase sharply their borrowing at the Federal Reserve Banks. By November 1931, member-bank borrowings reached over $1.5 billion, as compared with around $300 million in the spring of that year. During the same time the discount rate was increased from 1½ per cent to 3½ per cent. Market rates of interest, both short-term and long-term, responded sharply upward to these developments.

The System's failure to meet this crisis by supplying reserves through heavy open-market purchases was due to the fact that, because of the law then governing collateral for Federal Reserve notes, such a buying program would have necessitated the suspension of reserve requirements against Federal Reserve deposits. This was a decision that the authorities were apparently not prepared to face at that time.

In February 1932, Congress modified the collateral requirements against Federal Reserve notes so as to allow United States Government securities to be so used. The System at once bought the unprecedented volume of about $1 billion of Government securities and thereby pulled member-bank borrowing down sharply. In mid-1933 an additional $500 million of purchases were made and Federal Reserve holdings of Government securities reached $2,400 million by October 1933. Member-bank borrowing all but disappeared, and interest rates again declined abruptly. For several years after mid-1932, except for a brief period during the bank holiday in March 1933, bill yields averaged under one-half of 1 per cent. Yields on long-term high-grade securities settled down again to the levels reached in the first half of 1931.

INACTIVITY—1934-37

For nearly twenty years after October 1933, the Federal Reserve did not use open-market operations for the primary purpose of affecting member-bank reserves. From 1933 until March 1937, the System purposely held its total portfolio of Government securities at $2,430 million. Member banks were not borrowing at the Reserve Banks, and indeed during that period they held excess reserve balances that ranged up to $3 billion, so the System saw no need to buy additional securities. Neither was the System's portfolio large enough to permit it to absorb the excess reserves of member banks, should it have wished to use it for that purpose.

Although open-market operations were kept on an inactive status for a long period after 1933, the easing of credit generated by both the heavy open-market purchases in 1932 and 1933 and the reserves supplied by a large gold inflow worked gradually to develop lower and lower interest rates. Bill yields reached about one-quarter of 1 per cent by mid-1934 and they held in that area through 1936. Yields on three- to five-year Government securities dropped from about 3 per cent in December 1933 to about 1 per cent in December 1936. Long-term yields also declined sharply.

"ORDERLY MARKETS"—1937-41

Although open-market operations were not used for nearly twenty years for the purpose of affecting member-bank reserve positions, another use was developed in the 1930's and in the war and postwar years. At first the Federal Reserve began to intervene in the Government securities market to keep that market "orderly"; ultimately, first in the war and then in the postwar period, the objective became to maintain a fixed pattern of yields on Government securities.

The first important occasion for intervention on a large scale to affect directly the market for long-term Government securities arose in connection with the Board's action over the first part of 1937 to raise reserve requirements to the maximum authorized by law. This action, of course, was taken to absorb some of the large volume of excess reserves. Although it was stated at the time that the action was a preventive measure, and not a restrictive one, some holders of intermediate-term and long-term Government bonds concluded that it was advisable to take profits on these while they could, and bond prices began to decline sharply. After some hesitation the System intervened and stemmed the price break by purchasing such securities. Bond yields subsequently resumed a steady decline that lasted until mid-1939, aided by the fact that the System added to its portfolio in the fall of 1937 as a depression remedy and reduced reserve requirements in 1938, as well as by a large gold inflow that added heavily to the excess reserves of member banks.

With the outbreak of war on September 1, 1939, a second major occasion arose for direct intervention in the intermediate- and long-term United States Government security market. The shock of war was reflected in a drastic break in the prices of Government bonds and other securities. Once again the Federal Reserve bought heavily in the intermediate-term and long-term sector of the Government security market, this time to stop a panic reaction to the developments in Europe. About $500 million of these securities were purchased and the market promptly recovered. Shortly thereafter the System resold the securities and the portfolio was restored to its previous size of about $2.5 billion. No further action of this kind was undertaken until well after our entry in the war.

Each of these occasions for direct intervention in the longer-term area of the market may be said to have been successful in accomplishing what was intended. In the first case the System did not wish its precautionary action of absorbing some of the redundant excess reserves to result in a tightening of the capital market or an increase in long-term interest rates. The open-market intervention was taken, in a sense, to stop a development in the Government securities market that was working against the System's easy credit policy. The same can be said for the action undertaken to stem the break in confidence that followed the outbreak of war in Europe. But together these experiences formed a background which set precedents for direct intervention by the System to maintain a fixed level of interest rates at later times, when the forces that were operating to change those rates were basic, not just transitory.

PEGGED MARKETS—1942-51

During World War II the primary objective of Federal Reserve open-market operations was to supply the banking system with adequate reserves for financing the war. Avoiding inflation was a secondary consideration. The wartime program for open-market operations was established early in 1942. Initially the Federal Reserve wished to peg the long-term rate of interest, but the Treasury was somewhat doubtful that this should or could be done. However, when the Treasury accepted the fixed-rate idea for war finance, it insisted that the entire rate structure be pegged at the prevailing pattern. After some slight compromise, it was agreed that the rate structure prevailing in March 1942 should be maintained. This rate pattern involved ⅜ per cent on ninty-one-day Treasury bills, ⅞ per cent one one-year certificates, and 2½ per cent on long-term bonds.

Maintenance by open-market operations of this sharply ascending structure of rates created some special problems over and above those that would have been associated with any rate-pegging operation. A fixed buying rate of ⅜ per cent was established on Treasury bills. To stimulate commercial banks to buy bills the Federal Reserve also established an arrangement that gave banks the right to buy back from the System, at the same rate, any bills it sold to the System, thereby in effect making bank holdings of bills the equivalent of interest-bearing excess reserves. Nevertheless, over the war period almost all Treasury bills gravitated to the Federal Reserve Banks. Since one security was as liquid as another under the System's pegging program, banks and others soon learned to hold the higher-yielding securities and even to sell these to the System as they became shorter-term and shift out again in maturity in order to maximize total return.

To sustain the low yields on longer-term securities, the Federal Reserve found it necessary to make small purchases during most of 1942, but only once during the war period was there a need for massive intervention by the open-market account. In the latter part of 1942, the System bought about $1 billion of 2 per cent 10-year bonds so as to insure the success of a Treasury offering of these securities. Within a few months, however, they were resold in the market. As we have seen, as soon as the mechanics and the implications of the open-market pegging program were understood, it was the short-term rate, particularly the bill rate, that needed help, not the intermediate- or long-term areas.

During the war the Federal Reserve increased its holdings of Government securities from $2.5 billion to $25 billion. The primary objective of open-market policy, that of financing the war, was readily accomplished and at low interest rates. Perhaps more could have been done to finance the war in a less inflationary way. However, the worst inflationary results of the war's financing came after the war, when the wartime program for pegging interest rates by open-market purchases was continued as a feature of the postwar economy.

After the war the overriding financial fact was the size of the Federal debt. The Treasury, the Administration, the Congress, the Federal Reserve, and the general public were all overawed by it. It was difficult then to comprehend how a debt of that size could be handled should the money and capital markets be set free to find their own levels with the Federal Reserve exercising only general influence over the total bank credit supply. Few in the Federal Reserve System, or outside of it, were disposed to move quickly to such a status. Federal Reserve officials, however, wished to take some small steps in that direction in the hope that the System might regain a measure of control over the availability of Reserve Bank credit and the total supply of bank credit and money.

A reluctant Treasury finally agreed to a gradual rise in short-term rates. In the summer of 1947 the Treasury-bill rate was cut loose from the ⅜ per cent peg. By the end of that year the bill rate reached

1 per cent, where it was again pegged for a time. Meanwhile, over a period of several months, the ⅞ per cent rate on one-year certificates was allowed to edge up to 1⅛ per cent.

These maneuvers, modest as they were, were enough to bring into question the stability of the low yields on intermediate- and long-term securities that had prevailed since the end of war financing. These yields began to rise sharply in the last few months of 1947, and the Federal Open Market Committee began to buy such bonds to cushion the price declines. On December 24, 1947, the Committee established, at levels below the then prevailing market, a pattern of prices on intermediate- and long-term bonds that it was prepared to defend and maintain by its buying. In defending this price structure over the following ten months, the Committee purchased over $8 billion of such bonds, although the effect of these purchases on member-bank reserve positions was about offset by sales of short-term securities and increased reserve requirements at New York and Chicago banks. Purchases of long-term bonds continued until after the 1948 national election, by which time the election results and a deteriorating business picture reversed public psychology and altered the demand-supply situation in the capital market.

During the first half of 1949 the System resold several billion dollars of long-term bonds, but it discontinued this operation at about mid-year since the sales were tending to prevent the capital market from easing, a development that would have been desirable in view of the declining business situation. When sales were discontinued by the Committee, bond prices advanced sharply and yields declined.

By early 1950 the Federal Reserve recognized that business was picking up and it began again to sell long-term bonds, thereby gradually depressing their prices and increasing long-term yields. It continued to support the short term sector of the market, and sales of bonds were offset by purchases of short-term issues. Short-term yields, however, were again permitted to rise gradually until midyear.

With the outbreak of the Korean war the growing dissatisfaction of the Federal Reserve officials with the System's price and yield pegging operations was heightened by the fear that prevailing open-market policies would greatly stimulate, rather than help curb, a severe inflationary movement. In an effort to break away from the prevailing rate pattern, the System raised the discount rate in August 1950 and allowed short-term interest rates to rise sharply. At the same time, however, the Secretary of the Treasury countered with an announcement of a refunding based on the old rate levels. To protect the Treasury's refunding, the Federal Reserve purchased all of the maturing issues offered to it and sold other short-term securities to the market at higher rates than were carried by the new Treasury offering. This operation brought into the open the growing difference of opinion between the Federal Reserve and the Treasury regarding the role that open-market operations and monetary policy should play in the economy.

Although short- and intermediate-term interest rates were allowed to firm further over the second half of 1950, the System still found it necessary to buy a substantial volume of short-term securities to keep short-term yields from rising sharply. The Open Market Committee also began to buy long-term bonds again in order to defend the 2½ per cent long-term rate. From the outbreak of the Korean war in mid-1950 through February 1951, the Federal Reserve purchased a net of over $5 billion of Government securities of all kinds. Part of these purchases were offset by a gold outflow and an increase in the reserve requirements of member banks in New York and Chicago. Nevertheless, there occurred a substantial bank credit and monetary expansion. In addition, savings institutions were raising funds by selling bonds to the Federal Reserve and making loans that helped support private spending, while at the same time the Federal Reserve System was vainly trying to curb this spending with selective credit controls. These developments, and the substantial rise in commodity prices that was occurring, set the stage for the Treasury-Federal Reserve Accord in early March and the subsequent revival of open-market operations as an anticyclical instrument.

THE TREASURY-FEDERAL RESERVE ACCORD

The Treasury-Federal Reserve Accord provided for the cessation of direct Federal Reserve support of Government security prices, subject to certain transition arrangements set forth in an agreement with the Treasury. With respect to long-term Governments, the Treasury agreed to offer those investors holding two huge issues of bonds (June and December 1967-72) an exchange into a nonmarketable 2¾ per cent bond, which in turn was convertible at any time at the holder's option into a 1½ per cent marketable note. The objective of this offering was to cut down the amount of long-term marketable bonds overhanging the market. As a transition measure the Treasury agreed to set aside $400 million, and the Federal Reserve $200 million, to support the long-term market during the period that this refunding offer was open. Investors turned in a substantial block of bonds to accept the new issue, and a large amount of long-term marketable securities was thereby removed from the market. The $600 million of support funds were quickly used up, however, and prices of long-term bonds were than allowed to drop below par. All direct support of the long-term market by the Federal Open Market Committee ended in June 1951.

With respect to the short-term area, the authorities agreed that direct open-market support would also end. Yields in the short-term market were to be allowed to form about the discount rate—then 1¾ per cent. It was understood as a part of the Accord that, unless compelling circumstances should require it, no change would be made in the Federal Reserve discount rate for the remainder of 1951.

In essence the Accord took away from the money and credit market the immediate and unlimited access to Reserve Bank credit that it had previously had through sales of Government securities to the Federal Reserve System. Thereafter Federal Reserve credit was available at the initiative of the market only through the Reserve Bank discount windows (via member banks) at a cost established by the System. Since member banks are not willing to become indebted to the Federal Reserve on an unlimited and indefinite basis, and since the Federal Reserve also is not prepared to lend on such a basis, access to Federal Reserve credit again became subject to over-all control by the monetary authorities. There was a period of transition during which the System was a reasonably generous supplier of funds through open-market purchases of short-term securities, but the reins on the total supply of Reserve Bank credit gradually came firmly into the System's hands. Open-market operations again became an anticyclical instrument, instead of a mechanism for freezing the price of credit to the Treasury and ultimately to all other borrowers as well.

CLASSICAL OPERATION SINCE 1951

After the Accord, open-market operations were restored to the pattern followed in the 1920's. Purchases and sales have been made in order to produce and maintain whatever member-bank reserve position has been considered appropriate to the business and credit situation. For about a year following the Accord there was little need either for an easing or for a tightening of the credit markets. The contraction in liquidity that occurred with the end of pegged security prices seemed a sufficient monetary brake on earlier inflationary pressures. Member-bank borrowings at the Reserve Banks averaged around $300 million during most of 1951 and the first quarter of 1952.

Pressure on member-bank reserve positions was allowed to build after mid-1952, however, as business activity picked up and credit demands expanded. In the latter part of 1952 and the first five months of 1953, member-bank borrowing at the Federal Reserve was generally in excess of $1 billion. In this revival phase of credit policy there was a certain amount of misunderstanding among some member banks over how and when the borrowing privilege should be used. This situation, together with an excess profits tax that made borrowing very profitable for those banks that were subject to the tax, kept the high level of member-bank borrowing that was reached late in 1952 from having great restrictive significance.

By early 1953, both the member banks and the operating officials of the Federal Reserve System were becoming more familiar with the principles governing the borrowing privilege at the Reserve Banks. A given level of member-bank borrowing, therefore, began to have an increasingly restrictive effect. Open-market operations were used to absorb most of the reserves supplied by the return of currency after the turn of the year, and member-bank borrowing remained over the billion-dollar level through May 1953. Free reserves—that is, excess reserves less borrowings from the Federal Reserve—held at around minus $600 million. Pressure of credit demands and the tightness of bank reserve positions were reflected in an upsweep in short-, intermediate-, and long-term yields. This movement culminated in May and early June 1953, when prices of bonds broke sharply.

In early June the System bought a large amount of Treasury bills to correct the deteriorating market situation. Shortly thereafter, when the prospect of declining Government defense outlays made the business outlook less robust, the Federal Reserve Board reduced reserve requirements. No offsetting action was taken by the open-market Account. Member-bank borrowing at the Federal Reserve banks was thereby trimmed to around $500 million (free reserves to about zero). Over succeeding months member-bank borrowings declined sharply and free reserves rose correspondingly, reflecting partly less active demands for credit and partly a vigorous open-market policy of credit ease.

The shift after mid-1953 from an open-market policy designed to maintain member-bank borrowing in excess of $1 billion dollars (and free reserves around minus $750 million) to a policy that virtually eliminated member-bank borrowing (with free reserves ranging over $1 billion) was accompanied by a dramatic decline in interest rates in all maturity sectors and by a substantial increase in the availability of credit, particularly bank credit. Rates on Treasury bills dropped from around 2¼ per cent to less than 1 per cent, and yields on inter-mediate-term and longer-term Governments also declined sharply. Yields on high-grade corporate and municipal bonds fell about one-half of 1 per cent (50 basis points).

An open-market policy of active ease was continued until late 1954, when the decision was made to pull back somewhat on the free re-serves of member banks in view of the improved business situation and outlook. Open-market operations were slowly oriented toward supply-ing less reserves than were being absorbed through monetary expan-sion. By about June 1955, borrowings became equal to excess re-serves. (Free reserves were zero.) Thereafter, as the business boom intensified, pressure of open-market policy and the active demand for bank credit lifted borrowings to nearly $1 billion (free reserves of from minus $300 million to $500 million on an average). This open-market program of restraint was maintained with occasional moderate shifts in intensity until October 1957. It was reinforced by a series of increases in the discount rates of the Reserve Banks. Credit, par-ticularly bank credit, became increasingly less readily available, and interest rates increased more or less steadily over this three-year period. Rates on Treasury bills rose three percentage points to a peak of over 3½ per cent, and intermediate- and long-term yields rose about 1½ percentage points. By mid-1957, short-term and long-term yields were about equal, and intermediate-term yields were even higher, reflecting the special pressures of bank selling to maintain re-serve positions.

In October of 1957 the Open Market Committee began to give recognition to an easing in the demands for bank credit and a topping-off in business activity by allowing the reserves thus being released to remain in the banking system, but no positive open-market action was taken to ease the pressure on bank reserve positions. On November 14, however, the Federal Reserve authorities decided that a quick, dramatic move was needed to signal the change in credit policy in view of the rapidly deteriorating business picture and the congested situation in the capital markets. The System chose for this signal a reduction in the discount rate from 3½ per cent to 3 per cent. Thereafter, open-market policy was shifted gradually. By the early part of 1958 the deficiency in free reserves was wiped out and member-bank borrowing was pulled down to around $500 million. Over the following several months, member-bank borrowing at the Reserve Banks was largely eliminated and the average of free reserves was lifted to more than $500 million. The Reserve Banks' discount rates were also reduced further to 1¾ per cent by mid-April.

The initial response to this easing in credit policy was a sharp decline in all market yields. Later, as open-market action pulled banks almost entirely out of debt to the Reserve Banks, an expansion of bank credit began to create a condition of increasing ease in all sectors of the credit market. Short-term yields fell under 1 per cent and yields of securities maturing in up to five years were pulled down correspondingly. Long-term yields declined sharply until January 1958; thereafter, for several months there was little further decline despite additional easing in shorter-term yields, reflecting the continuing heavy demands for long-term credit by municipal and corporate borrowers and the sale by the Treasury of two issues of long-term bonds. The total flow of funds into the long-term market was substantial, however, and the availability of credit in the capital market was materially easier than had been the case prior to mid-November 1957.

MARKET SECTOR FOR OPEN-MARKET OPERATIONS

If the intention of the Federal Open Market Committee is to influence the general availability and cost of credit, it can do this by affecting the volume of reserves that member banks are obliged to borrow at the Federal Reserve. For this purpose, open-market operations can be conducted in Government securities of any maturity or in any other assets that may be eligible for ownership by the Federal Reserve Banks. Traditionally, however, such operations have been conducted in paper of rather short maturity, and since 1952 it has been the policy of the Federal Open Market Committee to deal exclusively in short-term securities, in Treasury bills if possible.

The practice of dealing only in sort-term securities was adopted formally in March 1953, following a broad inquiry by an Ad Hoc

Subcommittee of the Federal Open Market Committee. This sub-committee, which was headed by the Chairman of the Board of Governors, studied the relation of the Federal Open Market Account and its operation to the entire Government securities market. It made a number of recommendations to the Federal Open Market Committee that were designed to strengthen the market for Government securities, thereby improving it as a mechanism for open-market operations and for Treasury debt management.[10]

The Ad Hoc Subcommittee's study was made shortly after the Federal Reserve discontinued its practice of interfering directly in both the long-term and the short-term sectors of the market for the purpose of pegging the prices and yields on Government securities. This intervention, the subcommittee found, had left its mark on the Government securities market, and even after the Accord there remained an uncertainty about System intentions that was detrimental to the development of "depth, breadth, and resiliency of the market." The subcommittee recommended, therefore, that the System confine its operations to very short-term securities, preferably bills, where the direct impact of System transactions on the market would be at a minimum. It also recommended that instructions given by the Federal Open Market Committee to the Manager of the Account be changed to make it clear that the System did not intend to interfere lightly in the long-term market under the guise of "maintaining orderly markets." Under the new instructions, such action is to be taken only to correct a "disorderly situation" and then only after other measures have failed and upon due deliberation by the entire Federal Open Market Committee.

Prior to the subcommittee's study, it had been the practice of the Federal Reserve to intervene in the market to support "rights" values on maturing securities during a Treasury refunding operation. The subcommittee found this practice to be detrimental to the efficient operation of the Government securities market and to run counter to System responsibilities for formulation and execution of credit and monetary policy. It recommended that the practice of direct intervention to support Treasury refinancing operations be discontinued, leav-

[10] *Federal Open Market Committee, Report of Ad Hoc Subcommittee on the Government Securities Market,* November 12, 1952. Reprinted in Congress of the United States, Subcommittee on Economic Stabilization of the Joint Committee on the Economic Report, *United States Monetary Policy: Recent Thinking and Experience,* 83rd Congress, 2nd Session, 1954, pp. 257-307.

ing the Treasury to insure the success of its refinancings by the proper pricing of its new offerings.

These recommendations were accepted by the Federal Open Market Committee in March 1953. Since that time the System has only once found it necessary to intervene in the long-term market because of disorderly market conditions, despite the fact that prices of long-term bonds have undergone some substantial swings. The capital market no longer expects, wants, or needs such intervention. Only twice has the Open Market Committee decided to intervene directly to assist a Treasury financing, and the Treasury has successfully carried out refinancings under all kinds of market conditions without direct System assistance.

There are still some students of monetary policy who believe that the Federal Reserve should "broaden" the scope of its open-market operations beyond its objective of affecting the general availability and cost of credit. Their contention is that, by intervening directly in the intermediate- and long-term sectors of the market, the System could guide the impact of its operations so as to achieve more promptly than otherwise either higher or lower interest yields on intermediate- and long-term securities, bringing the yields quickly to whatever levels System authorities might regard as appropriate to the prevailing business and credit situation.

It is, of course, always tempting to advocate direct Government interference with market processes in order to substitute official judgment for that of the market place or at best to achieve at once what the market might take time to bring about. Usually, however, such proposals are not pressed strongly when bond prices are declining. At such times the tendency is rather to encourage the System to buy bonds in order to cushion the drop, even though such a move would run counter to prevailing credit policy. The economic argument for direct intervention in the long-term market is more likely to be advanced when market yields are not declining fast enough or far enough to suit the advocate.

The major question involved in such an operation by the Federal Reserve is not whether the System could bring about the desired yield declines by direct intervention, although the opponents of this kind of action do not agree that it could always do so. The basic questions raised in opposition to such intervention are rather whether the monetary authorities would be prepared to accept the disruption in the private capital markets that such an action might engender, whether these markets then could satisfactorily function at the artificially imposed lower-yield levels to bring lender and borrower together, and whether the Treasury under such circumstances could finance in any size outside the short-term area.

OPEN-MARKET OPERATIONS AS AN INSTRUMENT OF CREDIT CONTROL

Over the period of the 1920's and again since the Accord in 1951, experience has shown that the climate or tone of the credit markets is clearly responsive to shifts in the reserve positions of member banks. During the 1920's, when member-bank borrowing at the Reserve Banks rose to about $500 million, the atmosphere of the money market became one of restraint, interest rates increased, and the general availability of credit tended to be curtailed. Conversely, as such borrowing dropped significantly below that level, the tone of the money market became easy, rates declined, and credit generally was more readily obtainable. Since the Accord, there has been the same pattern of response to changes in the need for banks to borrow at the Reserve Banks. Relatively moderate shifts in the average amounts of such borrowing have had marked effects on the entire credit climate. To some extent, moreover, these responses have been independent of the absolute level of the discount rate, or of interest rates generally.

The fact that the tone of the market is responsive to the level of member bank borrowing at the Reserve Banks gives an unique character to the role of open market operations in the effectuation of credit and monetary policy. They can be used flexibly to offset the net impact on bank reserves of other sources of demand and supply of reserve funds in such a way as to result in an increase or decrease of member bank borrowing, or, if desired, to maintain a level of such borrowing that is fairly constant frem week to week, or month to month. This means that when the Federal Open Market Committee decides that a tone of tightness, or ease, or moderation, in the money markets would promote financial equilibrium and economic stability, it has the means at hand to make the decision effective.[11]

Open-market operations are not just one of several alternative instruments of credit policy. They are the only instrument by which the System can continuously adjust and maintain that tone of ease or restraint in the credit markets which is appropriate to the developing economic situation. To be most effective, open-market operations

[11] *Ibid.,* p. 259.

should be used complementarily with discount rate changes. In recent years they have also been dovetailed with occasional downward adjustments in reserve requirements. Neither of these other instruments, however, can serve as substitutes for open-market operations in the implementation of Federal Reserve credit policy decisions. Open-market operations "constitute the only effective means by which the elasticity that was built into our monetary and credit structure by the Federal Reserve Act can be made to serve continuously the needs of the economy. Without them, that elasticity would often operate capriciously and even perversely to the detriment of the economy."[12]

SUGGESTED READINGS

BOPP, KARL R., "Three Decades of Federal Reserve Policy," *Federal Reserve Policy,* Postwar Economic Studies, No. 8, Washington, Board of Governors of the Federal Reserve System, November 1947.

BURGESS, W. RANDOLPH, *The Reserve Banks and the Money Market,* rev. ed., New York, Harper & Brothers, 1936.

CHANDLER, LESTER V., *Benjamin Strong, Central Banker,* Washington, D.C., The Brookings Institution, 1958.

Federal Open Market Committee, Report of Ad Hoc Subcommittee on the Government Securities Market, November 12, 1952. Reprinted in Congress of the United States, Subcommittee on Economic Stabilization of the Joint Committee on the Economic Report, *United States Monetary Policy: Recent Thinking and Experience,* 83rd Congress, 2nd Session, 1954, pp. 257-307.

GOLDENWEISER, E. A., *American Monetary Policy,* New York, McGraw-Hill Book Company, Inc., 1951.

RIEFLER, WINFIELD W., *Money Rates and Money Markets in the United States,* New York, Harper & Brothers, 1930.

————, "Open Market Operations in Long-Term Securities," *Federal Reserve Bulletin,* November 1958, pp. 1260-74.

ROOSA, ROBERT V., *Federal Reserve Operations in the Money and Government Securities Markets,* New York, Federal Reserve Bank of New York, July 1956.

[12] *Ibid.*

Chapter 8

SELECTIVE CREDIT CONTROLS

1. DISTINCTION BETWEEN GENERAL AND SELECTIVE CREDIT CONTROLS

In THE United States, the term "general credit controls" usually means those controls which are designed to affect directly the volume of bank reserves and hence the money supply. The ability of banks to enlarge the money supply is limited by their need to hold cash reserves against their deposit obligations. For member banks, these cash reserves must take the form of demand deposits with the Federal Reserve Banks, in an amount determined by the reserve requirements established by the Board of Governors of the Federal Reserve System. General credit control consists of the regulation, by the Federal Reserve, of the need for such reserves and of their supply, availability, and cost. The instruments of general credit control are the discount rate, open-market operations, and variable cash reserve requirements.

In the United States, the term "selective credit controls" usually refers to measures designed to restrict the use of credit for specific purposes, such as the purchase of securities, of durable consumer goods, and of houses. Selective credit controls in this country generally are regarded as a method of restraining demand during periods of strong inflationary and speculative pressures. In other words, they may be said to be oriented toward the problems which arise in wartime or in the boom phase of the business cycle.

In some countries, however, and notably in Latin America, selective credit controls frequently have been designed for a much broader role, because they often have had the dual objective of encouraging banks to make certain types of loans (generally to industry and agriculture) while simultaneously discouraging them from making certain other types of loans (generally to merchants and importers of nonessential consumer goods). Thus they have been designed to cope with problems of balance-of-payments equilibrium and long-run economic development, rather than with a specific phase of the business cycle.

There is another kind of regulation of specific uses of credit that is found in banking legislation in most countries. Its purpose is to establish sound credit standards for the sake of protecting depositors. For want of a better name, it may be called "supervisory credit control." Examples of such provisions are (1) maximum limits on the size of individual real estate loans, in relation to the value of the mortgaged property; (2) maximum maturity limits on real estate loans; (3) restrictions on the creation of bankers acceptances for purposes other than to facilitate the movement of goods; and (4) restrictions on the amount of a bank's loans to any single borrower. Restrictions of this sort ordinarily are not regarded as selective credit controls, however, because their primary purpose is not to regulate the *total volume* of the specific types or uses of bank credit to which they refer (even though, indirectly, they actually may do so). Because that is not their function, such provisions usually are fixed inflexibly by banking legislation and are not subject to modification by the central bank in accordance with changing credit and economic conditions. If they were subject to such variation, they would have to be classified as selective credit controls. Their focus, as has already been indicated, is on the welfare and soundness of the individual bank, in the interest of its depositors.

In terms of economic impact, general credit controls are less general and selective credit controls are less selective than they commonly are considered to be. General credit controls—operating, as they do, through the commercial banking system—affect commercial banks more directly than they do other financial institutions. When the lending activities of banks are being curbed by general credit controls, other types of lending institutions (such as savings and loan associations and credit unions) find it especially profitable to encourage the public to shift from bank deposits to the types of financial assets issued by such institutions. The reason for this is that some of the would-be borrowers who are unable to obtain accommodation from banks, because of Federal Reserve restriction of the volume of bank credit, then turn to nonbank lenders. These, faced with a strong demand for loans at attractive rates of interest, find it profitable to raise the rates of interest they pay on their own obligations, in order, thereby, to obtain a larger volume of loanable funds by inducing the public to acquire and hold such obligations in lieu of bank deposits. In engaging in this competition, these institutions are not restricted by reserve requirements—they are restricted only by their ability to sell their obligations at a low enough rate of interest to permit the proceeds to be loaned out at a profit. Because of this competitive advantage of nonbank financial institutions in tight-money periods, they are in a strong position to expand their lending activities at the relative expense of the banking system. In other words, a larger amount of the total volume of credit extended by lenders is financed by a faster rate of turnover of bank deposits and a smaller amount is financed by an increase in the volume of bank deposits.

General credit controls also tend to affect long-term borrowers more than short-term borrowers, because higher interest rates have a proportionately greater effect on the size of monthly interest payments of long-term borrowers than of short-term borrowers and are a more important consideration in the cost-profit calculus of the long-term borrower. Moreover, in a period of "tight" monetary policy, pressure on bank liquidity positions tends to make banks curb their long-term loans to a greater extent than their short-term loans, with the result that a higher proportion of total long-term lending tends to be accommodated by nonbank lending institutions, which are under somewhat less pressure in this respect.

Notwithstanding the foregoing observations about the unequal *incidence* of general credit controls on various types of lending institutions and borrowers, it should be emphasized that, whenever the Federal Reserve is enforcing a "tight money" policy, the supplies of loanable funds from all sources, in varying degrees, tend to be "tight" relative to demands, with a resulting general (though not uniform) tightening of lending terms or increase in cost, or both, to all types of borrowers.

Similarly, selective credit controls really are somewhat less selective in their impact than they might seem to be. This observation has three aspects. First, the impact of a selective credit control to some extent may fall on the *forms* of borrowing rather than on the pattern of expenditures. Second, the impact which a selective credit control has on the pattern of spending ordinarily is not entirely restricted to the specific spending area at which the control is aimed. Third, selective credit controls have a general-credit-control effect because one of their consequences is a tendency to restrict the *total* demand for credit, thereby easing the pressure on the total available supply of loanable funds.

With respect to the first of these three aspects, the following example may help to illustrate the problem. Suppose that restrictions on the extension of credit for the purchase of securities limit borrowing against securities to 50 per cent of their value. This would not mean that buyers must necessarily finance at least 50 per cent of their security purchases with their own savings; instead, some of them might obtain the 50 per cent cash margin by using other forms of credit more extensively than they would have done had there been no selective credit control on securities' purchases. Thus, they might finance a higher proportion of their purchases of appliances, automobiles or houses with credit, or they might obtain general-purpose personal loans, or they might use charge-accounts more intensively, in order to raise money for purchases of securities. The principal end result of the selective credit control conceivably could be a change in the *form* of borrowing, rather than any substantial reduction in the total amount of actual borrowing and spending for the purpose which the authorities wish to curb. In practice, such shifts undoubtedly have occurred as a consequence of selective credit control, but there is no conclusive evidence in the United States experience that would indicate that substitutions of one form of credit for another have been quantitatively very important.

Even if more intensive use is not made of other types of credit, the would-be borrower in the example cited above might buy the securities he desired and might finance the cash margin by eliminating some of the other expenditures he had in mind, such as an expensive vacation. In this case, which refers to the second of the three aspects mentioned above, the credit control on security purchases would not have curbed a contemplated purchase of securities, but rather a contemplated vacation. Whenever credit is extended to a borrower, therefore, what the loan really finances is that purchase which would not have been made in the absence of the loan. Many times there probably is little direct or discernible relationship between the ostensible purpose of a loan and the marginal expenditure of the borrower. In fact, frequently the borrower himself does not know which of his contemplated expenditures he would forego if his application for credit were denied. This is especially true, of course, whenever the borrower is confident of success in obtaining credit and sees no need for a careful weighing of alternative lines of action in advance of failure. Again, there is no satisfactory evidence as to what the quantitative importance of such realignments of expenditure plans has been in this country, but it seems reasonable to conclude that their importance has not been especially great.

The third aspect of selective credit controls is that they inevitably tend to restrict the *total* demand for credit, and thus tend to ease the pressure on the total available supply of loanable funds. For borrowers in the aggregate, restrictions on the availability of credit for any specific major purpose are not likely to create an equivalent increase in demand for other types of credit, so some net reduction in total demand is to be expected, although it is impossible to predict how much.

Thus, selective credit controls may set in motion a chain of readjustments both in the use of credit and in patterns of expenditures far beyond the area of initial impact, just as do general credit controls.

2. PURPOSE OF SELECTIVE CREDIT CONTROLS

In the United States, selective credit controls usually have been regarded as ancillary or supplementary to general credit controls. Their use has been regarded as appropriate for special situations in which general credit controls alone could not restrict certain specific types of credit fast enough, or could do so only at the expense of simultaneously restricting credit to other areas of the economy unduly. It should be noted, however, that in the periods in which consumer and real estate credit controls were imposed in this country, the full and effective use of general monetary policy was being hampered by a Federal Reserve policy of supporting the price of Government securities.

In some foreign countries selective credit controls have been used as substitutes for the traditional instruments of general credit control. This has been the case especially in underdeveloped countries. There the absence of a highly organized and extensive government securities market has precluded the monetary authorities from using open-market operations in such securities as an effective means of regulating the volume of bank reserves. In those countries, selective credit controls often have a positive as well as a negative objective; in other words, they are also used to encourage certain types of credit. Among the methods chosen for this purpose are (a) especially low interest rates at which the commercial banks may discount the favored types of credit at the central bank, and (b) permission to the banks to include certain types of loans or investments as part of their required "reserves" against deposits.

In the United States, however, selective credit controls have been ancillary rather than principal instruments of credit *restriction,* and have had rather limited and usually temporary objectives. These objectives have been to prevent a rate of debt-financed purchases of certain goods (such as automobiles or houses) or of certain financial assets (such as common stock) and a rate of debt accumulation which the Federal Reserve authorities regard as inimical to the national welfare in terms of the effects on the volume of income and employment and on the stability of prices, and possibly also in terms of the effects on the solvency of the nation's financial institutions. Thus, the concern of the authorities may be linked to a fear that excessive debt-financed demands for the products of certain key industries will lead to a sharp rise in their prices and/or to an unsustainably high level of output and rate of expansion of productive facilities, thus creating an unhealthy situation in these industries and for the nation's economy as a whole. There may also be concern that the expansion of a particular type of credit in a period of "boom psychology" is a result of unsound competition among lenders, with liberalization of down-payment and maturity requirements proceeding to a point where the quality of the credit structure and hence the ultimate solvency of lending institutions may be endangered. Similarly, the authorities may believe that debt-financed purchases of securities have reached a point where they may lead to rampant speculation in the stock market, with attendant dangers to the nation's economic and financial stability.

In each of the foregoing situations, the concern over instability in certain pivotal sectors of the economy almost always is coupled with a conviction that the over-all demand for credit is excessive,[1] and that it is being aggravated to an important degree, or perhaps even is being caused, by excessive use of specific types of credit—such as consumer instalment credit and credit for carrying common stocks—which are relatively insensitive to monetary actions designed to restrict the total volume of credit.

---

[1] Occasionally, such as in the fall of 1929, excessive demand for credit for speculation in securities may occur at a time when total demand for goods and services for credit is not clearly excessive.

So long as total demands for credit in relation to the available supply of physical resources are not so large as to be inflationary, it is unlikely that demands for any specific type of credit will rise to a level that constitutes a grave danger to the stability of the economy or to the quality of the nation's credit structure. It is when the economy is fully or nearly fully employed that there is danger that a sharp increase in a specific area of credit may trigger an inflationary process that will feed on itself and engulf the entire economy. Thus, situations in which there is an alleged need for selective credit controls—in the United States, at least—usually are situations of substantially full employment and of strain on the total supply of credit. An important exception to the foregoing statement needs to be made with respect to stock market credit. There can be circumstances, and in fact there have been, in which it is desirable to restrict the use of stock market credit rather tightly even though Federal Reserve over-all credit policy may be relatively easy. The reason for this is to be found in the special susceptibility of the stock market to credit-financed speculation.

In periods of wartime emergency in which the production of the credit-controlled goods is limited by materials' allocations and production restrictions and in which price controls are in effect, the basic aims of selective credit controls are to assist in the attainment of the objectives of general credit control measures by helping (a) to relieve pressure on the production and materials' controls, (b) to facilitate the distribution of the controlled goods at legal prices, and (c) to prevent an increase in the demand for *uncontrolled* goods, services, and assets, which otherwise might be financed indirectly by extensions of credit for purchases of the *controlled* goods and assets.

In other periods, when selective credit restrictions are not used in conjunction with production and price controls, their basic objectives may be summarized as follows:

1. To facilitate general credit controls and to reduce their uneven impact by reaching specific areas of excessive credit which are not very sensitive to general credit control.

2. To keep demand for the products of certain key industries, such as the automobile and residential construction industries, or for common stock, from soaring to such unsustainable heights that the eventual downward readjustment will involve such a sharp contraction in demand as to endanger the nation's over-all economic stability.

3. To protect lending institutions from entering into competition over down-payment and maturity terms to such an extent as to endanger the solvency of these institutions.

Three things should be noted about these objectives. First, there is considerable overlapping and interrelationship among them— seldom would one of them be sought to the complete exclusion of the other two. Second, notwithstanding the foregoing observation, there can exist some degree of conflict among them, inasmuch as the choice, timing, duration, intensity, coverage, and scope of a selective credit control measure and its application could very well vary to some extent, depending upon the degree of importance given to each of these three objectives by the authorities. Third, the objectives of selective credit controls pertain to circumstances which are likely to exist only in boom phases of aggregate-business activity; thus, the role of selective credit controls is a special and one-sided one, unlike the continual role of general credit controls which have important responsibilities for stimulating demand in periods of recession and depression as well as for restraining it in periods of boom.

Some of the issues raised in this section will be discussed at greater length in the section on problems of administering selective credit controls, but it is worth noting now that there is no single simple objective of selective credit controls, and this is perhaps the main reason why not only the use of such controls but also evaluation of their merits and defects is subject to widespread disagreement and controversy.

3. TYPES OF SELECTIVE CREDIT CONTROLS

American experience with selective credit controls has been limited to three types of controls: (a) regulation of stock market credit, (b) regulation of consumer credit, and (c) regulation of real estate credit. There have, however, been other methods of influencing the availability of credit on a selective basis which might be considered, in a sense, to be selective credit controls. The Voluntary Credit Restraint Program inaugurated in March 1951 represented a formal and elaborate attempt to use "moral suasion." Nevertheless, when the term "selective credit controls" is used in the United States, what usually is meant are the first three types of controls enumerated above. Accordingly, sections 4, 5, 6, and 7 of this chapter will deal only with those three types of controls. Section 8, however, will deal with the history and experience of the Voluntary Credit Restraint Program of 1951, perhaps the most important use of "moral suasion."

Regulation of Stock Market Credit

The purpose of stock market credit control has been to prevent the excessive use of credit, whether supplied by banks or other lenders, for purchasing or holding securities. In the American economy, the stock market can play a pivotal role, and at times it has done so. The prices at which stocks are quoted, and the ease with which new issues can be absorbed by the market, influence the ability and the plans of corporations to obtain capital; they reflect investors' attitudes about the prospective growth and profitability of firms, and, by affecting the value of an important form of wealth, they have important repercussions on the spending plans of those who hold such securities. The stock market also is a potential focal point of speculative inclinations. Accordingly, to permit unlimited use of credit for the purchase or carrying of stocks would be to encourage speculation and to jeopardize the stability of the entire economy. Moreover, excessive use of credit for stock market speculation occasionally may occur at times when conditions in industry, commerce, and agriculture do not call for a general tightening of credit—in fact, conditions in those sectors may require an easy money policy.

Because of the special problems surrounding the use of credit for the purchase and carrying of securities, this type of credit has been subjected to direct control by the Federal Reserve Board since 1934. The control takes the form of setting so-called "margin requirements." These consist of the percentage of the value of stocks which a buyer is expected to supply from his own resources. For example, if the "margin requirement" is 70 per cent, a bank or broker is permitted to lend the buyer no more than 30 per cent of the value of the stocks given as collateral; the remaining 70 per cent must come from elsewhere.

Regulation of Consumer Credit

Consumer credit bulks large in our total credit structure. Its availability is decisive in the sale of a substantial portion of the output of consumers' durable goods. For these reasons, a sharp increase in consumer credit in periods in which the productive capacity of the economy is being overpressed can initiate or strongly aggravate a serious inflationary situation. There have been three occasions—

during World War II, from September 1948 to June 1949, and from September 1950 to May 1952—in which controls over consumer credit have been imposed. These controls have taken the form of establishing the maximum maturities and minimum down payments required for purchases of consumer goods on credit. The regulations applied to all lenders and sellers, and not merely to banks.

Regulation of Real Estate Credit

Real estate credit has some of the same characteristics as credit for purchasing consumer durable goods. Lending techniques are reasonably well specialized and standardized with respect to loan purposes, collateral, equity requirements, and maturity. It is a type of loan which bulks large in the total credit picture. It can be a source of serious inflationary pressure in periods in which the economy is operating under forced draft, especially if free use of the instruments of general credit control is hampered by a monetary policy which endeavors to support the prices of Government securities.

The following section will sketch the history of each of the foregoing types of selective credit controls. The history of these controls is important because, to a much lesser extent than was true of the development of the standard instruments of general credit control, their imposition was related more to certain specific and temporary circumstances than to general theoretical or long-term considerations.

4. HISTORY OF SELECTIVE CREDIT CONTROLS

Stock Market Credit

Federal Reserve Board authority to regulate the use of credit for the purchase and carrying of securities is a consequence of a situation that developed at the end of the nineteen-twenties and in the early nineteen-thirties. Economic activity in the United States, in real terms, reached a peak before 1929, but in that year stock prices and brokers' loans continued their upward march, and at a faster tempo. This created a serious dilemma for the Federal Reserve authorities; namely, how to restrain the speculative use of credit in the stock market without bearing down unduly on credit for production and trade.

The Board endeavored to meet this situation by issuing a public statement, on February 7, 1929, to the effect that "a member bank is not within its reasonable claims for rediscount facilities at its Federal Reserve Bank when it borrows either for the purpose of making speculative loans or for the purpose of maintaining speculative loans." The Board's statement seemed to have some effect, though with a lag of a couple of months. In April and May such loans moved downward, after having fluctuated irregularly and without a definite trend in the first eight weeks following the Board's statement. Nevertheless, in June, July, and August, speculation in securities again became rampant. The demand for security loans mounted rapidly and the level of stock prices advanced approximately 25 per cent. Interest rates on brokers' loans rose to very high levels, averaging over 8½ per cent during the spring and summer of 1929, but the high rates did not succeed in restraining credit speculation.

Since the attempts of the Board to restrain the flow of funds into security loans were nullified by the willingness of speculators to pay such high rates of interest, they were abandoned. An important reason for the lack of success was that most of the expansion in loans to brokers in the summer of 1929 was not made with banks' own funds but with funds provided by foreign banks, individuals, and domestic corporations to banks acting as agents only. The banks assumed responsibility for making the loan and supervising the collateral while the loan was outstanding; in return, the banks received their remuneration in the form of a commission. This type of credit was not within the direct reach of the Federal Reserve's controls over member banks.

In the fall of 1929, the stock market was hit by strong bearish forces. By the middle of November, the level of stock prices was 40 per cent below the peak reached in early September. "Within a week lenders outside the New York banks withdrew over 2 billion dollars of loans to brokers and dealers. Since the restrictive policy of the Federal Reserve System was occasioned exclusively by credit developments in the securities market, the liquidation was accompanied by an immediate reversal in that policy. . . ."[2]

After the stock market debacle, which attained even greater proportions from April 1930 through June 1932, a clamor arose for legislative action to prevent future speculative excesses in the use of credit for securities transactions.

[2] Karl R. Bopp, *Three Decades of Federal Reserve Policy*, Postwar Economic Studies No. 8, Washington, D.C., Board of Governors of the Federal Reserve System, November 1947, p. 9.

The first step was taken in the Banking Act of 1933; the Federal Reserve System was directed and empowered to prevent undue use "of bank credit for the speculative carrying of or trading in securities, real estate, or commodities, or for any other purpose inconsistent with the maintenance of sound credit conditions." The Federal Reserve was to implement this responsibility and authority by refusing to extend its credit to offending member banks and by exercising a newly created power to establish the maximum percentage which a bank's loans collateralized by stocks and bonds could be in relation to the bank's capital and surplus. In addition, member banks were prohibited from acting as agents of nonbank lenders in making security loans to brokers and dealers—the type of operation which had been responsible for the bulk of the expansion of stock market credit in the summer of 1929.

The action taken in the Banking Act of 1933 was greatly extended and strengthened by certain provisions of the Securities Exchange Act of 1934. This legislation provided for the regulation of securities exchanges and of brokers and dealers in securities. Its purpose was to prevent manipulation and other unfair practices in securities dealings. However, the Act also undertook to regulate the extension of credit for the purchase or carrying of securities. There was some doubt, in the preparation of the legislation, whether this power should be vested in the Securities and Exchange Commission, which was to be responsible for the administration of the provisions pertaining to the regulation of the securities exchanges and of trading practices, or in the Federal Reserve Board. The final decision, however, was to vest the credit-control authority in the Board, because of the nature of the matter and because of the Board's reputation as the most experienced and best equipped credit agency of the Government.

The Securities Exchange Act also prohibited nonmember banks from making loans to brokers "for the account of others"—a prohibition which, as has already been mentioned, was imposed on member banks by the Banking Act of 1933. In addition, the Act prohibited brokers from borrowing directly from nonbank lenders.

The margin-requirement provisions of the Securities Exchange Act were aimed directly at the excessive extension of credit, *by any type of lender,* for the purchase of securities alone; whereas the Banking Act of 1933, as was noted above, attempted to deal with the undue use of bank credit for speculation in securities, real estate, or commodities.

The Securities Exchange Act stated that "for the purpose of preventing the excessive use of credit for the purchase or carrying of securities, the Federal Reserve Board shall . . . prescribe rules and regulations with respect to the amount of credit that may be initially extended and subsequently maintained on any security (other than an exempted security)[3] registered on a national securities exchange." The Act also supplied a formula which was to serve as a standard upon which the Board's regulations should be "based," but adherence to the formula was not mandatory, and the Board was given specific authority to make the requirements higher or lower than the standards established by the statutory formula.

Thus, the Securities Exchange Act of 1934 was a major landmark in the evolution of credit controls in the United States. It marked the first attempt to single out a specific field of credit, instead of a specific type of lender (i.e., member banks), and to control a type of credit *directly*, rather than indirectly through the supply or cost of bank reserves. Finally, it represented the culmination of a long-evolving recognition (which began in the early twenties) that monetary policy can be faced with divergent developments of major dimensions in various sectors of the economy, and that control over the supply and cost of member-bank cash reserves may be inadequate to cope with them.

The statutory formula provided in the Securities Exchange Act was as follows. Credit extended on a given security should not exceed whichever of the following two quantities be the greater: (1) 55 per cent of the current market price of the security, or (2) 100 per cent of the lowest price of the security since July 1, 1933, but not more than 75 per cent of the current market price. This rule was adopted by the Board in its initial Regulation T, which applied to brokers and dealers. It meant that the margin requirements for individual stocks ranged from 25 per cent to 45 per cent of their current value. A survey showed that, as of July 31, 1934, the average effective margin requirement amounted to about 28 per cent. According to the 1935 Annual Report of the Board of Governors, "The theory on which the statutory margin formula was based was to provide for a constant increase of restraining influence as the prices of stocks advanced from their lows." By the beginning of 1936, the average margin requirement, under the operation of the formula, had risen to 42 per cent.

[3] Mainly Federal, state, and local government securities.

Effective February 1, 1936, the Board used its discretionary authority to modify the statutory formula by raising the upper limit of the margin formula to 55 per cent, from the 45 per cent limit previously in force. As a consequence of this action, the average margin requirement was elevated from about 42 per cent of current market value to about 48 per cent. A substantial expansion in stock market credit, beginning in the middle of 1935, and an upward movement in stock prices, prompted the increase in margin requirements in early 1936. An additional consideration was the existence of over $3 billion of excess reserves of member banks, which might be used—in part at least—to finance purchases of securities.

Effective April 1, 1936, the Federal Reserve Board abandoned the statutory formula by establishing a uniform requirement in Regulation T of 55 per cent of market value. This action resulted in an average increase of 5 percentage points above the average requirements then in force.

The same uniform margin requirement was also imposed on banks, effective May 1, 1936, with the issuance of Regulation U. In its 1936 Annual Report, the Board explained that

The statutory formula, stated as a standard but not prescribed in the Securities Exchange Act of 1934, would be burdensome for most banks since few banks have a large volume of security loans and most of them are not under the necessity of being familiar with market quotations or the details of the securities loan business, and a flat percentage of market value, therefore, would be better adapted to the existing banking situation. The statutory formula had been found by experience to be involved and difficult to understand, both in respect to its provisions and in respect to its purposes. Furthermore, it was agreed that in Regulation U a loan value should be given to unregistered stocks. The use of the statutory formula as a basis for fixing the loan value of an unregistered stock would be impracticable . . . and it would be undesirable to have the loan value of unregistered stocks fixed on a different basis from that of registered stocks.

Table 1 shows the record of Federal Reserve Board actions, from 1934 through October 16, 1958, on the authority granted to it under the Securities Exchange Act.

Consumer Credit Controls

Consumer credit controls first made their appearance in the United States during World War II. The legal authority for the regulation of consumer credit emanated from the President's Executive Order 8843

TABLE 1.   MARGIN REQUIREMENTS[1]
(Per cent of market value)

	Regulation T		Regulation U
	For Extension of Credit by Brokers and Dealers on Listed Securities	For Short Sales	For Loans by Banks on Stocks
Oct. 1, 1934-Jan. 31, 1936	25-45[2]	[3]	—
Feb. 1, 1936-Mar. 31, 1936	25-55[2]	[3]	—
Apr. 1, 1936-Oct. 31, 1937	55	[3]	55[4]
Nov. 1, 1937-Feb. 4, 1945	40	50	40
Feb. 5, 1945-July 4, 1945	50	50	50
July 5, 1945-Jan. 20, 1946	75	75	75
Jan. 21, 1946-Jan. 31, 1947	100	100	100
Feb. 1, 1947-Mar. 29, 1949	75	75	75
Mar. 30, 1949-Jan. 16, 1951	50	50	50
Jan. 17, 1951-Feb. 19, 1953	75	75	75
Feb. 20, 1953-Jan. 4, 1955	50	50	50
Jan. 4, 1955-Apr. 22, 1955	60	60	60
Apr. 23, 1955-Jan. 15, 1958	70	70	70
Jan. 16, 1958-Aug. 4, 1958	50	50	50
Aug. 5, 1958-Oct. 15, 1958	70	70	70
Effective Oct. 16, 1958	90	90	90

[1] Regulations T and U limit the amount of credit that may be extended on a security by prescribing a maximum loan value, which is a specified percentage of its market value at the time of extension; margin requirements are the difference between the market value (100 per cent) and the maximum loan value.

[2] Margin requirements were within the range indicated, the exact requirement on each security being determined by the relation of its current price to the lowest price during a preceding period. The maximum loan value (see note 1 above) was 75 per cent of current market value or 100 per cent of lowest price in period since July 1, 1933, whichever was the smaller, except that it could always be as much as 55 per cent (changed on February 1, 1936, to 45 per cent) of current market value. Average requirements on listed stocks have been estimated as follows: October 15, 1934—31 per cent; January 31, 1936—42 per cent; February 1, 1936—49 per cent; March 31, 1936—50 per cent.

[3] Requirement under Regulation T prior to November 1, 1937, was the margin "customarily required" by the broker.

[4] Regulation U became effective May 1, 1936.

NOTE: Regulations T and U also provide special margin requirements on "omnibus" accounts and loans to brokers and dealers.

of August 9, 1941. This order declared that it was necessary to regulate the volume of instalment credit available for purchases of consumers' goods, in order (a) to facilitate the transfer of productive resources to defense industries; (b) to assist in curbing unwarranted price advances and profiteering which tend to result when the supply of consumers' durable goods is curtailed without a corresponding curtailment of demand; (c) to assist in restraining general inflationary tendencies, to support or supplement taxation imposed to restrain such tendencies, and to promote the accumulation of savings available for financing the defense program; (d) to aid in creating a backlog of demand for consumers' durable goods; and (e) to restrain the development of a consumer debt structure that would repress effective demand for goods and services in the post-defense period.

The Federal Reserve Board was designated as the agency responsible for administering the consumer credit control program. However, the Executive Order established a coordinating committee consisting of the Secretary of the Treasury, the Federal Loan Administrator, the Administrator of the Office of Price Administration and Civilian Supply (or such alternate as each should designate), and such other members as the President should subsequently appoint. The Board was instructed to maintain liaison with the committee and, in formulating policies with respect to down payments, maturities, terms of repayment, and other such questions of general policy, to consult with the committee and to take into consideration any suggestions or recommendations it might make. The Board was authorized to issue regulations with respect to:

(1) The maximum amount of credit which may be extended on, or in connection with any purchase of, any consumers' durable goods;

(2) The maximum maturity, minimum periodic payments, and maximum periods between payments, which may be stipulated in connection with extensions of credit;

(3) The methods of determining purchase prices or market values or other bases for computing permissible extensions of credit or required down payments; and

(4) Special or different terms, conditions, or exemptions with respect to new or used goods, minimum original cash payments, temporary credits which are merely incidental to cash purchases, payment or deposits usable to liquidate credits, and other adjustments or special situations.

Pursuant to the authority granted to it under the Executive Order, the Board of Governors of the Federal Reserve System issued an implementing regulation, which went into effect on September 1, 1941.

A schedule of "listed articles" subject to the controls was prepared. Inclusion of an article in the list "was based mainly on considerations of the amount of scarce resources that the articles specified might divert from the production of munitions, and the amount of instalment credit that their purchase might generate."[4] Table 2 shows the complete list of articles covered by the regulation, together with the corresponding minimum down payment and maximum maturity requirements. Major amendments made at later dates also are shown.

The standards imposed in the initial regulation were designed to coincide, for the most part, with the terms then generally in effect in the sale of the items concerned. Thus, the regulation attempted to "hold the line" rather than to impose any drastic tightening of existing standards, although it was known that there was a certain amount of credit being extended on more liberal terms, which would thenceforth be prohibited.

Nearly seven months later, on March 23, 1942, the first basic change—a tightening and extension of the controls—was made in the original requirements (see Table 2). Another tightening of terms and extension of coverage occurred on May 6, 1942. In June and October of 1945, certain liberalizations were made. On December 1, 1946, there was a major revision and easing of the controls.

Effective November 1, 1947, Congress terminated the consumer credit controls, as part of a general move to eliminate the price, production, and credit controls which had been imposed during the War. The pertinent legislation stated "That after November 1, 1947, the Board of Governors of the Federal Reserve System shall not exercise consumer credit controls pursuant to Executive Order Number 8843 and no such consumer credit controls shall be exercised after such date except during the time of war beginning after [August 8, 1947] . . . or any national emergency declared by the President after [August 8, 1947]."

In the weeks and months immediately following the removal of consumer credit controls, prices continued to rise rapidly, at both wholesale and retail levels. Tremendous demands for automobiles and other consumer durable goods were believed by many observers to be largely responsible for the strength of the upward pressures on prices. Moreover, although the vast accumulations of liquid assets by the public during the war years could by themselves have financed a large volume of purchases of these products, demand was being inflated still further by a substantial growth of consumer instalment credit—a growth which was occurring at a much faster rate than was consumer spending on durables.

[4] Board of Governors of the Federal Reserve System, *Consumer Instalment Credit*, Vol. 1, *Growth and Import*, Washington, D.C., Government Printing Office, 1957, Part I, p. 291.

TABLE 2. MINIMUM DOWN PAYMENTS AND MAXIMUM MATURITIES UNDER REGULATION GOVERNING CONSUMER INSTALMENT CREDIT SEPTEMBER 1, 1941-NOVEMBER 1, 1947, AND SEPTEMBER 20, 1948-JUNE 30, 1949

Type of Credit	Sept. 1, 1941–March 22, 1942		March 23, 1942–May 5, 1942		May 6, 1942–Nov. 30, 1946		Dec. 1, 1946–Nov. 1, 1947[1]		Sept. 20, 1948–March 6, 1949[2]		March 7, 1949–April 26, 1949		April 27, 1949–June 30, 1949[3]	
	Down Payment (per cent)[4]	Maximum maturity (months)	Down Payment (per cent)[4]	Maximum maturity (months)	Down Payment (per cent)[4]	Maximum maturity (months)	Down Payment (per cent)[4]	Maximum maturity (months)	Down Payment (per cent)[4]	Maximum maturity (months)	Down Payment (per cent)[4]	Maximum maturity (months)	Down Payment (per cent)[4]	Maximum maturity (months)
Instalment sales:														
Air conditioners, room units	20	18	33⅓	15	33⅓	12	33⅓	15	20	[5]	15	21	10	24
Air conditioning systems, home	15	18	33⅓	15	33⅓[6]	12[6]								
Aircraft (including gliders)	33⅓	18	33⅓	15	33⅓	12								
Attic ventilating fans	15	18	33⅓	15	33⅓	12								
Automobiles (for carrying less than 10, including taxis)	33⅓	18	33⅓	15	33⅓	15	33⅓	15	33⅓		33⅓	21	33⅓	24
Auto batteries and accessories					33⅓	12								
Auto tires and inner tubes, passenger					33⅓	12								
Bedding, blankets, curtains, draperies, household linens, towels					33⅓	12								
Bicycles			33⅓	15	33⅓	12								
Binoculars, field glasses, opera glasses, and hand telescopes					33⅓	12								
Boats, inboard and outboard motors designed for use therewith, other than commercially designed	33⅓	18	33⅓	15	33⅓	12								
Clocks			20	15	33⅓	12								
Cooking stoves, ranges	20	18	20	15	33⅓	12	33⅓	15	20		15	21	10	24
Dishwashers	20	18	33⅓	15	33⅓	12	33⅓	15	20	[5]	15	21	10	24
Electric appliances (not elsewhere listed) for household or personal use					33⅓	12								
Floor coverings			20	15	33⅓	12	20	15	20	[5]	15	21	10	24
Furnace and heating units	15	18	20	18	33⅓[6]	12[6]								
Furniture	10	18	10	15	20	12	20	15	20	[5]	15	21	10	24
Heating stoves, space heaters	20	18	20	15	33⅓	12								
Ironers	20	18	33⅓	15	33⅓	12	33⅓	15	20	[5]	15	21	10	24
Jewelry					33⅓	12								
Lamps	[a]	[a]	[a]	[a]	33⅓	12								
Lawn mowers			33⅓	15	33⅓	12								
Lighting fixtures					33⅓[6]	12[6]								
Luggage, purses, handbags, toilet cases, and umbrellas					33⅓	12								

Materials and services (not elsewhere listed) for home repairs and improvements, provided deferred balance not over $1,500 (changed from $1,000 on May 6, 1942)		18		18	[b] [7]	12[7] / 18[8]								
Motion picture and still cameras and equipment			33⅓	15	33⅓	12								
Motorcycles	33⅓	18	33⅓	15	33⅓	15								
Musical instruments (metal)	20	18	33⅓	15	33⅓	12								
Organs, electric	10	18	10	18	33⅓	12								
Pianos	10	18	10	18	20	12								
Plumbing fixtures	15	18	20	18	33⅓[6]	12[6]								
Portable lights					33⅓	12								
Radios, phonographs, or combinations	20	18	33⅓	15	33⅓	12	33⅓	15	20	[5]	15	21	10	24
Refrigerators	20	18	33⅓	15	33⅓	12	33⅓	15	20	[5]	15	21	10	24
Sewing machines	20	18	33⅓	15	33⅓	12	33⅓	15	20	[5]	15	21	10	24
Silverware			33⅓	15	33⅓	12								
Sports equipment					33⅓	12								
Suction cleaners	20	18	33⅓	15	33⅓	12	33⅓	15	20	[5]	15	21	10	24
Tableware and kitchen equip.					33⅓	12								
Television									20	[5]	15	21	10	24
Washing machines	20	18	33⅓	15	33⅓	12	33⅓	15	20	[5]	15	21	10	24
Watches					33⅓	12								
Water heaters	15	18	20	18	33⅓[6]	12[6]								
Water pumps	15	18	20	18	33⅓[6]	12[6]								
Wearing apparel and furs[1]					33⅓	12								
Yard goods					33⅓	12								
Combinations of stoves, ranges, dishwashers, ironers, refrigerators, and washing machines									20		15	21	10	24
Instalment loans:														
To purchase listed articles[9]														
Other		18		15		12 / 18[11]		15		15[10] / 18[12]		21		24
To pay charge account arising from sales of listed article, or to pay single-payment loan						6								
Single-payment loans						3								
Charge accounts						[13]								

SOURCE: *Consumer Instalment Credit*, Part 1, Vol. 1, "Growth and Import," pp. 292–94.

[a] Classified as furniture.
[b] No minimum.
[1] Regulation ceased to be operative on Nov. 1, 1947, in accordance with resolution of Congress approved Aug. 8, 1947.
[2] Regulation reinstated effective Sept. 20, 1948, under authority of Public Law 905, approved Aug. 16, 1948.
[3] Regulation inoperative after June 30, 1949.
[4] Down payment determined after deduction of trade-in, except for automobiles.
[5] Maximum maturity for all listed articles was 15 months where principal amount of credit was $1,000 or less and 18 months where credit was more than $1,000.
[6] Deleted, effective June 11, 1945; see footnote 7.
[7] Effective June 11, 1945, materials deleted (footnote 6) were added to the group "Materials and services for repairs and improvement, etc." and the maximum maturity of the entire group was increased to 18 months.
[8] Deleted, effective Dec. 1, 1945.
[9] Where credit was to purchase listed articles, requirements were same as on instalment sales of the respective articles.
[10] For credit of $1,000 or less.
[11] Effective Oct. 15, 1945.
[12] For credit of more than $1,000.
[13] 10th day of second month after sale.

On November 17, 1947, less than three weeks after the termination of consumer credit controls, the President presented a strong program of anti-inflationary action to a special session of Congress. At the top of the President's list was a request that consumer credit controls be reinstated. Congress adjourned in June 1948, without having granted the necessary authority for restoration of the controls. Another special session of Congress was called by the President at the end of July 1948 for the express purpose of considering anti-inflationary legislation because concern over inflation had continued to grow. The President's specific recommendations were much the same as those he had made in November of 1947, and included consumer credit controls.

This time Congress granted the necessary authority, by means of a joint resolution which was approved by the President on August 16. Under its terms, Executive Order 8843 could be reinstated until June 30, 1949, but only with respect to instalment credit.

Effective September 20, 1948, a new regulation governing instalment credit purchases was issued. Its principal purpose was to retard the rate of growth of instalment credit, which had continued to rise steeply, partly under the stimulus of a competitive lengthening of the maturity terms of such loans. Table 2 summarizes the principal features of the regulation.

Sales of consumers' durables weakened in the period following the reimposition of controls. At first it was not clear whether the weakening was nothing more than a reaction to the rush of anticipatory buying that had taken place just before the controls went into effect. As other symptoms of slackening business activity became apparent early in 1949, however, a need for liberalizing instalment credit terms became apparent. The Federal Reserve Board, effective March 1949, raised the maximum maturity limits from fifteen and eighteen months to twenty-one months in all cases. Down-payment requirements were lowered from 20 per cent to 15 per cent, except for autos, where the ratio remained at one third.

The recession in business activity continued in the succeeding months. This led the Board to undertake a further relaxation of terms in April (see Table 2).

After this last relaxation, the terms required by the Board were as liberal as those which most lenders would have granted had there been no controls; in fact, in some instances the terms permitted by law may have led to competitive pressures on lenders to grant such terms—pressures which might not have been so effective had the Board not set such "standards."

On June 30, 1949, in accordance with the terms of the joint congressional resolution of August 16, 1948, the Board's authority to control the extension of consumer instalment credit lapsed.

In 1950, to use the opening words of the Board's Annual Report for that year, "inflationary pressures again became a challenge to credit and monetary policy. The general economic situation became especially inflationary following the outbreak of hostilities in Korea and the inauguration of a far-reaching program of national defense in the United States. . . . At the time of the international crisis businesses and consumers, with high and rising incomes and ample credit, were already buying a record volume of goods and services. After June, civilian buying expanded sharply. It was stimulated by anticipation of shortages and supported by a continued rise in incomes, extensive use of credit, and considerable drawing on accumulated liquid assets. Prices advanced rapidly."

Authority to control consumer credit was restored to the Board under Title VI of the Defense Production Act, which was approved on September 8, 1950. The President had recommended such action in his July 19 message on Korea and in his midyear Economic Report of July 26. Moreover, the Federal Reserve Board, in its statement on the Defense Production Act of 1950 before the Senate and House Banking and Currency Committees, also had urged Congress to grant it temporary authority to regulate consumer credit. As soon as the Defense Production Act was approved, the Board immediately reissued Regulation W, effective September 18. The form was much the same as it had been when it expired on June 30, 1949 (see Table 3), but the terms, as a whole, were less liberal.

In the face of mounting inflationary pressures and of an increasingly grave situation in Korea, Regulation W was revised and made more restrictive in October 1950. These revised terms remained in effect until July 31, 1951, when certain relaxations in terms were forced upon the Board by the Defense Production Act Amendments of 1951, especially with regard to household appliances (see Table 3).

By the spring of 1952, economic conditions warranted a major relaxation or suspension of Regulation W. After conferences with other interested Government agencies, and with sellers of the regulated articles, Regulation W was suspended on May 7, 1952. The statement issued by the Board of Governors announcing the suspension of the controls recommended that the authority for the regulation be

TABLE 3. MINIMUM DOWN PAYMENTS AND MAXIMUM MATURITIES UNDER REGULATION GOVERNING CONSUMER INSTALMENT CREDIT SEPTEMBER 18, 1950-MAY 7, 1952

Listed article or loan	Minimum Down Payment[1] (Per Cent)			Maximum Maturity (Months)		
	Sept. 18, 1950- Oct. 15, 1950	Oct. 16, 1950- July 30, 1951	July 31, 1951- May 7, 1952	Sept. 18, 1950- Oct. 15, 1950	Oct. 16, 1950- July 30, 1951	July 31, 1951- May 7, 1952
Listed articles:						
Passenger automobiles	33⅓	33⅓	33⅓	21	15	18
Major appliances[2]	15	25	15	18	15	18
Furniture and floor coverings	10	15	15	18	15	18
Home improvement materials, articles, and services[3]	10	10	10[4]	30	30	36
Loans:						
To purchase listed articles	[5]	[5]	[5]	[5]	[5]	[5]
Unclassified				18	15	18

SOURCE: Consumer Instalment Credit, Part 1, Vol. 1, "Growth and Import," p. 300.
1 For automobiles, payable in cash, trade-in, or both; for other listed articles, payable in cash, September 18, 1950-July 30, 1951, inclusive, and in cash, trade-in, or both, beginning July 31, 1951. Exempted from down-payment requirements: September 18-October 15, inclusive, listed articles costing less than $100; beginning October 16, those costing less than $50; beginning April 8, 1952, those costing less than $100.
2 Includes radios, television sets, refrigerators, food freezers, phonographs, cooking stoves, ranges, dishwashers, ironers, washing machines, clothes driers, sewing machines, suction cleaners, room-unit air conditioners, and dehumidifiers.
3 Includes heating, plumbing, and other household fixtures.
4 Requirement eliminated as of March 24, 1952.
5 Requirements same as on instalment sales of the respective articles.

continued after June 30, 1952, so that the regulation could be reinstated if subsequent developments should necessitate such action.[5] Nevertheless, in the repeal of the Defense Production Act Amendments of 1952, the authority terminated.

Real Estate Credit Control

Under the Defense Production Act of 1950, the President was granted temporary authority to regulate credit for new construction. It should be noted that the authority extended only to new construction and did not apply to sales of existing housing (unlike the control of automobile sales under Regulation W, which covered used as well as new vehicles).

The President delegated his authority to the Board of Governors of the Federal Reserve System; however, the Board was required to obtain the concurrence of the Housing and Home Finance Administration in any regulations it might issue applying to residential real estate.

This was the first use ever made in the United States, or apparently anywhere, of regulation of real estate lending as an instrument of selective credit control. The situation which gave rise to this control was the inflationary atmosphere created by the Korean war, together with the need to channel labor and materials from residential and nonessential commercial construction into the defense program.

Pursuant to the authority delegated to it by the President, the Board issued Regulation X on October 12, 1950. It established maximum loan values, maximum maturities, and minimum amortization terms for credit extended for the construction or purchase of one- and two-family houses on which construction had been started after August 3, 1950—the date specified in the Defense Production Act. The provisions of Regulation X were prepared in cooperation with the Housing and Home Finance Administrator, who was responsible for the issuance of parallel regulations governing the terms of loans insured or guaranteed by the Federal Housing Administration and the Veterans Administration. The controls were extended, on January 12, 1951, to include all new residential construction, and about a month later Regulation X was further extended to cover commercial structures. The parallel regulations issued by the Housing and Home Finance Administrator restricted the terms of borrowing on purchases of both *old and new* dwellings financed with Federally underwritten mortgages, while, as has already been noted, Regulation X applied only to new construction.

[5] *Ibid.,* p. 302.

Because financing arrangements (including applications for federally insured and guaranteed mortgages) entered into prior to the effective date of Regulation X were exempt from the restrictions, the full impact of the real estate credit control measures was not felt immediately. A substantial percentage of the new housing units started in the last quarter of 1950 and the first half of 1951 were exempted for this reason.

On March 5, 1951, Regulation X was amended to permit relaxation of its terms by the Board and the Housing and Home Finance Administrator in areas designated as critical defense areas by the Interagency Critical Areas Committee of the Defense Production Administrator.

Table 4 shows the maximum loan values and maturities on real estate construction credit subject to Regulation X; the terms both of the initial version and of the subsequent revisions of the Regulation are presented. It should be noted that the table does not specifically indicate the terms of FHA and VA financing, since these were subject

TABLE 4. MAXIMUM LOAN VALUES AND MAXIMUM MATURITIES ON REAL ESTATE CONSTRUCTION CREDIT SUBJECT TO REGULATION X[1]

Value per Family Unit	Maximum Loan Value[2]	Maximum Maturity
	One- to four-family unit residential properties and farm residences	
	October 12, 1950, to September 1, 1951 (3- to 4-family units not included until January 12, 1951)	
Not more than $5,000	90 per cent of value per family unit	25 years for properties valued at $7,000 or less[3]
More than $5,000 but not more than $9,000	$4,500 plus 65 per cent of excess of value per family unit over $5,000	
More than $9,000 but not more than $15,000	$7,100 plus 60 per cent of excess of value per family unit over $9,000	20 years for properties valued at more than $7,000[4]
More than $15,000 but not more than $20,000	$10,700 plus 20 per cent of excess of value per family unit over $15,000	

TABLE 4—Continued

Value per Family Unit	Maximum Loan Value[2]	Maximum Maturity
	October 12, 1950, to September 1, 1951	
More than $20,000 but not more than $24,250	$11,700 plus 10 per cent of excess of value per family unit over $20,000	
Over $24,250	50 per cent of value per family unit	
	September 1, 1951, to June 11, 1952	
Not more than $7,000	90 per cent of value per family unit	
More than $7,000 but not more than $10,000	85 per cent of value per family unit	
More than $10,000 but not more than $12,000	80 per cent of value per family unit	25 years for properties valued at $12,000 or less[3]
More than $12,000 but not more than $15,000	$9,600 plus 40 per cent of excess of value per family unit over $12,000	20 years for properties valued at more than $12,000[4]
More than $15,000 but not more than $20,000	$10,800 plus 20 per cent of excess of value per family unit over $15,000	
More than $20,000 but not more than $24,500	$11,800 plus 10 per cent of excess of value per family unit over $20,000	
Over $24,500	50 per cent of value per family unit	
	June 11, 1952 to September 16, 1952	
Not more than $7,000	95 per cent of value per family unit	
More than $7,000 but not more than $10,000	$6,300 plus 75 per cent of excess of value per family unit over $7,000	

TABLE 4—*Continued*

Value per Family Unit	Maximum Loan Value[2]	Maximum Maturity
June 11, 1952 to September 16, 1952		
More than $10,000 but not more than $15,000	$8,550 plus 55 per cent of excess of value per family unit over $10,000	25 years for properties valued at $12,000 or less[3]
More than $15,000 but not more than $21,000	$11,300 plus 45 per cent of excess of value per family unit over $15,000	20 years for properties valued at more than $12,000[4]
More than $21,000 but not more than $25,000	$14,000 plus 25 per cent of excess of value per family unit over $21,000	
Over $25,000	60 per cent of value per family unit	
Multi-unit residential properties		
January 12, 1951, to June 11, 1952		
Not more than $7,000	83 per cent of value per family unit	None
More than $7,000 but not more than $15,000	$5,810 plus 53 per cent of excess of value per family unit over $7,000	None
More than $15,000 but not more than $23,500	$10,050 plus 20 per cent of excess of value per family unit over $15,000	None
Over $23,500	50 per cent of value per family unit	None
June 11, 1952 to September 16, 1952		
Not more than $7,000	90 per cent of value per family unit	None
More than $7,000 but not more than $10,000	$6,300 plus 55 per cent of excess of value per family unit over $7,000	None

TABLE 4—*Continued*

Value per Family Unit	Maximum Loan Value[2]	Maximum Maturity
	June 11, 1952 to September 16, 1952	
More than $10,000 but not more than $15,000	$7,950 plus 54 per cent of excess of value per family unit over $10,000	None
More than $15,000 but not more than $20,000	$10,650 plus 50 per cent of excess of value per family unit over $15,000	None
More than $20,000 but not more than $25,000	$13,150 plus 37 per cent of excess of value per family unit over $20,000	None
Over $25,000	60 per cent of value per family unit	None
Value of property[5]	Nonresidential properties	
	February 15, 1951 to September 16, 1952	
All values	50 per cent of value of property	25 years[3]

SOURCE: Thirty-Ninth Annual Report of the Board of Governors of the Federal Reserve System, 1952.

[1] Prescribed by Board of Governors of the Federal Reserve System under authority of the Defense Production Act of 1950 as enacted September 8, 1950, and as amended. Effective beginning October 12, 1950, for one- to two-family residences; January 12, 1951, for three- to four-family and multi-unit residences; and February 15, 1951, for nonresidential properties; suspended September 16, 1952.

[2] If the total amount of credit extended does not exceed $2,500, the loan is not subject to Regulation X.

[3] If amortized through substantially equal monthly, quarterly, semiannual, or annual payments which fully liquidate the original principal amount in the prescribed period.

[4] An alternative to the method of amortization described in footnote 3 is allowed which annually reduces the original principal amount by not less than 5 per cent until the outstanding balance has been reduced to 50 per cent or less of the value of the property. Not applicable to nonresidential properties.

[5] In the case of credit extended with respect to nonresidential property involving more than one nonresidential structure, the maximum loan value may be applied separately with respect to each such structure, or with respect to the entire property, at the election of the registrant.

to regulations issued by the Housing and Home Finance Administrator.[6]

The 1952 Amendments to the Defense Production Act declared that a "period of residential credit control relaxation" should be announced whenever the number of permanent nonfarm family dwelling units fell below a seasonally adjusted annual rate of 1,200,000 for three consecutive months. During the period of relaxation, the maximum down-payment restriction on residential property could not exceed 5 per cent. In June, July, and August of 1952, housing starts dropped below this level. The Board of Governors suspended Regulation X, effective September 16, 1952. At the same time, the Housing and Home Finance Administrator relaxed the terms on Government-aided real estate credit. The underlying statutory authority terminated in June 1953, and since that date, the Federal Reserve Board has had no authority to regulate real estate credit.

5. TESTS FOR APPLYING SELECTIVE CREDIT CONTROLS

In his reply to one of the questions posed by a Congressional committee in 1952, the Chairman of the Federal Reserve Board made the following statement, which succinctly describes the conditions prerequisite to effective selective control of credit:

To be effective, select regulation of credit must relate to an area which is reasonably definable in terms of such things as the purpose of the credit, the collateral for it, or the nature of the credit contract. Trade practices should be specialized and sufficiently standardized so that the regulation can be applied in terms of a continuation or extension of those procedures rather than a drastic disruption of them.

Furthermore, the credit area subject to regulation must be important enough in terms of size and volatility so that its regulation can help to reinforce general credit measures; and the flow of credit should be responsive to practicable adjustments in the borrower's equity or loan maturity. The selective credit regulation must not unduly impede permitted credit transactions and there must be a minimum possibility of successful evasion in the case of other transactions. Lastly, the constructive results of regulation must be great enough to outweigh the burdens associated with it—both on those subject to it and on those administering it.[7]

[6] For these terms, see Federal Reserve Bulletin: August 1951, p. 909; November 1951, p. 1382; and June 1952, p. 660.

[7] *Monetary Policy and the Management of the Public Debt,* Joint Committee on the Economic Report, 82nd Congress, 2nd Session, Washington, D.C., Government Printing Office, 1952, Part 1, p. 403.

Of the three types of selective credit control used to date in the United States, regulation of stock market credit most successfully meets the foregoing tests. The regulation of consumer and real estate credit meets most of these tests moderately well, although the problems of administration and equity have been considerably greater.

6. PROBLEMS OF ADMINISTERING SELECTIVE CREDIT CONTROLS

The problems of administering selective credit controls are quite formidable. They fall into the following categories.

1. In order to be administratively manageable, the regulations and rulings must be so broad in scope and uniform in application as to result, unavoidably, in inequities, hardships, and seeming absurdities in many individual cases. This is especially true of consumer credit controls. The larger the number of such cases, the greater will be public resistance—and hence noncompliance. These problems are likely to grow the longer the controls are in effect. Moreover, they are likely to be much greater in peacetime than in wartime, when patriotic sentiments evoke a larger measure of tolerance of inconveniences and inequities.

Another aspect of this problem pertains to "fringe areas" or "fringe lenders." These are cases in which the transactions are akin to but not identical with those subject to control, or in which the lender only occasionally and incidentally engages in the extension of credit of the type under control. Here again, the problem arises most often in the case of consumer credit control. An example is leasing arrangements with options to buy and to have all of the rental payments applied toward the purchase price. Another example is the case of an individual who wishes to dispose of a personal automobile or appliance and is willing to extend credit terms to the buyer.

2. Another problem arises from the necessity of requiring extensive keeping of records by sellers and lenders, in forms which permit the authorities to ascertain whether or not there has been compliance with their rules and regulations. This problem is magnified, of course, whenever sellers and lenders have not customarily kept such records.

3. Enforcement is greatly complicated if (a) the number of lenders is very large, or (b) the lenders are of a wide variety of types and sizes. Take consumer credit, for example; the lenders may be banks, finance companies, department stores, specialty stores, and so forth. Another example is mortgage lenders, who may be banks, insurance companies, building and loan associations, private individ-

uals, mortgage companies, or other kinds of institutions. The larger the number of lenders and the wider the disparities in their characteristics, the more difficult it is to devise workable regulations that can be applied equitably to all and be enforced effectively.

It should be noted that consumer and real estate credit controls have been used in this country only in time of war or of postwar adjustment, in which conditions are more favorable to public co-operation than would be true in more nearly normal circumstances. Whether these controls—and especially consumer credit regulation —would have been effective in a situation such as existed in 1955 is a moot question. The patriotic sentiment would have been lacking; consequently, enforcement would have been hampered. The controls would not have been backed by materials allocations controls. And finally, the public might have displayed remarkable ingenuity in diverting funds from other sources for the purchase of the controlled articles.

There are other problems of administering selective credit controls, in addition to those already mentioned, but perhaps they can best be treated as part of the next section.

7. ADVANTAGES AND DISADVANTAGES OF SELECTIVE CREDIT CONTROLS

Advantages

The principal arguments usually advanced in favor of selective credit controls in peacetime are:

1. They can cope with situations in which general credit controls are of limited effectiveness and have an inequitable impact. Fluctuations in certain important types of credit, it is claimed—namely, stock market credit, consumer instalment credit, and real estate credit—can cause economic instability, or at least contribute substantially to it, and excessive expansion of such types of credit in boom times tends to make subsequent recessions unavoidable. Accordingly, excessive expansion of these kinds of credit should be curbed. General monetary controls are not always able to do this, because they sometimes do not have sufficient restrictive impact on such types of credit, and an offsetting restriction of other types of credit by means of general credit controls not only creates serious problems of equity but runs the risk of curtailing the flow of loanable funds to business and to agriculture

to such an extent as to cause economic recession. Moreover, general credit controls have a limited restraining effect on nonbank lenders, whereas selective credit controls can cover all types of lenders. Reliance solely on general monetary controls in such circumstances can be compared to the use of an anticancer drug which kills not only cancerous tissues but also the healthy cells on which life depends. Selective credit controls, on the other hand—so their advocates assert—can treat the specific disease without killing, maiming, or stunting the growth of the patient.

2. Selective credit controls can prevent a dangerous deterioration in the quality and soundness of the loans of lending institutions in periods of rising prices and booming sales. By so doing, the interests of those who place their savings with such institutions are protected, and the economy as a whole benefits. In the absence of selective credit controls, intense competitive pressures are likely to force lenders to liberalize their credit terms to a dangerous degree, with consequent damage not only to the solvency of the nation's thrift institutions but also to those who have entrusted their savings to them. Those who need to borrow will also suffer if their needs cannot be accommodated because of the illiquid or insolvent position of lending institutions. Thus, the entire economy will be adversely affected if excessive lending to securities speculators and to consumers becomes widespread.

Disadvantages

The arguments usually advanced against selective credit controls briefly are as follows.

1. Selective credit controls are difficult to administer and enforce effectively and fairly. They present too many opportunities and inducements for evasion and circumvention. They impose an unreasonable burden of record keeping on lenders, which is especially burdensome for small lenders.

Those in favor of selective credit controls usually object to these arguments, and even some of those who oppose such controls on other grounds do not accept them as being sufficiently valid. They say that the problems of compliance with and enforcement of selective credit controls have been exaggerated out of proportion to their true importance, and that after the public became accustomed to such controls, there would be no more evasion than is experienced with usury and small-loan statutes, tariff duties, or the federal income tax.

2. If they block spending in the regulated areas, selective credit

controls may, to a considerable extent, divert spending pressures to other areas that then become equally dangerous to over-all economic stability.

3. The imposition of consumer credit and real estate credit controls involves a decision by the Government, or by the Federal Reserve authorities, that the production and purchase of certain specific types of goods should be restricted. This is a discriminatory interference with individual freedom of economic choice and with an allocation of productive resources compatible with the criteria of a private-enterprise competitive society. It is recognized that the Government has an obligation to prevent total demand for goods and services from exceeding the volume of output that can be brought forth at the minimum price level consonant with the maintenance of "full" employment. For this purpose, the Government has adequate instruments of general monetary and fiscal policy. Except in wartime, however, the Government should not presume to dictate what kinds of *specific* demands for goods should be curbed—this should be left to the judgments of the market place. Some of the opponents of selective credit controls carry this position a step further. They question whether unregulated growth of consumer purchases of durables and of houses really is more unstabilizing for the economy than regulated growth would be. Thus, at the heart of some of the disputes there lie differing views on the economic consequences of consumer and real estate credit.

4. For practical reasons of enforcement and equity, selective credit controls are not capable of highly flexible manipulation, and thus are a rather cumbersome method of control in contrast with the principal instrument of general monetary control, namely, open-market operations.

8. VOLUNTARY CREDIT RESTRAINT PROGRAM OF 1951

The Voluntary Credit Restraint Program was a new experiment in selective credit regulation. The Program represented an effort by the monetary authorities to cope more effectively with the general inflationary boom generated by the Korean war and especially to restrain credit that might interfere with the defense program. The novelty of the Program was that it provided a means whereby banks and other lending institutions could participate directly in the Government's struggle to limit credit extension to the most essential needs of the economy, and could do so with protection from the antitrust laws.

The Program was not intended to operate in isolation; it was an adjunct to the use of general credit controls and to selective regulation of consumer and real estate credit.

The legal authorization for the Program was Section 708 of the Defense Production Act of 1950, which empowered the President to encourage financing institutions to enter into voluntary agreements and programs to restrain credit in keeping with the objectives of the Defense Production Act.

The implementation of the authority of the President under Section 708 of the Defense Production Act was delegated by him to the Board of Governors of the Federal Reserve System, but with the stipulation that the Board should consult with the Attorney General and the Chairman of the Federal Trade Commission, and that the approval of the Attorney General should be obtained before actions were taken on the voluntary agreements and programs contemplated by the Act. The purpose of this condition was to prevent actions that would represent unwarranted restraints of competition on the part of the lenders participating in the Program.

In the latter part of 1950, the Board invited representatives of the respective associations of bankers, life insurance companies, and investment bankers to confer with it to prepare a plan of operation. From these conferences emerged a Program for Voluntary Credit Restraint and a National Voluntary Credit Restraint Committee which included representatives of the aforementioned three groups and had as its chairman a member of the Board. Later, representatives of mutual savings banks and savings and loan associations were added to the national committee, which in turn appointed a total of forty-three regional subcommittees that were to be in direct touch with the individual cooperating lending institutions. Most of the regional committees included personnel from the local Federal Reserve Bank.

The Program began actually to function with the issuance of a statement, on March 12, 1951, by the Federal Reserve Board, addressed to all financing institutions in the United States, requesting their cooperation with a Program and a Statement of Principles prepared by the conferring representatives of the financial associations referred to above.[8]

The Statement of Principles set forth the following basic objective of the Voluntary Credit Restraint Program:

[8] See *Federal Reserve Bulletin,* March 1951, pp. 263-66.

It shall be the purpose of financing institutions to extend credit in such a way as to help maintain and increase the strength of the domestic economy through the restraint of inflationary tendencies and at the same time to help finance the defense program and the essential needs of agriculture, industry and commerce. . . . Under present conditions of very high employment of labor, materials and equipment the extension of loans to finance increased output will have an initial inflationary effect; but loans which ultimately result in a commensurate increase in production of an essential nature are not inflationary in the long run whatever their temporary effect may be. It is most important, however, that loans for nonessential purposes be curtailed in order to release some of the nation's resources for expansion in more vital areas of production.

No precise rules and regulations were prescribed under the Program, since it was to be a voluntary rather than a legally mandatory undertaking. It was assumed, however, that few lenders of any importance would refuse to cooperate, especially if the recommended lending standards were (a) realistic, (b) sufficiently flexible to enable them to be adapted to local circumstances, (c) nondiscriminatory with respect to borrowers of the same general class, and (d) adequately disseminated. The national and regional committees endeavored to satisfy these tests, and to a considerable extent succeeded. Although more specific guides were set forth, the basic test to be applied to any given loan request could be expressed briefly by the question: "Does it commensurately increase or maintain production, processing, and distribution of essential goods and services?"[9]

On April 17, 1952, the Program For Voluntary Credit Restraint was amended to provide that it would no longer seek to restrict, nor would it apply to, the borrowing of states and local governments. This action resulted from a request from the President of the United States to the Director of Defense Mobilization that such action be taken.[10] In the opinion of some observers, this step greatly weakened the effectiveness of the Program and made cooperation of lending institutions difficult to retain, since some local government borrowing requests (such as for permission to issue veterans' bonus bonds) were regarded by many lenders as being no more essential to the "production, processing and distribution of essential goods and services" than

[9] Board of Governors of the Federal Reserve System, *The Federal Reserve System—Purposes and Functions,* Washington, D.C., 1954, p. 66.

[10] Thirty-Ninth Annual Report of the Board of Governors of the Federal Reserve System (1952), Washington, D.C., 1953, p. 80.

were some of the requests for credit by private borrowers which had to be denied under the Program.

The Voluntary Credit Restraint Program remained in effect until May 12, 1952, when it was suspended by the Board at the recommendation of the Voluntary Credit Restraint Committee. The need for the Program seemed to have vanished. The statutory authority for the Program terminated at midyear.

Opinions on the effectiveness of the Program have ranged from complimentary to derogatory. For the most part, however, the most commonly held view is that, in the special circumstances of the Korean boom, the Program made a useful though limited contribution, especially with respect to types of lending which are not adaptable to mandatory selective credit controls—such as short- and long-term borrowing by large business firms for multipurpose uses. In addition, the Program undoubtedly tended to curb the extension of bank credit for speculative purposes, such as undue inventory accumulation.

Among the problems and criticisms encountered in administering the Program were (1) the difficulties of devising clear-cut standards which would or could be interpreted uniformly by all lenders; (2) the charge that lenders placed the onus on the Program (and on the Federal Reserve Board) for the rejection of loan requests which they would have turned down anyway; (3) the fear that the conscientious and meticulously scrupulous lenders would lose valued business to less conscientious and scrupulous competitors, and (4) a concern that the Program, despite the safeguards established, would set the groundwork for subsequent collusive practices by lending institutions, which would be contrary to the public interest in preserving competition among lenders. Perhaps some of these considerations were in the mind of the Chairman of the Federal Reserve Board when he testified that "Experience with the Program shows that two related observations deserve special emphasis. The first is that a program of voluntary credit restraint is most useful only under conditions of pronounced inflationary pressure which reflect a large defense program, war, or similar emergency conditions. Under more normal situations reliance should be confined to the use of other credit instruments, especially general credit measures."[11]

[11] *Monetary Policy and the Management of the Public Debt*, p. 450.

SUGGESTED READINGS

BOARD OF GOVERNORS OF THE FEDERAL RESERVE SYSTEM, *Consumer Instalment Credit*, Washington, D.C., 1957, 6 vols. Part I, *Growth and Import*, 2 vols.; Part II, *Conference on Regulation*, 2 vols.; Part III, *Views on Regulation;* Part IV, *Financing New Car Purchases: A National Survey for 1954-55.*

————, *The Federal Reserve System, Purposes and Functions*, Washington, D.C., 1954, Chapter IV.

W. L. SMITH, "Consumer Instalment Credit," *American Economic Review*, December 1957, pp. 966–84.

U. S. CONGRESS, JOINT COMMITTEE ON THE ECONOMIC REPORT, *Monetary Policy and the Management of the Public Debt, Replies to Questions and Other Material for the Use of the Subcommittee on General Credit Control and Debt Management*, Washington, D.C., 1952, 2 parts. See Part 1, Chapter I, replies to questions 24 and 43; Chapter II, replies to 3, 38–42, and 52, and Part 2, Chapter IV, replies to 21–25; Chapter V, reply to 9; Chapter X, replies to 2–3; Chapter XI, reply to 9.

Chapter 9

EFFECTS OF FEDERAL RESERVE POLICY ON COMMERCIAL BANKS

To UNDERSTAND either monetary management or trends in banking, it is necessary to examine carefully how banking is affected by the actions of the Federal Reserve authorities.

Most discussions of monetary policy are primarily concerned with its implications for economic conditions generally, rather than for banking in particular. This is as it should be, since the goal of Federal Reserve policy is to contribute to the stability of the economy as a whole. Monetary policy affects nonbank credit as well as bank credit. For that matter, its influence extends beyond the realm of credit and modifies the plans and expectations of businessmen and consumers.

Nevertheless, the commercial banking system is in a particularly strategic position with respect to monetary management. The Federal Reserve's actions ordinarily affect directly only the commercial banks, and it is through these effects upon banking that their influence is transmitted to other types of lenders and investors. What happens to bank credit is highly important, therefore, even though it is only part of a large and complicated picture. The banking system is the medium through which monetary policy operates; and if we wish to understand what the Federal Reserve authorities can and cannot accomplish, we need to know how banks respond to their actions.

Similarly, bankers and students of banking need a knowledge of these relations too. When we say that Federal Reserve policy influences the supply, availability, and cost of credit, we are in effect saying that it influences the volume of bank deposits, the volume of bank loans and investments, and the rates of return received by banks on their various classes of earning assets. In short, monetary

177

policy has important effects upon the amount and composition of bank assets and liabilities, upon bank lending and investment policies, and upon the level of bank earnings.

NEED FOR CAREFUL ANALYSIS

These relations between monetary policy and banking are complex and difficult to measure. Consequently, many people have serious misconceptions regarding them—and this applies to many outside of banking who, unfortunately, have little knowledge of how the banking business actually functions.

The influence of Federal Reserve policies is by no means always clearly apparent even to bankers themselves. The banker naturally thinks primarily in terms of his individual bank. For instance, when his bank's deposits increase, this seems to him to be largely a matter of his customers having more funds to keep on deposit with him and also, naturally, the success of his efforts to encourage larger balances and to attract new accounts. He may not always appreciate that some of these additional deposits may have been created as a result of actions taken by Reserve Banks. And it may not always occur to him that his deposits would have shown a greater increase if the Reserve System had been following an easier credit policy.

Similarly, when a banker finds that his balance at his Federal Reserve Bank has built up somewhat and that he has more on deposit at the Federal than he is legally required to hold in relation to his deposits—in other words, that he has acquired some excess reserves—this may appear to him to have occurred simply as a result of a favorable balance in the normal everyday exchange of checks and other payments between his bank and other banks. Yet, for the banking system as a whole, of course, an increase in reserves is usually a reflection of monetary policy.

Another reason why the influence of monetary policy is often obscure is because other factors which affect banking are usually so much more obvious and dramatic. After all, monetary policy influences primarily the supply side of the credit picture, whereas it is the demand for credit that is the more dynamic element in the supply-demand equation. Also, the role of monetary policy is usually permissive—essentially passive—rather than positive. More often than not, it is a matter of *permitting* market forces—chiefly changes in demand—either to tighten credit to some degree or to ease it to some degree. In fact, one might say that the chief preoccupation of the monetary authorities is usually to decide the degree to which they should permit market forces to influence the cost and availability of credit.

Still another reason why the effects of monetary policy upon banking are hard to appraise is because our banking system consists of some 13,500 different banks which operate under widely diverse conditions and whose policies are determined by thousands of individual bank officers and directors. To certain developments, of course, most bankers tend to react in much the same manner. In many circumstances, however, the reactions of individual bankers scattered throughout the country are no more uniform than those of any other heterogeneous collection of individuals. Indeed, they may be less uniform than for many groups because banks are so greatly and so differently affected by varying local conditions.

Moreover, the banking business itself consists of countless individual transactions, and in each transaction involving an extension of bank credit the banker is inevitably preoccupied with the factors bearing upon that particular transaction. In deciding whether or not to lend to any particular applicant, a banker's thinking may in some instances be subconsciously influenced to some degree by monetary policy, but even when it is, he is seldom aware of it.

Anyone, therefore, who thinks of the banking system as being an automatic mechanism which responds mechanically and with predictable precision whenever the monetary authorities push certain buttons in Washington will understand neither monetary policy nor banking developments. Things just do not work that simply.

To see how they really do operate, let us first consider the nature of the relations between monetary management and commercial banks, and then examine how banking has actually been affected by Federal Reserve policies in recent years.

REGULATION OF BANK RESERVE POSITIONS

The present era of monetary management in the United States dates from the Federal Reserve-Treasury "Accord" of 1951, when the Reserve authorities were freed from their obligations to support Government bond prices at par. Since that time, the credit control machinery, rusty from long disuse, has been in process of renovation and adaptation to the changed environment in which it must now operate. Both the monetary authorities and the banks have been learning how to live with flexible monetary policy under modern conditions.

It goes without saying that the monetary developments of these years will not be precisely repeated in the future. Nevertheless, in many respects the character of the relations between the Federal Reserve and the commercial banks, as they presently exist and may exist in the future, can now be discerned fairly clearly.

Monetary policy in the United States has become largely a matter of regulating the reserve positions of member banks. Since all member banks are required to maintain legal reserves in the form of balances at the Federal Reserve Banks equivalent to specified percentages of their deposits, the direct impact of monetary management is on the total quantity of the banks' deposits and hence, of course—since bank balance sheets must balance—on the total quantity of bank credit, i.e., the volume of bank loans and investments.

Other effects of monetary policy on the banks—effects on their lending and investment policies and on their operating results—are largely indirect and derive from this regulation of their reserve positions and its influence on the total quantity of the banks' assets and liabilities. Some of these indirect effects are significant from the standpoint of monetary management, of course, but nevertheless the primary concern of the monetary authorities is with doling out reserves to the banking system either with a spoon or with a ladle, depending on economic conditions, or at times mopping up excessive reserves. They seek hereby to adjust the quantity and flow of money to the needs of the economy.

It is generally appreciated that the expansion of bank deposits and bank credit is *limited* by bank reserve positions. However, it may be worth emphasizing that, in addition, the Federal Reserve authorities can effectively encourage bank credit expansion, and that as a result they can largely determine the quantity of bank deposits and bank credit.

The reason for this is that, generally speaking, whenever banks obtain additional reserves, they can be counted on to invest them quite promptly as long as they can find suitable ways of investing them. If no more attractive investment media are available, short-term Treasury securities are always suitable because they are highly liquid and entail almost no risk.

To be sure, many banks do not try to invest every dollar of their excess reserves, because it is not worth while for them to do so. They prefer to keep a little margin of extra funds at the Federal Reserve Banks as a matter of operating convenience. This explains why, even when credit conditions are quite tight, the excess reserves of member banks usually total up to several hundred million dollars. This looks like a substantial volume of excess reserves, but it is widely distributed among thousands of member banks and does not amount to much per member bank.

However, whenever a banker sees his excess reserve increase beyond what he regards as a normal working margin, he immediately thinks of investing it. This process is practically automatic in larger banks where the sums involved make it worth while to assign an officer to "run the bank's money position." One of this officer's chief tasks is to see to it that any excess reserves acquired by his bank are promptly invested. In smaller banks it may sometimes take a little more time for the banker to get around to investing extra funds.

There was one exceptional period, the middle and late 1930's, when the member banks did not invest additional reserves that flowed into the banking system. The reason was that the expansion potential of the huge volume of excess reserves created by the inflow of gold during that period far exceeded the total available supply of short-term Treasury obligations. Banks bid so vigorously for the available supply of these securities that the yield on ninety-day Treasury bills was forced down to about one-tenth of 1 per cent per annum—which only about covered the bookkeeping expense involved in such an investment. The banks obviously would have absorbed far larger quantities of bills if the Treasury had made them available.

Today, however, the volume of short-term Treasury obligations is far greater than it was during the 1930's, and there is little prospect that it will decline substantially for many years to come. Under these circumstances, the Federal Reserve, in addition to being able to restrict the expansion of bank deposits and bank credit, can effectively encourage expansion whenever it wishes simply by injecting more reserves into the banking system or by lowering the reserve requirement percentages.

It should be pointed out that the control of the Federal Reserve over the quantity of bank deposits is not appreciably diminished by the fact that member banks can obtain some additional reserves on their own initiative by means of borrowing from Federal Reserve

Banks. True, the borrowing privilege does enable an individual member bank to cushion itself to a limited degree and temporarily against an adverse shift in its reserve position. However, since there is a strong tradition against continuous borrowing at the Federal (and since this tradition could be effectively enforced by the Reserve authorities if the need should arise), the amount of reserves that member banks can obtain by borrowing is limited. Moreover, the reserves that member banks obtain by borrowing can be offset by the Reserve authorities in the same way that they offset other nonmanaged factors which affect bank reserves—usually through open-market operations. Indeed, the volume of member-bank borrowing is a sensitive indicator of the pressure of demands for credit at the member banks and therefore serves the Reserve authorities as an important guide for policy formulation.

In the world of realities, of course, the extent to which the monetary authorities are actually free to regulate bank credit is limited by practical considerations. For example, it is hardly conceivable that in this day and age the Reserve authorities would follow a severely deflationary policy. They cannot disregard the effects of their actions either on the availability or on the cost of credit. Neither can they ignore their unwritten responsibility to assist the Treasury, when necessary, with its financing operations. Nevertheless, within fairly broad boundaries, the Reserve authorities do exercise a very considerable degree of control over the reserve position of the banking system and hence over the volume of bank deposits and bank credit.

SIGNIFICANCE OF QUANTITATIVE CONTROL

Regulation of the quantity of bank deposits and bank credit obviously has important effects upon the composition of banking assets, upon bank investment and lending policies, and upon interest rates and bond prices.

Perhaps its most significant impact is on the composition of banking assets, notably on bank holdings of Government securities. Bankers, of course, regard lending as the most important part of their business, whereas investing in securities represents a residual use of funds. Generally speaking, banks buy and hold securities only to the extent that they have surplus funds they are unable to lend. To be sure, they wish to retain some minimum amount of Government securities for liquidity and other purposes. In the main, however, changes in bank holdings of Government securities usually reflect changes in the difference between the total amount of funds the banks have available to lend and invest and the amount they are able to lend.

This means that by restricting total bank credit when loan demands are strong, the monetary authorities can in effect force the banks to reduce their holdings of securities in order to accommodate these demands. Conversely, by supplying the banks with funds when loan demands decline, the monetary authorities can bring about an expansion of bank investments. In general, loans fluctuate with loan demand, whereas fluctuations in the volume of bank investments primarily reflect the effects of monetary policy.

As a result, commercial banks are at times on balance substantial buyers of Government securities and at other times are net sellers. At times they are interested in lengthening out the maturities of their investment portfolios and at other times they restrict their investments to short-dated obligations.

These shifts in bank investment activities have an important marginal effect upon prices and yields of Government securities and hence upon the entire bond market and the whole spectrum of interest rates. They also directly affect the flow of credit through various channels by at times absorbing and at times increasing the volume of lendable funds at the disposal of nonbank lenders and investors. The effects of monetary policy are thus transmitted to nonbank credit via the operations of the commercial banks in the Government securities market.

In addition, changes in the volume of bank investments obviously affect the liquidity of the banks and may therefore at times have some influence on their lending policies. In general, of course, banks do not modify their lending policies unless there is a really marked change in their liquidity positions. Nevertheless, the average banker does watch the trend of his liquidity position as measured by his holdings of liquid assets, and when these measures show a marked and apparently persistent shift, he may decide to become either more conservative or more liberal in his lending activities.

Finally, monetary policy obviously has important effects upon operating earnings and net profits through its impact on rates of return on both loans and investments and also on bond prices. At times monetary policy puts banks under pressure to liquidate securities at losses in order to be able to accommodate loan demand. In some cases, the reluctance—or even inability—of banks to realize such losses may lead them to tighten their lending policies.

EFFECTS OF VARIOUS CREDIT CONTROL INSTRUMENTS

The three chief instruments employed by the Federal Reserve authorities in regulating bank reserve positions consist of open-market operations, the discount rate, and the reserve requirement ratios. Of these, open-market operations are most frequently used and most important.

Effects of Open-Market Operations

Open-market purchases of Government securities by the Federal Reserve Banks expand member-bank reserve balances and, conversely, open-market sales absorb reserves. These operations may be employed either to offset the effects of other factors that influence bank reserves or to bring about a change in bank reserve positions. For many years open-market operations have been the chief determinant of the volume of bank reserves and hence of the volume of bank credit.

Open-market operations are, of course, a highly flexible method of control. They can be speeded up, slowed down, or even reversed, from one day to another—or even from hour to hour. A large proportion of open-market transactions are undertaken to offset the effects of nonmanaged factors that affect bank reserves—fluctuations in Federal Reserve float, gold movements, and the like. On the other hand, for any given period, the net volume of purchases and sales of Government securities by the Federal Reserve Open Market Account inevitably reflects current monetary policy.

In recent years, open-market policy has been aimed primarily at keeping the net reserve position of the banking system—i.e., total excess reserves minus total borrowed reserves—within a range considered suitable to the degree of credit restraint or ease desired at the time. The managers of the Open Market Account keep running estimates of what nonmanaged factors will do to bank reserves and then, taking these factors into account, aim at a predetermined target in terms of net excess reserves or net borrowed reserves.

The effects of these operations on the reserve position of the banking system as a whole are reflected in the figures released each week by the Reserve System. These over-all figures naturally hide the diversity of the effects of open-market policy on various groups of banks. For instance, open-market operations usually have their initial impact on banks located in the large financial centers and may have little immediate influence on the reserve balances of country banks. Nevertheless, experience has shown that the aggregate figures for all member banks are meaningful and do have considerable value as an indicator of the availability of bank reserves.

Open-market operations have an enormous impact, of course, on the market prices and yields of Government securities. These effects come about directly as a result of the purchases and sales made by the Federal and also indirectly as a consequence of the purchases and sales made by the banks due to the changes that take place in their reserve positions. And through these effects on Government security yields, open-market operations influence the level and pattern of most interest rates.

Rates in the organized short-term money market are highly sensitive to open-market policy. When Federal Reserve operations cause an increase in the reserve balances of money-market banks, the latter naturally try to put these funds to work and they may aggressively bid against each other for the available market supply of short-term Government securities, thereby pushing market yields sharply downward. This buying of securities by banks does not reduce reserve balances but simply shifts them to other banks. The creation of reserve balances through open-market operations therefore has a multiple effect on bank buying of short-term Governments. This chain reaction is reversed, of course, when bank reserve positions are tightened by open-market sales by the Reserve Banks.

The relation between bank reserve positions and Government security yields is by no means constant and fixed. This is true even in the case of short-term yields. The relation between bank reserve positions and long-term rates is even more variable. The willingness of banks and other investors to buy securities at progressively lower yields is greatly influenced by, but not precisely determined by, the quantity of reserves made available to the banks through the open-market transactions of the Federal Reserve System.

In short, Federal Reserve open-market policy is inevitably a major factor affecting bank reserve positions at all times. It thereby exerts a powerful influence on the expansion of bank deposits and bank credit and on rates of return on bank loans and investments.

Effects of Changes in the Discount Rate

The Federal Reserve discount rate—the cost of member-bank borrowing from Federal Reserve Banks—has become largely an adjunct of open-market policy. Changes in the discount rate may be used at times, as in the fall of 1957, to signal a reversal of monetary policy. Often, however, changes in the discount rate are simply a belated confirmation of changes which have already taken place in money-market rates and which have been strongly influenced by Federal Reserve open-market policy.

Changes in the discount rate nevertheless do affect member banks in several ways. First, they influence the relative attractiveness of borrowing from the Federal. When the discount rate is increased, banks are to some degree discouraged from borrowing, and vice versa. Secondly, discount rate changes afford concrete evidence of the intentions of the Federal Reserve authorities and therefore affect the expectations of investors with respect to the course of interest rates. An increase in the discount rate tends to stiffen other interest rates, and, conversely, a reduction tends to ease other rates. Discount rate changes are usually reflected rather quickly in short-term open-market rates and are sometimes followed by changes in the rate on prime business loans.

Effects of Changes in Reserve Requirements

Changes in member-bank reserve requirements are another potent method of altering the reserve position of the member banks. Authority to vary the reserve requirement percentages of member banks was originally granted to the Board of Governors on the theory that this power would be used only under unusual circumstances calling for a large-scale adjustment in the country's available bank reserves. It was not intended to be an instrument of short-run credit control.

On a number of occasions, the Reserve Board has departed from this original concept and has used changes in the reserve requirement percentages as a means of regulating bank reserve positions. However, this does not indicate that the Reserve authorities have come to regard this instrument as a desirable method of influencing the availability of bank credit. Reserve requirements were *raised* for this purpose only during World War II and during the early postwar years, when the Federal Reserve was committeed to supporting Government bond prices at par and therefore could not use open-market operations effectively to curb credit expansion.

It is significant that the only changes that have been made in the reserve requirement ratios since the Federal Reserve-Treasury Accord of 1951 have been downward. Although the avowed policy of the Board of Governors during 1952 and early 1953 and again during 1955-57 was to combat inflationary tendencies, reserve requirements were not raised. On the other hand, requirements were lowered in mid-1953, again in 1954, and again in 1958 at times when the Reserve authorities were pursuing easy money policies.

The significance of this seems to be quite clear. Reserve requirements were raised to unusually high levels during the 1930's to cope with an unprecedented inflow of gold and the consequent burgeoning of member-bank reserves. The need for these high reserve requirements disappeared with the tremendous wartime expansion of bank credit and currency. Nevertheless, we emerged from the war and postwar period without having appreciably reduced the reserve requirement percentages. Moreover, it is apparent that existing requirements will become increasingly inappropriate as our economy continues to grow.

Over the years, therefore, the Federal Reserve authorities may from time to time lower the reserve requirement ratios. Most of these reductions will probably be timed to implement an easy money policy. However, once the ratios have been brought down to a more appropriate level, they are not likely to be changed except under extraordinary circumstances.

The chief significance of further reductions in reserve requirements will be that they will put the banking system in a better position to accommodate future demands for bank credit. If they are made during periods of monetary ease, they will probably not be fully offset at the time by open-market operations and will therefore accentuate tendencies toward easier bank reserve positions and lower interest rates. Initially, most of the funds released by such reductions will be invested in Government securities at low rates of return. Eventually, however, the banks should be able to shift some part of these funds into higher-yielding investments and loans.

HOW CREDIT RESTRAINT AFFECTS BANKING

The years 1955-57 provide a revealing case study of the relations between monetary management and banking during a period of credit restriction. Developments during these years adhered closely to the classic pattern of cyclical boom, including heavy demands for bank loans. The monetary authorities concentrated their attention primarily on restricting the growth of the money supply. They dribbled additional reserves into the banking system via open-market operations in a limited manner. With deposit velocity rising, as it usually does during a boom, the Reserve authorities held down the increase in demand deposits to less than average for normal growth.

Effects on Bank Investments

Consequently, the huge increase that took place in bank loans was financed largely by a reduction in bank holdings of Government securities. The chief aim of monetary policy was clearly not to clamp down on bank lending but rather to force the banks to liquidate Governments to offset the effect of loan expansion on the money supply. In other words, monetary policy operated primarily through its effects on bank investment policies. Instead of being buyers of Government securities on balance, as they had been during 1954, the banks became sellers on balance on a large scale.

They also shifted from a policy of lengthening the maturities of their holdings in 1954 to a policy of confining almost all of their new purchases to short-term issues. About 90 per cent of the banks replying to a survey conducted by the American Bankers Association in May 1957 reported that they had purchased hardly any medium or long-term Government bonds during the preceding twelve months. About two-thirds of them indicated that their purchases of municipal securities had also been limited to short maturities.

These changes in bank investment policies were the natural result of insistent demands for bank credit plus a restrictive monetary policy. It was primarily through these effects on bank investments that the growth of the money supply was curbed and that the impact of monetary policy was transmitted to nonbank lenders and investors, especially in the capital market.

Bank earnings improved somewhat, but not as much as might be assumed in view of the substantial rise in money-market rates. Bank asset growth was restricted; operating costs continued to rise; and the banks raised their interest rates paid to savings depositors. Intense competition held down bank lending rates much more than might be expected in view of the unprecedented demands for a limited supply of bank credit.

Few banks foresaw the magnitude of the loan demand that did develop and many liquidated their lower-yielding short-term securities first. By 1957 the investment portfolios of many banks had been denuded of short-term obligations and their remaining holdings showed a substantial market depreciation. Security profits were replaced by losses, some of which were doubtless realized because bankers wished to share them with the Department of Internal Revenue.

Effects of Treasury Financing

During 1955-57 there were some interesting developments in the relations between the Federal Reserve System and the commercial banks with respect to Treasury financing operations. With private borrowers bidding aggressively for credit, the Treasury relied heavily on short-term financing and therefore repeatedly needed help from the banking system.

One might assume that this would have seriously impaired the efforts of the Federal Reserve to restrain bank credit, and some observers believe that it did. Others, however, while granting that the necessity of helping the Treasury complicated the task of the monetary authorities, held that the effects of these operations on bank credit were temporary and did not seriously interfere with Federal Reserve policy.

What happened was that time and again the banks took on substantial amounts of new Treasury issues, and the additional reserves required to finance these acquisitions came in part from Federal Reserve open-market operations and in part from increased borrowings by member banks from the Federal Reserve. The willingness of banks to borrow for this purpose enabled the Treasury to accomplish these financings without requiring the Reserve Banks to relax greatly their pressure on bank reserve positions. As a result, the banks soon resumed selling Governments, and the expansion of bank credit resulting from the financings proved to be temporary. In essence, the banks acted as middlemen in distributing new Treasury securities among nonbank investors.

Effects on Bank Lending

During this period, there were also some interesting changes in bank lending policies. Two surveys conducted by the American Bankers Association among its members in 1955 and in 1957 shed considerable light on the nature of these changes and why they took place.[1]

Before presenting the results of these surveys, it should be emphasized that it is impossible to say to what extent they reflect the influence of monetary policy versus other factors. No one knows what would have happened to bank credit and to the entire economy during this period if no restraint had been placed on monetary expansion. However, it seems obvious that if monetary policy had not been operative, inflationary tendencies would have been intensified, perhaps markedly. This in turn would have resulted in larger demands for bank credit than actually did develop. Indeed, it might well be argued that the greatest effect of monetary policy on bank credit was through its contribution toward curbing the development of speculative excesses based on credit.

In any event, the replies received from bankers indicated that they became more conservative in their lending policies during this period and that this was attributable to two main reasons: the development of boom conditions and the restrictive credit policy of the Federal Reserve System. These two factors are inextricably interrelated. Bankers reacted to the rising demand for credit in much the same way the monetary authorities did. One banker replied that whereas monetary policy had probably had some influence on his lending policies, "it might be more accurate to say that we were influenced by those factors which caused the change in monetary policy rather than by the change in monetary policy itself."

From the standpoint of the individual banker, it is almost impossible to say just what the effects of monetary policy are upon his institution. Looking at the banking system as a whole, it is clear that Federal Reserve policy restricted the growth of bank deposits; and this meant that as loans increased, banks' ratios of loans to deposits rose more rapidly than would otherwise have been the case. The survey results show that the rise in loan-deposit ratios was one of the chief reasons why bankers became more conservative in their lending operations. Yet, viewed by the banker in Worcester, Tallahassee, or Klamath Falls, this appeared to be largely a local development.

Despite the difficulty of tracing its effects, most bankers did report that monetary policy had been among the factors influencing them in

---

[1] See E. Sherman Adams, "Monetary Policy and the Present Credit Situation," *Banking,* November 1955, and "Monetary Restraint and Bank Credit," *Banking,* September 1957.

the direction of greater conservatism. This was particularly true among larger banks. On the other hand, analysis of the survey results strongly suggests that monetary policy may actually influence the policies of smaller institutions to a greater extent than they themselves realize.

So, without trying to assign any specific weight to the effects of monetary policy, let us examine what happened to bank lending policies during 1955-57.

The survey replies clearly indicate that throughout this period, with loan-deposit ratios rising, more and more banks felt that they were approaching a fully loaned position. Also, with bond prices trending downward, there was an increasing reluctance to take additional losses from selling securities to obtain more funds to lend. In addition, bankers' attitudes were influenced to some degree by the very fact that the Federal Reserve was following a policy of curbing credit expansion.

Consequently, most banks became more selective in their lending policies. The change was a gradual one, very gradual indeed during 1955, much more marked thereafter. During 1955, in fact, due to competitive conditions, many banks relaxed their lending policies with respect to consumer intallment loans. Also, in answering the A.B.A. survey taken in the last quarter of 1955, they emphasized that in the types of lending where they had become somewhat more strict, their shift in that direction had been only moderate. As long as most banks still held an adequate supply of short-term Governments, Federal Reserve policy had little effect on their lending activities. During 1956 and the first part of 1957, however, as bank liquidity positions progressively deteriorated, there was a decided trend toward greater selectivity in all categories of bank lending.

This was particularly true for most medium-sized and large banks, especially the latter. In certain financial centers, New York in particular, loan demands were extraordinarily strong, and at the same time many large corporations drew down their balances to take advantage of the increasingly attractive returns available in the short-term money market. As a result, some of the big money market banks were caught in a squeeze of rapidly rising loans and declining deposits. To be sure, these banks' customers could frequently obtain the credit they wanted from banks in other cities, but this very process helped to spread the tightening of credit throughout the banking system.

About three-fifths of the banks reporting that they had become more selective in their lending stated that this involved stricter review of loan applications from a credit standpoint. Almost as many indicated that they were giving greater consideration to their past relations with loan applicants. About one-third reported a definite policy of providing faster repayment schedules, and about the same number stated they were giving more weight to the willingness of borrowers to maintain good balances. Only about one bank out of four indicated that it was doing much in the way of scaling down the amounts of loan requests.

Some banks reported they had tightened up on term loans either from the standpoint of maximum maturity or with respect to their willingness to make additional loans of this type. In the area of instalment lending, greater selectivity usually took the form of cutting down on the exceptions granted to standard terms.

To what extent did this greater selectivity in bank lending actually curb the rise in bank loans? Two-thirds of the banks with deposits under $500 million said "hardly at all," and most of the remaining third estimated that loan expansion after 1955 may have been held down to the extent of "perhaps 5 to 10 per cent." Even among the largest banks, only a comparatively small minority estimated that their loan expansion had been held down by more than 10 per cent.

In evaluating these replies, it should be kept in mind that in making these estimates, bankers were thinking in terms of the loan applications they actually received during this period. As previously mentioned, demands for credit might have been much larger than they actually were if the Reserve authorities had not been curbing monetary expansion. Also, during a period of credit restraint, banks naturally refrain from entering new fields of credit extension. Nevertheless, the survey does clearly suggest that the availability of credit to bank customers was not restricted during this period to anywhere near the extent that many people assumed. Despite all the talk about "tight money," most banks were continuing to accommodate almost all requests for loans from credit-worthy customers.

This, of course, is not surprising. Generally speaking, bankers feel a deep sense of responsibility to meet the legitimate credit needs of their communities to the extent that they can safely do so. This obligation applies particularly to business customers who have maintained good balances over the years so they can borrow when they need to. And in many cases, of course, banks have definite commitments to lend in the form of lines of credit.

Indeed, many bankers, especially in smaller institutions, do not even think in terms of making their lending policies more strict or more liberal from year to year. Many a banker would define his loan policy as being a continuing policy of serving the credit needs of his community at all times. He knows from long experience that when he analyzes a loan application, the key considerations should be the purpose of the loan and ability to repay. His appraisal of ability to repay may be influenced at times by changes in economic conditions, but he does not always think of this as being a change in his lending policy.

In larger banks, where lending authority is widely dispersed, there is need for more precise policy definitions. This may be one reason why larger banks report more change in their lending policies than smaller banks. On the other hand, these institutions were undoubtedly under much greater pressure to tighten their lending policies during this particular period because of the extraordinarily heavy demands for credit from large business concerns and the flow of funds away from some of the financial centers.

Additional evidence on this matter is presented in Table 1, which shows the percentage distribution of answers received from bankers in mid-1957 to the question: "How would you characterize the availability of bank credit in your locality?" As can be seen, more than one-third of the banks with deposits under $50 million reported that bank credit in their localities was still "readily available," and most of the others characterized the situation as being merely "somewhat tight." In short, despite the trend toward greater selectivity in bank lending policies during 1955-57, credit was still quite readily available to most bank customers at mid-1957, except at a comparatively small number of large money-market banks.

Some people may interpret these survey results as indicating that monetary policy was not as effective as it should have been in holding down the volume of bank loans. The question is admittedly a debatable one. However, it should be borne in mind that a large part of the expansion of bank loans was used to finance increased production and was therefore highly desirable from the standpoint of combating inflationary trends. Moreover, bank loans should clearly not be singled out as a special target for restraint. Monetary policy in this country operates through many channels besides bank lending, and the Federal Reserve authorities have shown no desire to discriminate against bank loans as against other types of credit. Indeed,

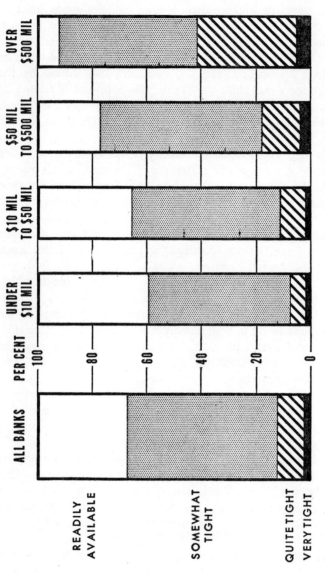

TABLE I

REPORT ON AVAILABILITY OF BANK CREDIT
Percentage distribution of answers by banks as to how they would characterize the availability of bank credit in their respective localities in mid-1957.

it would be most unfortunate if monetary policy were to bear with undue severity on borrowers who are dependent upon commercial banks as their source of credit.

Effects on Various Types of Credit

Another question, widely discussed in recent years, is whether a policy of monetary restraint seriously curtails the availability of credit to particular types of borrowers. The A.B.A. surveys shed some interesting light on this question.

The results already presented suggest two pertinent conclusions, namely, (1) that during 1955-57, the effects of monetary policy on the customer loan market, though bearing more heavily on large banks than small, were nevertheless quite widely diffused throughout the banking system; and (2) that while the availability of bank credit tightened to some extent during this period, the customer loan market did not by any means bear the whole brunt of credit restraint.

Additional evidence relating to this question is presented in Table 2, which shows the changes that took place in bank lending policies during 1956 and early 1957 with respect to various types of borrowers. This tabulation clearly shows that the tendency toward conservatism was reflected in all these major types of bank credit.

Loans to agriculture were affected less than any other category and the replies received from bankers indicate that this type of credit is not likely to be influenced to any appreciable extent by monetary policy. A North Dakota banker wrote: "Our loaning policy does not change with the national money market. What affects us is local crop conditions."

The table does indicate, however, that banks slowed down on mortgage loans more than on other types of credit. This was especially true of Government insured and guaranteed mortgages, and this, of course, did not reflect the effects of monetary policy but rather the attempt on the part of the Government to shelter this type of credit from the effects of monetary policy by holding down the interest rates on these mortgages. As other rates of return rose, these loans naturally became relatively less and less attractive.

As the table shows, banks also cut back on their lending on conventional mortgages more than on most other types of credit. However, the replies suggest that this may largely reflect the fact that banks had expanded their mortgage holdings quite heavily during the preceding years. As a result, many banks found that their mortgage

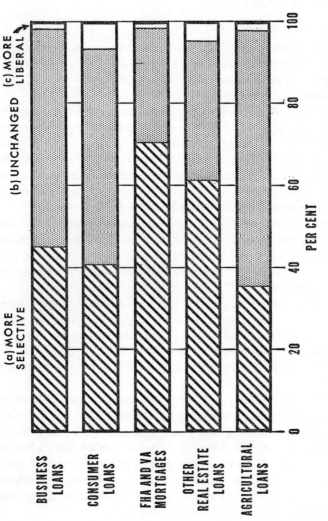

TABLE II

HOW POLICY VARIED WITH DIFFERENT TYPES OF LOANS

Percentage of banks reporting in 1957 that since 1955 their lending policies with respect to various types of loans (a) had become more selective; (b) were unchanged; or (c) had become more liberal.

Source: Department of Monetary Policy, American Bankers Association

portfolios were at or approaching legal limits and that they did not have as much money available for these loans as formerly.

A few bankers—a very small minority—reported that during this period they tightened up more on loans to sales finance companies than on other types of business loans. This was because their own consumer loans were growing rapidly and they wished to avoid acquiring too heavy a commitment in finance company plus consumer paper. On the other hand, many banks added substantially to their holdings of open-market paper of finance companies during this period.

Credit for Small Business

Another question that has received much attention is whether monetary restraint seriously harmed small-business borrowers.

It is not surprising that this is assumed to be the case by many people who know little about the banking business. In theory, it sounds quite logical that if bankers are forced to ration a limited supply of credit, they might be inclined to favor large-business customers at the expense of smaller concerns.

However, this assumption fails to take into account the structure of the banking industry in this country, the importance of small-business loans to American banks, the attitude of bankers toward lending to small business, the closeness of the relations that are built up between banks and small-business customers, the fact that many small concerns are just as credit-worthy as large ones, and many other relevant facts of banking life in the United States.

Also, of course, as far as the 1955-57 period is concerned, it is obviously significant that small- and medium-sized banks, whose business loans consist predominantly of credits extended to small concerns, were much less affected by the general tightening of credit than the larger banks serving large corporations. Likewise, as already mentioned, the great majority of banks, and again especially the small- and medium-sized institutions, reported that greater selectivity in their lending policies actually had little influence on the volume of their lending.

To obtain additional evidence on this point, the A.B.A. asked its members whether stricter credit review of loan applications tends to curtail lending to small business more than to large corporations. About five out of six bankers stated that it did not. To be sure, this leaves a minority of one out of six reporting that it did. On the other hand, some bankers pointed out that there is frequently a tendency in the opposite direction of giving special consideration to loan applications from small companies.

Many bankers did report greater reluctance to lend to new concerns than to established customers. However, new business incorporations during 1955-57 were at record levels—about a third higher than during the preceding three years. To the extent that the formation of additional businesses may have been discouraged during this period by difficulty in obtaining bank credit, the net result may have been quite salutary from the standpoint of established small-business concerns—not to mention the economy as a whole.

Much more detailed information on this question was developed as part of the study of small-business financing conducted by the Federal Reserve System in 1957-58.[2] This mass of data will naturally be interpreted differently by different people. To many, however, the conclusion will seem warranted that the tightening of bank credit during 1955-57 did not seriously handicap small business.

HOW MONETARY EASE AFFECTS BANKING

When the Federal Reserve pursues an easy money policy, the effects on the commercial banks are largely a reversal of the impact of monetary restraint. To examine these effects, let us look at what happened in 1953-54 and in 1957-58.

In May and June of 1953 the Reserve authorities shifted from a restrictive credit policy and eased bank reserve positions by large-scale purchases of short-term Government securities in the open market. At the end of June, confronted with the necessity of helping the Treasury with a large financing operation for new money, they announced a reduction in member-bank reserve requirements.

As it became increasingly apparent that the business boom was giving way to recession, the Reserve authorities eased credit more and more aggressively and publicly characterized their policy as being one of "active ease." Their aim was not simply to make sure that credit was readily available at reasonable rates; they were intent upon really pumping reserves into the banking system and actively encouraging an expansion of the money supply.

The banks found themselves well supplied with reserves and as-

---

[2] Board of Governors of the Federal Reserve System, *Small Business Financing*, Washington, D.C., 1958. See especially Part II, Vol. 1.

sured that the supply would continue to be ample. In April 1953, member banks had had a net reserve deficit of $650 million. By the following January, they had net excess reserves of around $800 million. In effect, the Reserve authorities were following a policy of injecting more and more reserves into the banks as fast as the banks could get these additional funds invested.

Yields on short-term Government obligations dropped precipitously, accelerated by cuts in the discount rate. Rising bond prices shifted bank security portfolios from the red into the black.

The influence of Federal Reserve policy was reflected in the fact that total bank deposits and total bank loans and investments actually increased during this period. The chief impact, of course, was on bank investment policies. The banks used most of their additional reserves to expand their holdings of securities. And with sharply lower yields prevailing on short-term Governments, they lengthened out the maturities of their investments on a substantial scale.

There was also some effect on bank lending policies. Although declining business tended to make bankers generally cautious, many banks loaned somewhat more freely than during the first part of 1953. Ready availability of bank reserves forestalled possible pressures to liquidate bank credit.

Developments in late 1957 and early 1958 followed a similar pattern, though with some variations. When the Reserve authorities finally decided in November 1957 that the bloom was off the boom, they used a reduction in the discount rate as a dramatic signal of this decision. Investors and speculators took this signal seriously and proceeded to push up bond prices with unprecedented vigor. Within two months after the first cut in the discount rate, long-term Government bonds had advanced eight points.

The sharpness of this rise in bond prices may have been one reason why the Reserve authorities did not start immediately to ease bank reserve positions aggressively. Nevertheless, by the end of May 1958, member-bank reserve requirements had been cut three times and member banks held net excess reserves of more than $500 million, compared with a net reserve deficit of about $500 million seven months earlier. The discount rate had been reduced four times and the rate on Treasury bills had again been pushed below 1 per cent.

With respect to the volume of bank credit, the main impact was again on bank investments. During the six months following the initial cut in the discount rate in mid-November 1957, Government security holdings of reporting member banks showed an increase of almost $6 billion, which contrasted with a decline of about $400 million during the comparable period the year before. Similarly, banks added substantially to their holdings of state and municipal securities, whereas they had been reducing these investments a year earlier.

Bank lending policies were affected to some extent, though this is much harder to measure. Bankers naturally tend to become more cautious when business turns downward. On the other hand, as credit conditions ease, the inhibiting effect of credit restraint is at least removed. Here and there individual banks may decide to embark on new types of lending or to resume making certain types of loans they had restricted when they were rationing credit—mortgage ware-housing, for example. More important, however, is the tendency gradually to relax the various restrictive practices adopted during the period of credit restraint.

Bankers are in agreement that these changes in their lending policies do not have much influence as a positive stimulus to bank customers to borrow more than they otherwise would during a recession. Never-theless, ready availability of bank reserves eliminates the deterrent effects of credit restriction and is a safeguard against the development of a spiral of monetary deflation.

LONGER-RANGE IMPLICATIONS FOR BANKING

Let us consider briefly some of the longer-range effects that mone-tary policy may have on commercial banking in the United States over the years ahead—assuming no global war and assuming no great change in the character of monetary management.

In the first place, the long-run growth of the banking business will obviously be affected by the fact that the monetary authorities will at times restrict and at times stimulate the expansion of bank credit and bank deposits. In this connection, it should be borne in mind that the Federal Reserve authorities are primarily concerned with in-fluencing the volume of *demand* deposits, rather than total deposits or total bank credit. Moreover, the volume of savings deposits at commercial banks is not directly affected by monetary control. The future growth of these deposits will depend primarily, not on Federal Reserve policy, but on the degree of success that commercial banks are able to achieve in competing with other institutions for personal savings.

In regulating the volume of demand deposits, the monetary authorities will try to prevent the money supply from expanding so rapidly that it contributes to inflation or so slowly that it contributes to deflation. In determining the appropriate rate of monetary expansion during any particular period, they will naturally take into account many factors—inflationary or deflationary trends in the economy, changes in the velocity of money turnover, and so forth. Over a period of years, however, unless there should be a lasting change in money velocity, it is to be expected that the long-run growth in demand deposits should roughly parallel the growth in the dollar volume of business transacted in the United States—as measured, say, by gross national product.

It is also apparent that monetary management will greatly affect the profitability of the banking business. For one thing, banks will find that their ability to expand their business may be restricted at the very times when customer demands for their principal product, bank credit, are strongest and when expansion would be most profitable. This may inhibit the long-run profitability of banking and mean that banks may not grow as rapidly as some other types of financial institutions.

Even more important to bank earnings will be the effect of monetary management on the average level of interest rates over the years, and especially during periods of business recession. Public attitudes and public policies in the United States show a strong bias in favor of low interest rates, and some observers believe that this bias is reflected at times in monetary policy. It would be rather remarkable, indeed, if the attitude of the monetary authorities toward interest rates could help being influenced to some degree by the prevailing psychology and also by the magnitude of the public debt. For that matter, some students of central banking believe that there is a built-in tendency for monetary policy to have an easy-money bias a goodly part of the time.[3]

[3] For example, Professor R. S. Sayers, Sir Ernest Cassell Professor of Economics, University of London, has observed: "There is, for instance, the inherent difficulty of taking the right decision sufficiently early. The central banker has to try to act in anticipation of events, whereas the graphs prepared by his statistical department reveal the events only weeks or months afterwards. When the central banker has to choose between two courses, one of which is politically disagreeable, he is strongly tempted to doubt the diagnosis that urges the disagreeable course. All too readily he postpones the disagreeable, pending clearer omens. On the other hand, he is apt to hasten action that relieves pressure on the credit situation, because such action ordinarily has political attractions. The difficulty of early diagnosis coupled with ordinary

From the standpoint of bankers and bank stockholders, experience in recent years has not been altogether reassuring. This record is admittedly subject to varying interpretations, but it has seemed to some observers that the tendency has been for monetary policy to accelerate declining interest rates during periods of recession and to retard the rise in rates during periods of active business.

If this should be the case in the future, it might have rather serious implications for bank earning power. On the other hand, this would depend largely upon the duration of our periods of recession and of good business. If it turns out that periods of recession and low interest rates are of relatively short duration and our periods of economic expansion are of long duration, then the net result should be a fair level of interest rates over the years. Also, the extent to which the Federal Reserve can retard rising interest rates when it is determined to hold down the money supply is obviously limited.

To sum up, we might say that over the years ahead, it is apparent that Federal Reserve policy will continue to have a major impact upon commercial bank investments, a lesser but still significant influence upon bank lending, and very important effects upon rates of return and bank profits. Nevertheless, there seems to be no reason why American banks will not be able to function satisfactorily, and at a better-than-subsistence level, under modern monetary management.

SUGGESTED READINGS

ADAMS, E. SHERMAN, "Monetary Policy and the Present Credit Situation," *Banking*, November 1955, pp. 36–41, 155.

——, "Monetary Restraint and Bank Credit," *Banking*, September 1957, pp. 68–72, 142.

ALHADOFF, DAVID A., *Monopoly and Competition in Banking*, Berkeley and Los Angeles, University of California Press, 1954, especially Chapters VIII and IX.

BOARD OF GOVERNORS OF THE FEDERAL RESERVE SYSTEM, *Small Business Financing*, Washington, D.C., 1958. See especially Part II, Vol. 1.

"INTEREST RATES AND CREDIT AVAILABILITY AT COMMERCIAL BANKS," *Monthly Review*, Federal Reserve Bank of Kansas City, February 1957.

MONETARY STUDY NO. 2, *How Our Reserve Banking System Operates*, New York, Economic Policy Commission, American Bankers Association, 1954.

human weakness thus gives to central banking an inflationary bias, undermining the value of the monetary unit." *Central Banking After Bagehot*, London, Oxford University Press, 1957, p. 3.

MONETARY STUDY NO. 4, *The Effects of Federal Reserve Policies,* New York, Economic Policy Commission, American Bankers Association, 1955.

Relations Between the Central Banks and Commercial Banks: A Series of Lectures at the Tenth International Banking Summer School, Garmisch-Partenkirchen, September 1957, Frankfort on Main, Fritz Knapp Verlag, 1957.

SAYERS, R. S., *Central Banking After Bagehot,* London, Oxford University Press, 1957.

WHITE, W. H., "Interest Inelasticity of Investment Demand," *American Economic Review,* September 1956, pp. 565–587.

Chapter 10

EFFECTS OF FEDERAL RESERVE POLICY ON NONMONETARY FINANCIAL INSTITUTIONS

ONE of the most important financial developments of this century has been the growth in number and variety of institutions which act as intermediaries between the suppliers of funds and the users of funds. There has been a steady movement away from direct investment by savers and a steady growth in the use of financial intermediaries as channels through which savings flow to the various money and capital markets.

During the period 1900-1929, about 40 per cent of net personal savings (excluding savings in the form of durable goods) flowed through financial intermediaries; in recent years, the proportion has risen to 80 per cent. In 1900, only about one-tenth of total assets held by individuals consisted of claims against financial intermediaries; today, about one-quarter of individuals' assets is held in this form.[1]

The growth and specialization of financial intermediaries have come about in response to changing needs on the part of both capital suppliers and capital users. The growing number of individuals in the middle income brackets has increased the need for savings institutions of a type readily available to the average wage earner and adapted to his investment ability and knowledge. There has also been increased demand by savers for assets which combine a specialized use value with a savings feature, e.g., life insurance policies. From the standpoint of the users of funds, the growing size of corporations has led to demands on the capital market which can be met only through the pooling of the savings of thousands of individuals. And new

[1] Raymond W. Goldsmith, *Financial Intermediaries in the American Economy since 1900*, Princeton University Press for National Bureau of Economic Research, 1958, pp. 306-7.

financing requirements, e.g., consumer installment buying, have given rise to institutions specializing in particular types of lending. In recent years, about 60 per cent of all externally supplied funds has flowed through financial intermediaries, compared to 46 per cent early in this century. Over and above developments in the private financial mechanism, the growing size of government agencies, both as users and as suppliers of funds, has greatly changed our financial structure as well as the types of assets held by financial institutions.

Financial intermediaries as a group have grown more rapidly than the economy and more rapidly than the liquid savings generated by the economy. Goldsmith estimates that total assets of financial intermediaries increased from $19 billion in 1900 to almost $560 billion in 1952, an average growth rate of 6.7 per cent a year. In 1900, the assets of financial intermediaries accounted for about one-ninth of national assets, whereas this ratio had grown to one-fifth in 1952.[2]

As might be expected in view of the different services performed by various types of financial intermediaries, some types have grown much more rapidly than others. The most rapid rate of growth has been shown by government lending agencies and government insurance funds. Among the private intermediaries, there have also been wide differences in rate of growth, from the rapid rise of such institutions as credit unions, private noninsured pension funds, and mutual funds to the relatively slow growth exhibited by such institutions as mutual savings banks, closed-end investment companies, and mortgage companies.

Nonmonetary financial intermediaries as a group have grown, during the present century, at a somewhat more rapid rate than has the commercial banking system. This slower growth of commercial banks has not been in the savings aspect of their business (commercial bank time deposits grew more rapidly in the period 1900-1958 than did the liabilities of other financial intermediaries), but has resulted from the relatively slow growth of demand deposits. The less rapid growth of demand deposits has been due, in turn, to the more efficient use

[2] Goldsmith lists the principal financial intermediaries as the commercial banks, mutual savings banks, property insurance companies, life insurance companies, fraternal insurance organizations, savings and loan associations, trust departments of commercial banks, security brokers and dealers, mortgage companies, the Federal Reserve Banks, government pension funds, government lending institutions, credit unions, investment companies, finance companies, investment holding companies, land banks, and private self-administered pension funds. Of these, only the first nine types were in existence, or of any significance, at the turn of the century.

of our money supply, i.e., to a higher velocity or turnover of demand deposits.[3]

THE NATIONAL COMMISSION ON MONEY AND CREDIT

The growth of nonbank financial institutions, described in the preceding section, has naturally attracted more and more attention from economists, from the financial community, and from government agencies. Twenty years ago it was not unusual for books dealing with money and credit to include no mention of financial institutions outside the commercial banking system. Even at that time this constituted a distorted view of the financial world as it existed in reality. But in the postwar period, the nonbank financial institutions have been accorded an increasingly prominent position in discussions of the monetary and credit structure.

Along with greater recognition of the contribution of nonbank institutions to our total financing mechanism have come inquiries into the place which these institutions occupy, or should occupy, in the framework of theoretical discussions of the supply of credit, the flow of loanable funds, and the relation between the capital market and the level of business activity and prices.

Interest in the operations of nonbank financial institutions has been one of the factors behind suggestions in recent years that a National Monetary Commission be appointed to review our whole banking and financial system. In December 1956, an Advisory Committee to the Senate Banking and Currency Committee recommended the establishment of such a commission.[4] Early in 1957, President Eisenhower asked Congress to establish a National Monetary and Financial Commission, with the comment that "Recent changes in our financial structure and practices call for careful study of the adequacy of existing facilities for meeting the Nation's capital and credit requirements and of the means for exercising appropriate controls over credit."[5]

[3] A further discussion of relative rates of growth of financial intermediaries will be found later in this chapter.

[4] *Study of Banking Laws:* Report of the Advisory Committee for the Study of Federal Statutes Governing Financial Institutions and Credit, to the Committee on Banking and Currency of the United States Senate, Washington, Government Printing Office, December 17, 1956, p. 49.

[5] *The State of the Union Address* of the President of the United States, 85th Congress, 1st Session, House of Representatives, Document No. 1, p. 5.; and *Economic Report of the President,* transmitted to Congress, January 23, 1957, Washington, Government Printing Office, 1957, p. 49.

Following this presidential recommendation, several different Congressional committees attempted to secure jurisdiction over the proposal, and there were various suggestions that the subject be assigned to an already existent Congressional committee, to a committee composed partly of Congressmen and partly of non-Government representatives, and to a committee of "independent citizens." The proposal for a monetary commission was also seized upon by various interests who saw in it, not an objective study of the country's financing mechanism, but an opportunity to "investigate" the financial community in general, to attack the Federal Reserve Board, to oppose all credit restraint, or to injure financial institutions which were competitive with their own. The net result was that, for the time being at least, Congress dropped the commission study proposal.

In November 1957, however, the Committee for Economic Development announced that, with the assistance of a grant from the Ford Foundation, it intended to establish a National Commission on Money and Credit.[6] Appointment of the twenty-five Commission members, drawn from the fields of business, labor, agriculture, education, and government, was announced in May 1958. Care has been taken to make the Commission an independent body, with as objective an approach as possible. The Commission will of course be assisted by a research staff, which will also draw on opinions and research outside the Commission.

The area to be studied by the National Commission on Money and Credit is a broad one. No aspect of the country's monetary and financial mechanism is excluded. The Commission will consider monetary policy, fiscal policy, taxation, and government financing agencies, as well as the private financial mechanism. Among the many important subjects to be studied will be the place of nonbank institutions in our financial structure and the effect which these institutions may have on the level of business activity and prices. Since this chapter is primarily concerned not with the internal workings of nonbank financial institutions but with their place in the economy as a whole, a fruitful approach will be to consider some of the questions which may be raised by the National Commission on Money and Credit, and provide such answers as appear possible at this stage of our knowledge.

The following questions will probably rank high on the agenda of the Commission:

[6] *Announcement of a National Commission on Money and Credit,* Committee for Economic Development, 711 Fifth Avenue, New York 22, N.Y.

1. In what ways does the growth of nonbank financial institutions affect the level of business activity or the level of prices? Does the possession of liquid assets other than demand deposits affect the spending intentions of the holders of those liquid assets? Does a decline in the value of liquid assets, e.g., a fall in stock prices, affect the volume of purchases of goods and services?

2. Do nonbank financial institutions "create" their own liabilities in the same sense that commercial banks "create" demand deposits? Do commercial banks "create" time deposits in the same sense that they "create" demand deposits?

3. If the growth of the liabilities of nonbank financial institutions affects the level of business activity and prices, do present monetary controls exert effective pressure on the growth of these nonbank institutions?

4. Do present monetary controls unfairly inhibit the growth of commercial banks, while permitting unhampered growth of nonbank financial institutions?

LIQUID ASSETS AND THE SUPPLY OF MONEY

The money supply in the United States is usually defined as the sum of all coins, paper money, and demand deposits available to the public. These are the liquid assets normally used for spending, so that the quantity of these assets available to the public has an obvious influence on the level of prices and business activity. Coins, paper money, and demand deposits are not, however, the only means by which liquid balances can be held. The growth of nonbank financial institutions, and the development of new and varied financial instruments, have provided the public with a wide assortment of liquid assets through which savings can be held in readily available form. Although these latter types of liquid assets are not used directly for spending, and are therefore usually not considered part of the "money supply," they are nevertheless readily convertible into money.[7]

Because such liquid assets as government securities, time deposits at commercial banks, savings deposits at mutual savings banks, and share accounts at savings and loan associations may easily and quickly

[7] Whether certain very liquid assets, such as time deposits, are or are not part of the money supply is more a question of semantics than of economics. Most economists find it convenient to define money as including only those instruments which serve *both* as a medium of exchange *and* as a store of value, i.e., which are used both for spending and for saving.

be converted into money, there is little question that the volume of these assets available to the public does have an influence on the volume of spending, and hence on the level of business activity and prices. Although they are, strictly speaking, nonmonetary assets, monetary theory and monetary policy must nevertheless take account of their existence and of the influence which they exercise on business activity and prices.

Two brief examples may be offered at this point to illustrate the way in which changes in the dollar volume of nonmonetary liquid assets may affect business activity and the general level of prices. Some liquid assets, such as common stocks, are traded in organized markets and are subject to substantial changes in value. A fall in the price of common stocks involves the destruction of a portion of liquid assets held by investors. The fall in stock prices need involve no change in the money supply, yet it frequently has an adverse effect on business activity, partly because it may be taken as a signal that business profits are due for a decline, but also partly because common stock investors now feel less prosperous—a portion of the savings which they believed were available to them has evaporated. The personal spending, and in some cases the business spending, of these investors is likely to be adversely affected with depressive results on business activity and prices.

A second example of the destruction of liquid assets occurs when the Federal Government achieves a cash surplus and uses this surplus to reduce the outstanding Treasury debt. A reduction in the public debt does not necessarily change the money supply. The taxes may, in fact, come from the same individuals who hold the government securities which are to be redeemed, in which case the individual as a taxpayer pays the funds to himself as a bondholder. Although the redemption may involve no change in the money supply, it does involve the destruction of liquid assets. The Government has, in effect, ordered the taxpayer-bondholders to tear up their government securities. It is clear that this destruction of liquid assets may have an adverse effect on private spending plans, and thus exert a depressive influence on business activity and prices.

THE CREATION OF LIQUID ASSETS

It has sometimes been argued that even though the volume of nonmonetary liquid assets exercises some influence on prices and business activity, and even though nonbank financial institutions obviously supply funds to the economy, the activities of these institutions can nevertheless be ignored for considerations of broad monetary policy because they do not "create" credit as do the commercial banks, but simply channel credit, which had previously been created by the commercial banking system, to those uses where it is in most demand. In other words, it has been argued that because nonbank institutions do not produce changes in the total quantity of credit, the central monetary authority need not concern itself with their operations but should concentrate entirely on the commercial banking system, which does produce the changes in the total quantity of credit.

As will be shown later, the practical conclusion flowing from this argument—that the Federal Reserve can effectively influence the total quantity of credit by applying pressure on the commercial banking system alone—is correct. But there are some serious theoretical misconceptions in the argument itself which should be cleared up before arriving at the practical conclusion.

Is it true that demand deposits are unique in that they alone can be "created" or "extinguished" by the commercial banking system, whereas this is not possible in the case of time deposits, for example, or savings deposits at mutual savings banks and savings and loan associations? The basic requisite for the creation of demand deposits by the commercial banking system is that the banks be permitted to operate with a fractional cash reserve. If commercial banks were required to maintain 100 per cent cash reserves against demand deposits, the commercial banking system would then be unable to "create" or "extinguish" demand deposits. The banking system would simply take in one very liquid asset, cash, and exchange it for another very liquid asset, demand deposits. This process would not involve an increase or decrease in the total volume of money, nor the total volume of liquid assets, but would constitute simply the exchange of one type of asset for another of approximately equal liquidity.

In actual practice, however, banks are permitted to operate with less than 100 per cent cash reserves, so that they are able, in cooperation with borrowers, to create new liquid assets not previously in existence and also extinguish these assets when the demand for credit subsides. A full explanation of the process of credit creation and extinction has been given in Chapter 4. This explanation will not be repeated here, but attention is called to the fact that the creation of demand deposits involves basically the creation of a liquid asset (the demand deposit) in exchange for an illiquid asset (the promissory note of the borrower). This process is sometimes described by saying that the bank substitutes its credit (which is liquid) for the credit of the borrower (which is not liquid).

The question to be investigated in this section is whether this process of liquid-asset creation is unique with demand deposits, or whether it can occur also with respect to other types of liquid assets. As a first step, it may be asked whether a commercial bank can "create" a time deposit in the same sense that it can "create" a demand deposit.

The usual process by which demand deposits are "created" is through the bank's lending activity. The bank creates a demand deposit in exchange for the promissory note of the borrower. There is no corresponding reduction in liquid assets in the hands of the public (as there would be, for example, in the case of a deposit of cash in exchange for a demand deposit), so that the total of liquid assets in the hands of the public is greater than before the loan was made. There has been a true "creation" of liquid assets.[8]

The borrower in the above example could, of course, have taken a time deposit in exchange for his promissory note, in which case the bank would obviously have created the time deposit in exactly the same way as it created the demand deposit. But since borrowers do not normally take time deposits as the proceeds of a loan, the conclusion has sometimes been drawn that time deposits are not normally "created." This conclusion is not valid, and results from observing only the superficial procedure of liquid-asset creation without inquiring into the basic process.

The basic reason why a commercial bank can create demand deposits is that the bank is not required to maintain 100 per cent *cash* against its deposit liabilities; it can instead hold borrowers' promissory

[8] It is sometimes stated that an individual bank cannot create credit, whereas the banking system as a whole can. This statement is not literally correct because it is obvious that individual banks *do* create credit. What is meant is that, because an individual bank may lose deposits to other banks, credit creation by each individual bank is limited by the degree to which other banks are creating credit. A good portion of credit creation occurs *within* an individual bank, through check clearing between deposits in the same bank. Beyond this internal credit creation, the banker can proceed with credit creation only so far as his clearinghouse balance indicates that he is not expanding credit faster than are other banks. That is, too rapid credit creation will result in an adverse clearing balance vis-à-vis other banks and, because of the loss of cash reserves, will hold the individual bank in phase with other banks.

notes as assets matching a portion of deposit liabilities. Now, it should be obvious that demand deposits can be created in two ways. First, the bank can grant a deposit liability without taking in cash. This is the normal procedure in making a business loan, or a large consumer loan. Second, the bank can release cash to circulation without reducing its deposit liabilities. This is the normal procedure in the purchase of securities, or in the making of small consumer loans where the borrower wishes cash rather than a checking account. In either of the above two situations, the total of liquid assets available to the public is increased—in the first case by increasing this bank's deposits, with its cash remaining the same; and in the second case by reducing this bank's cash, with its deposits remaining the same. In the first case, the total of liquid assets available to the public is increased because cash has not been withdrawn from circulation, yet demand deposits have increased. In the second case, the total of liquid assets available to the public is increased because demand deposits have not been reduced, yet cash originally held idle in the bank's vaults has been released to circulation.

In actual practice, both of the cases discussed above are normal and usual. Each is going on continually in the banking system, and it would be difficult to say which is the more important of these two techniques for liquid-asset creation. The significant principle to note is that for liquid-asset creation to occur there must be (a) the creation of a debt instrument (i.e., someone must borrow), and (b) the bank must either surrender cash or grant to the borrower a claim against the bank. Which of the latter two alternatives occurs is not significant for the process of liquid-asset creation. Liquid assets are created if the borrower acquires a newly created demand deposit, or if he withdraws the loan in cash. (Or, to make the story complete, if he causes a cash drain on this bank by writing a check against the newly created deposit).

From the above discussion it should be clear that a commercial bank can "create" time deposits in the same sense that the bank can "create" demand deposits. If a bank receives a $1,000 time deposit and subsequently releases to circulation, through a loan, any of the $1,000 cash behind this time deposit, then the total of liquid assets available to the public is greater than before the cash release occurred. The process could occur without even a temporary change in demand deposits, if the withdrawal came about through a cash loan and the cash were subsequently lodged in a time deposit in this or any other bank. Or the process could occur through the temporary establishment of a demand deposit, its extinguishment through withdrawal in full by check, and the deposit of this check in a new time deposit. Looked at in this light, it is seen that the demand deposit is simply a means of releasing a portion of the cash behind the original time deposit. Even though demand deposits are unchanged at the end of this example, time deposits are increased, and they have been increased by spreading the cash behind the original time deposit so as to support additional time deposits, the borrower's note being accepted to cover the portion of time deposits not covered by cash. The liquid asset (time deposit) has thus been substituted for the illiquid asset (borrower's promissory note), the prime condition of the substitution being that cash need not be 100 per cent of time deposits.

Savings banks and savings and loan associations can also create liquid assets in exchange for borrowers' promissory notes. This can be illustrated through the following example. Assume that the savings and loan industry is operating with what it considers a minimum ratio of cash to deposits (or share accounts). Assume that the Federal Reserve Bank purchases $1 million Treasury bills from an individual or from a business corporation. (For simplicity, the intermediation of the government security dealer is ignored). Assume that the seller of the Treasury bills deposits the $1 million proceeds in a savings and loan association. Savings and loan associations maintain their cash reserves in the form of deposits, either at a Federal Home Loan Bank or at a commercial bank. Assume that the savings and loan association deposits the $1 million in a commercial bank. As a result of the Federal Reserve Bank purchase, deposits at the savings and loan association have increased $1 million, demand deposits at the commercial bank have increased $1 million, and the cash-to-deposit ratio of both the savings and loan association and the commercial bank has been increased.[9] The commercial banking system can now proceed to expand (create credit) in the familiar way; but *in addition* to the commercial bank credit creation, the savings and loan association is also now in a position to create credit.

Assume that the savings and loan association makes a mortgage

---

[9] It could be argued that, at this point, the savings and loan association has created $1 million, since it is clear that, had the association not been involved in the example, the Federal Reserve purchase of bills would have involved only a $1 million increase in commercial bank deposits. But since the case for savings and loan credit creation can be made independently, it will be assumed that all credit creation up to this point has been by the Federal Reserve Bank.

loan for $500,000, and delivers to the borrower a check in that amount drawn on its commercial bank account. At this moment, the savings and loan association has increased the total volume of liquid assets available to the public. It has not decreased the volume of its own deposit liabilities, but it has relinquished to the public control over a part of a demand deposit originally held behind its deposit liabilities. It should be observed that this credit creation is separate and distinct from any credit creation by the commerical bank or by the Federal Reserve Bank.

The above credit creation need not end the process, any more than the similar activity by the commercial bank will call a halt to the subsequent process of credit creation. If the mortgagor now pays the $500,000 to an individual who is selling him a piece of property, and this individual then deposits the amount in a second savings and loan association, the cash-to-deposit ratio of this second savings and loan association will then be raised and it will be in a position to create credit by releasing a part of the cash behind this most recent deposit liability. The process can then go on, until the original cash deposit at the commercial bank has formed the basis for, perhaps, twenty times that amount of savings and loan deposits. This subsequent credit creation need involve no credit-creation activity by the commercial banking system, although, as was pointed out earlier, the commercial banking system could *independently* be expanding on the basis of the original $1 million cash received.

It is quite possible that at some point the recipient of the proceeds of a mortgage loan by a savings and loan association may pay the proceeds to an individual or corporation which will deposit it in the commercial banking system. At this point, the commercial banking system would pick up the process and continue it just as it had been going on in the savings and loan industry. Similarly, credit creation begun in the commercial banking system can jump over into the savings and loan industry and continue within that industry.[10]

The credit-creation process which has been described above for commercial bank demand deposits, commercial bank time deposits, savings bank deposits, and savings and loan deposits can also occur in other financial institutions, and even in nonfinancial institutions. Any institution (or individual) whose liabilities are more liquid than

[10] An important distinction occurs here, however, and is discussed later in footnote 16. At this point, it should be noted that even when credit creation jumps to another industry, this does not halt its continuance within the commercial banking system.

the promissory notes which it takes in, and which is able to maintain less than 100 per cent cash against those liabilities, can create credit. This is so, of course, because the term "create credit" means simply that the stock of liquid assets in the hands of the public is increased.

The answer to the second of the questions listed above as likely to be considered by the National Monetary Commission is therefore that credit creation occurs throughout our economic system and can be accomplished not just by commercial banks but by most financial institutions and by many nonfinancial institutions and individuals.

NONBANK FINANCIAL INSTITUTIONS AND FEDERAL RESERVE POLICY

The fact that institutions other than commercial banks can create liquid assets is obviously important to monetary policy. If liquid assets other than demand deposits have some influence on prices and the level of business activity, and if the volume of liquid assets in the hands of the public can be varied through the activities of nonbank institutions, it is conceivable that nonbank institutions could frustrate a monetary policy which was effectuated solely through pressure applied to the commercial banking system. The question might be raised whether the powers of the Federal Reserve Board should be extended so that the Board could apply direct pressure to all liquid-asset creation wherever it might occur in the economy. Gurley and Shaw have, in fact, jumped to this conclusion, and recommended what they call "financial control" as the successor to "monetary control."[11]

The general stream of thought, of which the work of Gurley and Shaw constitutes a part, forms a healthy questioning and refinement of monetary theory. On the other hand, the public policy recommendations which have accompanied some of these theoretical discussions do not appear to have been carefully thought through. The remainder of this section is devoted to a number of important theoretical and practical points regarding nonbank financial institutions which have been overlooked in previous discussions of this subject.

Direct Control of Liquid-Asset Creation

Those who advocate more direct control of liquid-asset creation wherever it may occur throughout the economy greatly underestimate the extent of the power necessary to accomplish this task. Credit creation occurs in almost every segment of the business world. It has been

[11] John G. Gurley and E. S. Shaw, "Financial Aspects of Economic Development," *American Economic Review,* Vol. XLV, No. 4, p. 537.

popular to speak as though credit were created only by financial institutions. This is of course a great oversimplification. Trade credit extended by nonfinancial corporations is an important element in the monetary-financial structure. In some years—particularly years of tight money—credit extended by individuals to the mortgage market becomes very important. Furthermore, liquid assets need not be in the form of debt, but may be equities. Whenever a corporation issues new stock, and then releases to circulation the cash realized through the security flotation, it increases the total supply of liquid assets in the hands of the public. An increase in the total outstanding supply of the stock of nonfinancial corporations may have a much greater influence on prices and business activity than the credit-creating activities of some types of financial institutions whose liabilities are not considered particularly liquid by the general public. Similarly, a rise in stock values on the Exchange constitutes an increase in the value of liquid assets in the hands of the public. There is no question that changes in the value of stock have an important psychological influence on spending plans and thus on prices and business activity.

The examples cited above are by no means a complete enumeration of all the various ways in which the supply of liquid assets in the hands of the public may change. The examples do, however, give some idea of the extent and degree of control which would be necessary in the modern economy to exert direct pressure on credit creation wherever it occurs. It is clear that it would be necessary to control all extension of debt, whether by financial institutions or by nonfinancial institutions and whether by corporations or by individuals. It would also be necessary to control not only the volume of net new issues of stock but also the general level of stock prices. Quite apart from the question of freedom, the task imposed on the central monetary authority in controlling and policing the economy in this fashion would be tremendous. Fortunately, as will be explained later, it is not necessary to control each type of credit creation directly. The question is discussed here only to show that those who advocate this approach have apparently not realized the pervasiveness of credit creation in the economy.

The Degree of Liquidity of Different Assets

There has also been insufficient emphasis on the fact that it is the *degree* of liquidity of different assets which measures their importance for monetary policy. Any asset which can be sold, or will command other goods and services in exchange, has some degree of liquidity.

The influence which a given asset has on prices depends, however, on (a) how readily the asset can be turned into cash or otherwise used to command other goods and services in exchange, and (b) how frequently the public thinks of this asset as a potential cash generator or "purchasing asset." There is, for example, a ready market for used automobiles in this country, so that automobiles can under normal circumstances be turned into cash quite easily. They have, in other words, a certain degree of "liquidity," and it must therefore be granted that the existence of a stock of used automobiles in the hands of the public has some effect on prices. It would be unrealistic, however, to charge the Federal Reserve with the function of controlling the volume of used automobiles in the hands of the public. Even though this stock of automobiles has some effect on prices, the fact that the public does not ordinarily think of used automobiles as a cash-generating or "purchasing" asset means that, *as liquid assets*, they do not have an important effect on prices.[12]

The characteristics of an asset which cause it to have a monetary influence are therefore (a) a high degree of liquidity, and (b) little or no use value. The most important types of assets which fit this category are coins and currency, commercial bank demand deposits, commercial bank time deposits, deposits or share accounts in savings banks and savings and loan associations, and all continuously traded debt and equity securities *in the hands of the spending public*.[13] These

---

[12] In addition to having certain of the characteristics of a liquid asset, an automobile has a use value. That is, it can be used, not only to acquire other goods and services in exchange, but also to generate services itself. Where an asset has use value, its employment as a cash generator or purchasing medium will be minimized. An example of an intangible asset which has a certain degree of liquidity and also has a high use value is a life insurance policy. Most life insurance policies have a "cash value," i.e., cash may be realized, either by surrender of the policy or by borrowing under the policy loan provision. The protection purpose, or use value, for which the policy was bought, however, minimizes its liquid-asset characteristics in the mind of the policyholder. Life insurance companies "create assets" when they issue life insurance policies and lend or invest a good portion of the net proceeds of those policies, but the asset which they create has a low liquidity in the minds of the public, partly because the asset itself is nontransferable, partly because cash can be realized from the asset only under certain conditions laid down in the policy contract, and partly because the asset has a high use value.

[13] It might be noted that securities held by financial institutions, such as banks and savings and loan associations, are not purchasing assets according to the above definition, because these securities do not increase the spending plans of the financial institutions which hold them. It is the deposits of these institutions, and not the securities held against them, which influence spending. Similarly, vault cash is not a purchasing asset as long as it is held by a bank.

assets might be called "purchasing assets" because they are held primarily not for any use value which they themselves possess but because they give command over other goods and services.

Although all the liquid assets mentioned in the previous paragraph influence prices and business activity to a significant degree, there are nevertheless wide differences even within this group in the degree of monetary influence. Two rough guides to the degree of monetary influence are (a) the relative convenience of the asset as a purchasing medium, and (b) the frequency of turnover, or "velocity," of the asset. All the assets listed above can be used, without great inconvenience, to secure other goods and services. But there is no question that coin, paper money, and demand deposits are in the most convenient form for exchanging for other goods and services. The next group in order of convenience is made up of time deposits at commercial banks, and savings deposits and share accounts at savings banks and savings and loan associations. Somewhat less convenient, but nevertheless reasonably available for exchanging purposes, are debt and equity securities having a continuously traded market.

Wide differences in the degree of monetary influence of the above assets are also shown by differences in their velocity, although this characteristic is less useful in the case of securities. Demand deposits outside New York City have had an annual rate of turnover of over twenty times in recent years. Time deposits at commercial banks, on the other hand, have a velocity of only about 0.7 per year. Savings deposits at commercial banks turn over about 0.5 per year, and deposits at savings banks and shares of savings and loan associations have a turnover rate of about 0.25 per year.[14] Velocity is, unfortunately, not helpful as a measure of monetary influence in the case of securities because "withdrawals" from the securities market are frequently for trading purposes rather than for the purchase of goods and services.

The above discussion indicates that sweeping demands for direct monetary controls on all financial institutions have not properly taken

[14] George Garvey, *The Development of Bank Debits and Clearings and their Use in Economic Analysis,* Washington, D.C., Board of Governors of the Federal System, 1952, and "Velocity of Time Deposits," *Journal of the American Statistical Association,* Vol. 48, No. 262, June, 1953, pp. 176-91.

For recent data on the velocity of commercial bank demand deposits, see the *Federal Reserve Bulletin;* for recent data on savings and loan association withdrawal ratios and turnover rates, see Federal Home Loan Bank Board *Savings and Home Financing Source Book.*

account of the fact that (a) many financial institutions create assets which have virtually no monetary influence; (b) assets having some monetary influence are frequently created by nonfinancial institutions, or even by individuals; and (c) even among those assets having significant monetary influence, there is so wide a difference in velocity as to suggest strongly that monetary policy can be effectively administered through concentration on the volume of demand deposits.

Federal Reserve Policy and the Non-Bank Community

Perhaps the most serious defect in the demand for "financial control" as the successor to "monetary control" arises from a failure to appreciate the influence which present Federal Reserve credit control techniques bring to bear on the nonbank community. There is implicit in the argument for financial control the invalid assumption that nonbank financial institutions are not importantly affected by Federal Reserve policy, and that during a period when the Federal Reserve Board is attempting to curb credit extensions these nonbank institutions can frustrate Federal Reserve policy by continuing to move ahead unhampered in their creation of liquid assets. A more careful examination of our financial structure, however, shows that Federal Reserve policy does in fact exert strong pressure on nonbank institutions, both because of the relations of these institutions with the commercial banking system and because of the effect on their investment policies of changes in the price of debt instruments.

It will be recalled that the process of liquid-asset creation is made possible because the credit-creating institution is permitted to maintain less than 100 per cent in cash reserves against its liabilities. (Its liabilities being the liquid assets which it has created.) Financial institutions, including commercial banks, normally operate close to the minimum cash reserve position required either by law, by custom, or by their own estimate of the day-to-day need for cash. Although some further liquid-asset creation could always be squeezed out of the system without an addition to cash reserves, a major increase in the volume of liquid assets can normally occur only if there is an increase in cash reserves. In the case of commercial banks, for example, once they have expanded deposits to the legal maximum relative to reserves at the Federal Reserve Banks, further creation of credit can occur only if member-bank reserves are increased (perhaps through an inflow of gold, or the purchase of government securities in the open market by the Federal Reserve Bank of New York).

The situation of nonbank financial institutions is similar to that of commercial banks, except that, whereas the basic reserves for the commercial banks are maintained as deposits with the Federal Reserve Banks, the basic reserves of nonbank institutions are maintained as deposits (normally demand deposits) with the commercial banks. Just as the volume of the deposit liabilities of the Federal Reserve Banks sets an upper limit to the liquid-asset creation of the commercial banks, so the volume of the deposit liabilities of the commercial banks sets an upper limit to the liquid-asset creation of the nonbank financial institutions. The total credit structure may therefore be thought of not simply as a single inverted pyramid, but as two inverted pyramids one on top of the other. The Federal Reserve stands at the base of the lower pyramid and provides ultimate liquidity to the whole credit structure. By controlling the volume of their own deposit liabilities, the Federal Reserve Banks set an upper limit not only to the deposit liabilities of the commercial banks but also to the liabilities of all those institutions which use the deposit liabilities of the commercial banks as cash reserves.

As an illustration, assume that the Federal Reserve exerts sufficient pressure on member-bank reserves so that the normal growth of deposit liabilities of the commercial banks is halted, and the total of these deposit liabilities is held approximately constant over the course of a year. This means not only that commercial banks are unable to create additional deposits but also that the reserves of the whole nonbank community are held constant. If the nonbank community is already operating with minimum reserves—as will probably be the case under the assumed Federal Reserve policy—then it will be extremely difficult for the nonbank sector *as a whole* to expand credit further.[15] Individuals and institutions in the nonbank sector will no longer be able to gain reserves through an expansion in the total of such reserves; they must now bid these reserves away from alternative holders. The reserves of individuals as a group can expand only if the reserves of nonbank institutions as a group decline. A given industry, such as the savings and loan industry, can gain reserves only at the expense of other industries or individuals. The ability of the nonbank sector of the economy to expand credit under these circumstances is

---

[15] If cash reserves are not at an absolute minimum, a small amount of additional liquid-asset creation could occur. This process of squeezing liquidity out of the whole economic system is the normal result as Federal Reserve restraint is applied. It is the intent of the Federal Reserve not to bring credit creation to an abrupt halt, but to make it more and more difficult to expand on the basis of limited cash reserves.

obviously quite different from the situation obtaining when Federal Reserve policy is permitting an expansion in the deposit liabilities of the commercial banks, and thus in the cash reserves of the nonbank sector.

In addition to the effect of Federal Reserve policy on the cash reserves of nonbank institutions, these institutions are also importantly affected by the changes in the price of debt instruments caused by changes in monetary policy. The ability of financial institutions to make new loans is dependent primarily on the volume of their normal cash flow, but is also greatly influenced by their willingness to unload existing assets. A policy of credit restraint on the part of the Federal Reserve is promptly reflected in declining prices for Government securities, so that financial institutions become reluctant to take the loss which would be necessary in order to augment their normal cash flow through sales of Governments. The fact that fluctuations in Government security prices impose strong pressures on the lending policies of financial institutions is supported not only by the opinions of lending officers but also by clear statistical evidence in studies made by the Federal Reserve Board.

Although it is easy to show the effect of Federal Reserve policies on the Government-security-portfolio decisions of private financial institutions, it is more difficult to demonstrate statistically that the total liquid asset creation activities of nonbank financial institutions are importantly affected by Federal Reserve policies. This difficulty is not, however, confined to nonbank institutions but exists also where an attempt is made to show the effect of Federal Reserve policies on commercial bank deposit-creation activities. A Federal Reserve policy of credit restraint is normally imposed during a period of rapid growth of the economy, accompanied by inflation or the threat of inflation. During such a period of rapid growth, there is of course a strong demand for credit so that the assets of both bank and nonbank institutions would be expected to be growing at above average rates. Logically, therefore, a policy of Federal Reserve credit restraint could be expected to be accompanied, at least during its early stages, by *above* average growth in credit, not because the credit restraint policy has no effect, but because the credit restraint policy is normally invoked during boom times. In other words, the statistics do not reveal what would have happened in the absence of credit restraint, so that it is impossible to measure statistically the effect of the credit restraint.

It is possible, however, to determine whether cyclical changes in

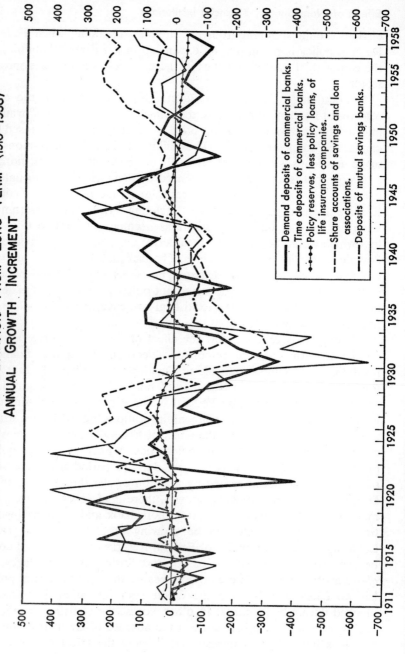

ANNUAL INCREMENT IN LIABILITIES OF MAJOR FINANCIAL INSTITUTIONS
AS A PERCENTAGE DEVIATION FROM LONG TERM (1910-1958)
ANNUAL GROWTH INCREMENT

Demand deposits of commercial banks.
Time deposits of commercial banks.
Policy reserves, less policy loans, of life insurance companies.
Share accounts of savings and loan associations.
Deposits of mutual savings banks.

the growth rates of nonbank institutions follow somewhat the same course as cyclical changes in the growth rate of commercial banks. The accompanying Chart shows percentage deviations from the long term growth trends of the liabilities of commercial banks, mutual savings banks, savings and loan associations, and life insurance companies. It will be seen that there is a similar cyclical deviation in the growth of the liabilities of these financial institutions, with changes in the growth of demand deposits exhibiting a clear lead both on the downturn and on the upturn.[16] This similarity of pattern with a lead by commercial banks is what would be expected on the basis of prior discussion in this chapter. Variations in the rate of growth of the nonbank community are dependent on prior variations in the rate of growth of commercial banks, because the deposits of the commercial banks, which form the cash reserves of the nonbank community, set a maximum limit to liquid-asset creation outside the banking system.

From the preceding discussion it may be concluded that present Federal Reserve credit control techniques exercise a strong influence on credit creation wherever it may occur throughout the economy. There appears to be little evidence that present monetary control techniques should be superseded by some type of "financial control." Although there is still a great deal to be learned about the proper use of Federal Reserve monetary policy, the most productive avenue for future study lies in the direction of a more careful understanding of

[16] Some authors have confused the question of cyclical variations in the growth of different types of financial institutions with the long-term growth trends themselves. Differences in long-term growth trends of various financial institutions are not a matter of direct concern to the Federal Reserve Board, since that Board is not charged with the duty of determining the public's preference for different types of financial institutions. The Board *is* concerned with the long-term growth of commercial bank demand deposits because, as has been explained, these deposits form the cash reserves for the entire economic community. On the question of relative long-term growth trends, it might be noted that while the commercial banking system is under the disadvantage of bearing the first impact of credit restraint, it also has the advantage of having its long-term growth guaranteed, a guarantee not accorded to any other single type of financial institution. It is also clear that nonbank financial institutions as a group cannot grow unless there is a corresponding growth in the demand deposits of commercial banks. This follows from the fact that (a) if a demand deposit is withdrawn from a commercial bank and deposited in a savings and loan association, for example, this deposit is not lost to the commercial banking system because the savings and loan association is also a depositor at a commercial bank, and (b) nonbank financial institutions as a group cannot grow unless their cash reserves (demand deposits with the commercial banking system) also grow.

the application of present techniques, rather than toward a multiplicity of new controls.

SUGGESTED READINGS

Books

GOLDSMITH, RAYMOND W., *A Study of Saving in the United States,* Princeton, Princeton University Press, 1955.

————, *Financial Intermediaries in the American Economy Since 1900,* Princeton, Princeton University Press, 1958.

HELLER, BODDY, and NELSON, *Savings in the Modern Economy,* Minneapolis, University of Minnesota Press, 1953.

INSTITUTE OF LIFE INSURANCE, *Life Insurance Fact Book,* 488 Madison Avenue, New York.

LINTNER, JOHN, *Mutual Savings Banks in the Savings and Mortgage Markets,* Cambridge, Harvard University Press, 1948.

PROCHNOW, HERBERT, *American Financial Institutions,* New York, Prentice-Hall, Inc., 1954.

U.S. SAVINGS AND LOAN LEAGUE, *Savings and Loan Fact Book,* 221 N. LaSalle Street, Chicago.

Articles

ASCHEIM, JOSEPH, "Commercial Banks and Financial Intermediaries: Fallacies and Policy Implications," *Journal of Political Economy,* Vol. LXVII, No. 1, February 1959, pp. 59–71,

CROTEAU, JOHN T., "The Large Credit Union," *Journal of Finance,* Vol. XI, No. 3, September 1956, pp. 347–62.

CULBERTSON, J. M., "Intermediaries and Monetary Theory: A Criticism of the Gurley-Shaw Theory," *American Economic Review,* Vol. XLVIII, No. 1, March 1958, pp. 119–31, and "Reply" by Gurley and Shaw, pp. 132–38.

GURLEY, J. G., and SHAW, E. S., "Financial Aspects of Economic Development," *American Economic Review,* Vol. XLV, No. 4, September 1955, pp. 515–38.

————, "Financial Intermediaries and the Saving-Investment Process," *Journal of Finance,* Vol. XI, No. 2, May 1956, pp. 257–76.

HAYWOOD, CHARLES F., "A Comment on 'The Federal Home Loan Bank System and the Control of Credit,'" *Journal of Finance,* Vol. XIII, No. 4, December 1958, pp. 542–44, and "Reply" by Gordon W. McKinley, pp. 545–46.

KLAMAN, SAUL B., "Mortgage Companies in the Postwar Mortgage Market," *Journal of Finance,* Vol. XII, No. 2, May 1957, pp. 148–58.

MCKINLEY, GORDON W., "The Federal Home Loan Bank System and

the Control of Credit," *Journal of Finance,* Vol. XII, No. 3, September 1957, pp. 319–32.

O'LEARY, JAMES J., "The Institutional Savings-Investment Process and Current Economic Theory," *American Economic Review,* Vol. XLIV, No. 2, May 1954, pp. 455–70.

ROBERTSON, ROSS M., "The Commercial Banking System and Competing Nonmonetary Intermediaries," *Monthly Review,* Federal Reserve Bank of St. Louis, Vol. XXXIX, No. 5, May 1957, pp. 61–69.

————, "Do We Really Need a National Monetary Commission?" *Business Horizons,* University of Indiana Bureau of Business Research, June 1957.

SHELBY, DONALD, "Some Implications of the Growth of Financial Intermediaries," *Journal of Finance,* Vol. XIII, No. 4, December 1958, pp. 527–41.

SMITH, WARREN L., "On the Effectiveness of Monetary Policy," *American Economic Review,* Vol. XLVI, No. 4, September 1956, pp. 588–606.

TOBIN, JAMES, "Asset Holdings and Spending Decisions," *American Economic Review,* Vol. XLII, No. 2, May 1952, pp. 109–23.

Chapter 11

SERVICE AND SUPERVISORY FUNCTIONS OF THE FEDERAL RESERVE SYSTEM

Introduction

IT is difficult today to appreciate the hindrances and expenses once imposed upon economic activity by recurrent currency shortages, sometimes culminating in money panics; by the cumbersome transfer of cash from bank to bank, or from city to city, in order to pay check-clearing balances; by the ten or fifteen or twenty days needed for collecting a check drawn on a bank in a not-far-distant city; by the exchange charges that were levied on the holder of a check; by the gnawing fear of a bank failure. Where once there was sand in the economic machine, there is now a smoothly functioning lubricating system.

The preamble to the Federal Reserve Act can remind us of the sand, however:

. . . To provide for the establishment of Federal reserve banks, to furnish an elastic currency, to afford means of rediscounting commercial paper, to establish a more effective supervision of banking in the United States, and for other purposes.

Two of the three specified purposes in establishing the Federal Reserve Banks seem to have been concerned with the subject matter of this chapter; the other, originally closely connected with the "elastic currency," has grown until the subject of credit policy and its execution accounts for the bulk of this volume. It is a measure of the success our monetary and banking system has achieved in correcting the shortcomings so evident before 1914 that the success is now taken for granted, and attention is now almost completely concentrated on the objective of economic growth and stability, perceived only in embryo when the Act was passed.

THE MONEY-PAYMENTS MECHANISM

It is a truism among economic writers that a barter economy is wasteful since it requires a producer needing something he cannot himself produce to spend time and effort locating another who has what is needed and who will also take what is offered, and that the invention of money resulted in a more efficient economy. Extending this analysis, one comes to the conclusion that—in this limited sense at least—the best money mechanism should require the least time and effort of the user. Or, to return to the metaphor of the sand and lubrication, it should produce the least possible amount of friction in the economic machine. Such an analysis would go far to explain the Federal Reserve System's interest in the money-payments mechanism: why air transport is used to cut check collection time; why Federal Reserve Banks pay the cost of shipping checks, coin, and currency; why they have people working around the clock; why they engage research engineers to help develop more efficient machines; why they maintain a leased wire system that makes possible the transfer of funds between member banks anywhere in the nation within an hour. Well over half of the employees of the Federal Reserve Banks work on the money-payments mechanism.

CHECK CLEARING AND COLLECTION

About a century ago, total bank deposits in the United States exceeded currency and coin in circulation for the first time; since then the gap has widened. Today demand deposits alone are four times the amount of money in circulation, and it is estimated that checks drawn on such deposits are used for more than 90 per cent of all money payments made. The number of checking accounts in this country has increased during the last twenty years from less than 27 million to almost 54 million;[1] in the same period the number of checks drawn has approximately tripled. On an average business day, about 40 million checks are being deposited or cashed in this nation's banks, with about 8 million being deposited or cashed in the same bank (or one of its branches) on which it is drawn. The other 32 million

[1] *Federal Reserve Bulletin*, May 1958, p. 533.

checks a day are collected through the facilities of the banking system. Because they are, for the most part, collected swiftly and efficiently, they have become widely acceptable—and even preferred, since they entail less risk of loss or theft than would coin and currency—as a means of payment.

In 1957 it is probable that 10 billion checks were used to make payments aggregating $3.3 trillion.[2] The Federal Reserve Banks handled about a third of these checks, with the remainder being collected largely through the correspondent banking system, local clearinghouses, or within the banks (and their branch offices) on which they were drawn. One of the reasons for the great growth in the use of checks has been the contribution of the Federal Reserve System in functioning as a national clearinghouse for settlement of balances and in developing and encouraging speedier collection at par (the face amount of the check).

For the most part, a Federal Reserve Bank acts as a kind of middleman between the bank in which a check is deposited and the bank on which it is drawn. From banks within its District, a Federal Reserve Bank receives checks drawn on other banks both within and outside the District. It also receives from other Federal Reserve Banks, and from direct-sending[3] banks in other Districts, checks drawn on banks in its District. All the checks drawn on banks within its District must first be sorted according to the drawee banks, and then sent to those banks (or be presented to the drawee banks through the local clearinghouse). Checks drawn on banks outside the District are sorted according to the Federal Reserve Bank or Branch through which they are to be collected, and are then sent to that point.

The machine operators performing this sorting operation also list the amount of each check on an adding machine tape, identifying the bank from which received and to which sent, and stamp the endorsement of the Federal Reserve Bank on the back of the check. The tape record makes it possible to "prove" the dollar amount of incoming checks against the sum of the outgoing, as well as to verify the amount a depositing bank claims it has sent to the Reserve Bank.

[2] *American Banker,* January 22, 1958, p. 2; February 19, 1958, p. 1.

[3] A bank that regularly has a substantial volume of checks to be collected by a Federal Reserve Bank or Branch outside its own area may be requested, in the interest of speedier presentment and payment, to sort out such checks and to send them directly to the collecting Reserve Bank or Branch (or, if in the same city as a Reserve Bank or Branch, to consolidate its shipments with those of the local Federal Reserve office). The cost of such direct sendings is paid by the Federal Reserve.

Generally speaking, a Federal Reserve Bank will accept checks for collection from member banks and from "nonmember clearing banks" in its District.[4] It will also receive from other banks checks "drawn on all member and nonmember clearing banks of its District, and checks drawn on all other nonmember banks of its District which are collectible at par in funds acceptable to it."[5]

Checks are called cash items, and packages of checks sent to a Federal Reserve Bank, together with an accompanying list of the amounts of individual checks, are called cash letters. (Cash items may also include Government checks, postal money orders, and certain other items collectible at par in funds acceptable to a Reserve Bank.) Banks sending cash letters to a Federal Reserve Bank do so under the terms and conditions set forth in Regulation J of the Board of Governors and in the operating circular or letter of the Reserve Bank. These terms and conditions specify the responsibilities of the Reserve Bank and of the depositing bank, and the extent of the liability each assumes, thus detailing the contractual arrangements under which the checks will be handled.

AVAILABILITY SCHEDULE AND FLOAT

Probably the most important of the terms is the availability or time schedule. This operating circular (letter) specifies the time at which credit will be given in the depositing bank's reserve (or nonmember clearing) account for checks received by the Federal Reserve Bank. Thus, checks drawn on banks that are members of the New York Clearing House will be credited on the same business day if received by the New York Reserve Bank in sufficient time for it to process and present them at the final clearing (10 A.M.) that day. Checks drawn on banks in most other Federal Reserve Bank and Branch cities are credited one calendar day after receipt, and checks on banks outside such cities are credited two business days after receipt.[6]

---

[4] A nonmember bank that maintains "with its Federal Reserve Bank a balance sufficient to offset the items in transit held for its account by the Federal Reserve Bank." Regulation J, as amended, effective January 1, 1949, Section 1.

[5] *Ibid.* Checks drawn on nonpar banks (those that remit less than the full amount of a check, deducting a small percentage as a fee for handling or as an exchange charge) are not accepted for collection. Member banks must remit at par. On December 31, 1957, there were 1,741 nonpar banks in the United States and Alaska. *Federal Reserve Bulletin,* February 1958, p. 203.

[6] See "Operating Circular No. 5," Federal Reserve Bank of New York, for full details.

Although no Federal Reserve Bank defers credit for checks more than two business days after receipt, there are many checks which cannot be collected within that period, principally those deposited in banks in one Federal Reserve District but drawn on banks that are located in other Districts and outside of cities having Federal Reserve Banks or Branches, as, for example, a check deposited in an Albany bank that is drawn on a Santa Fe bank. This is the most important reason for failure to collect checks within the time schedule. In addition, delays in transportation or inability of a Reserve Bank to process and ship all checks on the day they are received will occasionally result in collection delays. When a Federal Reserve Bank gives credit in a depositing bank's account, even though it has not yet actually collected payment for the check or checks involved, float is created. This float, which constitutes funds valid for satisfying reserve requirements, is outstanding as long as the checks remain uncollected beyond the day when, according to the time schedule, credit is given for them. (Usually, this excess period is only a day or two.) Since, as we have seen, the Reserve Banks handle for collection more than a trillion dollars' worth of checks in the course of a year, float can mount to substantial proportions; recently, it has ranged from daily low points of about $700 million to peaks near $2 billion.

There is a clearly discernible monthly pattern in check writing: the Federal Government issues most of its checks at the beginning of the month, while individuals and businesses tend to write more checks about the middle of the month than in the first or last weeks of the month. As a result, banks find themselves with a more-than-average volume of checks to process in mid-month, and a less-than-average volume a couple of weeks later. During the days of peak volume, it may happen that not every check is processed on the day it is received, and the float rises, thus giving the banking system reserve funds. The float rises to especially high levels during December, when mail delays and, frequently, bad weather slow down transportation at a time when the banking system is struggling to cope with an extremely large volume of checks. (As it happens, the December bulge in float is not altogether unwelcome to the Federal Reserve System, since it serves to offset the simultaneous drain on banks' reserve accounts resulting from the expansion of money in circulation.)

The Federal Reserve Banks collect approximately $5 billion of checks on an average day, but there may be $1 billion of float on each such day, despite swift air transportation and specially arranged trucking service between airports and the Banks. There has been criticism of the float, on the ground that uncollected funds should not be credited to member banks' accounts, there to serve as valid reserves against the banks' deposit liabilities. It is not practicable, however, to account individually for each check, crediting the collected proceeds only as word is received that the drawee bank has remitted funds for that check; such a procedure would require a multiplication of staff in the commercial banks as well as in the Reserve Banks.[7] An alternative that has been advanced is to extend the availability schedule, that is, to change some Federal Reserve cities from one-day points to two days, and some other cities from two days to three. Another problem inherent in float is, of course, that it complicates the task of the Manager of the System Open Market Account in his day-to-day operations. The float can rise or fall as much as $300 million from one day to the next, with consequent important effects on the money market. It is extremely difficult to predict accurately the amount of float on any given day, although considerable progress has recently been achieved through coordinated telegraphic reports to the Manager of the Open Market Account from all the Federal Reserve Banks and Branches.

RETURN ITEMS

When the Federal Reserve Bank sends a cash letter to a drawee bank, that bank is supposed to make payment for the checks presented on the day the letter is received. The payment may be made by authorizing the Reserve Bank to deduct the amount involved from the drawee bank's reserve (or nonmember clearing) account, or it may be made by draft on a correspondent bank located in the same city as the Reserve Bank. It usually happens that a bank remits for a cash letter before the checks involved have been examined and posted to ledgers, and that after examination and posting it is found that some checks are improperly endorsed, or are drawn against insufficient funds, or for some other reason will not be paid by the drawee bank. The bank thereupon returns these items to the Federal Reserve Bank, (usually) deducting the sum from the remittance due on the next day's cash letter. The Federal Reserve Bank, in turn, returns

[7] If the Federal Reserve Bank of Philadelphia had handled all checks processed in the first half of 1938 as collection items (individually), it would have needed a force of 6,864 employees instead of an actual force of 228. Wallace M. Catanach, *Check Collections,* New Brunswick, N.J., The Graduate School of Banking, 1939.

such an item to the bank from which it was originally received. If, as is most likely, that depositing bank has already received credit in its account for the check now returned, the amount of the credit is revoked. (The depositing bank will, of course, do much the same thing with the customer who deposited the check, who must in turn have recourse to the maker.)

INTERDISTRICT SETTLEMENT FUND

This procedure for paying or returning items will suffice when checks are deposited in and drawn on banks in the same Federal Reserve District. When, however, a check is drawn on a bank in one District and deposited in a bank in another, the payment must be (normally) deducted from the reserve account of one bank (A) by its Reserve Bank (X), then transmitted to another Reserve Bank (Y) for credit to the account of the depositing bank (B). This transfer of funds from one Federal Reserve Bank to another is done through the Interdistrict Settlement Fund, a gold certificate account maintained in Washington, to which all the Reserve Banks have contributed. Each day, therefore, a Reserve Bank will calculate the total of all checks it has sent to all the other Reserve Banks, or, to put it another way, the amounts payable to it by each of the other Federal Reserve Banks.[8] It will then notify the Settlement Fund through the Federal Reserve privately leased wire system of these amounts. The net differences, calculated in Washington, are then paid, or received, by debits and credits to individual Reserve Bank accounts in the Fund. In effect, therefore, movements of money from one part of the country to another are made by transfers of gold holdings from one Reserve Bank to another.

Large commercial banks in banking centers also collect checks, both for member and nonmember banks. Many member banks, for example, prefer to send their checks to correspondent banks for collection because they do not then have to sort the checks, as they might be required to by the Federal Reserve Bank. One large commercial bank in New York City handled more than 350 million checks for

[8] This is, obviously, a much simplified statement for purposes of describing the principles involved. It would be necessary to calculate also the total of items sent directly to other Federal Reserve Banks by direct-sending banks of the District, the day credit is to be made available according to the time schedule, the amounts of cash letters consolidated in the Reserve Bank's shipment, the amount of items returned, etc.

collection in 1957, compared with 600 million items processed by the Reserve Bank in New York. These correspondent banks, with specialized equipment and several shifts of trained employees, sort the checks received, clear those drawn on banks in the same city through the local clearinghouse, (usually) send those drawn on par-remitting banks in the same District to the local Reserve Bank or Branch, and sort others by Federal Reserve Districts in order to consolidate such shipments with those the local Reserve Bank sends to the airport for dispatch to the other Reserve Banks and Branches.

Whether collected through the correspondent banks or the Reserve Banks, the emphasis during sorting and sending is always on speed, so that the depositor of the check can have the use of his money, or be informed of nonpayment of the check, as soon as possible. Prompt presentment to the drawee bank also militates against kiting operations, which can involve banks and depositors in substantial losses. In order to speed up presentment, another procedure has developed considerably in recent years: the clearing arrangement, under which banks in a county, for instance, will agree to send checks drawn on other banks in the same county directly to the drawee banks. The sending bank also transmits to the Reserve Bank a statement of checks sent to other banks in the arrangement, and the Reserve Bank calculates the net clearing balances for each of the banks in the arrangement, and makes the necessary debits or credits to their accounts (in much the same way as is done for a local city clearinghouse).

NONCASH ITEMS

Noncash items include maturing notes, acceptances, certificates of deposits, bills of exchange, drafts, bonds, coupons, warrants, and other evidences of indebtedness and orders to pay.[9] Federal Reserve Banks accept such items from member and nonmember clearing banks, acting as agents of the banks in presenting the items at the time and place payable.[10] A Reserve Bank usually asks a local member bank to act as its collection agent for items payable outside a Reserve Bank or Branch city; generally speaking, there is little or no charge for this

[9] See Regulation G, Board of Governors, and relevant Operating Circulars of Federal Reserve Banks for full details of acceptable items and terms and conditions of collection.

[10] Except for obligations (matured bonds and due coupons) of the United States and its agencies, or of the International Bank for Reconstruction and Development, which a Federal Reserve Bank pays as fiscal agent.

service, except for out-of-pocket expenses incurred. While the volume of this business is much smaller than that of cash items, it is nonetheless considerable. In 1957 the Federal Reserve Banks handled more than 18 million noncash items worth $5.5 billion.

Except for bankers' acceptances and (bond) coupons, credit for the net proceeds of collection is given only upon receipt of actually and finally collected funds.

WIRE TRANSFER

A Federal Reserve Bank will make telegraphic transfers of funds (bank balances) to other Reserve Banks or Branches in multiples of $1,000 for member banks to member banks without charge. In addition, Reserve Banks will telegraphically transfer funds for member banks, in any amount, and for the use of any company or individual, for a charge that approximates but does not exceed the commercial wire rate for the telegram involved in the transfer.[11] (Transfers of funds will also be made by mail at no charge on request by a member bank, but these transfers are today much less significant than the wire transfers.) The volume of wire transfers of funds has grown sharply and steadily during the last decade; in 1957 the Reserve Banks handled 2¼ million transfers aggregating $1,300 billion, compared with 1.15 million for $316 billion in 1947.

Probably the most important reason for the growth in the volume of funds transferred by wire in the last decade has been the development of the Federal funds market. As interest rates rose from the low levels of World War II, and as banks and their corporate customers became aware of the ease and speed with which large sums could be moved throughout the country, or be mobilized in one place, to take advantage of such rates for a day or a week (the earnings on each million dollars, in the Federal funds market or in Treasury bills, is about $28 each day for each per cent of interest rate), the total dollars transferred by wire mushroomed. Another aspect of this development is, of course, the economizing by depositors on cash balances and the steady postwar rise in velocity of deposits. The growth is also linked to the expanding use of wire transfer facilities for Treasury securities (discussed below) and the functioning of a truly national money and securities market place in New York City. For the student of the

[11] See, for example, Operating Circular No. 10 of the Federal Reserve Bank of New York.

money market, one of the most interesting sights in a visit to the Federal Reserve Bank of New York is the facsimile transmission mechanism linking that Bank to the large downtown member banks, for here one can see almost the only visible manifestation of the money market, as orders to transfer funds emerge continuously from the machines. More than $2 billion move from bank to bank over this equipment on an average day, with the sums rising much higher during a period of Treasury financing. Settlement for these transfers between Federal Reserve Districts is made through the Interdistrict Settlement Fund, as in the case of checks.

CURRENCY AND COIN OPERATIONS

As we have seen, one of the chief reasons for the creation of the Federal Reserve System was to "furnish an elastic currency," the marked absence of which had much to do with the Money Panic of 1907. In the minds of the framers of the Federal Reserve Act there was a direct link with the rediscounting of commercial paper, which was to become part of the backing for the currency so furnished; that is, as member banks rediscounted some of their farmer and businessman promissory notes with a Federal Reserve Bank, the latter could increase its issue of currency. Thus, it was believed, the amount of money in circulation would rise as the economic need for money rose and would contract as economic activity receded. (In addition to the commercial paper backing, there was also of course a requirement for a 40 per cent gold cover.)

In 1932 the Glass-Steagall Act permitted the Reserve Banks to use Government securities as collateral for their notes. (This permission, which had to be renewed frequently until 1945, was then made permanent.) Another change (1945) reduced the gold cover to 25 per cent. (This is, of course, the legal minimum; in 1958, the Federal Reserve Banks had gold backing of almost 50 per cent behind their combined note and deposit liabilities.) At present, therefore, there can be little doubt that the Reserve System can furnish the economy with an elastic currency (with almost $10 billion of excess gold reserves, it is able to issue up to $40 billion of currency should it be needed), and that one of the objectives of creating the System has been achieved. Indeed, as other chapters of this volume indicate and as our postwar financial history has demonstrated, the problem of this generation is more likely to be one of a too-elastic money supply.

All United States coin is produced by the Treasury Department through its Bureau of the Mint, which operates (in 1958) mints at Philadelphia and Denver.[12] The mints maintain a "reservoir" of coins, shipping from time to time to the thirty-six Federal Reserve Banks and Branches located throughout the country, where smaller reservoirs are also maintained, so that demands of banks and the public can be quickly satisfied. The Reserve Banks and the Treasury estimate annually the probable needs for coin (and, together with the Board of Governors, for currency) so that adequate and economical production schedules can be planned for the ensuing year. No attempt is made, of course, to limit the amount of money in hand-to-hand circulation, the objective of both the System and the Treasury being always to satisfy the requirements of the public.

Virtually all coin (and currency) is issued through the Federal Reserve Banks to commercial banks and, through them, to the public. The Federal Reserve Banks pay the face value of all coin received from the mints, crediting the payment to the Treasury's accounts on their books. (The Reserve Banks subsequently receive payment from banks to whom they pay the coin, by debiting the reserve or nonmember clearing accounts.) Since the cost of the silver and other metal in the coin, and the expense of manufacturing, is less than the face value, the Treasury obtains an income from the coining process.[13]

In addition to coin, the Treasury also produces, through the Bureau of Engraving and Printing, two kinds of paper currency: silver certificates (currently) issued in $1, $5, and $10 denominations; and United States notes, issued in $2 and $5 denominations.[14] The silver certificates represent pledges of silver held by the Treasury and are redeemable in silver on demand; they are produced as the Treasury buys domestically mined silver under the Silver Purchase Act of 1934, so that the outstanding amount of these certificates has risen steadily year by year.[15] The United States notes, by contrast, have been held at approximately $300 million for almost a century; first issued as fiat money to help finance the Civil War, they have since received some gold cover.

[12] In 1957, these mints produced $71 million of subsidiary silver (half-dollars, quarters, and dimes), and $22 million of minor coin (nickels and cents). Bureau of the Mint, monthly reports.

[13] About $50 million in 1957; see *Treasury Bulletin*, March 1958, p. 60.

[14] At the end of 1957, there were $2.4 billion of silver certificates outstanding, and $347 million of United States notes, compared with a total of $28.6 billion of Federal Reserve notes.

[15] In the ten years ending with 1957, the volume of silver certificates rose $150 million.

The Federal Reserve Banks pay for Treasury currency as they do for coin.

FEDERAL RESERVE NOTES

The nation's needs for currency above the amount the Treasury can issue (which is of course limited by the amount of silver purchased and the authorized maximum of United States notes) are met by Federal Reserve notes. These are issued in denominations of $5, $10, $20, $50, $100, $500, $1,000, $5,000, and $10,000, in response to public demand, and must have as collateral backing at least 25 per cent in gold certificates, with the balance of up to 75 per cent in Government securities or certain other eligible paper specified in the Federal Reserve Act. The gold certificates represent pledges of gold held by the Treasury (the nation's "monetary gold stock"); the Federal Reserve Banks have paid for these certificates by crediting the Treasury's account with the $35-per-ounce value of the gold. Normally, when a foreign country sells gold to the Treasury, the Treasury pledges the gold with the Reserve Banks and thus recovers the amount of the payment made to the seller of the gold; when a foreign country buys gold from the Treasury, the latter must redeem the gold certificate held by the Federal Reserve, and then recover the redemption cost when the foreign country pays for the gold.

Federal Reserve notes are produced, like the Treasury currency, under the direction of the Comptroller of the Currency at the Bureau of Engraving and Printing, which uses the same special paper and much the same kind of engraving plates. The notes are issued by (and through) the individual Federal Reserve Banks, each note bearing a seal, letter, and numerical designation identifying the Bank of issue. Each Reserve Bank, therefore, shows in its statement of condition the amount of its notes outstanding as a liability, and of course each Bank pledges 100 per cent collateral in gold certificates and securities (or other eligible collateral) for the full amount of its notes outstanding. The collateral is pledged with the Federal Reserve Agent (who is also chairman of the board of directors of the issuing Bank), who in this capacity acts as agent of the Board of Governors of the Federal Reserve System. Customarily, a reservoir of currency is maintained at the Bureau of Engraving and Printing, and another reservoir at the Federal Reserve Banks and Branches in the custody of the Agent. These supplies of Federal Reserve notes are unissued; that is, they may not be put into circulation (and will not be released by the Agent) until collateral has been pledged by the issuing Bank. Federal Reserve notes are also a first lien on all other available assets of the Reserve Banks, and are guaranteed by the United States Government. The Reserve Banks pay only the cost of producing their notes (about one cent per note, no matter what the denomination) and the expense of shipment from Washington to the Reserve Bank or Branch; this expense amounted to more than $6 million in 1957, a year when Federal Reserve notes outstanding rose by about $60 million.

The currency needs of the country vary considerably during the year, rising by well over a billion dollars between Thanksgiving and Christmas and then falling by a larger amount to an annual low point before Easter. In addition, there are minor peaks at each month's end, and other peaks before holidays. A Federal Reserve Bank seeks to make sure it has enough issued currency in its vaults to meet these seasonal needs. Before 1954, when the Federal Reserve Act was amended, this problem was complicated by a prohibition against a Reserve Bank's paying out the notes of another Reserve Bank; since such a payment is now permitted, a Bank has fewer occasions when it must have recourse to the Agent's supply of unissued currency.[16]

Because member banks may not count coin and currency in their possession as part of their required reserves (see Chapter 5), they seek to keep these cash holdings to a minimum. They will, therefore, send any amounts they estimate to be greater than they need to take care of their customers to the Reserve Bank for credit to the reserve account.[17] If the member bank is located in or near a Reserve Bank or Branch city (and thus can quickly get cash in the event of need), it may deposit one day and withdraw only two or three days later. Except for banks located in Federal Reserve cities, the cost and risk of shipment both ways are assumed by the Federal Reserve Bank.

A statute (Public Law 86–114, approved July 28, 1959) now gives the Federal Reserve Board discretionary authority pursuant to regulation to permit member banks to count all or part of their currency and coin on hand (so-called vault cash) as reserves required to be maintained under Section 19 of the Federal Reserve Act. This provision, which is now effective, thus ends the prohibition dating back to 1917 on the inclusion of cash on hand in member bank reserves.

[16] The amendment also made possible significant economies by reducing the amount of sorting and other handling required, the cost of transportation and printing, and other minor expenses.

[17] There are other reasons for a bank to keep its cash to a minimum: available vault space, risk of loss or theft, cost of insurance coverage, for example.

This change in the previous law will in time prove important to member banks generally, and particularly to country member banks. It should be noted that the Board has unlimited discretion to determine when and to what extent all or one or more classes of member banks may count vault cash in computing their reserve requirements. It was the intention of the Congress that this authority would be exercised by the Board as monetary conditions at a given time warrant.

When coin or currency is deposited by a bank,[18] the Reserve Bank must verify the amount (by counting); sort as to fitness for additional circulation; detect and remove counterfeit, foreign, or other unacceptable money; and repackage the fit notes and coins for payment. The notes and coins judged unfit, because of wear or mutilation, for further circulation are destroyed, the coins being sent to a mint for melting, the Treasury currency being destroyed by the Reserve Banks, and the Federal Reserve notes being sent to the Treasury for verification and destruction.[19] To replace the unfit money withdrawn from circulation, and to satisfy any additional needs, the Reserve Banks issue new coin and currency. If a Reserve Bank has an amount of fit currency on hand greater than it is likely to need for a time, it can retire some of its own notes by returning them to the Agent (who will release an equal amount of collateral), or it can return the notes of other Reserve Banks to the Banks of issue.

FISCAL-AGENCY OPERATIONS

Almost from their beginning, the Federal Reserve Banks have served as fiscal agents, custodians, and depositaries for the United States Government and its various departments and agencies. Most of this work is of course done for and in close cooperation with the Treasury, the Banks being reimbursed for most of the expense incurred.[20] Since the Treasury, the Post Office, the Defense Department,

[18] Depositing banks are asked to segregate coins and currency by denominations, and to package them in specified units. See, for example, Operating Circular No. 3, Federal Reserve Bank of New York.

[19] Federal Reserve notes to be destroyed must be sorted according to the Bank of issue, so that the liability of the issuing Bank, and the collateral pledged, may be reduced correspondingly. The canceled notes are sent to the office of the Comptroller of the Currency, where they are actually destroyed.

[20] In 1957 these reimbursed expenses amounted to about $18 million. One reason that Reserve Banks are paid for services for the Government is that expenses must be included in the Governmental budget and that Congress must appropriate the necessary funds; if the services were free, there would be no Congressional review of the appropriateness of the Governmental activity involved.

the Commodity Credit Corporation, the Federal National Mortgage Association, and many other Governmental instrumentalities have financial transactions throughout the country, the widely dispersed banking services, trained personnel, vault facilities, and advice of the Reserve Banks and their Branches are useful to the Government.

The great bulk of Federal Governmental spending is done by checks drawn against balances maintained by the Treasury in the Federal Reserve Banks; in 1957 almost 500 million such checks were issued. Most of the Government's income is also in the form of checks, paid to directors of Internal Revenue, for instance, who may deposit them with Federal Reserve Banks for credit to the Treasury accounts. Most of the Treasury's receipts now go first into tax and loan accounts; these accounts are in commercial banks that have qualified (under Treasury regulations) as special depositaries.[21] The Reserve Banks administer these accounts on behalf of the Treasury, maintaining records, making sure that the depository has collateral (usually Government securities) at the Reserve Bank at least equal to the amount of the deposits, and notifying the depositary when the Treasury decides to shift some of its balances at special depositaries to its accounts at the Federal Reserve Banks (as it must do to replenish the balances against which checks are constantly being drawn).

Because the movement of money from private checking accounts or from the tax and loan accounts in commercial banks to the Treasury accounts at the Federal Reserve Banks represents a loss of reserves to the banking system (the amounts being deducted from member banks' reserve accounts), and because large sums can be involved ($5 billion or more at quarterly tax-payment dates, an amount in excess of a quarter of all bank reserves), every effort is made to keep such disturbing movements to a minimum. In practice, the Treasury attempts to keep a balance of about $500 million at the Reserve Banks, replenishing it at the same rate that money is spent, and making "calls" on the special depositaries relatively frequently for relatively small amounts.[22]

[21] About 11,000 of the nation's 14,000 banks have qualified as special depositaries. *Monthly Review*, Federal Reserve Bank of New York, April 1, 1958, which also provides a more detailed explanation of the operation of the tax and loan accounts.

[22] It is estimated that in 1957 more than $50 billion moved through the tax and loan accounts; the balance in the accounts varied between $6 billion and $1 billion.

ISSUE AND TRANSFER OF SECURITIES

These tax and loan accounts may also receive funds in payment for new securities issued by the Treasury. In this connection, the Federal Reserve Banks also perform another function as fiscal agent of the United States. When the Treasury decides to offer a new security, it will request the Reserve Banks to print an announcement of the offering and to distribute copies to all those (banks, savings and loan associations, insurance companies, corporations, brokers, dealers, etc.) known to be interested. Applications to subscribe to these issues are received by the Reserve Banks, which transmit the information to the Treasury. The latter then calculates how much it wishes to allot on each subscription (such issues are invariably oversubscribed), and the Reserve Bank notifies each applicant. A similar procedure is followed when the Treasury is refunding (that is, offering a new security or securities in exchange for a maturing one), except that allotment is normally not involved. In any case, the method of payment for the securities is specified by the Treasury: in maturing securities, in cash (that is, funds at a Reserve Bank or the Treasury on the payment date), or in a credit to a tax and loan account. (Payment for Savings Bonds is normally received by a bank and credited to the tax and loan account of the Treasury.) Finally, as payment is made, the Reserve Banks will issue the new securities, acting as the Government's fiscal agent. During the life of the security, the Reserve Banks will be ready to make denominational exchanges (for example, to issue five $1,000 bonds for a $5,000 one, or vice versa), to pay interest coupons as they fall due, and to redeem the security upon maturity.

In order to make denominational exchanges and to transfer securities by wire, the Federal Reserve Banks keep a supply of unissued Treasury securities on hand.[23] A typical transaction in which securities may be transferred by wire might be the sale of a Treasury bill by a securities dealer in New York City to a bank in Salt Lake City. The dealer would deliver the Treasury bill to the Federal Reserve Bank of New York, requesting that it be delivered to the Salt Lake City Branch of the Federal Reserve Bank of San Francisco, where it

---

[23] At the New York Reserve Bank, in the major money and securities market of the nation, such unissued stock of Government securities normally amounts to $60 billion or more, while the volume of securities issued, exchanged, and redeemed in the course of a year might reach $400 billion.

is to be paid for by the investing bank. The New York Reserve Bank would thereupon wire the Salt Lake City Branch to issue a Treasury bill, of like maturity and denomination, against payment by the buyer to be wired to New York; concurrently, the New York Bank would "retire" the Treasury bill delivered to it. Such a transaction might be completed within an hour. The facilities thus made available assure buyers and sellers of Government securities anywhere in the country that they can deal in the market most advantageous to them, regardless of location, and they also assure the Treasury that it always has a truly national market for its securities. Before the development of this wire transfer service, shipment of securities from the place of purchase, or to the place of sale, meant substantial expense in time and money (three or four days, and as much as $150 per $1 million of securities.) [24]

In addition to their fiscal-agency work in connection with marketable issues of the United States Government, the Federal Reserve Banks also play an important part in the Savings Bond program. They designate, under Treasury regulation, both issuing agents and paying agents, keep the voluminous records involved, supply the issuing agents with stocks of Savings Bonds, reimburse paying agents for the bonds they redeem and for their expenses, and, of course, act as issuing and paying agents themselves. As fiscal agents, the Reserve Banks also work with certain Government departments (the military services, Atomic Energy Commission, General Services Administration, etc.) that guarantee loans made by financing institutions to the departments' contractors who lack adequate working capital. In this work, the Reserve Banks advise on the terms of the loan contract, service the loan during its life, and administer payments made under terms of a loan. [25]

The Federal Reserve Bank of New York acts as fiscal agent of the International Bank for Reconstruction and Development, exchanging and redeeming its securities much as it does for the Treasury. It also acts as depositary and custodian, not only for the World Bank, but also for the International Finance Corporation, the International Monetary Fund, and the United Nations. In this same international finance

[24] By contrast, wire transfer is made, usually without charge, of Government securities maturing within a year; when a fee is charged, it is only $5 or $10 (which goes to the Treasury). See Operating Circular No. 17, Federal Reserve Bank of New York.

[25] See Regulation V, Board of Governors of the Federal Reserve System.

area, it operates as the agent of the Treasury in gold and foreign-exchange transactions.

ECONOMIC AND FINANCIAL PUBLICATIONS

All of the Federal Reserve Banks and the Board of Governors collect and study economic information, primarily for the purpose of formulating and administering credit policy. Most of this information is made available to the public in press releases and in publications in order to improve understanding of the economy and of the reasons for Federal Reserve policy. The Federal Reserve System "believes that public understanding helps to make effective a credit and monetary policy designed to foster stable economic development and a stable dollar. The more fully the public understands the issues involved, the simpler and easier credit and monetary administration can be. Accordingly, System publications undertake to present objective, authoritative, and comprehensive discussions of economic and financial trends, together with related statistical series."[26]

Among the more important publications of the Board of Governors are the monthly *Federal Reserve Bulletin,* the monthly *Federal Reserve Chart Book on Financial and Business Statistics,* and the Annual Report. Each of the Reserve Banks publishes a *Monthly Review,* covering business and credit conditions, usually in the District of the Reserve Bank, and most of the Banks publish Annual Reports that review and comment upon developments during the year. In addition, there are special releases (later incorporated in the *Bulletin,* for the most part) that present statistics weekly on the assets and liabilities of the Reserve Banks, changes in factors affecting member bank reserves, the assets and liabilities of member banks in 107 of the leading cities, and so on. These data provide early indications not only of changes in banking conditions but also, through such statistics as those on loans to business firms, of trends in business conditions. Weekly releases are also provided by each of the Reserve Banks on department-store sales, and the Board publishes such significant monthly data as the index of industrial production, the volume of consumer credit outstanding, and the dollar amount of debits to demand deposit accounts (from which the velocity of checkbook money is derived). The Board and the Banks also publish special booklets

[26] Board of Governors of the Federal Reserve System, *The Federal Reserve System—Purposes and Functions,* Washington, D.C., 1954, p. 164.

and monographs from time to time, usually the products of studies undertaken for the use of the System. In short, the economic research staffs of the System (numbering almost 500 people) produce or use a vast quantity of economic data and make many studies of trends and developments; much of this information is then made available to the public at little or no cost.

SUPERVISORY FUNCTIONS

Banking is a business with a strong element of public interest, largely for two reasons: as we have seen, banks are an essential part of our money mechanism because they can create a most important form of money (Chapter 4) and because they facilitate money payments, and banks are the source for the largest segment of short-term credit needed by business firms; farmers; consumers; Federal, state, and local governments; and others. A special kind of charter has therefore been required before a bank is allowed to begin operations, and afterward the bank is subject to continuing supervision and surprise examination. The principal purposes of this supervision are to try to make sure that banks are operated in such a way that the public's deposits are safe, that the essential credit needs of the economy can be satisfied, that the banks remain strong and vigorous so that they can contribute to the maximum extent possible to the smooth functioning of the economy, and that stockholders' investments are used prudently.

The task of bank supervision is both more urgent and more complicated because of the nature of our banking system in the United States. (In the United Kingdom, for example, there is no examination of banks.) First, there are more than 14,000 banks in this country (compared with fewer than a dozen of significance in Canada or Britain); second, there is a multiplicity of chartering and supervising authorities, and a mass of legislation specifying what banks may and may not do.[27] A further "direct cause of the type of bank supervision, with its detailed laws, regulations, and examinations, that has developed in this country, is the fact that the management of banks has been frequently entrusted to men without particular training for banking and the further fact that the earnings of many banks have been

[27] In addition to the Federal Government and the fifty states, the governments of Puerto Rico and the Virgin Islands, which are in the Second (New York) District, also charter and supervise banks.

too small to permit the employment of well-trained and capable officers."[28] The work of the supervisory authorities is essentially that of satisfying themselves that a bank's assets are sound, that it is being operated in accordance with applicable laws and regulations, and that its management is qualified.

CAPABILITIES AND LIMITATIONS

Bank supervision cannot be a substitute for management; the responsibility for decisions, as well as the power to make them, rests with bank directors and officers. But good supervision can help individual banks to improve, and it can help to raise the level of competence of the banking system. It can, and does, offer constructive criticism, make valuable suggestions derived from experience gained in examining other banks with similar problems satisfactorily handled, and lend experts to banks desirous of improving their operations or controls.

An examiner, when he and his associates make a surprise entrance into a bank, will seek to check all the assets and liabilities as they appear in the general ledger, evaluate the quality of the assets, appraise the ability of the management, ascertain and evaluate the general nature of the bank's policies, judge the soundness and prudence of the lending and investing policies, and, finally, produce a reasonable estimate of the present condition of the bank, its management, and its prospects.

There are many who confuse a bank examination with an audit, and who express surprise that an examination has not disclosed what soon after is discovered to have been a protracted defalcation. An examination, however, does not seek to verify the liabilities, as an audit customarily does. It is, of course, usually through the manipulation of actual or fraudulent depositors' accounts that an embezzlement is carried out and temporarily concealed. Nor can the examiner verify the genuineness of every signature on checks, deposit slips, or promissory notes. Indeed, the purpose of an examination is quite different from the purpose of an audit. One of the things an examiner does try to determine, however, is that the auditing procedures are adequate

[28] R. F. Leonard, "Supervision of the Commercial Banking System," *Banking Studies*, Washington, D.C., Board of Governors of the Federal Reserve System, 1941, p. 191.

and that satisfactory controls are maintained on both asset and liability accounts.

Probably the most important and the most difficult phase of the examiner's work is the appraisal of the loans and lending policy, and the investments and investment policy. Here, a careful study of the available facts—the nature of the loan, the record of interest payments, amortization, renewals or extensions, the nature of the collateral, the borrower's net worth and business, might be some of the things available in the bank's files, supplemented by a visit to the borrower's place of business or to real estate pledged—and then an equally careful application of judgment, based on wide and long experience, are indispensable. At the end of this process, an examiner may classify certain loans as less than satisfactory; the worst of these he may ask the management to write off against the reserves set up for this purpose. In addition to evaluating the soundness of the loans made, the examiner is at the same time able to form impressions of the management's lending policies, its competence in obtaining adequate credit information about the borrower at the time of extending credit and then maintaining current information about the borrower's financial condition during the life of the loan, and the efficiency of the office and paper work involved in granting, reviewing, and servicing loans. When an examiner has questions about the soundness of a loan, or about its current status, he will discuss these questions with the lending officers or senior management of the bank, thus gaining opportunity for further evaluation of the quality of management. An appraisal of the bank's investments is made from the same general point of view, except that here the usual financial manuals are readily available to check on credit (investment) rating. It is important, moreover, for the examiner to assess the soundness of judgment displayed by management in spreading the maturities of investments, particularly in arranging for maturities at times of recurring seasonal needs for funds, and—in the aggregate—allocating types of investments in a manner consistent with the nature and velocity of the deposit liabilities, as, for example, time and demand, individual and corporate, church and municipal.

An examination should also appraise the adequacy of the bank's capital in the light of its assets and liabilities, its type of operation, the economic characteristics of the community it serves, and the demands likely to be made upon it. Usually this consideration begins by dividing the bank's assets into riskless (cash, short-term Government securities), risk (loans, long-term and other securities), and fixed (real estate) assets, and then attempts to estimate reasonable sums for each degree of risk to which the bank—and, of course, the depositors and stockholders—is exposed. Closely related to the capital position is the adequacy of the bank's earnings relative to the amount and nature of its deposits, the possibility of losses to be absorbed, the current dividend rate, and the economic trends in the area it serves. Comparisons may be made with other banks in similar circumstances; this procedure obviously affords an easy way, though only one of several, to appraise the efficiency and quality of the management.

In summary, while the primary purpose of examination is to protect the public interest in the banking system, the approach is always to be as helpful as possible. When criticisms are made of loans, investments, operating practices, or policies, suggestions are also made for correction and prevention. The examiner's wide experience with other banks in comparable circumstances enables him to pass on the benefits of his knowledge and judgment. The examiner's report is made to the directors of the bank, so that these officials, who are legally responsible for the bank's operations, can have an independent and expert view of their institution.

SUPERVISORY AGENCIES

Bank chartering, regulation, examination, and supervision in the United States seem impossibly complicated and almost irrational to the foreigner making his first acquaintance with our banking system. Banks must of course receive a charter to do business, but each of the fifty states and in addition the national Government is empowered to, and does, charter and supervise banks. Moreover, a second agency of the Federal Government examines and regulates them, also. The shorthand description of this state of affairs is usually "the dual banking system." That such a spread of authority and responsibility should work at all, let alone as well as it does on the whole, is probably a tribute to the ability of reasonable men of good will to adjust themselves to an arrangement that stems from something fundamental to their political philosophies: the concept of a Federal union of sovereign states. This dual banking system of both state and national chartered banks also reflects the traditional American opposition to placing the control of money and credit in one person or agency (so that, typically, we have a decentralized central bank), lest control over money and credit lead to domination of all economic activity.

Thus, a group of men, dissatisfied with the banking facilities available to them in their community, or convinced that there is a profitable opportunity for a new bank, can turn to the Comptroller of the Currency (an official of the Federal Government's Treasury Department) in applying for a charter, or to the state's banking supervisor. In either case, the chartering agency will make a study of the economic need for, and the profit prospects for, a bank in the location specified in the application, as well as a credit and character investigation of the persons applying. If chartered, the bank will thereafter be examined periodically by the chartering agency, with the costs of the examinations assessed against the bank. In addition, since a national bank must be a member of the Federal Reserve System, and of the Federal Deposit Insurance Corporation, the Federal Reserve Bank of the District in which the proposed bank is to operate, and the FDIC, will be advised of the application and be given an opportunity to present their views to the Comptroller of the Currency. If applicants for a state charter also wish membership in the Federal Reserve System (and, therefore, in the FDIC also since a member bank must be insured), separate applications must be made. State member banks are thereafter examined by the Federal Reserve,[29] and insured nonmember banks by the FDIC.

This multiple examining, however, is more apparent than real. National banks, for example, are actually examined only by examiners, stationed about the country, working under the direction of the Comptroller of the Currency; copies of the reports of these examinations are available to the Federal Reserve and the FDIC. State member banks are examined, when practicable, jointly by teams drawn from the examining force of the local Federal Reserve Bank and the state supervisory agency, so that the bank is inconvenienced as little as possible. State nonmember insured banks are examined by the state examiners and those of the FDIC (which, like the Comptroller, has examining forces stationed in each of the Federal Reserve Districts). Finally, only the uninsured banks (a little more than 3 per cent of the total number of commercial banks) are examined only by the state chartering agency. Federal examiners from three national bank supervisory agencies therefore examine almost 97 per cent of the banks; in doing so, they operate under certain common standards

[29] The Federal Reserve Bank, however, makes no charge for examination.

accepted by agreement of the Comptroller of the Currency, the Board of Governors, and the FDIC in 1938. Since that time, a close and cordial cooperation between the Federal agencies and the National Association of Supervisors of State Banks has done much to establish high standards for banking and for bank supervision throughout the nation.

In addition to ascertaining the status of an individual bank, examination is also useful in giving the supervisory authorities some indication of the condition of all the banks under their jurisdiction. Mention has been made of the value of comparing one bank with another in similar circumstances; information obtained from a wide and representative sample of banks may also suggest the need for new regulations, interpretations, or general corrective action. Supplementary aids in this data-collecting process are periodic "calls" for statements of conditions, reports of earnings and dividends, or similar information. Such information, useful in the formulation of broader banking and credit policies, is collected and put into usable form by analysts who review the reports filed by examiners and by banks.

On occasion, critics of banks' lending and investing policies, or of the adequacy of Federal Reserve credit policy, have suggested that examination affords a valuable tool for exerting pressure on banks to relax standards of credit worthiness during a recession and to stiffen them during a boom. These suggestions have consistently been rejected by Federal Reserve officials, who have argued that the result would be a lack of any acceptable credit criteria and confusion among bankers and examiners, both of whom should center their attention on the prospects for repayment of the credit.

HOLDING COMPANIES

In addition to the general supervisory authority and responsibility discussed above, the Federal Reserve System has several special statutory duties: granting of trust powers, upon application, to national and State member banks (Regulation F); establishment of branches overseas by national banks and outside the head-office city by state member banks; regulation of loans by any bank for the purpose of purchasing or carrying securities (Regulation U); and supervision of holding companies (Regulations P and Y). Of these, the last duty is probably the most significant for the structure of banking in the United States.

In the Banking Act of 1933, the Federal Reserve Board was given authority to grant or deny permits to holding companies controlling a member bank to vote the stock of that bank. The law also provided for examination of the holding company, for maintenance of a liquid reserve by the company, and for restrictions on payment of dividends by the company. The Bank Holding Company Act of 1956 greatly increased the Board's authority over such companies, now defined in terms of control over two or more banks (member or nonmember). These companies were required to register with, and report to, the Board, and to subject themselves to examination. In effect, the Board is the chartering agency for bank holding companies, since applications must be made for new ones to be formed. Moreover, application must be filed when a registered holding company wishes to acquire control of another bank, and even, under some circumstances, to acquire bank shares. Holding companies were also required to divest themselves of ownership of any other companies not directly related to the banking business, and financial relations among the subsidiaries and with the parent holding company were subjected to regulation.

SUGGESTED READINGS

Bank Reserves—Some Major Factors Affecting Them (booklet), Federal Reserve Bank of New York, 1953. See "Demand for Cash during Holiday Periods" and "Federal Reserve Float."

BOARD OF GOVERNORS OF THE FEDERAL RESERVE SYSTEM, *Banking Studies*, Washington, D.C., 1941. Victor M. Longstreet, "Currency System of United States"; John E. Horbett, "Banking Structure of United States"; Robert F. Leonard, "Supervision of the Commercial Banking System"; Leo H. Paulger, "Policy and Procedure in Bank Examination"; and Edward L. Smead, "Operations of the Reserve Banks."

BOARD OF GOVERNORS OF THE FEDERAL RESERVE SYSTEM, *Federal Reserve System—Purposes and Functions*, 3rd ed., Washington, D.C., 1954. Chapter VI, "Relation of Reserve Banking to Currency"; Chapter XI, "Federal Reserve Service Functions"; and Chapter XII, "Supervision of Banks by the Federal Reserve."

The Treasury and the Money Market (booklet), Federal Reserve Bank of New York, 1954 (for fiscal agency services).

Chapter 12

REGULATIONS OF THE
BOARD OF GOVERNORS

RECOGNIZING that it would not be feasible to prescribe by statute complete details for regulating various phases of our banking system, and that any attempt to do so would result in too much rigidity in adjusting to constantly changing conditions, Congress has followed the practice in the Federal Reserve Act and elsewhere of laying down certain general principles and over-all policies and then authorizing the Board of Governors of the Federal Reserve System to issue Regulations for the purpose of carrying out and effectuating these principles and policies.

Although references are made in other chapters of this book to some of the Regulations of the Board of Governors of the Federal Reserve System, this chapter deals exclusively with the Regulations and their place in the over-all operations of the Federal Reserve System.

Authority for Issuance of Regulations

The general authority of the Board of Governors to issue Regulations is somewhat buried in the enumeration of powers given to the Board under Section 11 of the Federal Reserve Act. Paragraph (i) of this section provides as follows:

To require bonds of Federal Reserve agents, to make regulations for the safeguarding of all collateral bonds, Federal reserve notes, money or property of any kind deposited in the hands of such agents, *and said board shall perform the duties, functions or services specified in this Act and make all rules and regulations necessary to enable said board effectively to perform the same.*[1]

[1] 12 U.S.C. 248 (i). Italics added.

251

Throughout the Act, however, as well as in other statutes (such as the Securities Exchange Act of 1934, the Defense Production Act of 1950, and the Bank Holding Company Act of 1956), there are numerous provisions giving the Board of Governors authority to prescribe regulations in connection with specific matters. For instance, in Paragraph 8 of Section 4 of the Federal Reserve Act it is provided: "The Board of Governors of the Federal Reserve System may prescribe regulations further defining within the limitations of this Act the conditions under which discounts, advancements and the accommodations may be extended to member banks." In the subsequent discussion of the Regulations, reference will be made to some of the other pertinent statutes.

Considering the broad powers of the Board of Governors, it is clear that the authority to make rules and regulations is of great importance and, in effect, provides the mechanism for carrying out its various functions and services.

Preparation and Issuance of Regulations

An excellent statement regarding the procedures followed by the Board of Governors in the preparation and issuance of Regulations was made by Charles B. Dunn, a former General Counsel and First Vice President of the Federal Reserve Bank of Chicago, in an article written in 1941.[2]

. . . . After a thorough study of the legal, technical, and practical problems involved, a tentative draft of a regulation is prepared by the board's staff. Without being acted upon by the board, copies of this tentative draft are furnished to all twelve federal reserve banks, the Federal Advisory Council, a Committee of the American Bankers Association, the Comptroller of the Currency, the Federal Deposit Insurance Corporation, and any other interested governmental agencies, all of whom are invited to submit criticisms and recommendations in writing.

Each of the federal reserve banks confers with a number of its member banks and the tentative draft of the regulation is made the basis of study and discussion by a committee of the staff of the federal reserve bank after which their comments, criticisms and suggestions are transmitted to

[2] Charles B. Dunn, "The Organization and Functions of the Federal Reserve System," *The John Marshall Law Quarterly,* December 1941, p. 280. See also Section 2 of Rules of Procedure contained in a pamphlet entitled *Rules of Organization and Rules of Procedure,* issued by the Board of Governors. These Rules of Procedure are based upon Sections 3 and 4 of the Administrative Procedure Act (5 U.S.C. 1003 and 1004).

the board. Likewise, the other agencies submit their comments to the board for consideration.

After criticisms and suggestions have been received from all of these sources, they are assembled by the board's staff and thoroughly considered. If the revisions are very extensive, another draft of the regulation may be prepared and the same process repeated until differences of opinion are reduced to a minimum.

After members of the board have had ample opportunity to study and discuss the final draft of the regulation and the accompanying data submitted, the matter is brought up for consideration at a meeting of the board. If it is satisfied with the product, the regulation is adopted and promulgated in pamphlet form, copies being furnished promptly to all member banks, and, as far as practicable to every other person or organization affected by it. The effective date of the regulation is usually at least thirty days after the member banks have had time to receive copies. The text is then published promptly in the Federal Register and in the next issue of the board's monthly bulletin.

The board is always willing to give adequate consideration to requests from banks and other interested parties that the regulations be amended. They are also amended from time to time on the board's own motion in the light of changing conditions or in order to effect improvements in the light of experience. From time to time, as circumstances warrant, the regulations are revised and the same process usually is followed in connection with a revision or amendment if it includes any substantial or important changes. When, in the opinion of the board, a regulation serves no further useful purpose it is rescinded.

Since Mr. Dunn's article was written, the Board of Governors, in addition to the procedures which he described, usually publishes *proposed* Regulations in the Federal Register, thereby publicly inviting comments and suggestions before the Regulations are issued in final form. The only exceptions to this practice are those cases in which an emergency exists or where it is deemed unnecessary in the public interest.

From time to time the Federal Reserve Banks issue Operating Circulars containing data, information, and instructions based upon and supplemental to the Regulations. In addition, the Board of Governors prepares and issues rulings and interpretations with respect to questions that arise under the Regulations. These interpretations and rulings are usually issued in response to written requests from member banks or others affected by the Regulations.

Summary of Regulations

At present there are twenty-three Regulations, which are designated by letters running from A to Y, inclusive, except for Regulation W, dealing with Consumer Credit, which was suspended as of May 7, 1952, and Regulation X dealing with Real Estate Credit, which was suspended as of September 16, 1952. Although it would be possible to write at great length on many of the individual Regulations and their underlying legislation (as in the case of Regulation F, for instance, dealing with trust powers of national banks, or Regulation Y dealing with bank holding companies), there is set forth below a brief summary or discussion of each of the Regulations which are presently in effect, as well as a reference to the suspended Regulations W and X.[3]

REGULATION A   Advances and Discounts by Federal Reserve Banks

The importance of this Regulation is indicated by the following "General Principles" which were added in 1955 as a foreword to the actual text of the Regulation, and which incorporate much of the basic philosophy governing the extension of credit by the Federal Reserve Banks:

A principal function of the Federal Reserve Banks under the law is to provide credit assistance to member banks, through advances and discounts, in order to accommodate commerce, industry, and agriculture. This function is administered in the light of the basic objective which underlies all Federal Reserve credit policy, i.e., the advancement of the public interest by contributing to the greatest extent possible to economic stability and growth.

The Federal Reserve System promotes this objective largely by influencing the availability and cost of credit through action affecting the volume and cost of reserves available to the member banks. Through open market operations and through changes in reserve requirements of member banks, the Federal Reserve may release or absorb reserve funds in accordance with the credit and monetary needs of the economy as a whole. An individual member bank may also obtain reserves by borrowing from its Federal Reserve Bank at a discount rate which is raised or lowered from time to time to adjust to the credit and economic situation. The effects of borrowing from the Federal Reserve Banks by individual member banks are not localized, as such borrowing adds to the supply of reserves of the

[3] Copies of the Regulations in pamphlet form can be obtained upon request from any of the Federal Reserve Banks.

banking system as a whole. Therefore, use of the borrowing facility by member banks has an important bearing on the effectiveness of System credit policy.

Access to the Federal Reserve discount facilities is granted as a privilege of membership in the Federal Reserve System in the light of the following general guiding principles.

Federal Reserve credit is generally extended on a short-term basis to a member bank in order to enable it to adjust its asset position when necessary because of developments such as a sudden withdrawal of deposits or seasonal requirements for credit beyond those which can reasonably be met by use of the bank's own resources. Federal Reserve credit is also available for longer periods when necessary in order to assist member banks in meeting unusual situations, such as may result from national, regional, or local difficulties or from exceptional circumstances involving only particular member banks. Under ordinary conditions, the continuous use of Federal Reserve credit by a member bank over a considerable period of time is not regarded as appropriate.

In considering a request for credit accommodation, each Federal Reserve Bank gives due regard to the purpose of the credit and to its probable effects upon the maintenance of sound credit conditions, both as to the individual institution and the economy generally. It keeps informed of and takes into account the general character and amount of the loans and investments of the member bank. It considers whether the bank is borrowing principally for the purpose of obtaining a tax advantage or profiting from rate differentials and whether the bank is extending an undue amount of credit for the speculative carrying of or trading in securities, real estate, or commodities, or otherwise.

Applications for Federal Reserve credit accommodation are considered by a Federal Reserve Bank in the light of its best judgment in conformity with the foregoing principles and with the provisions of the Federal Reserve Act and Regulation A.

Section 2 of this Regulation provides that any Federal Reserve Bank may (a) make advances under the authority of Section 13 of the Federal Reserve Act to any of its member banks for periods not exceeding fifteen days on the promissory note of the member bank secured by direct obligations of the United States, or for periods not exceeding ninety days if secured by eligible paper (which is defined in Section 3 of the Regulation); or (b) may make advances under the authority of Section 10 (b) of the Federal Reserve Act for periods not exceeding four months upon the promissory note of any of its member banks secured to the satisfaction of such Reserve Bank, whether or not the collateral offered as security constitutes eligible paper. Advances made pursuant to (a) above are entitled to the discount rate then in effect at the Federal Reserve Bank granting the advance; whereas, advances made pursuant to (b) must be not less than one-half of 1 per cent higher than the discount rate.

The definitions of what constitutes eligible paper are fairly long and technical, but the most common type of paper used for this purpose is defined in paragraph (a) of Section 3 of the Regulation and consists of negotiable notes, drafts, and bills of exchange which mature within ninety days and the proceeds of which are used in producing, purchasing, carrying, or marketing goods, merchandise, or agricultural products.

It will be noted that, as pointed out in the "General Principles," access to the Federal Reserve discount facilities is a privilege rather than a right, and that Regulation A provides for advances only to member banks. However, a footnote indicates that in unusual or exigent circumstances advances may be made to others if secured by direct obligations of the United States. As a matter of practice, the advances to member banks secured by Government obligations are normally for the full fifteen-day period, but with a full right of prepayment on the part of the borrowing banks, so that they can adjust their borrowings from day to day.

Rates of discount are established by each of the Federal Reserve Banks, subject to review and determination of the Board of Governors, for discounts and advances within their respective Federal Reserve Districts. As an example of the general rate structure for advances under Regulation A and of how these rates may change from time to time, the following table, based upon Operating Circulars issued by the Federal Reserve Bank of Chicago to member and nonmember banks of the Seventh Federal Reserve District, shows the rates which were in effect in that district as of the dates indicated:

TABLE 1.   RATES OF DISCOUNT

(Operating Circular No. 10)

	As of Aug. 9, 1957 % Per Annum	As of Apr. 18, 1958 % Per Annum	As of Oct. 31, 1958 % Per Annum
Advances to member banks secured by obligations of the United States under Section 13	3½	1¾	2½

TABLE 1. *Continued*

	As of Aug. 9, 1957 % Per Annum	As of Apr. 18, 1958 % Per Annum	As of Oct. 31, 1958 % Per Annum
Discounts of eligible paper or advances thereon to member banks under Sections 13 and 13a	3½	1¾	2½
Advances to member banks under Section 10b secured by ineligible paper, including term loans, and other acceptable assets	4	2¼	3
Advances to individuals, partnerships, and corporations other than member banks, secured by direct obligations of the United States, under Section 13	4½	4	4

REGULATION B Open-Market Purchases of Bills of Exchange, Trade Acceptances, and Bankers' Acceptances Under Section 14

The title of this Regulation is generally descriptive of its contents, which consist of three relatively short sections. The first section simply refers to Section 14 of the Federal Reserve Act, which provides that, under rules and regulations to be prescribed by the Board, Federal Reserve Banks may purchase and sell in the open market, from or to domestic or foreign banks, firms, corporations, or individuals, bills of exchange eligible for discount, and bankers' acceptances, with or without the indorsement of a member bank.

The second section then prescribes the general character of bills and acceptances that are eligible for purchase by Federal Reserve Banks in the open market; and the third section provides for the furnishing of financial statements where bills and acceptances are not accepted or indorsed by any member bank.

REGULATION C Acceptance by Member Banks of Drafts or Bills of Exchange

This Regulation is divided into two sections, the first of which deals with the acceptance of commercial drafts or bills, and the second with acceptance of drafts or bills to furnish dollar exchange. Both sections set forth the types of drafts or bills that may be accepted, the maximum maturity (six months in the case of commercial drafts or bills under Section 1, and three months in the case of dollar exchange drafts and bills under Section 2), and limitations on the amount of acceptances from any one person or corporation, as well as on the aggregate amount of acceptances that a bank may have outstanding at any one time.

REGULATION D   Reserves of Member Banks

Regulation D, like Regulation A, is of great importance in carrying out the policy and basic functions of the Federal Reserve System. By raising and lowering the reserve requirements, the Board of Governors can exert a considerable degree of control over the amount of credit in the Federal Reserve System.

By reason of the higher reserve requirements for "demand deposits," as contrasted with "time deposits," the definitions of these two terms in Section 1 of Regulation D deserve careful attention. Without going into detail, it should be noted that demand deposits include all deposits except time deposits, which in turn are defined to consist of time certificates of deposit; time deposits, open account; and savings deposits.

Reserve requirements for demand deposits vary for different banks, depending upon whether the bank is located in a Central Reserve city, Reserve city, or elsewhere. For example, the reserves required to be maintained by member banks as of January 1, 1959, were as follows:

1. If not in a Reserve or Central Reserve City:
   a. 5 per cent of time deposits, plus
   b. 11 per cent of net demand deposits.
2. If in a Reserve city (except as to banks in outlying districts where reserves specified in paragraph 1 above may apply):
   a. 5 per cent of time deposits, plus
   b. 16½ per cent of net demand deposits.
3. If in a Central Reserve city (except as to banks in outlying districts where reserves specified in paragraph 1 or 2 above may apply):
   a. 5 per cent of time deposits, plus
   b. 18 per cent of net demand deposits.

The above requirements are set forth in Supplements to Regulation D and may be changed from time to time by the Board of Governors, "in order to prevent injurious credit expansion or contraction," within the following limitations prescribed by the Federal Reserve Act:[4]

1. As to time deposits—not less than 3 per cent or more than 6 per cent.
2. As to demand deposits:
   a. If not a Reserve or Central Reserve city, not less than 7 per cent or more than 14 per cent.
   b. If a Reserve city, not less than 10 per cent or more than 22 per cent.
   c. If a Central Reserve city, not less than 10 per cent or more than 22 per cent.

The designation of Central Reserve cities and Reserve cities is made by the Board of Governors, which notifies the various member banks from time to time of any change in classification. The only two Central Reserve cities are New York and Chicago, and as of January 1, 1959, the list of Reserve cities was as follows:

Indianapolis, Indiana	Wichita, Kansas
Des Moines, Iowa	St. Paul, Minnesota
Milwaukee, Wisconsin	Columbus, Ohio
National City (National Stock Yards), Illinois	Toledo, Ohio
	Tulsa, Oklahoma
Pueblo, Colorado	Fort Worth, Texas
Kansas City, Kansas	Washington, D.C.
Topeka, Kansas	Miami, Florida

and cities, except New York and Chicago, in which there is situated a Federal Reserve Bank or a branch of a Federal Reserve Bank. In recent years there has been a growing feeling that the classification of Central Reserve cities should be eliminated as being discriminatory against the banks in New York and Chicago and as no longer serving any useful purpose.[5]

The third and last section of Regulation D provides for computation of deficiencies in reserve balances, penalties for such deficiencies, and steps to be taken if a member bank does not pay due regard to maintenance of its reserves.

[4] 12 U.S.C. 462, as amended July 28, 1959. See *Federal Reserve Bulletin,* February 1958, "Seasonal Factors Affecting Bank Reserves," p. 122.
[5] Public Law 86-114, approved July 28, 1959 deals with reserves of member banks and contains a provision for the termination of the classification of Central Reserve cities on July 28, 1962.

REGULATION E   Purchase of Warrants

This Regulation implements Section 14(b) of the Federal Reserve Act, which provides that every Federal Reserve Bank shall have power to buy and sell tax-anticipation warrants in accordance with rules and regulations prescribed by the Board of Governors of the Federal Reserve System. It defines what warrants are eligible for purchase and sets up certain limitations on the amount of warrants that may be purchased by any Federal Reserve Bank and from any single municipality.

REGULATION F   Trust Powers of National Banks

This is the longest of all the Regulations. The pamphlet on Regulation F issued by the Board of Governors contains thirty-four pages. Its primary statutory authority is Section 11(k) of the Federal Reserve Act, and it covers subjects ranging all the way from application for a permit to operate a trust department and rules for managing a trust department to procedures for the surrender of trust powers. In many respects, Regulation F is the bible for trust departments of national banks, and no trust officer of a national bank should neglect to become familiar with its provisions. To attempt to summarize these detailed provisions would serve no useful purpose since in many instances it would be necessary to quote the exact wording of the Regulation.

REGULATION G

Section 1 of Regulation G defines "noncash items," which broadly can be said to include practically all evidences of indebtedness and orders to pay, except checks, drafts, and other items handled as cash items under Regulation J, provided they are payable in a Federal Reserve District. Section 2 provides from what sources each Federal Reserve Bank may receive such items for collection; and Section 3 sets out the terms of collection, such as warranties and agreements on the part of the sending bank, rules for presentation and forwarding of items, forms of payments accepted by a Federal Reserve Bank, and other related matters.

As an illustration of how one Regulation may replace another with changing conditions, it should be noted that the designation "Regulation G" had previously applied to a Regulation relating to the rediscount by Federal Reserve Banks of notes secured by Veterans Bonus Certificates. This earlier Regulation was rescinded in 1939 and the present Regulation G became effective February 1, 1940.

REGULATION H Membership of State Banking Institutions in the Federal Reserve System

Regulation H covers various phases of membership by state banks, including eligibility requirements, procedures for application and admission, privileges and requirements of membership, rules for establishment and maintenance of branches, and voluntary withdrawal from the System.

One of the conditions of membership (Section 7) is that the net capital and surplus funds of any such bank shall be "adequate in relation to the character and condition of its assets and to its deposit liabilities and other corporate responsibilities." This section then provides that if at any time in the light of all the circumstances the aggregate amount of a member state bank's net capital and surplus funds appears to be inadequate, the bank, within such period as the Board deems reasonable, shall increase the amount thereof to an amount which the Board determines to be adequate.

REGULATION I Increase or Decrease of Capital Stock of Federal Reserve Banks and Cancellation of Old and Issue of New Stock Certificates

This Regulation implements the various sections of the Federal Reserve Act which require each member of the System to subscribe for and maintain capital stock of the Federal Reserve Bank in its respective district in a sum equal to 6 per cent of its paid-up capital stock and surplus. Under the Regulation, one-half of the subscription is payable at or prior to the time of approval of an application for Federal Reserve Bank stock, and the remaining one-half of the subscription is subject to call when deemed necessary by the Board of Governors of the Federal Reserve System.

Upon the happening of certain events, such as a decrease in capital and surplus of a member bank, the liquidation of a member bank, or a voluntary withdrawal from the System, provision is made for the cancellation of the appropriate amount of Federal Reserve Bank stock and for a refund of all cash paid for it.

There are special provisions in Regulations H and I relating to mutual savings banks, which, in general, are required, as a condition to membership in the System, to apply for and agree to maintain Federal Reserve Bank stock in an amount equal to six-tenths of 1 per cent of their total deposit liabilities.

REGULATION J   Check Clearing and Collection

The scope of Regulation J is indicated by the following excerpt from Section 2:

In pursuance of the authority vested in it under these provisions of law, the Board of Governors of the Federal Reserve System, desiring to afford both to the public and to the various banks of the country a direct, expeditious, and economical system of check collection and settlement of balances, has arranged to have each Federal Reserve bank exercise the functions of a clearing house and collect checks for such of its member banks as desire to avail themselves of its privileges and for such nonmember State banks and trust companies as may maintain with the Federal Reserve bank balances sufficient to qualify them under the provisions of section 13 to send items to Federal Reserve banks for purposes of exchange or of collection.

Section 3 specifies what checks and other items may be received as cash items for collection by the Federal Reserve Banks; Section 4 deals with availability of credits; and Section 5 spells out the terms and conditions under which the Federal Reserve Banks will handle checks and other items as cash items for member and certain nonmember banks. These terms and conditions include the guarantee of all prior indorsements by the sending bank, the time within which items must be returned by the drawee bank, and other important rules covering the collection of checks.

This Regulation should be compared with Regulation G, which, as previously noted, deals with the collection of noncash items.

REGULATION K   Corporations Doing Foreign Banking or Other Foreign Financing Under the Federal Reserve Act

Regulation K applies to foreign banks and foreign financing corporations organized under Section 25(a) of the Federal Reserve Act (often referred to as "Edge Act Corporations"), and also to state-chartered foreign banking corporations in which member banks participate under Section 25 of the Act. The Regulation defines in specific terms the conditions and limitations under which corporations may carry on business in foreign countries and in the United States.

This is one of the longer Regulations issued by the Board of Governors and no attempt will be made to summarize its many provisions. It is interesting to note, however, that no corporation can be organized under Section 25(a) of the Federal Reserve Act with capital stock of less than $2 million, and that a banking corporation organized under that section may receive only such deposits within the United States as are incidental to carrying out transactions abroad.

REGULATION L   Interlocking Bank Directorates Under the Clayton Act

The first two sections of Regulation L set forth the prohibitions and exceptions contained in Section 8 of the Clayton Act (15 U.S. C. 19) with respect to interlocking bank-directorate relations. The third section then specifies certain additional exceptions permitted by the Board of Governors; and the fourth section deals with enforcement.

REGULATION M   Foreign Branches of National Banks and of Corporations Organized Under the Provisions of Section 25(a) of the Federal Reserve Act

In contrast to most of the other Regulations, Regulation M consists of only one page. In substance, it provides that whenever a national bank or an Edge Act Corporation (see discussion of Regulation K) has a branch or agency in a foreign country where there exists "a disturbed condition" which, in the opinion of the officer in charge, endangers the lives of the employees or the property of such branch or agency, he may suspend operations in whole or in part until the reason for such suspension has ceased to exist.

It is interesting to note that this Regulation was first issued in 1937 to permit the temporary suspension of American banks in Shanghai following their bombing by the Japanese in that year.

REGULATION N   Relations with Foreign Banks and Bankers

This Regulation prescribes the rules governing relations and transactions between Federal Reserve Banks and foreign banks or bankers or a foreign state. Except for routine transactions, it requires full information regarding such relations and transactions to be submitted to the Board of Governors, and prohibits negotiations or agreements between a Federal Reserve Bank and representatives of foreign banks or countries without prior permission of the Board.

REGULATION O   Loans to Executive Officers of Member Banks

Briefly, Section 22(g) of the Federal Reserve Act provides that no executive officer of any member bank shall borrow from any member bank of which he is an executive officer, except that, with the prior approval of a majority of his board of directors, any such officer may borrow from his bank up to $2,500. It also calls for reports by an officer to his board of directors of any borrowings from any other bank, and then states that the Board of Governors may prescribe all necessary rules and regulations.

Within these statutory limitations, Regulation O sets forth definitions, general provisions about prohibited loans, exceptions, reports to be made by executive officers, and penalties for violations.

There is considerable feeling that the statutory limitations on borrowings by executive officers of member banks are unnecessarily restrictive in the light of today's conditions; and legislation has been proposed which would amend Section 22(g) of the Federal Reserve Act so as to permit any executive officer of a member bank to borrow up to $5,000 from his own bank if he makes a written report to his board of directors, and up to $15,000 in the case of home mortgage loans, or $5,000 in the case of other borrowings from outside banks without making any report to his board.

REGULATION P   Holding Company Affiliates—Voting Permits

Regulation P, which is issued pursuant to Section 5144 of the United States Revised Statutes and Section 9 of the Federal Reserve Act, provides basically that no holding company affiliate, as defined, of a national bank or a state member bank may lawfully vote any shares of stock of such a bank for any purpose, other than to put it in voluntary liquidation, unless the holding company affiliate holds a valid voting permit issued by the Board of Governors of the Federal Reserve System.

According to Regulation P, the term holding company affiliate is defined to have the following meaning given to it by Section 2(c) of the Banking Act of 1933, as amended:

(c) The term "holding company affiliate" shall include any corporation, business trust, association, or other similar organization—

(1) Which owns or controls, directly or indirectly, either a majority of the shares of capital stock of a member bank or more than 50 per centum of the number of shares voted for the election of directors of any one bank at the preceding election, or controls in any manner the election of a majority of the directors of any one bank; or

(2) For the benefit of whose shareholders or members all or substantially all the capital stock of a member bank is held by trustees.

Notwithstanding the foregoing, the term "holding company affiliate" shall not include (except for the purposes of section 23A of the Federal Reserve Act, as amended) any corporation all of the stock of which is owned by the United States, or any organization which is determined by the Board of Governors of the Federal Reserve System not to be engaged, directly or indirectly, as a business in holding the stock of, or managing or controlling, banks, banking associations, savings banks, or trust companies.

REGULATION Q   Payment of Interest on Deposits

Under Section 19 of the Federal Reserve Act, which prohibits the payment of interest, directly or indirectly, by any member bank on demand deposits, the Board of Governors is authorized to define different types of deposits, to determine what shall be deemed to be a payment of interest, to limit the rate of interest which may be paid on time and savings deposits by member banks, and to prescribe all necessary rules and regulations.

Section 1 of Regulation Q contains detailed definitions of various types of deposits; Section 2 prohibits the payment of interest on demand deposits; and the remaining three sections deal with time and savings deposits. Interesting questions frequently arise under this Regulation in determining what constitutes an indirect payment of interest. Gifts to depositors to induce them to open new accounts and absorption of exchange charges are examples of practices which raise this question.

As of January 1, 1959, the following maximum rates for time and savings deposits were prescribed in a Supplement to Regulation Q issued by the Board of Governors:

1. 3 per cent compounded quarterly on (a) savings deposits, (b) time

deposits with a maturity of six months or more, and (c) Postal Savings deposits which constitute time deposits.

2. 2½ per cent compounded quarterly on time deposits with maturities of less than six months but not less than ninety days.

3. 1 per cent compounded quarterly on time deposits with maturities of less than ninety days.

REGULATION R   Relations with Dealers in Securities

The main purpose of Regulation R is to carve out an exception, with respect to dealers in Government securities, from the prohibition of Section 32 of the Banking Act of 1933 (12 U.S.C. 78), which provides that no person primarily engaged in the issue, flotation, or underwriting of stocks, bonds, or other similar securities can legally be at the same time an officer, director, or employee of a member bank, except in limited classes of cases where the Board of Governors may allow such service by general regulations when it finds that it would not "unduly influence the investment policies of such member bank or the advice it gives its customers regarding investments."

Thus, this Regulation affects only those member banks which desire to have security dealers or underwriters serving as their officers, directors, or employees.

REGULATION S   Industrial Loans by Federal Reserve Banks

Regulation S provides the mechanics for the making of loans and advances by Federal Reserve Banks pursuant to the provisions of Section 13b of the Federal Reserve Act. These loans and advances can be made only for "the purpose of obtaining working capital for an established industrial or commercial business." Such loans must mature in not more than five years and can be made either indirectly through a "financing institution" (which must participate to the extent of at least 20 per cent) or "in exceptional circumstances" directly to the borrowing business enterprise. Loans may also be made to a business enterprise in participation with a "financing institution."

Because of the existence of other Federal lending agencies, such as the former Reconstruction Finance Corporation and the present Small Business Administration, as well as the guaranteed loan program, which was designed to facilitate the financing of defense contracts (see discussion under Regulation V), all of which provide greater lending flexibility, to date there have been relatively few loans and advances made under Section 13b and Regulation S.

REGULATION T   Credit by Brokers, Dealers and Members of National
Securities Exchanges

Unlike the previously discussed Regulations, which are based primarily on various provisions of the Federal Reserve Act, Regulation T and subsequent Regulations find their statutory authority in other acts. Regulations T and U are issued pursuant to the Securities Exchange Act of 1934, particularly Sections 7 and 8. Section 7(a) of this Act provides, in part:

For the purpose of preventing the excessive use of credit for the purchase or carrying of securities, the Board of Governors of the Federal Reserve System shall, prior to the effective date of this section and from time to time thereafter, prescribe rules and regulations with respect to the amount of credit that may be initially extended and subsequently maintained on any security (other than an exempted security) registered on a national securities exchange.

Both Regulation T and Regulation U, which were substantially amended in June of 1959, are among the more complex Regulations. As indicated by its title, Regulation T governs the extension of credit by brokers, dealers and members of national securities exchanges to their customers. From time to time the Board of Governors issues Supplements to this Regulation prescribing (a) the maximum loan value for registered securities (other than "exempted securities") for general accounts; (b) the margin required for short sales in general accounts; and (c) the "retention requirement" for general accounts,[6] following a withdrawal of cash or securities from the account. By means of raising and lowering these factors, the Board seeks to control the extension of credit by brokers and dealers to their customers, depending upon its analysis of economic conditions. Reference is made to the discussion under Regulation U for the purpose of showing how the "maximum loan values" (which have been the same under both Regulations) have fluctuated since these Regulations first went into effect in 1934.

REGULATION U   Loans by Banks for the Purpose of Purchasing or
Carrying Registered Stocks

As indicated above, Regulation U is closely related to Regulation T. With few exceptions, Regulation U applies to all banks and trust

[6] A new requirement as of June 15, 1959.

companies doing business in the United States.

The general rule of Regulation U, as set forth in paragraph (a) of Section 221.1, is that no bank shall make any loan secured directly or indirectly by any stock for the purpose of purchasing or carrying any stock registered on a national securities exchange in an amount exceeding the "maximum loan value" of the collateral.

Section 221.2 of the Regulation sets forth eleven exceptions to the above mentioned general rule, and Section 221.3 contains miscellaneous provisions regarding the administration and construction of the general rule. For example, paragraph (a) of the latter section provides that in determining whether or not a loan is for the purposes specified in Section 221.1 of the Regulation or for any of the exempted purposes specified in Section 222.2, "a bank may rely upon a statement with respect thereto only if such statement (1) is signed by the borrower; (2) is accepted in good faith and signed by an officer of the bank as having been so accepted; and (3) if it merely states what is not the purpose of the loan, is supported by a memorandum or notation of the lending officer describing the purpose of the loan."

The following table illustrates how the Board of Governors has adjusted the loan value and margin requirement from time to time since 1934:

Effective Dates	Loan Value	Margin Requirement
Oct. 1, 1934 to Apr. 30, 1936	75%	25%
May 1, 1936 to Oct. 31, 1937	45%	55%
Nov. 1, 1937 to Feb. 4, 1945	60%	40%
Feb. 5, 1945 to July 4, 1945	50%	50%
July 5, 1945 to Jan. 20, 1946	25%	75%
Jan. 21, 1946 to Jan. 31, 1947	0%	100%
Feb. 1, 1947 to Mar. 29, 1949	25%	75%
Mar. 30, 1949 to Jan. 16, 1951	50%	50%
Jan. 17, 1951 to Feb. 20, 1953	25%	75%
Feb. 21, 1953 to Jan. 4, 1955	50%	50%
Jan. 5, 1955 to Apr. 22, 1955	40%	60%
Apr. 23, 1955 to Jan. 15, 1958	30%	70%
Jan. 16, 1958 to Aug. 4, 1958	50%	50%
Aug. 5, 1958 to Oct. 15, 1958	30%	70%
Oct. 16, 1958 to ———	10%	90%

It can be readily seen from the above table that during periods when the economy is depressed the loan value is fixed at a high percentage of the market value, thus facilitating loans for the purpose of purchasing and carrying listed securities; whereas during periods of prosperity and inflation the loan value may be reduced all the way to zero, thus prohibiting loans of this kind.

Included in the amendments which became effective on June 15, 1959 were: (a) the addition of a "retention requirement" with respect to the withdrawal of collateral from a "restricted loan"; (b) modification of the provisions relating to the so-called "statement of purpose"; (c) a change in the definition of "carrying"; and (d) the addition of a new section dealing with convertible securities. In the case of both Regulations T and U the "retention requirement" was initially set at 50%.

Under date of June 15, 1959 the Board of Governors issued a pamphlet setting forth thirty-two questions and answers in an effort to illustrate the interpretation and application of Regulation U.

REGULATION V   Loan Guarantees for Defense Production

Regulation V was issued pursuant to the Defense Production Act of 1950 and Executive Order 10161, dated September 9, 1950. Under Section 301(a) of the Defense Production Act of 1950, the President of the United States is given broad authority to assist in the financing of Government contracts "for the procurement of materials or for the performance of services for the national defense."

Under this authority, the President has designated the following guaranteeing agencies: the Departments of the Army, Navy, and Air Force, the Department of Commerce, the Department of the Interior, the Department of Agriculture, the General Services Administration, and the Atomic Energy Commission; and has authorized each of these agencies to guarantee, in whole or in part, any public or private financing institution against losses on any loan made for the purpose of financing defense production contracts. He also designated each Federal Reserve Bank to act on behalf of the guaranteeing agencies as Fiscal Agent of the United States in making guarantees, and authorized the Board of Governors to prescribe all necessary Regulations.

Regulation V, which was issued pursuant to the foregoing authority, sets forth the procedures for submitting and processing applications, outlines the responsibility of the Federal Reserve Bank in acting as

Fiscal Agent of the United States, and states that from time to time, after consulting with the guaranteeing agencies, the Board of Governors will prescribe rates of interest, guarantee fees, commitment fees, and other charges. In general, Regulation V in its present form follows the procedures developed from the administration of the V-Loan and T-Loan programs during World War II.

As of January 1, 1959, the maximum interest rate permitted for a V-Loan was 6 per cent and the guarantee fees vary from 10 per cent of the interest and any commitment fee paid to the financing institution where the Government guarantees 70 per cent or less of the loan up to 50 per cent where the Government guarantees over 95 per cent.

REGULATION W Consumer Credit

Since Regulation W is discussed in Chapter 8, suffice it to say here that it was issued under the authority of the Defense Production Act of 1950 (and on two earlier occasions under other legislation). It was designed to regulate any person (whether a bank, loan company or finance company, or a dealer, retailer, or other person selling consumers' durable goods) engaged in the business of extending installment credit in amounts of $5,000 or less.

As stated earlier in this chapter, Regulation W was suspended as of May 7, 1952.

REGULATION X Real Estate Credit

This regulation was suspended as of September 15, 1952, and was also issued under the authority of the Defense Production Act of 1950. Like its counterpart, Regulation W, which sought to regulate consumer credit, Regulation X sought to regulate real estate construction credit, both residential and nonresidential. Regulation of this type of credit was effected by requiring registration, establishing maximum loan values for different types of real estate, limiting maturities, and specifying minimum down payments and amortization requirements.

Because of the almost unlimited number of different types of transactions and special situations involved, Regulation X produced many difficult questions of interpretation and administration.

REGULATION Y
Bank Holding Companies

After many years of debate in Congress, the Bank Holding Company Act of 1956 was finally passed, and pursuant to Section 5b thereof the Board of Governors issued Regulation Y, effective September 1, 1956.

Under both the Act and Regulation Y, a bank holding company is defined to mean, generally, "any company which directly or indirectly owns or controls 25 per cent or more of the voting shares of two or more banks, or 25 per cent or more of the voting shares of any bank holding company." In substance, and subject to certain exceptions, the Act and the Regulation provide (1) that, without prior approval of the Board of Governors, no new bank holding company can be formed and no existing bank holding company can be expanded, (2) that within two years from May 9, 1956 (unless extended by the Board of Governors for not more than three additional years), each bank holding company must divest itself of nonbanking interests, and (3) that a subsidiary bank cannot extend credit to its holding company or to any other subsidiary of such holding company. Other provisions of the Regulation set forth procedures and rules for carrying out these basic principles.

Conclusion

From the foregoing, it will be seen that the Regulations cover a wide variety of subjects, affecting not only the Federal Reserve Banks and member banks, but many others, such as brokers and dealers in the case of Regulation T and financing institutions generally in the case of Regulation V.

Over the years the Reserve Banks and the Board of Governors have administered the Regulations in a relatively informal manner and have constantly sought for simplification in their procedures. Where violations have occurred, a warning from the Board of Governors or from a Federal Reserve officer or agent has usually resulted in prompt compliance, and in only a few cases has it been necessary to resort to penalties and formal proceedings. On the whole, the Regulations have provided a flexible and effective means of carrying out the provisions of the Federal Reserve Act, as well as other important functions delegated to the Board of Governors and the Reserve Banks under other statutes.

SUGGESTED READINGS

BACH, G. L., *Federal Reserve Policy-Making,* New York, Alfred A. Knopf, 1950, Chapter VI, pp. 95–103.

DUNN, CHARLES B.,"The Organization and Functions of the Federal Reserve System," *The John Marshall Law Quarterly,* December 1941, p. 280.

"FEDERAL-STATE RELATIONS UNDER THE BANK HOLDING COMPANY ACT OF 1956," *Yale Law Journal,* June 1957, p. 1093.

GOLDENWEISER, E. A., *Federal Reserve System in Operation,* New York, McGraw-Hill Book Company, Inc., 1925, Chapter XIII.

"THE BANK HOLDING COMPANY ACT OF 1956," *St. John's Law Review,* December 1956, p. 146.

"THE REGULATIONS OF THE BOARD OF GOVERNORS OF THE FEDERAL RESERVE SYSTEM," address delivered in 1938 by Walter Wyatt, former General Counsel of the Board of Governors (available in Library of Board of Governors of the Federal Reserve System, Washington, D.C.).

"THE REGULATIONS OF THE BOARD OF GOVERNORS OF THE FEDERAL RESERVE SYSTEM AND THEIR APPLICATION TO MEMBER BANKS," address delivered in 1939 by Paul C. Hodge, Vice President and General Counsel of the Federal Reserve Bank of Chicago (available in Library of the Federal Reserve Bank of Chicago).

War Loans, New York, Bank Management Commission and American Bankers Association, 1943.

Chapter 13

INTERNATIONAL RELATIONS AND THE FEDERAL RESERVE SYSTEM

INTRODUCTION: INTERNATIONAL FUNCTIONS OF THE FEDERAL RESERVE SYSTEM

THE Federal Reserve System is concerned with international problems, first, because of the interrelation between these problems and the problems of domestic monetary policy; and second, because of the specific functions in the international field with which the System has been entrusted by the Congress.[1]

The United States is by far the greatest financial and commercial power of the free world. Its merchandise exports and imports account for about one-sixth of world trade, and the international flow of its capital probably for a much larger share of all international capital movements. The health of the United States economy is therefore of the greatest importance for economic welfare abroad, and the domestic policies of the Federal Reserve System, through their effects on the maintenance of financial stability in the United States, deeply affect conditions all over the world.

Not only are the economies of foreign countries influenced by developments in the United States; developments abroad similarly influence the United States economy. It is true that in the United States international trade and finance form a smaller part of economic activity than in most foreign countries.[2] Nevertheless, there are many

---

[1] Cf. *Reply of the Chairman of the Board of Governors to Subcommittee on General Credit Control and Debt Management*, Washington, Joint Committee on the Economic Report, 1952, Part 1, pp. 273-75.

[2] In 1958, exports of United States goods and services amounted to $23 billion, or 5 per cent of the gross national product.

273

branches of industry and agriculture in which exports account for a large part, and occasionally for the bulk, of total output. Foreign developments also decisively affect the federal budget by determining the requirements of national security expenditures, including those involved in assistance to foreign nations. Finally, movements in foreign-held dollar balances and other short-term assets affect the reserve position of the member banks and the liquidity of the money market.[3]

In addition to these general concerns, the Federal Reserve System has special responsibilities in the following matters:

1. The Federal Reserve Banks act as correspondents for foreign central banks and governments and as fiscal agents for international institutions; they also are authorized, subject to supervision by the Board of Governors, to undertake certain financial operations abroad, and to make loans on gold collateral to foreign central banks and governments.

2. The Board of Governors supervises and regulates certain foreign operations of member banks (bankers' acceptances and foreign branches), and the operations of certain other corporations engaged in international financial activities (the so-called "Edge" and "Agreement" Corporations).

3. The Federal Reserve System is vitally concerned with gold problems, including the international movement of gold, since gold continues to function as the reserve basis of Federal Reserve notes and deposits, and thus indirectly also of member-bank deposits.

4. The Chairman of the Board of Governors is a member of the National Advisory Council on International Monetary and Financial Problems. In this way, the Federal Reserve System has some influence on the activities of the institutions with which the Council is concerned; these institutions include three international organizations (the International Monetary Fund, the International Bank for Reconstruction and Development, and the International Finance Corporation) and such United States government agencies as the Export-Import Bank of Washington, the International Cooperation Administration, the Development Loan Fund, and the Treasury's Stabilization Fund.

This enumeration shows that the Federal Reserve System plays a significant role in the international financial policies and operations of

---

[3] There are special Divisions at the Board of Governors and at the Federal Reserve Bank of New York which deal with the analysis of international developments of interest to the System.

the United States; nevertheless, its role is more explicitly circumscribed than in the case of many other central banks. Central banks of many foreign countries are empowered to "transact any banking business with foreign countries" (e.g., most recently, German Federal Bank law, Art. 19, para. 9). In contrast, the Federal Reserve Act defines in detail the powers of the System in regard to transactions abroad, and under the Gold Reserve Act of 1934 the Secretary of the Treasury, rather than the Federal Reserve System, decides on gold and Stabilization Fund transactions.

Within the Federal Reserve System, the ultimate responsibility for international financial policies and operations is vested in the Board of Governors, which exercises "special supervision over all relationships and transactions of any kind entered by any Federal Reserve Bank with any foreign bank or banker . . . and all such relationships and transactions shall be subject to such regulations, conditions, and limitations as the Board may prescribe" (Sec. 14, para. 8, of the Federal Reserve Act, added by the Banking Act of 1933).[4]

The following sections discuss the specific functions of the Federal Reserve System in the international field.

1. INTERNATIONAL FINANCIAL OPERATIONS OF THE FEDERAL RESERVE BANKS

Virtually all international operations of the Federal Reserve System are conducted by the Federal Reserve Bank of New York.[5] However, the other Federal Reserve Banks are given the opportunity of participating in the accounts held by foreign correspondents with the New York Bank, and they regularly make use of that opportunity.

Correspondent Relations

In December 1958, the Federal Reserve Bank of New York held accounts for the central banks or governments of seventy-four foreign countries (Federal Reserve Act, Sec. 14, para. 6) and acted as fiscal agent for such international institutions as the International Monetary Fund, the International Bank for Reconstruction and Develop-

[4] Cf. E. A. Goldenweiser, *American Monetary Policy,* New York, McGraw-Hill Book Company, Inc., 1951, pp. 274-78.
[5] A small number of gold transactions is executed by the Federal Reserve Bank of San Francisco as agent of the New York Bank.

ment, and the International Finance Corporation (Bretton Woods Agreements Act, Sec. 6; International Finance Corporation Act, Sec. 6).[6]

For the account of its foreign correspondents the Bank purchases (with its guarantee) and sells bankers' acceptances; purchases and sells securities and holds them in custody; purchases, earmarks, and sells gold; purchases and sells foreign exchange; collects checks, notes, bills, and other items payable within the United States; and receives and makes payments. However, it cannot accept any interest-bearing (time or savings) deposits, and it has only limited authority to make advances.

In its international operations, no less than in its domestic activities, the Federal Reserve System has to take account of its monetary policy as a whole (cf. Federal Reserve Act, Sec. 12A, para. 3). Therefore, the Bank reserves the right to prevent foreign operations in bankers' acceptances and U.S. Government securities from affecting the market in a manner inconsistent with the purposes of the open-market activities of the System, by executing the transactions directly through the System's Open Market Account rather than through the market.

On December 31, 1958, holdings of foreign countries and international institutions with the Federal Reserve Banks included $8.5 billion of earmarked gold, $5.8 billion of dollar deposits and U.S. Government securities, and $70 million of bankers' acceptances. The gold holdings exceeded 40 per cent of all gold holdings, and the dollar holdings were equal to nearly 60 per cent of all liquid dollar assets, of foreign monetary authorities and international institutions. Many foreign monetary authorities, however, hold part of their foreign exchange as working balances for commercial transactions, rather than as monetary reserves, and keep these balances with commercial banks. The fact that Federal Reserve Banks cannot pay interest on

---

[6] The Hague Agreement of 1930 envisaged the official participation of the United States in the Bank for International Settlements, including the appointment of a representative of the Federal Reserve System as ex-officio Governor (Statutes of the B.I.S., Arts. 6, 9, 15, and 28). This official participation has not materialized; however, the Federal Reserve Bank of New York acts as the Bank's correspondent (E. L. Dulles, *The Bank for International Settlements at Work,* New York, The Macmillan Company, 1932, p. 84), the Federal Reserve System has the right to object to any of the Bank's dealings in the United States market or in United States currency (Art. 20), and representatives of the Federal Reserve System frequently attend meetings of the B.I.S. as guests.

deposits offers an inducement to foreign monetary authorities to maintain time deposit balances with commercial banks.[7]

Exchange Operations

The Federal Reserve Banks do not operate in the foreign exchange market for their own account, although they do so for the accounts of the United States Treasury and of their foreign correspondents. The Federal Reserve Bank of New York acts as agent for the Treasury's Stabilization Fund; however, the Fund usually abstains from foreign-exchange transactions, and its sales and purchases of gold are initiated by foreign monetary authorities. The United States fulfills its commitment under the Articles of Agreement of the International Monetary Fund to maintain the par value of the dollar by its willingness to buy and sell gold freely in transactions with foreign monetary authorities for legitimate monetary purposes (see section 3, below); it does not try to influence the market exchange rate of the dollar in relation to other currencies.[8] This attitude contrasts with the practice of virtually all foreign countries with fixed par values, which maintain these values within the margin of 1 per cent, prescribed in the International Monetary Fund Articles of Agreement, by intervening in the exchange markets.

Transactions Abroad

In contrast to the large-scale activities of the Federal Reserve Banks in the United States as correspondents, depositories, and fiscal agents for foreign and international monetary institutions, their own operations abroad have virtually ceased.[9]

---

[7] This inducement is reinforced by legal provisions (Internal Revenue Code, Sec. 861a, 1, c, and 881) which exempt foreign central banks from income tax on the revenue from bankers' acceptances and time deposits. While some central banks are completely tax-exempt under tax treaties or as government agencies, many of them are taxable in regard to the yield of Government securities, and these banks find it often more profitable to invest in time deposits with commercial banks than in Treasury bills; the market for bankers' acceptances (see below) is too narrow to afford scope for large-scale investment.

[8] The Federal Reserve Bank of New York certifies daily to the Secretary of the Treasury the buying rates in the New York market for cable transfers of certain foreign currencies; however, this certification is exclusively for the purpose of determining the assessment and collection of import duties (Tariff Act of 1930, Title IV, Sec. 522).

[9] The President's Commission on Foreign Economic Policy recommended in January 1954 "that the Federal Reserve System explore with foreign central

Under the Federal Reserve Act, the Federal Reserve Banks may purchase and sell in the open market abroad (from or to foreign banks, enterprises, and individuals) cable transfers and bills of exchange; they may deal abroad in gold and make loans on gold collateral;[10] they may buy and sell abroad securities issued or guaranteed by the United States, and certain other securities of states, municipalities, and Government agencies; and they may establish and maintain accounts in foreign countries, and appoint correspondents and agencies abroad (Sec. 14, paras. 1, 2, 3, and 6). Actually, the last significant transactions abroad were undertaken in 1931, when the Federal Reserve Banks participated in international central bank credits to the United Kingdom, Austria, Germany, and Hungary, and made a deposit with the Bank for International Settlements to be used for the purchase of bills guaranteed by that bank; the largest such transaction was a credit of $125 million to the Bank of England. In previous years, the Federal Reserve Banks had participated in numerous credits (apart from loans on gold collateral), including one to the United Kingdom ($200 million in 1925); of these earlier credits, only one to Hungary ($2 million in 1929) was ever utilized. All the agreements provided for credit extension in the form of a purchase of bills, with the notable exceptions of the agreements with the United Kingdom (1925) and Hungary (1929), which provided for the sale of gold against foreign exchange (sterling and pengö, respectively), with the foreign currency accounts in turn to be used for the purchase of commercial bills.

The Federal Reserve Banks maintain accounts with three foreign central banks; at the end of 1958, these accounts totaled only $15,000 and had no economic significance.[11]

Gold Collateral Loans

The most important international transactions now executed by the Federal Reserve Banks for their own account are loans to foreign

---

banks the possibilities of standby credits or line of credit arrangements" as a means "of strengthening foreign reserves and . . . to assist in the gradual attainment of general convertibility" (Report, pp. 74-75).

[10] The Banks are also authorized to make advances "secured by direct obligations of the United States" (Federal Reserve Act, Sec. 13, para. 13, added by Banking Act of 1933). However, such advances bear interest rates that are higher than the discount rate, and are therefore less attractive to potential borrowers than loans on gold collateral.

[11] Upon request, the System makes staff members available to foreign central banks for technical assistance. The System also cooperates in some activities of the Center of Latin American Monetary Studies in Mexico, D. F.

central banks on gold collateral. In contrast to unsecured credits, or to drawings upon the International Monetary Fund, these loans do not add to the total amount of international means of payments available to the borrowing country, but merely transform one type of such means of payments, gold, into another, dollars. Under the policy of the Federal Reserve, such loans are made only on gold held under earmark at the Federal Reserve Bank of New York and only for temporary needs; they usually have a maturity of not more than three months and usually carry an interest rate equal to the discount rate at the Federal Reserve Bank of New York. For a country that needs dollars for longer periods, it is cheaper to sell gold than to borrow on gold collateral since the interest rate burden would exceed the cost of selling and repurchasing (one-fourth of 1 per cent each) the amount of gold in question.

Gold collateral loans usually involve relatively small amounts: in 1958 new gold loan arrangements totaled $43 million, of which $18 million was outstanding at the year-end; the largest amount outstanding at any one time was $185 million in October 1954.

2. SUPERVISION OF FOREIGN OPERATIONS OF MEMBER BANKS AND OF OPERATIONS OF CORPORATIONS ENGAGED IN FOREIGN BANKING

Foreign Operations of Member Banks

The Board of Governors supervises and regulates foreign operations of member banks in two respects: the acceptance of bills of exchange and the establishment of branches abroad.

Bankers' Acceptances

Any member bank may accept commercial drafts or bills of exchange growing out of the importation and exportation of goods, the shipment of goods between foreign countries, and the storage of readily marketable staples in a foreign country (Federal Reserve Act, Sec. 13, para. 7; Regulation C, Sec. 1) up to 50 per cent (or, with the permission of the Board of Governors, 100 per cent) of its capital and surplus.[12] Moreover, the Board of Governors may grant a member bank permission to accept bills of exchange drawn by banks in foreign

---

[12] Banks may also accept bills based on shipment or storage within the United States.

countries or insular possessions of the United States "for the purpose of furnishing dollar exchange as required by the usages of trade in the respective countries" (Federal Reserve Act, Sec. 13, para. 12; Regulation C, Sec. 2).[13]

Bankers' acceptances have been playing an increasing role in United States banking since the revival of foreign trade following the end of the Second World War. In December 1958, there were $1.2 billion of bankers' acceptances outstanding, most of them arising out of imports into and exports from the United States or the storage of staples in foreign countries; the volume of "dollar exchange" acceptances was about $80 million, and that of acceptances based on domestic transactions was about $250 million.

Foreign Branches

Member banks having capital and surplus of $1 million or more may, with permission from the Board of Governors, establish branches in foreign countries or overseas areas of the United States (Federal Reserve Act, Sec. 25, para. 1; Sec. 9, para. 3).[14]

As compared with banks of some other major countries, banks in the United States have few foreign branches. In December 1958, 11 United States banks (including "Edge" and "Agreement" Corporations; see below) had a total of 109 foreign branches (excluding those in United States overseas areas), of which 63 were in Latin America.

Corporations Engaged in Foreign Banking

The Federal Reserve System is concerned with two types of U.S. corporations that, without being member banks themselves, conduct an international or foreign banking business; the so-called Edge

[13] Under rulings of the Board of Governors, "dollar exchange" bills are required by the usages of trade in Australia, New Zealand, Indonesia, and Latin America, excepting Haiti, Mexico, and the Netherlands Antilles (Digest of Rulings of the Board of Governors, p. 151). Such bills, in contrast to commercial bills, are based on expected future rather than on present commercial transactions; they must be expected to be liquidated from exports or "other sources reasonably available . . . arising in the normal course of trade" (Regulation C, Sec. 2c).

[14] Restrictions upon activities of banks in the United States apply also to their foreign branches, although such restricted activities may be customary in the foreign country involved. Since this restriction sometimes hampers the competitive position of a foreign branch, the Board of Governors has recommended to the Congress that it be given authority to permit foreign branches to conduct activities customary abroad.

Corporations,[15] which are chartered by the Board of Governors; and corporations formed under state law, in which member banks participate as shareholders and which operate under agreement with the Board of Governors.[16]

Edge Corporations (Section 25 A of the Federal Reserve Act) must have a capital of not less than $2 million; all their directors must be U.S. citizens, and the holders of a majority of their shares must be U.S. citizens or corporations controlled by citizens and chartered under United States Federal or state laws.

Edge Corporations are of two kinds: Banking Corporations, which are engaged in deposit banking, and Financing Corporations, which are engaged in other types of financial activities. Banking Corporations may not engage in the securities business (apart from minor exceptions), and Financing Corporations may not engage in deposit banking (Regulation K, Sec. 4). Edge Corporations may not carry on any part of their business in the United States except such as is incidental to their international or foreign business. In particular, Banking Corporations may receive only such deposits within the United States as are incidental to or for the purpose of carrying out transactions abroad; and Financing Corporations may not engage or participate in the underwriting, sale, or distribution of securities in the United States (Regulation K, Sec. 6). Banking Corporations, but not Financing Corporations, are permitted to accept commercial drafts and bills of exchange growing out of foreign or international transactions, within limits similar to those imposed on member banks (Regulation K, Sec. 7).

Edge Corporations may establish branches abroad, but not within the United States, and may purchase and hold stock in other corporations, subject to the consent of the Board of Governors. However, the Board of Governors ordinarily will not grant consent for a Banking Corporation to purchase and hold stock in a corporation not engaged in banking or closely related activities, or for Financing Corporations to purchase and hold stock in a corporation engaged in bank-

---

[15] Senator Edge of New Jersey was instrumental in having the Federal Reserve Act amended in 1919 so as to permit the establishment of such corporations.

[16] In addition, there are corporations doing banking business abroad which have no connection with the Federal Reserve System; the most important corporation of this kind is the American Express Company, which neither operates nor is affiliated with a bank in the United States, but whose subsidiaries conduct extensive banking operations in many foreign countries.

ing; in no case may a subsidiary corporation be engaged in transacting business in the United States, except such as in the judgment of the Board of Governors is incidental to its international or foreign business (Regulation K, Secs. 5, 6, and 9).

Corporations (other than Edge Corporations) in which member banks participate as shareholders must restrict their operations by agreement with the Board of Governors (Federal Reserve Act, Sec. 25, para. 7; Sec. 9, para. 20); these corporations are generally subject to the same limitations as Edge Banking Corporations (Regulation K, Sec. 11). Both Edge and "Agreement" Corporations are subject to examination by the Board of Governors.

At the end of 1958 there were two Edge Banking Corporations: Bank of America, New York, a subsidiary of the largest commercial bank in the United States, Bank of America National Trust and Savings Association, San Francisco, California; and The First Bank of Boston (International), New York, a subsidiary of The First National Bank of Boston. Bank of America, New York, is the largest Edge Corporation, with total assets of $335 million; in addition to having a number of foreign branches and participations in some other foreign corporations, it controls the Banca d'America e d'Italia, the ninth-largest Italian bank. There were three Edge Financing Corporations and four "Agreement" Corporations, of which three conducted significant banking operations abroad, either directly or through subsidiaries.[17]

Edge Banking Corporations and "Agreement" Corporations have the advantage over foreign branches that their authority to do business abroad can be expanded by consent of the Board of Governors so as to include some activities which are customary abroad though beyond the power of United States commercial banks at home (Regulation K, Sec. 5a). They also enjoy some flexibility in acquiring stock in other foreign financial institutions. Moreover, the establishment of an Edge Corporation or an "Agreement" Corporation enables a member bank to establish a subsidiary (though with a restricted area of operations)

---

[17] One "Agreement" Corporation was owned by J. P. Morgan & Co., Inc., and conducted an extensive business in Paris. Another was owned by The First National City Bank of New York and in turn owned the principal bank operating in Liberia and a recently organized bank in South Africa. The third, indirectly owned by The Chase Manhattan Bank, owned another recently organized bank in South Africa.

in the United States outside of its home state.[18] The fact that Edge Corporations and "Agreement" Corporations thus have rather exceptional features explains the strict limitations upon the domestic business of such corporations included in Regulation K.

3. GOLD

Gold forms the basis of the American currency system: the dollar is by definition equal to one thirty-fifth of a troy ounce of fine gold. Moreover, each Federal Reserve Bank "shall maintain reserves in gold certificates of not less than 25 per centum against its Federal Reserve notes in actual circulation" and against its deposits (Federal Reserve Act, Sec. 16, para. 3).[19] The United States fulfills its commitment under the Articles of Agreement of the International Monetary Fund to maintain the par value of the dollar (Art. IV, Sec. 4) by freely selling and buying gold in transactions with foreign monetary authorities for all legitimate monetary purposes at the rate of $35 per ounce of fine gold (plus or minus a charge of one-fourth of 1 per cent).[20]

International Role of Gold

Gold remains the ultimate means of international payments.[21] In practice, dollars and sterling are used more frequently than gold in settling balances; however, gold is generally accepted by all monetary authorities, and it is readily convertible into any currency, including the dollar and the pound sterling.[22] In particular, the International

[18] Both Edge Banking Corporations were located in New York and owned by banks located outside New York State.

[19] Gold also must be held in reserve by the Treasury against some older United States paper money still in circulation, including United States notes, Treasury notes of 1890, and pre-1933 gold certificates. At the end of December 1958, the United States gold stock stood at $20.6 billion. Gold held against the gold certificate reserves of the Federal Reserve amounted to $20 billion and covered 42.1 per cent (instead of the statutory minimum of 25 per cent) of total Federal Reserve note and deposit liabilities; gold held as reserve against other money in circulation amounted to $0.2 billion. The rest of the gold stock represented "free" holdings of the Treasury's General Fund and the Stabilization Fund.

[20] Statement of the Secretary of the Treasury, October 4, 1949.

[21] Under Article IV, Sec. 1, of the Articles of Agreement of the International Monetary Fund, either gold or the U. S. dollar defined in gold as above forms the common denominator of the par values of the currencies of all Fund members.

[22] It might well be argued that the international acceptability of gold at present depends primarily on the willingness of the U. S. Treasury freely to convert gold into dollars at a fixed rate.

Monetary Fund is prepared to sell the currencies of any member in exchange for gold (Articles of Agreement, Art. V, Secs. 2, 6a and 7a). The members of the European Payments Union could, and frequently did, settle in gold that part of their monthly payments positions for which credit was not automatically extended.

Monetary gold held in the free world on December 31, 1958, amounted to $40 billion, of which the United States held slightly more than half. Nevertheless, it is sometimes suggested that the United States gold reserves are inadequate because of the size of dollar balances held by foreign authorities, corporations, and individuals, and by international institutions; on December 31, 1958, these balances (including not only short-term assets but also long-term U.S. government securities) amounted to $17.6 billion. It is true that if this entire sum were deducted from the United States gold holdings, the rest would not suffice to satisfy the statutory reserve requirements for Federal Reserve notes and deposits. However, these foreign dollar holdings should not be considered a lien on the United States gold stock. First, under present policies only official holdings of foreign countries—which in December 1958 amounted to about one-half of all foreign and international holdings—are repayable in gold. Second, a good part of these official holdings, as well as the great bulk of other foreign and international holdings, are needed as working balances (mainly for transactions with and in the United States), and their conversion into gold would be inconsistent with that purpose. Third, and most important, a large-scale demand for conversion of dollar balances into gold could be imagined only in the case of a political or financial catastrophe in the United States; however, in such a case not only foreigners but also domestic investors would presumably wish to withdraw their funds from the United States, and the problems created by large-scale domestic capital flight would dwarf those caused by requests for the redemption of foreign dollar holdings.[23]

Gold Movements and the Monetary System of the United States

Under the Gold Reserve Act of 1934 (Sec. 10), the Secretary of the Treasury is authorized, for the account of the Exchange Stabil-

[23] If an abnormal demand for redemption of foreign dollar balances into gold were due to a short-lived panic, it could be met, even though at the cost of impairing the legal gold reserve, since the Board of Governors is authorized to suspend all reserve requirements for a period not exceeding thirty days and to renew such suspension for periods not exceeding fifteen days (Federal Reserve Act, Sec. 11, para. 4).

ization Fund, to deal in gold "for the purpose of stabilizing the exchange value of the dollar." However, the gold par value of the dollar may not be changed without Act of Congress (Bretton Woods Agreement Act, Sec. 5), and under the Articles of Agreement of the International Monetary Fund (Art. IV, Sec. 2; Fund Rules and Regulations, F-4) the United States may not sell or purchase gold at prices deviating from that value by more than a specified margin (currently 1 per cent).

The Treasury's gold transactions affect the monetary policy of the Federal Reserve System. When the Stabilization Fund purchases gold from a foreign monetary authority, it usually pays for it out of its account with the Federal Reserve Bank of New York and immediately transfers the gold to the General Fund of the Treasury, whereby its Bank account is replenished by drawing on the account of the General Fund; the Treasury in turn usually issues an equal amount of gold certificates to the Federal Reserve Banks, using the proceeds to replenish its General Fund account with the Federal Reserve Banks. The ultimate effects of the purchase of gold from abroad are thus as follows: the Treasury has increased both its gold holdings and its liabilities to the Federal Reserve Banks (in the form of gold certificates) by the amount involved, leaving its deposit balance unchanged; the Federal Reserve Banks have increased both their holdings of gold certificates (and thus the power to expand their liabilities in the form of notes or deposits up to four times the amount involved) and their liabilities in the form of Federal Reserve deposits (held by the foreign seller of gold) by the amount involved; finally, the foreign seller of gold has increased its dollar holdings by the same amount. In other words, not only the lending power of the Federal Reserve Banks has been expanded—this would be important only if the actual reserve ratio were close to the legal limit of 25 per cent—but also the potential supply of money (represented by the deposits of the gold seller) has been increased.[24] If the Federal Reserve System wishes to avoid an increase in the supply of money, it has to counteract the purchase of gold by the Treasury by means of an open-market sale of securities out of its portfolio by the same amount. A sale of gold by the Treasury obviously has exactly the opposite effect on the money supply.[25]

[24] The increase in the money supply becomes actual when the gold seller transfers the proceeds from the Federal Reserve Bank to a commercial bank or converts them from Federal Reserve Bank deposits into currency.

[25] If the Federal Reserve System wished to let the "automatism of the gold standard" operate, it would refrain from counteracting the expansionary effects

The monetary impact of the changes in the gold stock of the United States is by no means academic: in the postward period, annual gold flows varied between a record net inflow of $2.2 billion in 1947 and a record net outflow of $2.3 billion in 1958, and the United States gold stock fluctuated between a year-end low of $20.1 billion in 1945 and a year-end high of $24.6 billion in 1949.

Domestic circulation of gold and, in fact, private domestic possession of gold coins or bullion (apart from collectors' coins or gold for industrial and artistic use) have been prohibited since 1933. Some observers, and especially the gold producers, have argued that it would be advisable to lift the prohibition on domestic gold coin circulation or at least on domestic trading in gold bullion. Their opponents have argued that in normal times the free-market price of gold would not depart from the legal par value and thus would not have any economic importance, while during a crisis a sudden increase in the demand for gold would draw gold from the monetary reserve into private hoards and thereby force a restriction in monetary circulation just at a time when the preservation of domestic liquidity and international solvency would be of the utmost importance.[26] Actually the clamor for freeing the trade in gold, which was rather loud at the time when gold in some foreign free markets showed a significant premium over and above its par value, has died down since in the most important markets gold is now traded at the equivalent of the United States par value.[27]

---

of gold purchases and the contracting effects of gold sales by the Treasury. According to gold-standard theory, the inflow of gold is a symptom of deflationary, and the outflow of gold a symptom of inflationary, departures from internal financial equilibrium, and these departures need to be corrected by expansionary and contracting monetary measures, respectively. However, this theory is valid only if the gold movements reflect exclusively the state of the balance of current international payments, and it cannot be applied when these movements, as at present, are often restricted by exchange controls, and in addition largely reflect capital transactions, especially those of a governmental nature, or the mere conversion of dollar assets into gold or of gold into dollar assets.

[26] A domestic free market in which the Treasury would not intervene could not directly withdraw gold from the U.S. monetary reserves. However, a divergence between U.S. official and market prices for gold might undermine confidence in the ability of the United States effectively to maintain the "par value" of the dollar.

[27] In those markets in which gold still commands a significant premium, the premium reflects either restrictions on the free importation of gold (e.g., in India), or a de facto depreciation of the local currency. The most important free gold market is in London (re-established in 1954); however, gold can be bought in that market only for nonsterling currencies convertible into dollars or "external account" sterling held by foreigners.

4. FEDERAL RESERVE PARTICIPATION IN THE NATIONAL ADVISORY COUNCIL ON INTERNATIONAL MONETARY AND FINANCIAL PROBLEMS

Organization and Functions of the Council

The Chairman of the Board of Governors is a member of the National Advisory Council on International Monetary and Financial Problems, together with the Secretary of the Treasury, the Secretary of State, the Secretary of Commerce, and the President of the Export-Import Bank of Washington. The Council was established by the Bretton Woods Agreements Act of 1945 "to coordinate the policies and operations of the representatives of the United States on the Fund and the Bank and of all agencies of the Government which make or participate in making foreign loans or which engage in foreign financial exchange or monetary transactions" (Sec. 4).

The Council obviously cannot try to coordinate the policies and operations of the International Monetary Fund and the International Bank for Reconstruction and Development themselves, but only those of the United States representatives on these institutions.[28] However, since the United States has the largest single vote in each of these institutions (25.5 per cent in the Fund, 28.5 per cent in the Bank), its representatives have a strong influence on the policies and operations of the institutions.

Under the Bretton Woods Agreements Act, the Council has primarily the duty to "recommend to the President general policy directives" and to "advise and to consult with the President"; in practice, it generally acts by means of direct consultation with the United States executive directors and their alternates on the Fund and the Bank and with the policy-making officials of the United States Government agencies involved.

Every six months the Council transmits to the President and to the Congress a report on its activities and especially on the participation of the United States in the Fund and the Bank; every two years it also transmits a special report on the Fund and the Bank, including recommendations about the policies and operations of these institutions and changes in their Articles of Agreement.

[28] The United States representatives on the Bank are also its representatives on the International Finance Corporation.

The Council has no staff of its own. Its Secretariat is staffed by Treasury personnel, and the work preparatory to Council decisions is done by a Staff Committee, including staff representatives of the member agencies and other Government agencies involved in the problem under discussion. The Council procedure is flexible. Some decisions are made in formal meetings; on routine matters the vote is taken without such a meeting. The Staff Committee meets about once a week. In this way a continuous and thorough coordination between the member agencies is achieved without consuming much of the time of the Council itself.

The Council is concerned with general matters of United States international financial policy, and with the policies and operations of the following international organizations and United States Government agencies.

International Monetary Fund

The Fund's main purposes are to promote international monetary cooperation; to promote exchange stability, maintain orderly exchange arrangements, and avoid competitive exchange depreciation; to assist in the establishment of a multilateral system of international payments and in the elimination of foreign exchange restrictions; and to make its resources available to members in order to enable them to correct maladjustments in their balance of payments (Articles of Agreement, Art. I).

The National Advisory Council is particularly concerned with the vote of the United States representative on proposals of member countries to establish or change the par values of their currencies, which are expressed in gold and in United States dollars (Art. IV, Secs. 1 and 5); on requests of member countries for approval of the maintenance or modification of exchange regulations and restrictions (Art. VIII, Sec. 2, and Art. XIV, Sec. 4); and on requests of member countries for drawings on the Fund's resources (Art. V, Secs. 3-5).

A country is entitled to a drawing only if it needs foreign exchange for a relatively short period. Drawings restricted to the country's "gold tranche" i.e., that part of its quota that has been paid by the country in gold,[29] are given the "overwhelming benefit of doubt" (International

---

[29] Each country is assigned a quota, ranging from $2,750 million for the United States to $0.5 million for Panama. In general, a country pays one-fourth of its quota in gold and the rest in non-negotiable noninterest-bearing government securities denominated in its own currency; these notes are presented for

Monetary Fund, Executive Board decision, February 13, 1952; Annual Report 1952, p. 89). Drawings exceeding the gold tranche, but not exceeding one-half of the country's quota, are granted liberally, though not without question (Annual Report 1957, p. 119). Drawings of further amounts are granted only under exceptional circumstances, e.g., if a country that had been in difficulties has given evidence of executing vigorously a stabilization program approved by the Fund (Annual Report 1957, p. 120). Most but by no means all drawings are made in U.S. dollars.

In order to give Fund members an opportunity to secure drawings without delay when needed, the Fund is prepared to enter into "standby arrangements," giving a member the right to draw an agreed amount within an agreed period without further examination (Executive Board decision, October 1, 1952; Annual Report 1953, pp. 95-96). Such standby arrangements have become increasingly important and now are a part of virtually every stabilization program approved by the Fund.[30]

International Bank for Reconstruction and Development

The Bank's main purposes are to assist in the economic development of its members; to promote private foreign investment by means of guarantees or participations; and to supplement private investment by loans out of its own resources. In practice, the most important function of the Bank is to aid underdeveloped countries, both by cooperating in the formulation of suitable development plans and individual

---

redemption by the Fund whenever the Fund needs the currency in question, primarily in connection with a drawing of that currency by another member. In early 1959 the Fund's Governors approved a general increase in quotas of 50 per cent.

[30] In the twelve months ending December 31, 1958, the Fund entered into new standby arrangements totaling $339 million, had actual drawings of $338 million, and received repayments ("repurchases") of $369 million. By far the largest individual transaction in the Fund's history was concluded in December 1956 with the United Kingdom; it consisted of a drawing of $561.5 million and an additional standby arrangement of $738.5 million, constituting together 100 per cent of the country's quota. This transaction was motivated by the exceptional position of the pound sterling as an international currency. On December 31, 1958, the Fund had $1.7 billion in drawings outstanding and $0.9 billion in standby arrangements still available for drawings of its members. Its uncommitted funds in gold or in currencies freely convertible into gold or dollars amounted to $1.8 billion; the rest of its total assets of $9.2 billion consisted primarily of other currencies, many of which are likely to become increasingly useful in consequence of the moves toward convertibility of all major European currencies made in December 1958.

development projects and by providing credits, wherever possible in conjunction with other public or private investors (Articles of Agreement, Art. I).

All loans granted by the Bank must be either made to, or fully guaranteed by, the government or the central bank of the borrowing country (Art. III, Sec. 4).[31] In general, the loans are to cover foreign exchange rather than local currency costs of the project involved; but in exceptional cases, the Bank may also provide funds for local expenditures, especially if a development project is likely to give rise indirectly to increased foreign exchange outlays (Art. IV, Sec. 3). In some instances, local currency funds arising from United States aid or agricultural surplus transactions (see below) have been used to cover local expenditures connected with projects, the foreign exchange costs of which were financed by the Bank; in the future, the Development Loan Fund (see below) may present increased opportunities for similar actions. It is one of the purposes of the National Advisory Council to encourage cooperation between the Bank and United States Government lending agencies.

International Finance Corporation

The International Finance Corporation was established in 1956 to supplement the activities of the International Bank by making investments in underdeveloped countries in a form resembling equity investments rather than fixed-interest loans. In contrast to Bank loans, its investments are available only to private enterprises, without Government guarantee. The Corporation is a frankly experimental institution with small resources.[32]

Export-Import Bank of Washington

The Export-Import Bank is fully owned by the United States Government; its purpose is "to aid in financing . . . exports and imports

[31] During 1958, the Bank disbursed loans amounting to $541 million and received repayments of $99 million. At the end of the year, it had loans outstanding of $3.3 billion of which $0.9 billion was undisbursed. Its liquid assets available for lending arise from members' subscriptions, proceeds of bond issues, and net receipts from repayment or sale of loans to other investors and current income; its total lending capacity is limited to the amount of its subscribed capital and its surplus, totaling $9.5 billion at the end of 1958. In early 1959 the Bank's Governors voted to recommend a general increase in members' subscriptions of 100 per cent.

[32] In December 1958 the Corporation had a capital stock of $94 million; by that time it had authorized thirteen investments averaging about $1 million each, all but three in Latin American countries.

and the exchange of commodities between the United States . . . and foreign countries . . . or nationals thereof" (Export-Import Bank Act of 1954, Sec. 2). In contrast to the International Bank, the Export-Import Bank generally insists that its funds be spent in the United States. In practice, it gives credits (or, to a very small extent, guarantees) to foreign importers of United States goods or, more rarely, to foreign institutions financing such imports; it thus relieves the United States exporter of a large part of the risk involved in the transactions. The Bank, like the International Bank and the International Finance Corporation, is not supposed to compete with private lending institutions, but to supplement and encourage private credits; and most of its credits, like those of the two international institutions, are medium- or long-term. About 40 per cent of its loans usually go to Latin America.[33] The Bank also administers the loans in local foreign currency made under the so-called Cooley Amendment to the Agricultural Trade Development and Assistance Act of 1954 (P.L. 480, 83rd Congress; see below).

It is a function of the National Advisory Council to avoid a duplication of functions betwen the Export-Import Bank and the international lending institutions, and to see to it that their credit terms and conditions are as far as possible consistent with each other. In general, the Export-Import Bank might be expected to be preferred as a source of dollar funds whenever a transaction is in the particular interest of the United States.

International Cooperation Administration

The National Advisory Council is concerned with the operations of the International Cooperation Administration, which administers United States aid programs, in regard to the choice between loan and grant aid, the terms and conditions of loans, and the disposal of the so-called counterpart funds, i.e., local-currency balances deposited abroad by foreign governments as counterpart for the receipt of grant

[33] On December 31, 1958, the Bank had a lending authority of $7 billion, outstanding loans of $3.3 billion, and undisbursed lending commitments of $1.6 billion; taking into consideration a small amount of outstanding guarantees, it had an uncommitted lending authority of $2.1 billion. In 1958, it disbursed credits of $646 million and received payments of $316 million. The transactions of the Bank do not usually constitute a drain on Treasury funds; the Bank regularly pays to the Treasury an annual dividend.

aid, which these governments may use only with the consent of the United States.[34]

The International Cooperation Administration also administers funds in local currencies resulting from the United States agricultural surplus disposal program (P.L. 480, 83rd Congress, as amended). Under the Cooley Amendment of 1957 (see above), up to one-fourth of these funds is to be lent to private enterprises (primarily United States enterprises) in the countries to which the agricultural surplus commodities are supplied. Most of the balance, as well as a large part of the funds arising from nonmilitary foreign aid, are lent to the public authorities of the countries involved, usually for purposes of development.

These loan transactions involve large sums, but they can only rarely be considered strictly from the point of view of the credit-worthiness of the borrowing country.[35] In recent years most of the funds have gone to the Near East and Far East, often to countries whose financial situation is rather equivocal.

Development Loan Fund

The Fund was established in 1957 for the purpose of making loans or guarantees or engaging "in other financing operations or transactions (not to include grants or direct purchases of equity securities)" for the development of the economy of "friendly foreign countries." The Fund is not to compete with private investment or with the Export-Import Bank and the International Bank for Reconstruction and Development. It is "administered subject to the applicable provisions of Sec. 4 of the Bretton Woods Agreement Act . . . with respect to the function of the National Advisory Council" (Mutual Security Act of 1954, as amended, Secs. 201, 202, and 206).[36]

[34] Secs. 111 (c) 1-2, and 115 (b) 6 of the Foreign Assistance Act of 1948; Secs. 522 and 523 of the Mutual Security Act of 1951; Secs. 142 (b) and 502 of the Mutual Security Act of 1954 (as amended) in conjunction with Sec. 101 (b) of the President's Executive Order of November 6, 1954.

[35] Some assistance legislation required that a specified minimum of aid be granted in the form of loans rather than grants. These requirements were repealed in 1955, but the Congress made it clear that it continued to expect "a maximum use of loans" (Report of the Senate Committee on Foreign Relations, Mutual Security Act of 1955, p. 22). By December 31, 1958, the Administration had concluded loan agreements totaling the equivalent of $2.6 billion under aid programs and $1.4 billion under the agricultural surplus disposal programs; about $2.7 billion had actually been disbursed.

[36] The Fund received in 1957 and 1958 appropriations of $700 million; it is expected to receive additional annual appropriations and it will act as a

The National Advisory Council, in its relations with the Fund, is concerned with problems similar to those arising in its relations with the International Cooperation Administration. The Fund makes primarily long-term loans for "overhead-type" projects (e.g., highway construction) and "profit-earning type" projects, frequently through local development institutions. Borrowers are regularly given the privilege of servicing and repaying loans in local currency, with a clause maintaining the dollar value of their payments constant; in this way, borrowing countries can prevent their debts to the Fund from impairing their ability to service and repay loans in dollars to foreign private investors, the Export-Import Bank, or the International Bank for Reconstruction and Development. However, the emphasis on repayment in local currencies with a "maintenance-of-value clause"—which also characterizes other recent lending policies under mutual security and agricultural surplus disposal legislation—may in time result in local-currency holdings of the United States Government reaching astronomical figures.

Exchange Stabilization Fund

The United States Treasury, through its Stabilization Fund established by the Gold Reserve Act of 1934, concludes from time to time "exchange agreements" with foreign countries, often supplementing stabilization programs approved by the International Monetary Fund, and sometimes in turn accompanied by credits of commercial banks. At the end of 1958 such agreements were in force with Mexico, Peru, Chile, Bolivia, and Paraguay. With the exception of the agreement with Mexico, they involved relatively small sums; no disbursements under exchange agreements were outstanding. It is one of the functions of the National Advisory Council to coordinate these activities of the Stabilization Fund with those of the International Monetary Fund.

SUGGESTED READINGS

ALTMAN, OSCAR L., "A Note on Gold Production and Additions to International Gold Reserves," *International Monetary Fund Staff Papers*, April 1958.

AXILROD, S. H., and TAMAGNA, F. M., "United States Banks and Foreign Trade Financing," *Federal Reserve Bulletin*, April 1955.

revolving fund in relending proceeds from repayments and net earnings. By the end of 1958 it had authorized loans of $581 million but disbursed only $6 million.

GARBER, M., and TAMAGNA, F. M., "The Private Demand for Gold, 1931–1953," *Federal Reserve Bulletin,* September 1954.

GOLDENWEISER, E. A., *American Monetary Policy,* New York, McGraw-Hill Book Company, Inc., 1951, Chapter XIII.

KLOPSTOCK, F. H., *The International Status of the Dollar,* Essays in International Finance, No. 28, Princeton University, May 1957.

KRIZ, M. A., *The Price of Gold,* Essays in International Finance, No. 15, Princeton University, July 1952.

NATIONAL ADVISORY COUNCIL ON INTERNATIONAL MONETARY AND FINANCIAL PROBLEMS, *Reports to the President and to the Congress,* Washington, D.C., Government Printing Office (since 1946).

SOLOMON, R., and TAMAGNA, F. M., "Bankers' Acceptance Financing in the United States," *Federal Reserve Bulletin,* May 1955.

TAMAGNA, F. M., and WILLIS, P. B., "United States Banking Organization Abroad," *Federal Reserve Bulletin,* December 1956.

U.S. CONGRESS, JOINT COMMITTEE ON THE ECONOMIC REPORT, *A Compendium of Materials on Monetary, Credit, and Fiscal Policies,* Washington, D.C., Government Printing Office, 1950, Chapter II, Part III, pp. 44-52.

WHITTLESEY, C. R., *Readings in Money and Banking,* New York, The Macmillan Company, 1952, Section 93.

Chapter 14

THE FEDERAL RESERVE SYSTEM, 1914-29

ARCHDUKE FERDINAND, heir to the Austrian throne, and his wife were assassinated at Sarajevo on June 28, 1914. One month later Austria declared war on Serbia. Within a few days Germany, Russia, France, and Great Britain had chosen sides. Early in August the German army crossed the Belgian border. It smashed its way through Belgium and into France, until halted at the Battle of the Marne in September.

The gathering war clouds, followed by actual hostilities, caused a series of shocks in the financial world. Heavy selling on the Vienna stock exchange forced it to close on July 27. The rush to sell spread to other centers. By the end of July, stock exchanges had ceased to operate in London, Berlin, Montreal, Toronto, Madrid, St. Petersburg, and in South American nations. The Paris Bourse suspended trading, though not officially closed until early September. Emergency measures were adopted in England and France to ease financial strain.

In the United States, oversized headlines announced the outbreak of war. During the succeeding days the front pages were full of war news. The average citizen followed all this with great interest, but usually with the feeling that these faraway happenings were of no particular concern to his daily life. Nevertheless, there were reverberations. For example, stock prices dropped sharply toward the end of July. The New York Stock Exchange shut its doors on August 1, not to reopen until December 11. Cotton fell along with stocks, and the cotton exchanges in New York and New Orleans were likewise closed for several months. Exporters soon found themselves in difficulty, as goods began to pile up in warehouses because of a shortage in ocean transportation.

Such was the world atmosphere when the members of the new

Federal Reserve Board took the oath of office on August 10, 1914.[1]
A more inauspicious time for the normal development of monetary
policy would be hard to imagine. The Reserve System's energies in
the first two years were devoted chiefly to organization and procedures. It had to feel its way along an unexplored course. Then, when
the United States entered the conflict, wartime demands came first.
Among other things, this meant that the System's credit actions were
tied to the needs of war financing. That situation continued until the
last of the five big war loans had been floated in 1919. In viewing
subsequent events, it is well to remember how the war delayed the
evolution of peacetime credit policy.

1. RELATION TO THE FEDERAL TREASURY

In framing the Federal Reserve Act, one of the matters for consideration was the relationship of the new system to the Treasury.
Two points were involved here. One was the correction of certain
faults in the machinery of Treasury operations. The other was the
broader question of how much direction, if any, should be exercised
over the Federal Reserve by the Government, including the Treasury
Department.

The first problem concerned the handling of Treasury funds. Under
the old system, the Treasury kept substantial amounts of coin and
currency in its own vaults and those of the nine subtreasuries located
in various cities. Changes in these amounts, arising from cash receipts
and disbursements, affected bank reserves; but were frequently made
without regard to the banking and credit situation. In addition, Government deposit balances were maintained with a large number of
banks which qualified as depositaries. The distribution of deposits was
left to the discretion of the Secretary of the Treasury. This gave rise
to pressure by banks to obtain increased balances; and on occasion, to
criticism of the Treasury for yielding to political influence in appor-
tioning funds. The report of the National Monetary Commission summarized the defects as follows:

The provision of law under which the Government acts as custodian
of its own funds results in irregular withdrawals of money from circula-

[1] The Federal Reserve Act became law on December 23, 1913, but it was
early August of 1914 before the last of the five appointive members of the
Board was confirmed by the Senate. The Federal Reserve Banks did not open
for business until November 16, 1914.

tion and bank reserves in periods of excessive Government revenues, and in the return of these funds into circulation only in periods of deficient revenues. Recent efforts to modify the independent Treasury system by a partial distribution of the public moneys among national banks have resulted, it is charged, in discrimination and favoritism in the treatment of different banks.[2]

Section 15 of the Federal Reserve Act was aimed to correct these faults by making the Reserve System a middleman between the Treasury and the banks. It authorized the deposit of Treasury funds with the Federal Reserve Banks, and directed them to act as fiscal agents of the Government when required by the Secretary of the Treasury. True, a proposal that *all* such funds must be kept with the Reserve banks was not adopted, so that the Treasury continued to maintain balances with depositary banks. But with the cooperation of the Reserve System, methods were devised to eliminate the earlier disadvantages of that arrangement.[3]

Under a subsequent law passed in 1920, the nine subtreasuries were abolished effective not later than July 1, 1921, and virtually all of their duties were assumed by the Federal Reserve Banks. How important the fiscal agency functions of the latter proved to be in wartime will be noted in the section dealing with World War I.

The second question involved the extent of direction by the Government over the new system. On one hand, political domination was strongly opposed by those who recognized that the proper exercise of monetary policy requires freedom from the pressure of politics. On the other, there was suspicion that control by the banks, as provided by the Aldrich plan, would mean too much "Wall Street" influence.

As finally passed, the Federal Reserve Act stood between the two extreme viewpoints. Government representation on the Federal Reserve Board was obtained by making the Secretary of the Treasury and the Comptroller of the Currency ex officio members.[4] The remaining five members were presidential appointees subject to confirmation by the Senate. However, the idea of decentralization was adopted by the provision for not more than twelve, nor less than

[2] Rudolph L. Weissman, *The New Federal Reserve System,* New York, Harper & Brothers, 1936, p. 24.

[3] Edwin W. Kemmerer, *The ABC of the Federal Reserve System,* Princeton, Princeton University Press, 1922, Chapter IX.

[4] The two ex officio memberships were later abolished by the Banking Act of 1935.

eight, Federal Reserve banks in the field, with a considerable degree of independence. The Federal Reserve Board, a Government body, was to appoint three of the nine directors of each Federal Reserve bank, with the other six to be elected by the member banks. Finally, all the stock of each Reserve Bank was to be owned by its member banks.

At first there was some fear that the Federal Reserve Board might become, in effect, a sort of bureau of the Treasury Department. William G. McAdoo, who became Secretary of the Treasury under President Wilson, is said to have held this belief originally, though opposed to mixing politics with the Board's decisions.[5] However, Federal Reserve-Treasury relations worked out satisfactorily, though with occasional differences of opinion.

2. WORLD WAR I, 1914-18

Early Problems, 1914-16

Fortunately for the fledgling Federal Reserve System, both the Federal Reserve Board and the Reserve Banks attracted the services of men representing a high level of ability. The terms of the five original appointive members of the Reserve Board were two, four, six, eight, and ten years. In that order they were Charles S. Hamlin, a lawyer who had become Assistant Secretary of the Treasury; Paul M. Warburg, of Kuhn, Loeb and Company, a deep student of banking; Frederick A. Delano, who had been a railroad executive and was then a member of the Industrial Relations Commission; W. P. G. Harding, able head of the largest bank in Alabama; and A. C. Miller, well-known teacher and economist who was then Assistant to the Secretary of the Interior.

The two ex officio members were William G. McAdoo as Secretary of the Treasury, and John Skelton Williams as Comptroller of the Currency. Mr. Hamlin was designated Governor of the Board, and Mr. Delano Vice Governor. Board members were assigned to offices on the west side of the Treasury Building, with a view of the White House lawn.

The first big task of the Board was to complete the organization of the twelve Federal Reserve Banks by appointing the three Class

---

[5] W. P. G. Harding, *The Formative Period of the Federal Reserve System,* Boston and New York, Houghton Mifflin Company, 1925, pp. 7-13.

C directors for each. It was naturally desired to get the banks started as soon as possible. At the same time, the Board felt the responsibility of securing the best men available. Much care was devoted to the selections, including consultations and visits to the field. By early October the work had been finished and the appointees announced. The other six directors of each bank had already been elected, and the new boards proceeded to choose their operating staffs. On November 16, 1914, the Federal Reserve Banks opened for business.

While this was going on, strains arising from the war in Europe demanded attention. One was the difficulty in meeting debts due and payable in pounds sterling, because of the high rate of exchange then prevailing. To devise a plan for relief, the Federal Reserve Board and the Treasury called a conference of clearing house representatives in September 1914. The result was the formation of a $100 million gold exchange pool, from which payments could be made rather than by the purchase of sterling at a substantial premium. Actually only a small part of the fund was used, as the rate on sterling declined and later went to a discount.

The outbreak of war also created hardships for cotton farmers. The 1914 cotton crop was the largest on record, but the export market was temporarily demoralized due to a shortage of shipping. That combination brought a quick slide in cotton prices, and growers clamored for aid. In response a cotton loan fund was arranged, with members of the Federal Reserve Board acting as a central committee. The plan was for subscribing banks in New York and elsewhere to lend on cotton at a loan value of about 6 cents per pound. The fund did not begin to function until the end of November, 1914. By then, local banks were able to finance a greater volume of loans, and some improvement in ocean transport had occurred. Consequently only a minor fraction of the fund was put to use.

The years 1915 and 1916 witnessed steady progress in the Reserve System's organization and its operating mechanism. Early in 1915 the question of reshuffling the territories of the Federal Reserve Districts came before the Reserve Board. Under Section 2 of the Act, the Reserve Bank Organization Committee (Secretary of the Treasury, Secretary of Agriculture, and Comptroller of the Currency) had previously selected twelve cities as locations for the Federal Reserve Banks, and had apportioned their respective Federal Reserve Districts. These decisions were subject to review by the Federal Reserve Board.

Dissatisfaction with Reserve District boundaries was soon apparent, and various requests for changes were presented to the Board. Two of them involved transfers of Federal Reserve Banks—namely, from Cleveland to Pittsburgh in the Fourth District, and from Richmond to Baltimore in the Fifth District. Discussions were likewise held within the Board as to whether the twelve districts should be reduced in number—possibly to the minimum of eight specified by the Act.

During 1915 the Reserve Board spent a good deal of time on these matters, and made several alterations in district territories. It also asked for an opinion by the Attorney General on the Board's powers with respect to the other points at issue. In April of 1916 Mr. Gregory, the Attorney General, ruled that the Board could order reasonable area readjustments; but had no authority to abolish or relocate a Federal Reserve Bank, or to reduce the number of districts. Thus the controversies were quieted.

In the field of operations, the Board established the Gold Settlement Fund in Washington in May 1915 as a clearinghouse for transactions between the Federal Reserve Banks. This made remittances from one Reserve Bank to another unnecessary. In 1916 a rather comprehensive plan was put into effect for clearing, and collecting at par, the checks deposited by member banks with their respective Reserve Banks. The scheme ran into opposition from banks which were accustomed to levying an exchange charge on certain items, and the satisfactory working out of the par collection system proved to be a lengthy and troublesome undertaking.[6]

Much thought was also given to improving and strengthening the Reserve System through changes in the Act. The Board made several suggestions along this line, and in the first three years the Act was amended on five occasions. The more important of these revisions were enacted on June 21, 1917. One lowered the minimum reserve requirements of member banks, but specified that all legal reserves must be maintained with the Federal Reserve Banks. Therefore gold and lawful money held in member-bank vaults could no longer be a part of legal reserves. The purpose here was to encourage concentration of gold reserves in the System, with an eye to enlarging the base for credit expansion for wartime purposes. Another amendment simplified the issuance of Federal Reserve notes against gold. A third was designed to make membership in the System more attractive to state banks. This resulted in a rise in the number of state-bank

[6] *Ibid.,* Chapter V.

members from 53 in June 1917 to 1,042 two years later.

Credit policy was not a major problem in 1914-16. Large gold imports, together with decreased reserve requirements under the Federal Reserve Act, enabled the member banks to expand credit without recourse to borrowing from the System except in a minor way. At the end of 1916 the Reserve Banks' combined holdings of bills discounted amounted to only $29 million. The discount rate varied according to the type of collateral. For most of the period it stood at 4 per cent on advances secured by commercial and other eligible paper maturing from thirty-one to sixty days.

While engaged chiefly in matters of organization and operation, the Reserve Board did give considerable attention in its first Annual Report to the place of the Reserve Banks in our economy. The report set up some notable guideposts for future policy. It asserted that the System should not await emergencies, but should endeavor to prevent them. At times the Reserve Banks should act to "secure a freer extension of credit," while at other times "prudence and a proper regard for the common good will require that an opposite course should be pursued and accommodations curtailed." This part of the report concluded with the following statement:

"It would be a mistake, therefore, and a serious limitation of their usefulness to regard the Reserve Banks simply as emergency banks. Regulation in ordinary times, as well as protection in extraordinary times, may be expected to become the chief service which these institutions will perform."

War Financing, 1917-18

Great black headlines announced the torpedoing of the *Lusitania* on May 7, 1915. Nearly 1,200 were lost, including 124 Americans. Public opinion was profoundly shocked, but in general not yet to the point of favoring our active participation in the war. In 1916 President Wilson was narrowly re-elected, with one of the campaign slogans being "He kept us out of war." But as time progressed, it became evident to thoughtful observers that this country was being steadily drawn nearer to the maelstrom. The process was hastened by the stepping up of Germany's submarine warfare early in 1917. Diplomatic relations with Germany were broken early in February, and war was declared on April 6, 1917.

The Treasury was quickly confronted with the formidable prospect of raising vast sums both for our own war effort, and for loans to our allies. It was apparent that in addition to higher taxes, heavy borrowings would be necessary. The Federal Reserve System's role was to assist the Treasury to obtain the funds required. Such aid was forthcoming both through the System's fiscal agency functions and through its credit actions.

Fiscal agency operations now assumed prime importance. In floating the five big Liberty bond issues, the objective was to sell as many as possible to investors. Since the public in general had little or no previous experience with Government bonds, this involved education as well as appeals to patriotism. In the nationwide war bond drives which followed, the Federal Reserve Banks played a leading part. Their respective governors became chairmen of the Liberty Loan committees in each Reserve District, and directed the campaigns which reached every section of the country. Allotments of subscriptions were made through the Reserve Banks. They also aided in the distribution and exchange of war bonds, war savings stamps, and thrift stamps.

The work in connection with these services was enormous. Public subscriptions to war bonds alone totaled around $17 billion from mid-1917 to October, 1918. In his annual report for 1918 the Secretary of the Treasury made this comment: "Much of the great work has been done by the Federal Reserve Banks. The Federal Reserve System has been of incalculable value during this period of war financing. . . . It would have been impossible to carry through these unprecedented financial operations under our old banking system. Great credit is due to the Federal Reserve Banks for their broad grasp of the situation and their intelligent, comprehensive cooperation."

The main feature of the System's credit policy, in supporting war financing, was the establishment of a preferential discount rate on loans to member banks secured by Government obligations. The purpose was to promote installment loans by member banks to the public for the purchase of war bonds.

For example, suppose that John Doe had subscribed for a $500 Liberty bond but lacked sufficient ready cash for full payment. His bank would extend a loan with the bond as collateral. The interest rate on his loan was the same as the coupon rate on the bond, so that he was not out of pocket on the transaction. The bank could then rediscount the paper with its Federal Reserve Bank at a slightly lower rate. When customers repaid their loans, the member banks were able to reduce their borrowings accordingly at the Reserve Banks.

That program helped considerably in placing the major portion of the war bonds in the hands of investors. Distribution by types of ownership is shown in Table 1.[7]

TABLE 1.   U.S. GOVERNMENT DEBT
(Ownership of direct and guaranteed securities
In millions of dollars)

	June 1916	June 1917	June 1918	June 1919
Federal agencies and trust funds	$ 2	$ 2	$ 56	$ 158
Federal Reserve Banks	57	66	255	292
Member banks	703	1,065	2,465	3,803
Other commercial banks	50	480	750	1,340
Mutual savings banks	10	100	300	670
Other investors	200	1,000	8,200	19,000
Discrepancy	−50	0	−40	−29
Total interest-bearing securities	$972	$2,713	$11,986	$25,234

It will be observed that the Government debt expanded roughly from $1 billion to $25 billion during the three-year period; and that in 1919, about 75 per cent of the total was held by nonbank ("other") investors. The table also indicates that direct holdings of Government securities by the Reserve System were relatively small. Open-market operations did not assume major importance until several years after the war.

The System's holdings of bills discounted rose from a few million dollars in 1916 to $1,766 million at the end of December 1918. There was a large increase in Federal Reserve note and deposit liabilities, made possible by the concentration of gold in the System after the June 1917 amendments to the Federal Reserve Act. Gold and gold certificates held by the Reserve Banks aggregated $2,001 million at the close of 1918, as against $736 million two years earlier. Even with this big expansion of gold reserves, the System's ratio of reserves to its combined deposit and note liabilities dropped from 81.4 per cent to 48.0 per cent in the same period.[8]

[7] Board of Governors of the Federal Reserve System, *Banking and Monetary Statistics,* Washington, D.C., The National Capital Press, 1943, p. 512.
[8] Under the original Act, the minimum reserve requirement against Federal Reserve notes was 40 per cent in gold; and against deposits, 35 per cent in gold or lawful money. The present minimum is 25 per cent in both cases.

Some other forms of assistance by the Federal Reserve should be mentioned. One was in connection with restrictions on gold and currency exports, which were in effect beginning September, 1917. The intent here was to conserve our gold supply as a base for credit operations of the Government, and to prevent shipments to points which might be advantageous to enemy nations.

Acting as agent for the Treasury, the Federal Reserve Board's duty was to pass on all applications to export coin, bullion, and currency. In examining each request, the Board applied two tests: (1) Would the transaction benefit the enemy, and (2) would the reduction in our gold supply be compensated by adding, through imports, to our store of necessary materials? Applications to ship gold to European neutrals were turned down. Other cases were approved or declined on their merits under the above tests. In all, permits were granted for export of some $46 million of gold and $86 million of currency, much of which went to Canada and Latin American nations.

Another activity was aimed to channel credit into essential industries. In September 1917, a committee of leading New York bankers took steps to limit stock market credit. A few months later the Federal Reserve Board created a Capital Issues Committee to restrict proposed new issues to essential lines. This committee, consisting of three members of the Board, had no official power to prohibit new security issues; but with the cooperation of the banks, its decisions were effective. Similar regional committees were set up in each of the Federal Reserve districts.

In May 1918, the functions of the Capital Issues Committee of the Board were taken over by the new War Finance Corporation, created by law to advance credit to necessary industries. Governor Harding[9] of the Reserve Board was one of the Corporation's five directors. He also served as its first Managing Director, being succeeded in 1919 by Eugene Meyer, Jr. The Corporation had its own capital issues committee of seven members, three of whom were on the Federal Reserve Board.

The Federal Reserve System was faced with heavy and difficult tasks during World War I. It performed them well—in fact remarkably well, considering that the System was new and had no background of experience. This was generally recognized, even by those who were critical of some of the System's later actions.

[9] Mr. Harding succeeded Mr. Hamlin as Governor in 1916. The latter continued as a member.

3. THE 1919-21 PERIOD

Great wars generate great inflations, and World War I was no exception. In 1918, commodity prices were far above the prewar level. After the Armistice there was first a brief reaction in business and prices. Then followed a year of booming business, free spending, rising prices, and speculative fever. The bubble burst in mid-1920, and was succeeded by the sharp depression of late 1920 and 1921.

Boom, 1919-20

The Armistice of November 11, 1918, marked the end of hostilities. It was received throughout the land with joyful celebrations. People wanted to forget their foreign adventure and "get back to normalcy." An illustration of this is found in the Senate's refusal to ratify the Treaty of Versailles in 1919, principally because of opposition to U. S. membership in the League of Nations as set up in the treaty. Not until July 1921 was a joint resolution passed by Congress declaring the war at an end.

Though most citizens were not aware of it, the war had wrought a major change in our financial position—namely, the transition from a debtor nation to the world's largest creditor nation. Throughout our history, a substantial part of the money needed to develop our natural resources and expand our industries had been borrowed from abroad. At the outbreak of World War I, European investors owned American securities estimated at around $5 billion.

In a few short years this situation was entirely reversed. Before we entered the war, vast quantities of war supplies were purchased here by the belligerents. Payments were made by the sale in this country of holdings of American securities, by extensive borrowing in the American market through private loans, and by shipping gold. Between November 1914 and April 1917, the gold stock in the United States rose from $1,520 million to $2,850 million. After the latter date our Government began to extend direct loans to the allies for purchase of war materials. By the middle of 1919 such advances amounted to nearly $10 billion.

With respect to the war and early postwar years, the significance of our transition from debtor to creditor was the doubling—or nearly so—of our gold supply. The receipt of so much gold, together with the transfer of the major part of it to the Reserve System and the reduced reserve requirements for member banks, was the foundation for credit expansion during and after the war. Total loans and investments of all banks increased from $20.8 billion in June 1914 to $28.3 billion in June 1917, and to $36.6 billion in June of 1919.[10] This rapid growth of credit was reflected in a similar rise in the money supply—that is, bank deposits plus currency outside banks.

The first few postwar months brought a temporary slump in business activity and prices, due to the quick drop in production for military purposes. Before long, however, our export trade boomed as orders for peacetime goods poured in from abroad, financed in part by Government loans to our war allies. Also, the backed-up domestic demand for civilian articles soon made itself felt. As a result, production and prices turned up in the spring of 1919, and credit growth was resumed.

Throughout the nation the reaction from war days caused a great wave of extravagance and speculation. Financial journals of that period commented frequently on the public's demand for luxuries such as high-priced silk shirts, and on the "extraordinary speculative activity in all sections." In late 1919 one observer wrote that "With no thought of price, with little provision for the future, our people almost without exception are demanding goods, especially luxuries."

Federal Reserve officials were well aware of the inflationary implications of a strong demand, both domestic and foreign, for civilian goods which in many cases were still in short supply. A. C. Miller, member of the Federal Reserve Board, stressed the presence of inflationary influences in a speech delivered in December 1918. Some of the Reserve Bank heads suggested that the discount rate be raised, and this was discussed at length by the Reserve Board in April 1919. (At the end of 1918 the rate on fifteen-day advances secured by commercial, agricultural, and livestock paper ranged from 4 to 4½ per cent at the twelve Reserve Banks.)

At this point the Board found itself between two crossfires. On one hand, the danger of further inflation called for a policy of credit restraint and a stepping up of the rate. On the other, the Treasury in 1919 was preparing to float the last of the five big war loans. It desired that the discount rate be kept low to aid in financing the Victory Loan at an interest rate (4¾ per cent) not substantially

[10] Board of Governors of the Federal Reserve System, *op. cit.*, p. 18; also p. 34 for deposits and currency.

above that of the Third and Fourth Liberty Loans, and below the rates on call money and commercial paper.

Faced with a difficult choice, the Reserve Board decided to go along with the requirements of Treasury financing, as it had done throughout the war. Not until November of 1919, after installment payments on the Victory Loan were completed, were increases in the discount rate approved—and then only cautiously to 4¾ per cent at most of the Reserve Banks.

Meanwhile "moral suasion" was directed at lenders to restrict credit extension to essential purposes. Warnings of unhealthy speculative trends were voiced by the Board in June 1919, and were repeated thereafter. However, they failed to have much effect. Member-bank borrowings from the System rose from $1,765 million (daily average) in December 1918 to $1,840 million in June 1919, and to $2,115 million in December of 1919. The strain on the System was such that several of the Federal Reserve Banks had to rediscount with other Reserve Banks, in order to maintain their required ratio of gold reserves to note and deposit liabilities.

At the beginning of 1920 the wholesale price index was more than twice its 1914 level, and speculation in commodities and real estate was rampant. In January all twelve Reserve Banks finally took vigorous action by raising the discount rate to 6 per cent, with approval of the Reserve Board, on the type of collateral already mentioned. But credit expanded further, and the prices of many articles ascended to new heights. (Sugar, for example, reached 26 cents a pound at retail in some localities.) By May, member-bank borrowings from the System had mounted further to $2,536 million. Rediscounting between Federal Reserve Banks continued on a large scale. In May the Board approved another increase in the discount rate to 7 per cent at the Federal Reserve Bank of New York and three others, effective at the opening of June.

Depression, 1920-21

The inflationary balloon exploded at last in the late spring of 1920. This was foreshadowed by a collapse of the Japanese silk market in March, which brought a rapid drop there in business and prices. Within two or three months raw-material prices broke elsewhere, followed by sharp declines in prices in general. In the United States the curve of business activity hesitated at first, then picked up speed on the downside. The course of events was well summarized later in a Congressional report, as follows:

With the exhaustion of the credits of European Governments in this country, the purchasing power of Europe in our markets began to fail. This resulted in a sharp decline in exports, particularly of farm products. The exhaustion of credit and capital, coupled with the decline in exports, gave the first impetus to the decline in prices. With the beginning of this decline the forces of reaction and depression began to operate. Goods were thrown on the market, orders were cancelled, the buyer's strike developed, unemployment ensued, and complete industrial depression followed.[11]

The 1920-21 depression was world-wide. In this country it was not as long as some others on record, but the descent was rapid and painful. From the high of 1920 to the low of 1921, the Federal Reserve index of industrial output dropped 32 per cent, most of which took place between August of 1920 and March 1921. Thereafter, production leveled off until recovery commenced toward the end of 1921.

Price declines were even more precipitate. The wholesale price index was nearly halved, with farm prices being especially hard hit. Wheat fell from an average price of $2.98 per bushel in May 1920 to $1.18 for the low month in 1921. Similarly, cotton tumbled from 42 cents to 12 cents a pound, and corn from $1.98 to 47 cents per bushel.

The depression, and especially the steep slide in agricultural prices, brought a series of violent attacks on the Federal Reserve System. As remarked by Governor Harding, the Federal Reserve Board had been blamed earlier for permitting inflation, but was now castigated for promoting deflation. In particular, it was accused of deliberate discrimination against the farmers through a policy of "murderous deflation" (despite the fact that the System's holdings of bills discounted continued to rise for several months after the spring of 1920). The bombardment was carried on both in Congress and outside. It included much totally unwarranted invective by Senator Heflin against Governor Harding personally, and strong criticism by John Skelton Williams both before and after his retirement in March 1921 as Comptroller of the Currency and ex-officio member of the Board.

Finally, at the Federal Reserve Board's own request, a resolution

[11] Harding, *op. cit.,* p. 298 (from the Report on Credit by the Congressional Joint Commission of Agricultural Inquiry, January 1922).

was introduced in the Senate for an investigation of all complaints and charges against the Board. This was referred to the Joint Commission of Agricultural Inquiry, previously set up by Congress to report on the whole agricultural situation. In August 1921, hearings were started by the Commission, which consisted of five members each from the Senate and House of Representatives.

The credit section of the Commission's report, submitted to Congress in January of 1922, contained a thoroughgoing discussion of Federal Reserve credit policies. No basis was found for the charge that the System's actions had discriminated against agriculture. The report also affirmed the difficult position of the System in respect to Treasury financing. But the opinion was expressed that "a policy of restriction of loans and discounts by advances in the discount rates of the Federal Reserve Banks could and should have been adopted in the early part of 1919, notwithstanding the difficulties which the Treasury Department anticipated in floating the Victory loan if such policy were adopted." Had this been done, "much of the expansion, speculation, and extravagance which characterized the postwar period could have been avoided."[12]

There is of course no way of knowing exactly what would have happened if the Federal Reserve System had put on the brakes earlier. However, in retrospect that would have been the proper step. Experience shows that the time to stop an inflationary spiral is before it works up a full head of steam. Mr. Miller of the Board later wrote that the System should have exercised effective credit restraint in 1919; and that such action would have "prevented many of the unhealthful developments in business and credit from gaining the headway which made action of so drastic a character as that which was taken in 1920 necessary."[13]

4. THE BOOM OF THE 1920'S

The decade of the 1920's commenced with the end of a full-sized speculative boom in commodities and the beginning of a severe depression. It closed with the collapse of a truly monumental speculative spree in stocks and the start of a much worse depression. In between was that interesting and boisterous era often termed the "roaring

[12] *Ibid.*, pp. 219-23, 296-305.
[13] A. C. Miller, "Federal Reserve Policy," reprint from *American Economic Review*, Vol. XI, No. 2, June, 1921, p. 12.

twenties." Newspapers had plenty of material for spectacular headlines—to mention a few, the Teapot Dome oil scandal, Lindbergh's
air flight to Paris, Zeppelin airship flights, bootlegging and gang warfare, the first talking picture, and the stock market debacle of late 1929.

Prosperity, 1922-27

The six years 1922-27 were characterized by industrial prosperity,
high employment, and rapid progress in mass production methods. The
Federal Reserve index of industrial output climbed to a new summit
without any deep setbacks. The only sizable downswing occurred
in 1923-24, but it did not prove to be drastic. The wholesale price
index leveled off in the latter part of 1921 after its rapid decline, and
moved within a comparatively narrow range thereafter.

Concerning the Federal Reserve System, the decade of the 1920's
marked the first real development of an independent credit policy. As
already noted, the System did not feel free to act on its own until
about the opening of 1920, after war financing by the Treasury had
been completed.

In 1923, open-market operations were officially designated as an
arm of credit control. Also, the Federal Reserve Board set forth a
number of guides to credit administration in its annual report for
1923. The more important points were (1) the inadequacy of the
reserve ratio as a guide; (2) rejection of stability of the price level
as the sole objective of credit policy; (3) the significance of both the
kinds and the total amount of credit; and (4) the principle that Reserve Bank credit is intended for productive use and not for speculative
purposes.

In the working out of monetary policy during 1922-27, the System's
course of action was complicated by the expansion of bank credit
resulting from very large gold imports. Loans and investments of
member banks climbed from $23.5 billion at the end of 1921 to
$34.2 billion in December 1927. (For all banks, the rise was from
$39.8 billion in mid-1922 to $55.6 billion at the close of 1927.) This
was made possible mainly by the addition of nearly $1 billion to our
gold stock from January 1922 to the spring of 1927. The major
portion went to increase member-bank reserve balances with the
System, thereby enlarging the base for credit expansion.

Financial conditions abroad created further problems. European
nations were struggling to stabilize their currencies and return to the
gold standard, which had been abandoned during the war. It was felt,

notably by Governor Benjamin Strong of the Federal Reserve Bank of New York, that such efforts should be assisted in the interests of world economic recovery. This influenced credit policy decisions in 1924 and again in 1927.

The year 1922 brought a strong business revival. Farmers were still unhappy, however, because the rapid drop in their incomes in 1920-21 had left them with a heavy burden of mortgage debt taken on at high prices. In many cases the borrowers were unable to meet payments on such debt, much of which was held by small banks in agricultural regions. This was a leading element in the wave of bank failures, principally in farm areas, which continued throughout the decade. Commercial bank suspensions totaled 5,879 for the entire ten-year period.

Troubles of the farmers led to agitation in Congress for the addition of a farmer member to the Federal Reserve Board. The result was an amendment to Section 10 of the Federal Reserve Act, passed in June 1922. It raised the number of appointive members from five to six and provided, in effect, for agricultural representation on the Board. In March 1923, the Act was further amended by liberalizing Section 13 with respect to discounts of agricultural paper by the Reserve Banks.

While the Reserve Board acquired a farmer member in 1922, it lost the services of Governor Harding, who had shown high qualities of leadership since the beginning. Mr. Harding's term expired in August 1922, and he was not reappointed. His successor as Governor of the Board was Daniel R. Crissenger, a purely political appointee who was not qualified to fill such a responsible position. The caliber of the Board was weakened, and for some years Governor Strong of the Federal Reserve Bank of New York became the dominant figure in the System's credit moves.[14]

During 1922 the Reserve Banks bought considerable amounts of Government securities to bolster their earning assets, since the latter had fallen to a low point and there was doubt as to whether the System's earnings would meet its expenses. In 1923 a major decision was made—namely, to coordinate open-market purchases and sales into national credit policy. The Federal Reserve Board announced that such transactions should be "governed with primary regard to

[14] In 1927 Mr. Crissenger was succeeded by Roy A. Young, previously Governor of the Federal Reserve Bank of Minneapolis. Governor Strong died in 1928.

the accommodation of commerce and business, and to the effect of such purchases or sales on the general credit situation." Thus open-market operations joined discount-rate changes as a control mechanism.

In 1924 the Reserve System lowered the discount rate, and directed open-market operations toward the easing of credit through heavy purchases of Government securities. This move was induced partly by sagging business at home. But an added motive was to support the desire of European nations to return to the gold standard, by helping to make dollar credits available and thus check the inflow of gold. The latter was temporarily successful, and England was able to resume the gold standard in 1925. However, from the domestic standpoint the wisdom of the action has been questioned by some authorities on the ground that it laid the foundation for the subsequent growth of credit, particularly of the speculative variety.

The next two years witnessed business recovery from the 1923-24 slump, a rising stock market, and a pronounced advance in loans to brokers. The Federal Reserve reversed its previous policy by raising the discount rate and reducing Government security holdings. Then in 1927 came the controversial decision to ease credit which stirred up criticism both within the System and outside.

The 1927 easy money policy was engineered by Governor Strong, following a conference at New York in the summer with Governor Norman of the Bank of England, Governor Schacht of the Reichsbank, and Deputy Governor Rist of the Bank of France. The discount rate was reduced, large open-market purchases were made, and in the last five months of 1927 total Reserve Bank credit outstanding rose from $1,115 million to $1,568 million (daily average). The primary objective was to help France to restore the gold standard and to aid the European financial position in general by encouraging gold exports. Thereafter our gold stock fell by about $500 million from mid-1927 to July 1928, when imports were resumed.

The Federal Reserve Board as a whole acquiesced in Governor Strong's policy, but it was opposed by A. C. Miller, and by some others in the System. One of the outside critics was B. M. Anderson, then economist of the Chase National Bank of New York, who later wrote a vivid account of the matter.[15] The core of the objections was that cheap money would stimulate a credit expansion which was

[15] Benjamin M. Anderson, *Economics and the Public Welfare,* New York, D. Van Nostrand Company, Inc., 1949, pp. 180-83.

already showing signs of being well overdone.

How much the 1927 action contributed to the speculative mania of the next two years is debatable; but in light of what followed, 1927 was a time for restraint rather than ease. The record shows that the stock market boom began to pick up steam after the middle of that year.

Boom and Bust, 1928-29

After thirty years the 1928-29 bull market still ranks as one of the most amazing episodes in history. The great New Era. Prosperity forever. Stocks up five points today. Tomorrow they will go up ten points. A tip that some mysterious "they" are going to put Skyblue common up fifty points. A tip that Joe Doe, who has inside information, is buying North Pole Industries common. The way to get rich quick is to borrow money and buy stocks on a shoestring margin. The Dow-Jones average of industrial common stocks crosses 200 in January 1928. It gallops to 300 in December. It soars to 381 in September of 1929. (And in July 1932, it languishes feebly at 41.)

At the start of 1928, industrial production was rising after a modest reaction in the last half of 1927. Credit growth continued, chiefly for speculative use as reflected in the sharp uptrend of brokers' loans. Stock prices had climbed well above the level of the previous summer. The evident symptoms of mounting speculative fever disturbed the Federal Reserve authorities, and early in the year the easy money policy was reversed by sales of Government securities and an increase in the discount rate.

Although credit restraint was maintained throughout 1928, it was unsuccessful in stopping the boom except for occasional shivers in the stock market. For one thing, the quick-road-to-wealth philosophy had gained powerful headway. For another, more and more stock market credit was represented not by bank loans, but by "outside loans to brokers"—that is, advances made by business concerns attracted by the high interest rate obtainable on call loans. This type of credit was not under the Reserve System's direct control.

With speculation showing no signs of abating, the System tried new tactics known as "direct action." On February 7, 1929, the Federal Reserve Board released a statement calling attention to the "excessive amount of the country's credit absorbed in speculative security loans." It said further that a member bank was "not within its reasonable claims for rediscount facilities at its Federal Reserve

Bank" when borrowing to make or maintain speculative loans. Moral suasion on member banks, however, had only a temporary effect on the stock market. Prices soon started up again; and loans to brokers, especially "outside" loans, continued to increase in almost perpendicular fashion.

Amid all the exuberance occasional warnings were heard, but not heeded. One was voiced by Paul M. Warburg, able member of the Federal Reserve Board from 1914 to 1918. In March 1929, he reported that the Reserve System had lost leadership "owing to its failure promptly and effectively to reverse the engines at the critical moment. The rudder then passed into the hands of stock-exchange operators, who have now for many months governed the flow of money not only in the United States, but in the principal marts of the world. History, which has a painful way of repeating itself, has taught mankind that speculative overexpansion invariably ends in overcontraction and distress."[16]

During all this period there was disagreement within the System over what should be done. Some feared that a policy of energetic restraint might upset business, where some indications of slackening had appeared. Others thought that the discount rate should be raised to discourage further speculation. In May such action was recommended by the Federal Advisory Council. At last on August 9 the Reserve Board permitted an increase in the rate at the Federal Reserve Bank of New York from 5 to 6 per cent, the first advance there in more than a year. But by that time the stock market had taken off on its final flight into the wide open spaces. Using the Dow-Jones industrial average, the high for June was 333.79; for July, 347.70; for August, 380.33; and on September 3, the peak of 381.17 (closing price).

At this dizzy height the stock market hesitated, retreated, and finally fell over the precipice in October. On that memorable day of October 29, 1929, no fewer than 16,410,000 shares of stock were sold on the New York Stock Exchange. A flood of margin calls forced sales at any price. The Dow-Jones industrial average closed at 230.07, down thirty points from the previous day and sixty-nine points from two days before. After a fitful rally, the industrial average skidded further to 198.69 on November 13. The carnival of folly was over.

During the stock market crisis the Reserve System acted promptly

[16] Paul M. Warburg, *The Federal Reserve System*, New York, The Macmillan Company, 1930, Vol. I, pp. 823-24.

and effectively to ease the credit strain. In November the discount rate of the New York Reserve Bank was cut to 5 per cent and again to 4½ per cent, large open-market purchases were made, and member-bank paper was discounted freely.

The stock market explosion was the forerunner of the long and deep depression of the 1930's. In fact, business activity had already commenced to slip before the market crash. For a while, in early 1930, the situation looked brighter. Stocks staged a vigorous recovery, and it appeared that the decline in business might level off. But before midyear, industrial production, employment, stock prices, and other indicators were again headed downward into depression.

SUMMARY

The Federal Reserve System began operations under the shadow of World War I. In the first two years its energies were devoted mainly to organization and procedures. After our entrance into the war, the System contributed efficient and valuable aid through its fiscal agency functions and other operations. Credit policy was tied in with the needs of Treasury financing throughout the war and until about the end of 1919. In 1920-21 the Reserve Board was severely criticized for promoting deflation. While much of this was unjustified, more vigorous credit action in 1919 might have softened the subsequent depression.

The decade of the 1920's brought the first real development of an independent credit policy. In 1923, open-market operations were added to the discount rate as a method of credit regulation. Twice, in 1924 and 1927, credit action was taken with an eye to the financial situation in Europe. During 1928-29 there was delay in applying restraint to speculation, for fear of the possible effect on business.

In appraising the years 1914-29, it should be remembered that the new and untried Federal Reserve System had to feel its way through a period characterized by unusual and difficult problems.

SUGGESTED READINGS

ANDERSON, BENJAMIN M., *Economics and the Public Welfare*, New York, D. Van Nostrand Company, Inc., 1949.

BOPP, KARL R., *Three Decades of Federal Reserve Policy*, Postwar Economic Studies No. 8, Washington, Board of Governors of the Federal Reserve System, 1947, pp. 1–9.

BURGESS, W. RANDOLPH, *The Reserve Banks and the Money Market*, New York, Harper & Brothers, 1936, pp. 110–20.

GOLDENWEISER, E. A., *Monetary Management*, New York, McGraw-Hill Book Company, Inc., 1949, pp. 45–56.

HARDING, W. P. G., *The Formative Period of the Federal Reserve System*, Boston and New York, Houghton Mifflin Company, 1925.

KEMMERER, EDWIN W., *The ABC of the Federal Reserve System*, Princeton, Princeton University Press, 1922, Chapters V and IX.

MILLER, A. C., "Federal Reserve Policy," *American Economic Review*, June, 1921, Part I.

SPRAGUE, O. M. W., and BURGESS, W. RANDOLPH, "Money and Credit and Their Effect on Business," in *Recent Economic Changes*, New York, published for the National Bureau of Economic Research, Inc., by the McGraw-Hill Book Company, Inc., 1929, Vol. II, Chapter X.

WARBURG, PAUL M., *The Federal Reserve System*, New York, The Macmillan Company, 1930, Vol. I, Chapters 7, 11; Addendum II; Appendix 37.

WEISSMAN, RUDOLPH L., *The New Federal Reserve System*, New York, Harper & Brothers, 1936, pp. 221–66.

Chapter 15

THE FEDERAL RESERVE SYSTEM DURING THE 1930's

THE thirties were as difficult a time for the Federal Reserve System as they were for the nation. The economy, which the System had been expected to stabilize, sank into deep depression. The banking system, whose soundness was the special concern of the Federal Reserve, collapsed ignominiously. The international monetary and credit mechanism, for which the System had done so much during the twenties, foundered in devaluations, exchange controls, and defaults. Though these calamities were scarcely the fault of the System, they severely disappointed the hopes that had been built up around monetary policy as a stabilizing force.

From this experience came reforms that in many ways strengthened the Federal Reserve. But the economy refused to react to the stimulation that monetary and credit policy could offer. Meanwhile, the painfully slow revival was accompanied by a growth in excess reserves that threatened to deprive the System also of its power to restrain some future boom. Thus, by the end of the decade, monetary policy saw itself displaced largely by fiscal policy. The Federal Reserve's own functions were shifting in the direction of regulating prices in the Government bond market instead of controlling money and credit. It was not until ten years later that monetary policy was fully rehabilitated.

1. THE STRUGGLE AGAINST THE DEPRESSION, 1929-33

The economic decline of the early thirties was, in terms both of duration and magnitude, one of the most severe contractions in

United States economic history. From its peak in June 1929 to the trough of the depression in 1932, the Federal Reserve index of industrial production[1] dropped from 125 to 58. The index of factory employment fell from a peak of 109 in August 1929 to a low of 61 in July 1932.[2] Unemployment increased from 2.6 million in December, 1929 to an all-time high of 15.7 million in March, 1933.

The three-year downswing proceeded without interruption except for a short revival in 1931. At that time, when the recovery hung in the balance, the breakdown of the international financial mechanism ushered in a new downward phase. In the spring of 1933, the country's economic crisis culminated in complete financial collapse.

Federal Reserve Action, 1929-30

The Federal Reserve System's reaction to the onset of the depression in 1929 was immediate. Following the stock market crash in October, the System purchased $375 million of Government securities. This action was designed principally to permit the banks to take over some of the loans to the stock market that were being called precipitously by nonbank lenders. Before the year was out, discount rates had been lowered from a range of 5–6 per cent before to 4½–5 per cent after the crash.

In 1930 the System continued to ease credit. In the course of the year, discount rates were brought down to a level of 2 to 3½ per cent. The Reserve Banks also purchased another $218 million of Government securities. These open-market operations enabled the banks to pay off a good part of their borrowings from the System, which dropped from $632 million at the end of 1929 to $251 million at the end of 1930. Loans and investments of member banks, however, shrank during the year and so did the money supply.

The 1931 Episode

During the first half of 1931 the System continued to ease credit. In January, several of the Reserve Banks once more lowered their discount rates, although five banks still maintained rates as high as 3½ per cent. In its efforts to supply the banks with reserves, the System was aided by an inflow of gold from abroad. As a result, member banks decreased their indebtedness to the Reserve Banks to a low of $132 million in April. Member banks also added to their

---

[1] Base year 1923-25 = 100, seasonally adjusted.
[2] Base year 1923-25.

holdings of Government securities. Loans, however, continued to decrease.

A modest revival began to be witnessed during the early part of 1931. The index of industrial production rose four points from December 1930 to April 1931; during the same period the decline in factory employment was almost stabilized. A continued decline in the wholesale price index and in bank loans, however, was indicative of underlying weakness. In May 1931, a slackening in industrial production was once more apparent.

As soon as the revival began to taper off, the System took renewed action to ease credit. In May, ten Federal Reserve Banks lowered their discount rates; at the end of June the System resumed the purchase of Government securities. The banks, however, used the funds mostly to increase their holdings of Government securities and to build up their excess reserves. Lending activity remained slack and outstanding loans continued to decline. During this renewed downward phase, the production index declined ten points from its high of 88 in April to 78 in August.

At this point, the deepening depression acquired momentum from the financial crisis abroad. The evolution of this crisis will be traced in the following section. By September 1931, it culminated in the abandonment of the gold standard by Britain. Confidence, already at a low ebb, received a further severe jolt. As fears of dollar devaluation began to gain ground, gold started to leave the United States.

The Federal Reserve responded to the gold outflow by reversing its easy money policy. This action has been much criticized because it aggravated domestic difficulties. In the light of present-day central bank philosophy, this criticism is probably justified. At that time, the System saw two reasons for acting as it did, one technical and largely adventitious, the other rooted in well established central bank tradition.

The technical reason for tightening credit in the face of a gold outflow derived from an awkward and ill-conceived provision of the Federal Reserve Act. The Act allowed the System to use both gold and eligible paper as backing for Federal Reserve currency, but to the extent that eligible paper fell short of the permissible maximum, proportionally more gold was required. Repayment of borrowings by the banks had decreased Federal Reserve holdings of eligible paper to around $300 million. This called for an increase in the gold backing. From February to August, gold formed 80 per cent or more of the collateral held against Federal Reserve Bank notes. As gold began to leave the country, the Federal Reserve faced a threat to its note cover, although that cover was at an extraordinarily high level.

The desire to preserve the gold cover of its notes, however, was not the only reason for the change in Federal Reserve policy. Traditionally, central banks have met balance of payments crises by tighter credit. This action is intended to reinforce the automatic gold standard mechanism by attracting funds from abroad and, over a longer period, restraining imports and encouraging exports. In taking measures to tighten credit, the System merely acted in the classical tradition. Thus, in October, following the depreciation of the pound, discount rates were being put up, by some Reserve Banks more than once. At the end of November, they ranged from 3½ to 4 per cent, as compared with 1½ to 3½ before the depreciation. Meanwhile, the gold loss reduced member-bank reserves and drove member-bank borrowings up from $333 million in September to $638 million in December 1931.

Domestically, the Federal Reserve's action in the fall of 1931 had its repercussions. Pressure was put on the banks at a time when they were already in difficulty. Bond prices declined following the System's tightening moves. This, in combination with inflexible bank examination practices, forced many banks into receivership. In the last four months of 1931 the number of bank suspensions rose sharply. The economy contracted further, and by the end of the year the index of industrial production stood at 74, a drop of ten points from 1930. The index of wholesale prices dropped another 14 per cent over the year and unemployment rose 4 million to almost 11 million.

The problem created by the rigidity of the Federal Reserve Act was resolved legislatively in February 1932 with the passage of the Glass-Steagall Act. The Act enabled the System to use government securities in addition to eligible paper as backing for its notes, subject, of course, to the continuing 40 per cent gold requirement. Thereafter the Federal Reserve, despite the continuing gold outflow, added steadily to its open-market portfolio. During the first nine months of 1932, the Reserve Banks bought $1 billion of government securities. The magnitude of this operation suggests how severely the System was hampered by the previous legal restriction. The fact that the Federal Reserve undertook these purchases while a gold outflow was in progress also indicates that adherence to traditional behavior in the face of a gold outflow was reversed rather easily.

Hand in hand with open-market purchases went further reductions in discount rates during the first half of 1932. In June 1932, discount rates ranged from 2½ to 3½ per cent. Meanwhile, member banks were able to decrease substantially their indebtedness to the Reserve Banks. They also used the reserves supplied by the Federal Reserve Banks to add to their government security holdings and to increase their excess reserves. In June, gold slowly began to return to the United States as fear of dollar devaluation diminished. Bank reserves were eased further by this reversal.

The Bottom Is Reached

The low point in industrial activity was reached in July 1932, when the index touched 58. Thereafter, for the next three months, activity began to rise. Factory employment also showed an increase. The 1932 revival, however, like its predecessor in 1931, was lacking in force. Wholesale prices continued to decline throughout the period. Toward the end of the year, the advance petered out and industrial production remained stagnant at a very low level.

In this brief 1932 recovery period, the Federal Reserve System played an inactive role. Discount rates remained unchanged; and after August, Reserve Banks' holdings of Government securities also remained substantially stable. Incoming gold then became the source of reserves for the banks. As in previous periods of reserve expansion, these funds were used by the banks to repay their borrowings from the Federal Reserve Banks and, in good measure, were allowed to go into excess reserves. At the end of 1932 the major economic indices, including the money supply, remained well below their 1931 levels.

Meanwhile, the difficulties of the banks increased. Toward the end of the year, bank suspensions again grew sharply. To the evils of falling bond prices and mounting loan defaults was added a growing demand for currency on the part of hoarders. Early in 1933 the banks began to feel extreme pressure. Bank suspensions increased markedly in January and February 1933. By early March the situation reached the crisis stage.

Thanks to the rapid rise in Federal Reserve note circulation, which was the result of widespread currency hoarding, the Federal Reserve System again found itself in a tight reserve position. The situation was aggravated as gold once more began to leave the country. By

March 3, the reserve ratio (gold to deposit liabilities and note issue) had declined to 45.3 per cent, close to its minimum of 35 and 40 per cent respectively. As in 1931, the System reacted to this threat in the traditional way. In a last futile gesture, a day before the banking collapse, the New York and Chicago Reserve Banks raised their discount rates. The action remained academic because banking operations came to a standstill on March 4. Perhaps it was symbolic that the last action in this phase of the depression should have reflected the limitations imposed upon monetary policy by tradition and rigid legislation. Major changes in both were ahead.

Other Credit Agencies

. Early in the fight against the depression it became clear that the Federal Reserve System could not cope with the need for emergency and salvage credit, which presented itself with growing urgency. To banks the System could lend only on eligible paper. The desperate needs of manufacturing, railroad, and other enterprises, threatened with imminent bankruptcy, were totally outside its purview. To meet these needs in some measure, a number of new lending agencies were rapidly improvised by the government.

One of the earliest of these agencies was the National Credit Corporation, created in October 1931. Funds for it were secured by subscriptions from the banking system itself, with the idea that the stronger banks should help the weaker ones. Loans by the Corporation in any one Federal Reserve district were limited to the amount of subscriptions obtained in that district.

The National Credit Corporation did not fulfill the hopes placed in it. One reason was the unfortunate organization on a regional basis. The districts where the need was greatest also had the least funds to lend. A second reason lay in the natural reluctance of the banks to publicize their difficulties to competitors by applying for assistance. Finally, with the RFC already in the formative stage early in 1932, many banks apparently preferred to wait and see if it would provide a better solution.

In February 1932, the banking system—as well as other sectors of the economy—received new governmental support through the Reconstruction Finance Corporation. Organized with an original capital of $500 million, and an additional borrowing power of $1.5 billion, the RFC made loans to hard-pressed banks and other financial institutions, and later also purchased their preferred stock.

The RFC was a powerful factor in slowing down the wave of bank failures in 1932. In that year, the agency loaned $850 million to approximately 5,600 banks and trust companies. As a result, commercial bank suspensions in 1932 were held to 1,453 against 2,293 in 1931; about 40 per cent of the 1932 suspensions occurred in January, before the RFC was in operation.

The RFC might have been still more effective had its lending policies in its early days been more flexible. Initially, following sound banking principles, the agency usually demanded the best assets of the borrowing banks as collateral. The banks were left with only their weaker assets and so did not get the full benefit of the RFC's financial assistance. Later the RFC modified its procedures by purchasing preferred stock, thereby ranking its claim behind that of the depositor instead of ahead.

Last among the more important early props to the credit system was the creation of the Federal Home Loan Banks. Their purpose was to deal with the grave difficulties into which real estate lenders had fallen; they made loans to building and loan associations, insurance companies, savings banks, and other credit institutions on the security of home mortgages.

The Collapse of the Banking System

In March 1933, the banking system, whose position had been weakening steadily throughout the depression, finally collapsed. On Inauguration Day, March 4, almost all the banks in the United States were closed. Many of them were never to reopen. For a modern economy this offered an extraordinary and unbelievable spectacle.

It was the depression that broke the banks, but the origins of the banking crisis can be traced back far into the twenties and even earlier. Evidence of this progressive deterioration is the increase in bank failures during the twenties, when suspensions averaged 500 per year against only about 80 per year during the preceding decade.

Many factors contributed to the gradual weakening of the banking system. Some involved structural defects; others stemmed from the economic conditions of the time. Both kinds were instrumental in bringing about the final breakdown.

Among the major structural defects lying behind the increase in bank failures during the twenties was the rapid increase in the number of small nonmember banks with inadequate capital resources. Many of these failures reflected the inability of the institutions to withstand any significant depreciation of their assets. Failures were especially frequent in rural areas, where the worsening farm situation was acutely felt by the banks.

A second problem affecting some of the larger banks derived from their relation to securities affiliates and from activities in the securities markets generally. These relations and activities influenced the banks' investment decisions, not always in the direction of soundness, and became a source of trouble.

Federal Reserve member banks, on the whole, fared much better during the twenties than nonmember banks. It is evidence of the effectiveness of the System that it was able, through its discount privileges, regular examinations, and the reserve and capital requirements imposed upon member banks, to avoid the high rate of failures that during the twenties affected nonmember banks. Nevertheless, the Federal Reserve itself contributed unintentionally to certain weaknesses among its members. These weaknesses, ironically enough, derived in part from the very security offered by the System through its rediscount privileges. By providing a feeling of security, the System inadvertently encouraged some banks to lower their liquidity in the erroneous assumption that the Federal Reserve would protect them against all difficulties. For national banks, moreover, membership in the System had brought a substantial lowering of reserve requirements. This meant that during the twenties, aside from the liquidity provided by the rediscount privilege, bank liquidity tended to be lower than in previous decades. In addition, the competition between the Federal Reserve and the state banking authorities led to practices in the area of capital requirements and bank examination that, perhaps, were not altogether unfairly characterized as "competition in laxity."

Superimposed on the structural weaknesses were several current economic factors. One was the farm situation produced by the first World War, when farmers had paid high prices for land based on crop prices that could not be sustained. A second was the real estate boom of the twenties that led to much speculation and unsound financing. A third was the eagerness of some banks to invest in the many high-yielding bonds issued at that time which did not stand up under the depression. Another was the competition among banks for deposits, leading to the payment of high interest rates, which once more became a motive for seeking out high-yielding but excessively risky investments.

When the crash came, these factors, structural and economic, began to weigh increasingly upon the banking situation. The first banks to close, as said before, were predominantly the small banks with a large percentage of local loans and mortgages. The larger banks, on the whole, were able to hold out until later in the depression, when their problems were compounded by large-scale currency withdrawals.

It was this final wave of currency hoarding that brought on the ultimate collapse. Currency in circulation had been increasing gradually since the onset of the depression. The early rise was in good measure due to the fact that the increased bank closings necessitated the holding of larger amounts of cash. Toward the turn of the year 1932, however, this gradual rise took on a different cast. The first indication of panic hoarding was the failure of currency, drawn into circulation during the Christmas holidays, to return fully to the banks. Beginning in February, the circulation jumped up markedly. The banks increasingly became unable to meet the unexpected demands. Their good assets were generally pledged and the remaining were in most cases illiquid. Banks far away from currency centers, moreover, were hampered by the difficulty of securing currency before their own supply was depleted.

To protect the banks against runs, bank holidays became prevalent on a local and later state-wide basis. But instead of restraining panic, these holidays only seemed to increase it. There was a constant nervous shifting of deposits, from banks thought unsafe or ready to close because of local holidays, to "safe" banks. When banks in one locality closed, neighboring banks suffered runs. Even the many sound banks that had pursued conservative investment policies could hardly cope with such a situation.

During the first week of March 1933, currency in circulation averaged $7 billion, compared with $5.3 billion a year earlier. On March 4 almost all banks had become subject to local or state holidays. Immediately after taking office, President Roosevelt declared a nationwide bank holiday, using powers derived from the Trading with the Enemy Act still in existence since the first World War. The national bank holiday lasted from March 6 to 9. On these days, the banks could transact only limited business as specified by the Secretary of the Treasury. After the ninth, the banks were slowly licensed to reopen by the Secretary of the Treasury as they were found in sound condition under the regulations of the Emergency Banking Act of 1933.

Confidence somewhat restored, the banking crisis passed quickly. Currency in circulation returned to the newly licensed banks and by June the level of currency in circulation was back to its pre-crisis level of about $5.5 billion. Many banks, however, never reopened and at the end of 1933 there were 3,360 fewer commercial banks in existence than in 1932. The experience of the collapse shaped the thinking of bankers for many years to come, and the extreme caution which resulted was a factor in the slowness of the following revival.

The Breakdown of the International Financial System

Hand in hand with the domestic difficulties that confronted the Federal Reserve went the breakdown of the international gold standard and of the world-wide credit system built on it, both of which the Federal Reserve had worked so hard during the twenties to re-establish. As the depression in the United States advanced, distress in Europe and elsewhere also mounted. Banks found themselves in growing difficulties, and war debts to the United States and short-term international commitments became increasingly hard to meet. The increase in the United States tariff rates in 1930 added to Europe's problems. In the spring of 1931, the closing of the Credit Anstalt, Austria's leading bank, marked the beginning of major bank defaults that soon engulfed Germany. International short-term money fled in panic from one country to another. Central bank gold reserves proved inadequate to facilitate these transfers, and exchange controls were imposed by several countries. President Hoover tried to salvage the situation by proposing a moratorium on all war debts, but the move came too late.

By the end of the summer, England found herself in acute foreign exchange difficulties. Faced with the prospect of withdrawals that would exhaust her gold holdings, especially on the part of France, England was forced to suspend the gold standard in September 1931. Following the British action, the run on gold spread to the United States. The resultant gold losses, and the Federal Reserve's response in tightening credit, contributed to the downturn at the end of 1931.

A second major blow was dealt to the international financial mechanism with the dollar devaluation of 1933-34. The episode began with a loss of gold of almost $300 million during the banking crisis of

February and March 1933. President Roosevelt believed it necessary to meet this by subjecting the export of gold to license. At first licenses were granted freely, but on April 20 the export of gold was prohibited, with certain exceptions, such as gold previously earmarked for foreign governments. This grave decision meant that the dollar had ceased to be a stable currency; it opened the way to the slow depreciation in its value which culminated in the fixing of a new parity in January 1934.

The decline of the dollar continued throughout 1933. In the fall of 1933 the Treasury began to purchase domestically mined gold at a gradually increasing price in order deliberately to speed the movement. This policy, it was hoped, would raise the domestic price level and stimulate exports. In November 1933, purchases of foreign gold were begun, in order to force the dollar down further. By December the United States buying price was $34.06 per fine ounce.

On January 30, 1934, under the Gold Reserve Act, the dollar was stabilized at $35 per fine ounce, against a previous parity of $20.67. The Treasury became the only legal holder of gold, except for that needed for artistic and commercial use. The Federal Reserve's gold was turned over to the Treasury in exchange for gold certificates.

Part of the profit which the Treasury derived from revaluing to $35 gold that it had acquired at $20.67 was employed to retire the currency privilege bonds on the security of which national banks had in the past been allowed to issue their own notes. This terminated in effect the circulation of national bank notes. Another part of the profit was used to establish the Stabilization Fund. Its purpose was to stabilize the international value of the dollar abroad, although the course of events was to show there was no need and not even a proper place for a fund of this sort in a monetary framework where the Treasury held large gold reserves and bought and sold gold at a fixed price.

The devaluation in retrospect proved to have been a measure of questionable wisdom. Insofar as it aimed at correcting an adverse balance of payments, it was addressed to a problem essentially minor and temporary that did not justify so far-reaching an action. The principal goal pursued—to raise the price level from its depression low—was indeed important and urgent. But the theory upon which the devaluation was based, and which postulated some direct and immediate relation between the price of gold and the price of commodities, proved altogether fallacious, as most economists had said it would. Some export prices did advance substantially, but the wholesale price index advanced only 8 per cent. A more substantial spurt in prices came a year or so later, as a product of the improving economic situation rather than of the devaluation.

2. THE REFORMS

The financial crisis over, energetic steps were taken to overhaul the monetary and financial mechanism of the country. The reform measures aimed to eliminate the weaknesses that had caused the breakdown of the banking and credit system, to correct the abuses that had become apparent, and to give the Federal Reserve System greater powers to deal with economic fluctuations. To further these ends the activities of commercial banks were regulated and their deposits insured. The securities business was subjected to extensive regulation. The Federal Reserve System itself underwent major revisions and received added powers to regulate credit and bank reserves. For the most part, these changes were incorporated in the Banking Acts of 1933 and 1935, the Securities Act of 1933, and in the Securities Exchange Act of 1934. The content and effect of these new laws will form the substance of the present section.

The Reform Legislation and the Banks

The reform legislation, as it affected the banks, was mainly of a restrictive character. It sought to eliminate some of the major factors that had led to weakness of bank assets in the past. By including a deposit insurance feature, the legislation also sought to strengthen the banks on their liability side.

To improve their investment practices, commercial banks were ordered to divest themselves of any securities affiliations (Banking Act of 1933). No officer, director, or manager of a member bank could be an employee of a security firm without the Federal Reserve Board's permission (Banking Act of 1933). This restriction was later extended to ordinary employees of member banks (Banking Act of 1935). Purchases of securities of a speculative nature were expressly forbidden and security loans were made subject to margin requirements issued by the Federal Reserve Board. New loans to officers, a frequent source of abuse, were forbidden.

The liabilities of the banking system were affected by two important changes. The most dramatic of these was the creation of the Federal Deposit Insurance Corporation (Banking Act of 1933). Its aim was to protect the small depositor against loss and at the same time to aid the banking system by removing one of the major causes of panic. The original Corporation was set up on a temporary basis and provided only up to $2,500 insurance on each deposit account. The permanent FDIC was organized in 1935, insuring deposits up to $5,000. An annual assessment of one-twelfth of 1 per cent of the total deposits of the insured bank was provided for in the 1935 Act. By its periodic examinations, the FDIC provided additional and highly effective supervision for a large portion of the banking system. Membership in the FDIC was open to all commercial and mutual savings banks capable of meeting certain minimum standards. Originally it was provided that all FDIC members with deposits of over $1 million were to join the Federal Reserve System by 1941. This requirement was dropped eventually owing to bank resistance.

The second major provision relating to liabilities was the prohibition of interest payments on demand deposits of all banks, and the limitation of interest on time and savings deposits payable by Federal Reserve member banks at the discretion of the Federal Reserve Board. This was intended to put a stop to excessive competition among banks for deposits, with its attendant consequence of excessively risky loan and investment policies.

The Reform Legislation and the Federal Reserve System

Major revisions were also made in the Federal Reserve Act. Three main objectives stand out: (1) to broaden the System's powers to deal with fluctuations in the economy, (2) to increase its flexibility for emergency action, and (3) to centralize more of the System's power in Washington and reduce the autonomy of the twelve regional banks.

Perhaps the most important power given to the System was that of changing reserve requirements of member banks up to twice the level of the requirements then in force (Banking Act of 1935). This power became very important owing to the great subsequent rise in excess reserves. It now ranks as one of the three principal tools of monetary policy, together with discount policy and open-market operations.

A second power entrusted to the System was that over credit in the securities market (Securities and Exchange Act of 1934). The Federal Reserve Board received authority to impose margin require-

ments on security loans of banks, brokers, and dealers. Soon afterward the Board implemented this power by issuing Regulation T,
which placed limitations on loans by brokers and dealers on security
collateral. Margin requirements on security loans of banks (Regulation U), however, were not stipulated until 1936.

A third power given to the System consisted of increased authority
to support the banking system in an emergency. In any future
emergency, loans could be made on the security of all "satisfactory"
assets (Banking Act of 1935). This faculty had been authorized
temporarily also by the Glass-Steagall Act of 1932, although no full
use of it had been made. Lack of such power previously had compelled the System to stand by idly as banks went under that had no
"eligible" paper but could offer other adequate security for emergency rediscounts. With this provision the Federal Reserve became a
more effective lender of last resort.

Revisions in the organizational framework of the Federal Reserve
System followed the centralizing trend of the times. The relation between the Federal Reserve Board in Washington, renamed in 1935
the Board of Governors of the Federal Reserve System, and the
regional banks was redefined to strengthen the hand of the Board.
The Open Market Committee, originally an informal group of representatives of first five and later all of the Reserve Banks, was trans-
formed into a statutory body with five Reserve Bank presidents and
seven Governors, giving the Board of Governors a clear majority
(Banking Act of 1935). Even so, the Open Market Committee was to
become a stronghold of Reserve Bank influence, for the new powers
over reserve requirements and stock market credit went exclusively
to the Board.

Another change, intended to strengthen the Board and to increase
its independence, was the removal of the Secretary of the Treasury
and the Comptroller of the Currency from Board membership. In
practice, the principal effect of this measure may have been to weaken
the liaison between Federal Reserve and Treasury at a time when the
growing public debt called for closer collaboration. To ensure
adequate stability of policy, the terms of the Governors were lengthened to twelve and eventually to fourteen years.

Finally, the System's power to regulate credit was defined more
clearly by making explicit the power of the Reserve Banks to deny
credit to member banks offering eligible paper (Banking Acts of
1933 and 1935). Previously, it could have been argued that the

possession of eligible paper conferred a right to Federal Reserve credit, as was done in a court case involving a Reserve Bank's refusal to discount the paper of a bank that increased its security loans, even though the Reserve Bank was upheld in this instance.

These changes undoubtedly did much to strengthen the monetary powers of the System. They also contributed to making the System a more effective operating agency. In this latter sense, they probably ran counter to the intentions of the founding fathers of the System, who had emphasized decentralization. But in effect they ratified and accelerated a trend that events and perhaps the inner logic of the organization had long been pushing—in the direction of greater power focused in Washington.

The strengthening of monetary tools and concentration of power came at a time, however, when events were running against monetary policy and the institutions charged with it. The Federal Reserve had failed to save the country from depression. It had not even been able to save the banking system, its chosen instrument and ward, from bitter collapse. Mounting excess reserves were making the future capabilities of monetary policy even more problematical. Thus, despite new powers and organizational improvements, the System's role was destined to remain on the downgrade for a number of years.

Matters might have been different if the System had boldly abandoned its pure central banking principles and had reached for monetary and credit power wherever such power was developing in new institutions. The System probably could without difficulty have taken control of the RFC had it wanted to. Mr. Eugene Meyer, who headed the Board at that time, was one of the intellectual creators and simultaneously also the first chairman of the RFC. The System might have been able to take charge of the functions of some of the other emergency credit agencies of the Government, of the FDIC and of the Stabilization Fund. It might then have had a much stronger position both within the economy and within the government. Monetary policy considerations might have been defended more effectively as a result, before and during the war as well as after.

But it is equally conceivable that such broadening of the concept of central banking might have distracted the System from its basic function of maintaining monetary and economic stability. This evidently was the view of those who decided against an attempt to achieve that broadening. As a result of their insistence on keeping central banking simon-pure, the System went through an agonizing period of diminishing influence and diminishing national regard for the needs of anti-inflationary monetary policy. But the successful revival of a free and effective monetary policy during the fifties may be thought to confirm the wisdom of the decision of the thirties to keep the central bank pure.

The Security Market Reforms

One of the first signals of the impending depression had been the crash of October 1929. The deepening slump had revealed a number of weaknesses and questionable practices in the securities field. Millions of investors had lost their money. No wonder, therefore, that the securities market was among the first segments of the financial mechanism to experience thoroughgoing reform through the Securities Act of 1933, which was passed a few weeks before the Banking Act of 1933 and the Securities and Exchange Act of 1934.

Three principal areas were emphasized in this legislation: (1) the issuance of new securities, (2) the relation between the issuer and the holder of already outstanding securities, and (3) trading in securities.

To protect the buyer of new securities and impede obviously unsound financing, an elaborate procedure was worked out. All new issues, with certain exceptions, such as those of intrastate corporations, railroads, and banks, had to be registered with the newly created Securities and Exchange Commission. The SEC passed only on the completeness of the information however, not on the financial soundness of the securities. Detailed disclosure was required, with severe penalties for officers and directors in case of incomplete or false statements.

To protect holders of already outstanding securities, the issuers were required to file periodic reports with the SEC. Better facilities were required to enable stockholders to make their votes effective in stockholders' meetings. Information was required regarding the financial interests of officers and directors.

Trading in securities, finally, was reformed extensively. The SEC was given broad powers to regulate the securities exchanges and the conduct of buyers and sellers. Speculation was curbed substantially. Stock market credit, as noted earlier, was placed under the control of the Federal Reserve.

At the time of their inception, bitter opposition was voiced to the new security laws. It was argued that the cost of preparing registration statements for the SEC, as well as the legal liabilities attaching to these statements, might severely hamper the offerings of new securities. While it is true that new security offerings were small during the thirties, this probably was due chiefly to the lack of business. Since then experience and cooperation have made the new rules workable. Excesses of the kind that occurred during the twenties have not been repeated. The reforms have increased public confidence in the securities markets and have, no doubt, contributed in good measure to the increasing ability of the markets to attract new investors.

3. THE RECOVERY PERIOD

Following the banking crisis of March 1933, the United States began its long, slow pull toward recovery. The Federal Reserve aided the recovery by sponsoring a setting of monetary ease, greatly intensified by a large gold inflow, but monetary policy proved insufficient to influence business conditions decisively. In 1937, after an incomplete recovery, the economy suffered a severe relapse. It snapped back again a year later, when renewed deficit spending and war preparations abroad supplied the needed impetus to expansion.

a. Revival and Boom

Until 1936, the Federal Reserve continued to follow a policy of extreme ease. Soon after the banking crisis had passed, the Reserve Banks resumed the purchase of government securities. By the end of 1933, the System's holdings had increased by $580 million. Discount rates were lowered at eight banks and at the end of the year ranged from 2 to 3½ per cent, with half the Reserve Banks posting a rate below 3 per cent, as against an average rate of 3½ per cent at the time of the banking crisis. Member-bank excess reserves at the end of the year stood at $859 million, an increase of $280 million over the previous December.

During the next two years, discount rates were lowered still further, to reach a range of 1½ to 2 per cent at the end of 1935. The System, however, made no further open-market purchases after the end of 1933. Instead it allowed the rising gold inflow to provide additional liquidity. From the end of February 1934 to December 1935, this inflow amounted to $2.6 billion. It supplied the banks with sufficient funds to reduce their discounts to the nominal amount of $5 million, and to increase their excess reserves to $2.8 billion.

Extreme monetary ease failed to produce an expansion in commercial bank loans. These continued to decline in 1934 and rose only insignificantly in 1935, ending with a net reduction over the two-year period of $1.1 billion. Commercial bank purchases of Government securities, however, which helped finance the annual deficits, amounted to $5.2 billion for the two years from June 1933 to June 1935. In consequence of these purchases, the gold inflow, and other lesser expansion factors, bank deposits rose by almost $10 billion over the two year period.

Business recovery in 1934 and 1935 was unsteady and slow. Extreme monetary ease proved insufficient to accelerate it. By the end of 1935, unemployment was still at 10 million. In 1936, however, the tempo of the recovery quickened. At the same time, evidence of speculation reappeared. Stock market quotations and raw-material prices began to advance rapidly. Although the recovery was still far from complete, the nature of the movement compelled the authorities to consider the need to restrain speculation.

In April 1936, the Federal Reserve Board took a first small step to restrain the stock market. Margin requirements for brokers' loans were raised from a range of 25-55 to a flat 55 per cent. Regulation U was promulgated, imposing margin requirements on security loans made by banks.

Meanwhile, the continuing inflow of gold kept excess reserves on the rise. By mid-1936, they stood at $3 billion, an amount that the sale of the entire open market portfolio of the Federal Reserve could not have absorbed. In view of the evidence of incipient boom, it appeared dangerous to the monetary authorities to be so far out of touch with the market. Consequently, in August 1936, the Federal Reserve moved to curtail excess reserves by raising reserve requirements 50 per cent. The Board made clear at the time that its purpose was not to restrict credit, but to bring excess reserves down to a level where the banks would have less of a cushion against credit control measures that might be taken at some future time.

The action brought excess reserves down temporarily to something over $1.5 billion, without further repercussions on the credit and business picture. But by December, the gold flow had advanced them once more to well over $2 billion, despite the seasonal currency outflow. At that point, the Treasury decided to stop the monetization of the gold it had to purchase. A procedure to "sterilize" new gold acquisitions was instituted. Instead of financing the purchase of gold by issuing gold certificates against it, which the Federal Reserve received and for which it credited the account of the Treasury, the Treasury began to reimburse itself for its gold purchases by borrowing from the market. The sterilization policy applied both to gold imports and to purchases of domestically mined gold. As a result of it, the factor most responsible for the growth in member bank reserves was eliminated. This was accomplished at the cost, however, of increasing the public debt and of turning over the control of bank reserves, at least in part, to the Treasury. The money supply, of course, was not affected by sterilization. It leveled off in 1937 for other reasons, after a steady rise since 1934.

As the speculative climate seemed to expand, the Federal Reserve took further action to cut down the remaining excess reserves. This was to be accomplished by another increase in reserve requirements, to their full legal maximum. The rise, announced in January, was scheduled in two stages, one half in March, the other in May.

This action proved unfortunate, though the seriousness of the consequences has often been greatly overrated. After the full increase in requirements had taken effect, excess reserves remained at close to $1 billion, with rediscounts practically zero. By all normal standards this was an extaordinary amount of liquidity. But the banks meanwhile had become accustomed to large excess reserves. Some individual banks, no doubt, were in a less comfortable position than the average. In consequence, some bond sales occurred; the Government bond market turned down, and the Federal Reserve found it advisable to offset its actions to some extent by purchasing about $100 million of securities. The mild drop in the bond market would scarcely have been sufficient to produce a dip in business, but a variety of other factors coincided at the time that took the steam out of the boom.

Recession

Government spending, which had provided the main support of the economy since the depression, was curtailed, while revenues rose, and in the first half of 1937 the Treasury had sizable net receipts. The Social Security tax, passed in 1936, began to affect consumption. The Undistributed Profits Tax acted to contract investment out of retained earnings. Rising wages and raw-material costs began to discourage business investment and new home construction.

Beginning with the summer of 1937, business turned down again, and continued to slide until the spring of 1938. In one of the swiftest and deepest declines on record, industrial production dropped back to 1934 levels, wholesale prices fell 10 per cent, unemployment rose 3½ million, and stock market values were cut in half.

The Federal Reserve had little ammunition to throw into the fight against this recession. Excess reserves were still substantial; rediscounts were negligible. Nevertheless, some Reserve Banks further lowered their discount rates in August 1937. A small volume of open-market purchases were undertaken in the fall to meet an anticipated expansion in currency that, however, failed to materialize. At the request of the System, the Treasury desterilized $300 million of gold, with a corresponding increase in excess reserves. In November, the Board reduced margin requirements on security loans from 55 to 40 percent in an effort to support the sagging stock market. These efforts, however, were obviously insufficient to halt the downswing. The gold flow reversed itself and turned outward.

In April 1938, the Board cut reserve requirements by one-eighth. The Treasury desterilized the gold it had previously withheld from monetization. Since excess reserves stood close to $1.5 billion at that time, while the gold tide was once again coming in, and the Treasury bill rate was approaching zero, there was little purchase in these actions. Beginning in 1938, however, the Federal Government for the first time initiated a program of deliberate deficit spending, designed to create purchasing power in general rather than meet certain particular needs, as had been the rationale of previous deficits. This fiscal policy action probably contributed substantially to the recovery that got under way in the summer of 1938.

In this manner, it became dramatically manifest that monetary policy had been displaced by fiscal policy. The Federal Reserve's tools had failed to deal adequately with the problems of a severe recession. Even more, the Federal Reserve's own preserve of monetary policy had been entered by the Treasury in order to deal with the extraordinary phenomenon of the "golden avalanche," as a well-known book then called the gold inflow.

Support of the Bond Market

The change in the position of monetary policy was epitomized by the last important policy action the System took during the thirties—the support of the bond market at the outbreak of the war in Europe. By mid-1939, bond yields had dropped to 2¼ per cent under the pressure of excess reserves then approaching $5 billion. The outbreak of war sent the market tumbling, with yields rising close to 2¾ per cent. The System stepped into the market to stabilize it. Within one month, it bought $375 million of government securities; it also offered to make advances to member banks on government securities at par at a favorable rate. Before the year was out, the System was able to dispose of most of the securities it had acquired in September.

With this action, the System had taken a fundamental step. Until then, open-market operations had aimed at controlling the volume of bank reserves and through them the supply of money and credit. The various parts of the interest rate structure—short, intermediate, and long term—had been allowed to find a mutual adjustment in response to the forces of the market. Now, the System had taken it upon itself to influence directly the price and yield of bonds and thus the term structure of interest rates.

In doing so, it was acting in accordance with a suggestion made by John Maynard Keynes years earlier, to the effect that monetary policy would be more effective if central banks did directly determine the relation of long- to short-term rates. It was also opening the door, however, to the wartime and postwar practice of pegging interest rates, which proved to be the abdication of all monetary policy. For almost ten years following America's entry into the war, the System's main function became the rigid fixing of long-term and, for a shorter period, also of short-term interest rates. The consequences, which do not belong in this chapter, are familiar. It was not until March 1951 that, through the "Accord" with the Treasury, the System regained its freedom of action and monetary policy once more was established as an important force in the economy.

SUGGESTED READINGS

Eccles, Marriner S., *Beckoning Frontiers*, New York, Alfred A. Knopf, 1951.

Meyer, Charles H., *The Securities Exchange Act of 1934, Analyzed and Explained*, New York, Francis Emory Fitch, Inc., 1934.

Nadler, Marcus, and Bogen, Jules I., *The Banking Crisis, The End of an Epoch*, New York, Dodd, Mead and Company, 1933.

Roose, Kenneth D., *The Economics of Recession and Revival, An Interpretation of 1937–38*, New Haven, Yale University Press, 1954.

Weissman, Rudolph L., *Economic Balance and a Balanced Budget, Public Papers of Marriner S. Eccles*, New York, Harper & Brothers, 1940.

Chapter 16

THE FEDERAL RESERVE SYSTEM SINCE 1940

THE period since 1940 has been characterized by a diversity of economic conditions. The organization and the powers of the Federal Reserve System, as they had evolved during the first quarter century of the System's existence, proved adequate to cope with the financing of the most costly of all wars, the transition back to a peacetime economy and rapid postwar economic expansion.

Experience since 1940 has demonstrated that this country had developed, between 1913 and 1939, a flexible, effective central banking mechanism, one capable of functioning under widely varying economic, fiscal, and political circumstances. As compared with the period before 1940, there was much less agitation for changes in law and organization and a shift in emphasis to the formulation and application of credit-control policies by the existing organization within the framework of established law and procedures.

The history of the Federal Reserve System since 1940 falls into five distinct periods. These are:

1. The era of war finance, 1940-45.
2. The System regains its independence, 1946-53.
3. Implementing "full employment," 1953-54.
4. Fighting boom and inflation, 1955-57.
5. "Leaning against the wind," 1957-58.

THE TRANSITION TO WAR FINANCE

The readiness of the Federal Reserve System in an emergency to subordinate other monetary policy objectives to the maintenance of orderly conditions in the Government security markets was demonstrated even before the outbreak of World War II. The Federal Open

Market Committee authorized its executive committee as early as April 19, 1939, to buy up to $500 million of Government securities if the market should be seriously disturbed by armed conflict abroad. Purchases of almost this entire amount were made by the Federal Reserve Banks during September 1939, chiefly in the days immediately following the outbreak of war in Europe.

Once selling of government obligations induced by the beginning of war in Europe had run its course, however, the Open Market Committee was under pressure to end its intervention in the Government security market. The October 9, 1939, meeting of the Federal Advisory Council issued the following recommendation:[1]

> While the Council fully recognizes the need in a grave emergency, such as that recently experienced, of taking steps designed to preserve an orderly market in Government securities, it also believes that the market price of Government bonds should be allowed to find its natural level, free of official intervention, as rapidly as possible consistent with an orderly market.

A later recommendation of the Council said:

> It is not believed to be consistent with sound central banking principles that the System retain an unduly large quantity of long-term Governments especially at a time when nearly all insurance companies and many banks are desirous of acquiring these securities. . . . The System should seize the opportunity in an orderly market to clear the decks so that when and if another grave emergency develops, it will be in a position to act without then having on hand an unnecessarily heavy inventory of long-term Government bonds.

Considering that excess reserves of member banks exceeded $5 billion at the time, due to heavy gold imports, it is not surprising that this advice was heeded. Government securities were sold by the Federal Reserve banks in the last quarter of 1939. Small support purchases were again made in the spring of 1940 when German armies invaded Denmark, Norway, and the low countries. Thereafter, however, business expansion, mounting Federal defense expenditures, and the rise in excess reserves to the $7 billion level shifted the attention of the Federal Reserve authorities to the twin threats of inflation and an unstable boom.

An unprecedented special report to Congress by the Board of Gov-

[1] Annual Report of the Board of Governors of the Federal Reserve System, 1939, p. 80.

ernors, the presidents of the Federal Reserve Banks, and the Federal Advisory Council on December 31, 1940, proposed that reserve requirements of member banks be fixed at the maximum percentages authorized in the Banking Act of 1935, and that the Federal Open Market Committee be authorized to raise requirements to double these percentages to absorb excess reserves. However, Congress did not act on this suggestion.

No major step was taken to restrain credit expansion and check the rising trend of commodity prices other than to raise legal reserve requirements once again to the statutory maximum on November 1, 1941. This canceled the reduction in requirements ordered in February 1939 to combat the business recession at that time. Also, Government security holdings of the Federal Reserve Banks were reduced moderately, so that they averaged $200 million less in 1941 than in 1940. Thanks to the expansion of deposits and currency and these limited restrictive measures, however, excess reserves of member banks were cut about in half during 1941.

THE FEDERAL RESERVE IN WORLD WAR II

The Board of Governors, in a statement issued the day after Pearl Harbor, promised to use its powers to assure an ample supply of funds for financing the war effort and to maintain conditions in the Government security market that would meet the Treasury's requirements.

It took several months to implement this pledge, which was carried out fully as the war progressed. The day after Pearl Harbor, the Federal Open Market Committee authorized its executive committee to add up to $400 million to the Government security holdings of the Federal Reserve Banks. At its December 12, 1941, meeting, a further increase of $500 million was authorized, but "with the understanding that when the market recovered and conditions justified, the securities added to the System account during the current week would be resold."[2]

The fear of inflation thus continued to affect the thinking of the Open Market Committee in the days following the attack upon Pearl Harbor. Support purchases of Government securities were in limited amount, and market prices were allowed to decline moderately in the three weeks immediately following our entry into the war.

[2] *Ibid.*, 1941, p. 65.

Members of the Federal Open Market Committee, in conferences with Treasury representatives during March and April 1942, agreed that "the Federal Reserve System would supply such reserves as were necessary to assure the successful financing of the war."[3] These reserves were to be provided, and at the same time Treasury financing through all channels was to be facilitated, by means of open-market purchases of Government securities sufficient to maintain "about the then existing curve of rates." In brief, the Government security market was to be pegged.

Federal Reserve purchases to make the pegs effective had two desired effects. First, the buying supported prices of Government obligations at or above the desired level. Secondly, the purchases provided additional reserves to member banks which enabled them to buy Government securities freely and persistently for their own account. Moreover, the expansion of bank deposits resulting from such purchases provided nonbank investors with funds that enabled them to subscribe to successive offerings of Treasury obligations.

By pegging of the Government securities market, the Federal Reserve System abandoned the effort to prevent inflation of the money supply, since the Treasury's wartime financial needs were so great.

"The principal weapons against inflation," said the Board of Governors in its 1942 report, "are taxation, increased savings, and controls over goods, prices and wages. For this reason the role of credit authorities in financing a war without inflation is necessarily subordinate to that of other Government agencies."[4]

In effect, the Federal Reserve System abdicated its powers to control the volume of bank deposits. The initiative in open-market operations was shifted from the Federal Reserve System to holders of Government securities. Bank reserves could be created at will through sales of Government securities to the Federal Reserve Banks, and the excess reserves thus secured provided the basis for a continuous expansion of commercial bank holdings of Government securities, and consequently of deposits, during the war.

The first step in pegging the Government security market was a directive issued by the Federal Open Market Committee to the twelve Federal Reserve Banks on April 30, 1942, to purchase for System account all Treasury bills offered them on a three-eighths of 1 per cent discount basis. Then, at the May 8 meeting of the Federal Open

[3] *Ibid.*, 1942, p. 104.
[4] *Ibid.*, p. 26.

Market Committee, the executive committee was directed "to arrange for such transactions for the System open market account, either in the open market or directly with the Treasury, as may be necessary for the purpose of maintaining about the present general level of prices and yields of Government securities or for the purpose of maintaining an adequate supply of funds in the market."[5]

To facilitate member-bank purchases of Government securities, four further steps were taken:

1. The discount rate at the Federal Reserve Banks was reduced to 1 per cent.

2. A preferential rate of one-half of 1 per cent was set for advances to member banks secured by short-term Government obligations.

3. Legal reserve requirements in central reserve cities were reduced from 26 to 20 per cent.

4. All bank supervisory agencies issued a statement on November 22, 1942, indicating they would not criticize banks for investing in Government securities, except those ineligible for bank investment by their terms, or for making short-term or amortized loans to finance subscriptions to new offerings of Government obligations.

These steps implemented a policy "of making available to the banks of the country sufficient reserves to enable them at all times to meet such demands as might be made by the Treasury."[6]

The Treasury required over $380 billion to finance Government expenditures between June 30, 1940, when the defense program was launched, and the end of 1945. Of this vast sum, taxes provided some 40 per cent, borrowing from nonbank sources 35 per cent, and borrowing from the commercial banking system the balance of 25 per cent.[7] Of this total of close to $100 billion absorbed by the commercial banking system, the Federal Reserve Banks acquired over $22 billion, thereby expanding member-bank reserves by a corresponding amount. The commercial banks increased their Government security holdings by $74 billion, from $17 to $91 billion, which resulted in nearly a tripling of bank deposits between 1939 and 1945.

APPRAISAL OF WARTIME FEDERAL RESERVE POLICY

The Federal Reserve System's record during World War II points to the following conclusions:

[5] *Ibid.*, p. 104.
[6] *Ibid.*, p. 1.
[7] E. A. Goldenweiser, *American Monetary Policy,* New York, McGraw-Hill Book Company, Inc., 1951, pp. 185-89.

1. Pegging of the Government security market proved a particularly effective device for facilitating Treasury financing. Under the pegs, the nation's financial machinery could help itself to bank reserves as needed. It is doubtful that the war could have been financed at so low an interest cost if the added reserves had been provided through member-bank borrowing from the Federal Reserve Banks, at however low a rate. Reliance on reductions in legal reserve requirements would not have been practical, as requirements would soon have been lowered to the vanishing point to provide needed reserves.

The pegging of Government security yields also made it clear that would-be purchasers of Government securities could gain nothing by postponing purchases, since yields on successive offerings could not rise, as had been the case during World War I.

2. The wisdom of retaining the specific yield curve for Government obligations that prevailed at the time the pegs were first imposed has been questioned. The three-eighths of 1 per cent bill rate and seven-eighths of 1 per cent certificate rate reflected the high level of excess reserves and the relatively low demand for loans of the immediate prewar period. At the other end of the curve, some argued that the 2½ rate was too high for long-term bonds, considering that these obligations were equivalent to cash so long as the pegs were maintained.

There can be little question, however, that the wide spread between short-term and long-term interest rates did put pressure on buyers of Government securities to lengthen maturities. At the same time, the fact that long-term bonds bore a coupon rate of 2½ per cent, rather than a substantially lower rate, was of assistance in eventually restoring a free market for Government securities, since it limited the decline to which long-term bonds became subject.

3. With the imposition of price and wage ceilings, the pegging of Government securities by the Federal Reserve System did not result in immediate price inflation. However, the near tripling of the money supply made eventual price inflation inevitable, in the absence of drastic measures to cut back the money supply after the war along the lines adopted in some European countries.

4. The lesson to be drawn from the World War II experience is that inflation can be minimized in such a national emergency only by reliance upon taxation or forced long-term, nonmarketable loans to finance a much larger proportion of Federal expenditures, or by eliminating shortly after the war, through taxation or forced non-marketable loans, a large part of the added bank deposits and cur-

rency created by wartime bank purchases of Government securities.

5. Under the pegging policy, the distinction between sales of Government securities to banks and to nonbank investors was not as significant as is usually assumed. Nonbank holders can unload their holdings on the Federal Reserve Banks at will so long as the pegs are maintained. The reserves thus created provide the basis for a continuous expansion of the money supply.

THE FEDERAL RESERVE SYSTEM REGAINS ITS INDEPENDENCE

As commodity prices rose and bank loans expanded following the end of the war, the Federal Reserve authorities became increasingly concerned over the passive and subordinate role that the pegging policy imposed upon them. Since pegging deprived the Federal Reserve System of any effective power to control credit, the chief financial instrument for restraining inflation in the immediate postwar years was the use of Treasury cash balances and budget surpluses to retire public debt.

A first step by the System toward regaining a measure of control over credit was the ending, in April 1946, of the one-half of 1 per cent preferential discount rate on advances to member banks secured by Treasury obligations maturing within one year. More significant moves were the Federal Open Market Committee directive of July 2, 1947, to the Federal Reserve Banks to end the fixed buying rate of three-eighths of 1 per cent for Treasury bills, and that of August 8 ending the seven-eighths of 1 per cent support level for certificates of indebtedness.[8] Thereafter, yields on both bills and certificates advanced well above the pegged rates. Longer-term Government securities continued to be pegged, however, and the Federal Reserve authorities agreed with the Treasury that the risks involved in ending the pegs were too great at that time. To regain control over bank reserves without abandoning the pegs for longer-term obligations, the Board of Governors asked Congress for power to raise legal reserve requirements further and to impose a supplementary or special reserve requirement in the form of Treasury bills and certificates to curb the ability of member banks to expand their loans.

Congress did not adopt these proposals, and granted temporary authority for raising reserve requirements moderately only in August

[8] Annual Report of the Board of Governors of the Federal Reserve System, 1947, pp. 92-94.

1948. As a first step away from the fixed pegs for long-term Treasury obligations, the Federal Reserve Banks had lowered support prices on Government bonds on December 24, 1947, but this move only swelled offerings of these securities to the Reserve Banks.

Measures taken during 1947 and 1948 to restrain credit expansion and inflation, despite the continued pegging of long-term Government bonds by the Federal Reserve banks, included:

1. Use of surplus Treasury receipts to retire Government securities held by the Federal Reserve banks, to soak up excess reserves of member banks and so limit bank credit expansion.

2. Raising yields on short-term Treasury issues to facilitate sales of such holdings by the Federal Reserve Banks to offset their purchases of long-term bonds for support purposes. A net increase in the Government security portfolio of the Reserve Banks was thereby avoided.

3. Discount rates at the Federal Reserve banks were lifted from 1 to 1½ per cent in two successive advances during 1948.

4. Legal reserve requirements of member banks were increased in 1948 to soak up excess reserves.

5. Consumer credit controls, terminated by Congressional action on November 1, 1947, were reinstated under new temporary legislation on September 20, 1948.

6. Margin requirements on listed securities, raised to 75 per cent in July 1945, were held at 100 per cent during 1946 and at 75 per cent from February 1, 1947, to the end of March 1949.

7. A program of voluntary credit restraint by commercial banks was sponsored by the American Bankers Association.

The Federal Reserve System was urged from many quarters to abandon pegging Government bonds at this time, in order to combat inflation more effectively. However, both because of the feared consequences of a major decline in Government bond prices and the desire to encourage expansion of production and building to relieve prevailing shortages, pegging was maintained.

When business activity slackened late in 1948, and bank loans were repaid in volume, Federal Reserve policy was reversed. In the spring of 1949, reserve requirements were reduced in successive stages, margin requirements were lowered to 50 per cent, and consumer credit restrictions were relaxed.

The outbreak of the Korean war in June 1950, and the huge rearmament program that followed, again made restraint of inflation the chief objective of Federal Reserve policy. A joint statement of the Board of Governors and the Federal Open Market Committee issued August 18 stated that the two agencies "are prepared to use all the means at their command to restrain further expansion of bank credit consistent with the policy of maintaining orderly conditions in the Government securities market." Discount rates were raised from 1½ to 1¾ per cent in August with a view to lifting yields on short-term Government obligations so as to discourage their sale by commercial banks. Legal reserve requirements were raised in January 1951. Earlier, consumer credit controls had been restored and home mortgage terms were subjected to selective control for the first time under Regulation X.

But large-scale Federal Reserve purchases of Government securities to peg bond prices and to assure the success of Treasury refunding operations weakened the effectiveness of these restrictive moves. Dissatisfaction with pegging and its hamstringing of effective credit control by Federal Reserve action mounted within the System. Conferences between Federal Reserve and Treasury spokesmen culminated in the momentous "full accord," announced March 4, 1951, on a "common purpose to assure the successful financing of the Government's requirements and, at the same time, to minimize monetization of the public debt."

To implement the full accord, the Treasury offered to exchange nonmarketable bonds, convertible into five-year marketable notes, for a large part of its outstanding marketable long-term bonds. This exchange was designed to lessen the potential volume of liquidation of long-term Government bonds with the ending of the pegs. The Federal Reserve System agreed that the Reserve Banks would buy long-term Treasury bonds in limited amounts in connection with the exchanges, but on a scale down if offerings proved large. The Open Market Committee indicated it would curtail purchases of short-term Treasury securities, so that member banks would have to resort to borrowing for needed reserves, "to minimize monetization of the debt."[9]

Following the full accord, Government bonds declined in price below par, open-market purchases by the Federal Reserve Banks were reduced, and member banks relied increasingly upon borrowing from the Federal Reserve Banks to secure required reserves. During December 1952, discounts and advances by the Federal Reserve Banks averaged $1.6 billion, the highest level to which they had risen since

[9] *Ibid.*, 1951, pp. 98-101.

1921. In January 1953, the discount rate was raised to 2 per cent.

Less emphasis was placed on selective credit controls, once the end of the pegs had made possible more effective quantitative credit control. Selective curbs on consumer lending under Regulation W and mortgage credit under Regulation X were suspended during 1952. In February 1953, margin requirements were reduced to 50 per cent.

With the change in Administration early in 1953, the last vestiges of the pegging policy were eliminated. The Federal Open Market Committee in March voted to confine operations for System account "to the short end of the market," which, as a practical matter, meant Treasury bills only. Also, a statement was approved that the Committee did not seek to support any pattern of prices and yields in the Government securities market, but "solely to effectuate the objectives of monetary and credit policy." The Committee also voted to refrain from support purchases of maturing or when-issued Treasury obligations in connection with individual Treasury financing operations.[10]

In April, the Treasury offered a long-term 3¼ per cent bond issue which depressed outstanding issues bearing lower coupon rates, and officials indicated that they intended to offer additional long-term bonds to stretch out the maturity of the public debt at whatever yields the market required. Sharp declines in bond prices followed from ill-advised publicity given this intention. Coming at a time when other forces were contributing to a business recession, the sharp decline in bond prices and rise in interest rates soon led to a drastic reversal of monetary policy.

More than seven years elapsed between the end of World War II and the Open Market Committee action of March 1953, which finally ended the pegging of the Government security markets by the Federal Reserve Banks and substituted a "bills only" policy that reduces the effects of open-market operations on Government security prices to an absolute minimum. The Federal Reserve System thus regained its freedom to combat inflation and boom, foster full employment, promote price stability, or pursue whatever objective it chose, without being hampered and impeded by the need to support Government security prices at any predetermined level.

[10] *Ibid.,* 1953, pp. 86-92. At its next meeting in June, the bills-only and support-purchases understandings of the Open Market Committee were rescinded, but only to leave wider discretion for its executive committee. This rescission did not cause any significant change in policy.

IMPLEMENTING "FULL EMPLOYMENT"

Signs that a downturn in business might be in the making became discernible in the spring of 1953. The new Republican Administration, eager to maintain a high level of employment, "deliberately took speedy and massive actions to build confidence and pave the way for renewed economic growth."[11] In May, before business activity had turned downward, the Federal Reserve Banks undertook a vigorous program of open-market purchases of Treasury bills, adding over $1.2 billion to their holdings of these securities by September. At its September meeting, the Federal Open Market Committee ordered that open-market operations be directed to "avoiding deflationary tendencies" and implementing a policy of "active ease." At the December meeting, following additional discussion and debate over what monetary policy should seek to achieve in a recession, the central objective of credit policy was stated by the Federal Open Market Committee to be "promoting growth and stability in the economy by actively maintaining a condition of ease in the money market."

In July, reserve requirements of member banks were reduced by $1.2 billion for the stated purpose "of sustaining economic equilibrium at high levels of production and employment."[12] These measures, two reductions in discount rates and a further large cut in reserve requirements in 1954 were part of a more comprehensive program to stimulate the economy which included tax reductions, extreme liberalization of terms of Government-guaranteed and -insured home mortgages and large-scale grants of the five-year amortization privilege for plant and equipment projects.

These measures proved only too effective, as the sequel showed. As in 1927, an incipient recession soon gave way to an intense boom. First, consumer spending for housing and durable goods, and then business spending on plants, equipment, and inventories, rose to new record levels, accompanied by accelerated debt expansion.

The boom of 1955-57, which witnessed the production and sale of 20,000,000 automobiles and 3,500,000 homes, $100 billion in new plant and equipment spending by business, a $15 billion rise in busi-

[11] Arthur F. Burns, *Prosperity Without Inflation*, New York, Fordham University Press, 1957, p. 30.
[12] Annual Report of the Board of Governors of the Federal Reserve System, 1953, pp. 84-85.

ness inventories, and large increases in personal and business debt, demonstrated that an easy money policy, when combined with other stimulants at a time when the economy is receptive, can have exaggerated results and so jeopardize the stable economic growth that is a key long-term objective of Federal Reserve policy.

FIGHTING BOOM AND INFLATION

By the beginning of 1955, it became evident that the antirecession program of 1953-54 was proving too effective, and that an inflationary boom was under way in consequence. The Federal Reserve System took a leading part in applying restraint to the developing boom.

The first move was taken at the meeting of the Federal Open Market Committee on December 7, 1954. At this meeting, the directive to the executive committee was changed by dropping the word "actively" from the previous directive that open-market transactions seek to promote "growth and stability in the economy by actively maintaining a condition of ease in the money market."

No public statement of this shift from "active ease" to "ease" in credit policy was issued at the time. Instead, as in most instances of a decision to change policy, rumors soon circulated in financial circles that a shift was taking place, and these rumors found their way into the financial pages of newspapers. The extent to which decisions to modify Federal Reserve policy should be announced publicly, so as to keep the public informed of such important decisions and give equal access to this information to all concerned, has been debated from time to time. Formal disclosure of policy reversals might cause an exaggerated significance to be attached to such decisions, and a tendency to discount further changes to an excessive extent. But similar consequences could result from the spread of rumors that may prove misleading or erroneous.

In the course of 1955, Federal Reserve policy was completely reversed from ease to restraint. The Federal Open Market Committee in January again changed the directive to its executive committee by removing reference to "a condition of ease in the money market" and substituting as its objective "conditions in the money market that would encourage recovery and avoid the development of unsustainable expansion."[13] Some reduction in Government security holdings of the Reserve Banks followed. At the same time, margin requirements

[13] *Ibid.*, 1955, pp. 89-90.

were raised from 50 to 60 per cent, and to 70 per cent in April. Discount rates at the Federal Reserve Banks were raised in three successive stages from 1½ to 2½ per cent.

When the Federal Open Market Committee abolished its executive committee in June 1955 and substituted the Federal Reserve Bank of New York as its agent, reference to "correcting a disorderly condition in the Government securities market" was eliminated from the new directive to its agent. The change emphasized anew the fact that the Federal Reserve System felt free to pursue its monetary policy objectives even if Government security markets were adversely affected to a serious extent.

A significant further shift toward a policy of restraint occurred in August, when the Committee directed the Federal Reserve Bank of New York to conduct open-market operations with a view "to restraining inflationary developments in the interest of sustainable economic growth."[14] Inflation was thus recognized as a threat to stable growth of the economy, and hence as a development that should be combated with vigorous measures that could temporarily jeopardize the high level of employment sought by the Employment Act of 1946. A limited amount of unemployment, as a price to pay to head off a "boom and bust" that could produce a much larger amount of unemployment in the future, was thus regarded as consistent with the requirements of the Employment Act.

As a result of reduction in member-bank reserves caused by open-market operations and an expansion of deposits resulting from a rapid rise in loans, member-bank borrowing from the Federal Reserve System increased sharply. During August, borrowing exceeded excess reserves for the member banks as a whole. Net borrowing of reserves became chronic while the policy of restraint lasted.

Due to the tight reserve position, member banks sold Government securities freely to offset the expansion of their loans, thus minimizing the resulting rise in the money supply. In consequence, the banks were under pressure to limit lending not only because of a shortage of reserves but also because of reduced liquidity. A third contributing influence was the declining ratio of capital funds to risk assets caused by loan expansion.

A test of the flexibility of Federal Reserve open-market policy came late in November, when the Secretary of the Treasury asked for assistance in effecting a refunding operation that threatened to be a failure

[14] *Ibid.*, pp. 101-2.

because of the rising level of interest rates. By a 9-to-3 decision, the Open Market Committee authorized the Federal Reserve Bank of New York to purchase on a when-issued basis up to $400 million of the 2⅝ per cent certificates of indebtedness then being offered in exchange, to assure the success of the refunding. This was a departure from the "bills only" policy. In doing so, however, the Committee went on record to say it was not abandoning its earlier policy, "but rather deviating from it only because of the unforeseen circumstances that had developed in connection with the current Treasury refunding operation."[15]

Flexibility in Federal Reserve policy was reflected also in the five changes in the directive from the Open Market Committee during 1956. In January, fearing a slackening of business, the Federal Reserve Bank of New York was directed to take "into account any deflationary tendencies in the economy." In March, with business investment gaining momentum, this was deleted. It was restored in May, but again deleted in August in response to booming business developments. In November, fearing that the policy of restraint might bring too severe a credit squeeze, a clause was added calling for recognition of "additional pressures in the money, credit and capital markets resulting from seasonal factors and international conditions." Discount rates were raised twice in 1956, from 2½ to 3 per cent.

Within this flexible framework, credit was tightened and interest rates raised during 1956 by the expansion in bank loans. Thanks to sales of bank holdings of Government securities, however, the rise in the active money supply, comprising demand deposits and currency, was only $1.5 billion in 1956, compared with $3.8 billion in 1955. The 1 per cent growth in the money supply, compared with a 5½ per cent rise in the gross national product, compelled the economy to resort to an increased velocity of turnover of money to conduct its transactions, in itself a considerable restraining influence because of the consequent pressure on liquidity.

The policy of monetary restraint was tightened further in several directions during most of 1957, despite indications that the boom launched by the several stimulants given the economy in 1953-54 was reaching its culmination. The steps taken included:

1. Maintenance of net borrowed reserves of member banks around the $500 billion level, a strong restraining influence on the banks, through a reduction in Government security holdings of the Federal

[15] *Ibid.*, pp. 109-10.

Reserve Banks during the first half of the year.

2. An increase in the discount rate from 3 to 3½ per cent in August, despite growing signs of a slackening of business activity.

3. Successive meetings of the Federal Open Market Committee during 1957, while noting evidences that the boom was losing its momentum, renewed its policy directive without change until the meeting of November 12.

4. The structure of interest rates advanced sharply to the highest levels reached since the early 1930's.

5. The money supply, comprising demand deposits and currency, was again held down by the tight money measures of the Federal Reserve System, and by the end of the year was actually lower than it had been at the beginning.

The policy of restraint, pursued steadfastly as in the past periods when the System was determined to curb a boom—1920, 1929, and 1937—proved effective. A cyclical recession began in the third quarter of 1957. The determination with which the policy of restraint was pursued in 1957 reflected the deep concern within the Federal Reserve System over "the notion that creeping inflation was an unavoidable and inevitable condition of modern economic life."[16]

The contrast between Federal Reserve policy in 1953 and in 1957, both years when a business recession began, is of considerable significance. In 1953, massive easy money measures were applied to head off a recession before the downturn began. In 1957, restrictive actions were continued and even intensified for a time, even though the peak in industrial production had already been passed. The Federal Reserve index of production did not exceed the record level of December 1956 in any month during 1957.

The inflationary boom that followed the 1953-54 massive anti-recession measures had raised questions about that kind of program in the minds of both the Federal Reserve authorities, and the Administration. A different approach had been decided on, both to combat inflation and to lessen the amplitude of future cyclical business fluctuations.

LEANING AGAINST THE WIND

The policy reflected in measures taken late in 1957 and in 1958 to combat the business recession was one of "leaning against the

[16] *Ibid.*, 1957, p. 3.

wind," rather than of halting a readjustment by massive doses of monetary and other stimuli. Federal Reserve policy had been earlier described in these terms by Chairman William McC. Martin of the Board of Governors before a Congressional committee hearing.

The Federal Open Market Committee at its October 22 meeting, while leaving the directive of restraint unchanged, did agree that the policy "should tend on the easier side from where it had been in recent weeks." At its November 12 meeting, reference to "restraining inflationary developments" was deleted and replaced by the words "fostering sustainable growth in the economy without inflation by moderating the pressures on banks' reserves." Only at its December 17 meeting was there unanimous agreement within the Committee on a directive calling for "cushioning adjustments and mitigating recessionary tendencies in the economy."[17]

Discount rates were reduced from 3½ to 3 per cent by four of the Reserve Banks on November 13, reversing the action taken three months previously. The other Reserve Banks followed suit by the end of the year. By May 1958, discount rates had been reduced to 1¾ per cent, a series of moderate reductions effected in reserve requirements, and margin requirements had been reduced from 70 to 50 per cent. A policy of active ease was thus again adopted. This time, however, relaxation of monetary policy lagged well behind the downturn in business, instead of seeking to head it off by anticipatory action, as was done in 1953. Moreover, easy money measures were applied in successive moderate, not massive, doses.

The net effect of these measures was to provide member banks with some $500 million of average net free reserves, in contrast to the $500 million or so of net borrowed reserves maintained through most of 1957. This marked easing of the banks' reserve position, and the contraction in business loans resulting from the recession, caused member banks to expand Government security and other holdings at a rapid pace. The large Treasury deficit also facilitated large-scale monetization of public debt and an expansion of the money supply which offset the declining velocity of circulation typical of recession periods.

The policy of "leaning against the wind" thus received a full-fledged test in the business recession that began in 1957. The emphasis was shifted from the prevention of cyclical readjustments to

[17] *Ibid.*, pp. 60-62.

a moderation of its severity and a shortening of its duration after the readjustment was well under way.

In other words, moderation rather than prevention of cyclical economic readjustments became the objective of Federal Reserve policy. But the rapid recovery and boom that ensued in 1958–59 raised questions whether even more limited monetary stimulation did not prove excessive when other economic conditions were favorable.

SUGGESTED READINGS

BOARD OF GOVERNORS OF THE FEDERAL RESERVE SYSTEM, Annual Reports, Washington, D.C.

BURNS, ARTHUR F., *Prosperity Without Inflation*, New York, Fordham University Press, 1957, p. 30.

CHANDLER, LESTER V., *Inflation in the United States, 1940–1948*, New York, Harper & Brothers, 1951, Chapters XIII–XIV.

GOLDENWEISER, E. A., *American Monetary Policy*, New York, McGraw-Hill Book Company, Inc., 1951, pp. 185–89.

JOINT COMMITTEE ON THE ECONOMIC REPORT, *Hearings before the Sub-committee on General Credit Control and Debt Management*, 82nd Congress, Second Session., Washington, D.C., Government Printing Office, 1952, pp. 685–710.

NADLER, M.; HELLER, S.; and SHIPMAN, S. S., *The Money Market and Its Institutions*, New York, The Ronald Press, 1955, Chapters 8–9.

SMITH, WARREN L., "On the Effectiveness of Monetary Policy," *American Economic Review*, Vol. XLVI, No. 4, September, 1956.

Chapter 17

CENTRAL BANKS AND MONETARY POLICY ABROAD

INTEREST in monetary management is world-wide today. Central banks have now been established practically everywhere and credit controls have become a part of the over-all economic policies of most countries of the free world.[1] How different from the immediate postwar years when monetary policy was generally out of favor and central banks were often regarded as only specialist appendages of treasuries, technically skillful but rather unimportant!

The objectives and concepts of central banking are basically the same everywhere outside of the Iron Curtain, as central banks endeavor to promote balanced economic growth of their countries through influencing the financial strands of the economy. The actual methods of central banks—and the success of their policies—however, have varied widely with the economic, financial, and political framework in which they operate. The policies of many foreign central banks have had much in common with those of the Federal Reserve System. But on the whole the techniques of central banking abroad have differed greatly from those in the United States.

[1] This chapter does not discuss central banking in Communist countries, since their economic systems preclude the use of monetary policy as we know it.

NOTE: Parts of this chapter are based on material presented at somewhat greater length in the author's booklet on *Foreign Central Banking: The Instruments of Monetary Policy* published by the Federal Reserve Bank of New York in November, 1957. As acknowledged in that monograph, thanks are due to the author's colleagues in the Research Department of the Bank for their assistance in contributing country data on some points discussed there.

THE ECONOMIC AND INSTITUTIONAL SETTING

Much of the dissimilarity between central banking here and abroad is due to differences in the structures of individual national economies. In the first place, many foreign countries have not reached our stage of economic development; and secondly, international trade and capital movements play a much more important role in foreign economies than they do in ours.

In degree of economic development, only the countries of Western Europe and a few countries of the British Commonwealth (and perhaps Japan) resemble the United States. Elsewhere in the world the market sector of the economy is still fairly narrow, and non-monetary barter transactions remain widespread. In these less developed economies the reach of monetary policy is necessarily limited, and the task of central banking has often been extended beyond credit control pure and simple to such fields as the establishment and encouragement of special financial institutions.

But even in the more advanced economies abroad, the central bank operates in an economic framework greatly different from that of the United States. Our imports and exports are important to our economy, and the state of our gold stock cannot be entirely dismissed from the calculations of our money managers. But for most foreign countries international trade is the life blood of their economies, and gold and foreign exchange reserves the gauge of their economic health.[2] Central banks abroad thus face special problems unknown in the United States. Most foreign economies are wide open to external influences which monetary policy is often powerless to counteract. The narrow margin of international reserves with which so many foreign countries operate makes it imperative for central banks abroad carefully to watch and quickly to react to changes in their gold and foreign exchange holdings. Sometimes conflicts arise between external and internal considerations, such as the need to stem an outflow of short-term funds through a raising of interest rates, on the one hand, and the desire to nourish a business upturn through continued easy money, on the other. More often than not, however, most foreign central banks have escaped this particular dilemma during

[2] It is not unusual among foreign countries that one-third of national production is sold abroad to obtain essential imports, or that external reserves are only large enough to pay for a few months' imports.

the first postwar decade. In fact, the closely knit economies of western Europe have felt the same kind of economic weather, with the result that shifts in monetary policy in various countries have come closely together in time.

Another difference in the economic setting here and abroad needs mentioning, even though it has been less fundamental. In the postwar climate inflation has been the predominant threat around the world. But government policies superimposed upon economic scarcities have often led to far greater inflationary problems abroad than we have known in this country. In western Europe the requirements of postwar reconstruction, in the less developed countries the need to lift the low living standards, have stoked the fires of inflation. The usual credit controls thus at times became powerless until more drastic remedies were applied. For the same reasons, postwar recessions abroad have generally been brief and mild, so that the monetary experience has been mainly one of fighting inflationary pressures rather than counteracting economic declines.

On the institutional side, the differences between the United States and foreign countries are no less far-reaching. The less developed countries naturally show the greatest contrasts with this country. Even among the economically advanced countries, however, only a few, notably the United Kingdom, have financial systems— commercial banks, nonbank intermediaries, money and capital markets—so developed and integrated as has this country. And when they have, the system is often sufficiently dissimilar as to lead central banking into avenues unknown here.

In many countries of the world the banking habit has not become as pervasive as it has in the United States, and most people never come close to a bank. Instead, their credit needs are served by small moneylenders and other rudimentary financial institutions, each operating almost in isolation. In countries like these, even if the central bank is able to influence the commercial banks, most credit operations are beyond its reach as the financial system remains unorganized and unintegrated. This state of affairs, however, has some compensations. With the banking habit less widespread, currency in circulation rather than checking deposits forms the preponderant part of the money supply. (Even in some Western European countries, demand deposits are only one-half of the money supply.) This preference for currency keeps down the deposit creating powers of the commercial banks, and may thus ease the credit control efforts of the central banks. At the same time, holdings of inactive balances are often small in many of these countries, and the resulting short-run stability in the velocity of money tends to increase the effectiveness of monetary policy.

But even in countries where commercial banking is more developed, the banking system may not be open to the influence of central bank operations. It may be so well supplied with liquid reserves or be in such a ready position to draw inexpensively on funds in major foreign centers that it may be independent of central bank credit. Moreover, the banking system may have such an ample supply of reserves that the central bank may not be able to put sufficient pressure on the banks through open-market operations or changes in reserve requirements to reduce their loans and investments; instead the central bank's policies may lead merely to some running down of excess reserves. Furthermore, there are many countries which, alongside with highly developed banking systems and other financial institutions, still have only thin money and capital markets.

Finally, a feature of the banking organization abroad has to be brought out that is not related to the stage of development, but rather to the way in which financial institutions have developed. The unit banking system so important in the United States is practically unique. The banking scene in most foreign countries is dominated by a few banking giants with nationwide branch networks, such as the "big five" in England or the "big four" in the Netherlands. As a result, many central banks abroad have found it feasible to exert their influence more through informal expressions of their views in discussions with the commercial banks and less through market operations, as will be noted further below.

THE POLITICAL AND LEGAL FRAMEWORK

The political and legal framework in which foreign central banks carry out their policies is likewise in most cases markedly different from that in the United States. But in practice these differences are rarely as overwhelming for the conduct of monetary policy as they seem to be on the surface. The vast majority of foreign central banks is fully government-owned today.[3] Of the close to fourscore central

[3] Before World War II, in contrast, government-owned central banks were in a minority. Since then about a dozen banks have been nationalized, while practically all new central banks created in the postwar period have been established as government-owned institutions.

banks abroad outside of the Communist world, only a handful is entirely privately owned and only in another dozen is there any private ownership of all. Yet this preponderance of government ownership does not necessarily mean that the central banks are completely subordinated to the Treasury.

Similarly, most foreign central bank laws now have specific provisions giving the government virtually absolute powers over the central bank. In the United Kingdom, for example, "The Treasury may from time to time give such directions to the Bank [of England] as, after consultation with the Governor of the Bank, they think necessary in the public interest." However, in the United Kingdom, as well as in most of the other countries, these legal provisions have never been used. Instead, many of these central banks retain a considerable amount of independence within the government, and at times have exerted great influence over general economic policy beyond monetary management. There are, nevertheless, some foreign central banks, particularly in the economically underdeveloped areas, that have little scope for exercising their judgment, not only in law but also in practice.

For the majority of the central banks abroad, the central bank-government relationship is aptly described in the words that the Governor of the Bank of England applied to his institution: "The Bank's relationship with the Government is like that of a good wife: it offers its advice freely and has been known to nag if the advice was not accepted. In the last resort, the Bank and the Government argue things out. If the Bank has a difference of view with the Government, it usually is able to reach agreement, but it recognizes that the Government has the final word on economic and monetary policy."

Even in the days when the great central banks of the world were entirely privately owned and run, they carried out policy "subject to the supreme authority of the government."[4] Since the war only a few central banks have taken steps running counter to the wishes of the government, and then only in special circumstances and for brief periods, after which full agreement with the government was again reached. (This was, for example, the case of discount rate increases in Germany and Sweden, in 1955 and 1957 respectively.) After all, now that most governments have assumed final responsi-

---

[4] In 1926 the Governor of the Bank of England explained the situation in those words, cited by R. S. Sayers in *Central Banking After Bagehot*, Oxford, Clarendon Press, 1957, p. 35.

bility for the trend of their economies, monetary control and other economic policies—the central bank and the government—have to work hand in hand.

Given this inevitable intermingling of government and central bank policies, it is not surprising that the political coloration of individual governments has been reflected in the use of credit controls. Generally speaking, central banks in countries with socialistic administrations have shown a preference for more direct controls. But it is significant that even these countries have turned to over-all monetary restraint, although with some delay and apparently some reluctance.

The tools that have been given to foreign central banks are similar but not identical with the powers entrusted by law to the Federal Reserve System. All foreign central banks today have statutory authority for discount operations, practically all are legally empowered to conduct open-market operations, and about half of them have the power to establish and vary commercial bank minimum cash ratios. No central bank abroad, as far as can be determined, however, has been given the specific authority to vary margin requirements on stock market credit, as has been done in the United States, nor the terms of real estate credit, as happened in this country in 1950–52. Consumer credit controls similar to those that had been in force here, for their part, have been entrusted to only a few central banks abroad, even though they exist in about a dozen foreign countries, where they are usually under the direct authority of the government. On the other hand, many foreign central banks have been legally authorized to establish other credit controls unknown in this country. Some of these are quantitative, such as ceilings on the aggregate volume of commercial bank loans and investments, while others are selective, such as import-predeposit requirements.[5]

As regards the "conventional" central banking instruments—discount policy, open-market operations, and reserve requirements—the statutory authority of many foreign central banks is wider than the authority of the Federal Reserve System. Thus, other borrowers besides banks sometimes have general access to central bank discounts and advances: government security dealers or discount houses in several countries that have relatively developed money markets, official development-credit institutions in a number of Asian and Latin American countries, and general business borrowers in a few

[5] For a discussion of this and other selective instruments, see below, pp. 372-377.

countries scattered around the globe. At the same time, practically any kind of paper is acceptable for rediscounting or as collateral for advances by a number of central banks, and the maximum legal maturity period of both discounts and advances is often as long as one year in the case of ordinary borrowing. As to central bank open-market operations, a number of central banks abroad can legally operate in other than government securities, while some, particularly in the financially less developed countries, have power to issue their own securities for monetary policy purposes.[6] Reserve requirement authority also is often broader than in this country: other assets besides deposits with the central bank, including government securities, may be eligible as required reserves, the range for the permitted variations of the requirements may be wide or even unlimited, and supplementary requirements may be imposed against increases in deposits.[7]

The granting of these special credit control powers to central banks abroad reflects the desire to overcome the various institutional obstacles—already touched upon—that tend to impede the effectiveness of the traditional instruments abroad. For the same reason, many foreign central banks have also applied, under their general statutory powers, various other credit control tools, such as the screening of individual bank loans or the giving of directives to commercial banks regarding their lending policies. The actual use of these and all other central banking instruments will be discussed below.

THE REDISCOVERY OF MONETARY POLICY

The postwar revival of central banking abroad began only during the world-wide wave of inflation that followed the outbreak of the Korean conflict in 1950. A few countries had turned to monetary policy earlier, but the ideological and theoretical climates of the years immediately after World War II combined to create a strong hostility to general credit controls almost everywhere, and economic conditions made their application difficult. It thus was not surprising that it took time before monetary policy emerged from the disrepute into which it had fallen during the Great Depression.

[6] Some central banks, however, are circumscribed by legislation as to the total amount and the maturity of government securities they may purchase. Nevertheless, the recent trend has been toward the relaxation and abolition of such controls.

[7] In some foreign countries, however, the ultimate authority over reserve requirements is vested in the government rather than the central bank.

In many countries centralized planning and detailed controls carried the day at the end of the war. Within such policies there was naturally no room for monetary management that exerts its influence through the market place. At the same time, monetary policy retained the stigma from the revolution in economic theory which during the 1930's made fiscal policy *the* tool of economic stabilization. But even those who saw the usefulness of central banking conceded that its role should be minimized during the rebuilding from the destruction and dislocation wrought by the war. The surplus internal liquidity inherited from the war by most economies—of the belligerents and the neutrals alike—posed an equally large obstacle to the use of ordinary monetary controls. Regardless of how vigorously taxes had been raised to help finance the vast wartime government expenditures, government debts were tremendously enlarged. In countries less directly hit by the war, the accumulation of balance-of-payments surpluses swelled internal liquidity in a similar degree. As a result, the liquid assets in the hands both of commercial banks and other lenders and of business and consumers were more than ample to finance the demands for goods and services that had to remain so greatly unsatisfied during wartime.

However, by the time the post-Korean inflation hit, conditions were ripe for a return to monetary policy. The combination of fiscal policy and direct controls that had been used to combat the almost continuous inflationary pressures of the first five postwar years had little success, and most foreign economies continued to be plagued by internal maladjustments and balance-of-payments deficits. The resulting reassessment by economic theorists of the role of central banking restored to it a considerable share of its earlier importance. Moreover, postwar reconstruction had been more or less completed, and the excess liquidity of many economies had largely been absorbed through the increase in production and unfortunately also in prices. At the same time, the experience of the few countries that had turned to monetary policy soon after the war, notably Belgium and Italy, gave encouragement to its advocates.

Within a few months of the outbreak of the Korean conflict, several of the more financially advanced countries (e.g., Denmark, the Netherlands, and Canada) resuscitated the old central banking tools, and others (e.g., the United Kingdom and Austria) followed before the end of 1951. (For comparison's sake, it should be noted, the Federal Reserve—Treasury accord that made a meaningful monetary policy possible in this country occurred in March 1951.) At the same time, the countries which had turned to monetary controls before (e.g., Belgium, Italy, France, and Germany) resorted to monetary restraint again and took steps to improve their central banking techniques further.

The experience of these countries encouraged others, and with the next wave of inflationary strains which followed the subsiding of the post-Korea inflation and lasted from late 1954 to 1957, a number of additional countries (e.g., New Zealand, Norway, Sweden, and Switzerland) shifted to central banking controls. By 1956, practically all the financially more developed countries abroad—most countries of Western Europe, the older overseas members of the British Commonwealth, and Japan—entrusted to monetary policy a major role in the safeguarding and promoting of their economic health. Since 1950, too, a growing number of the economically less developed countries of Asia and Latin America have sought ways of making monetary policy effective in their more unfavorable environments.

THE PATTERN OF INSTRUMENTS

Discount policy—the oldest central banking tool—led the revival of monetary policy abroad. But it lost its former pre-eminence and, as in the United States, it has come to be used mainly with other instruments. There has, however, been little similarity in the over-all pattern of central banking tools in foreign countries and in the United States. In this country, open-market operations have been the primary instrument, which has been supplemented by discount policy and reserve requirement policy. (In addition, several selective credit controls have been used in the United States; but except for margin requirements on stock market credit, they were discontinued after relatively brief periods.) Such a distribution of emphasis on the various credit control tools has only rarely been possible abroad. In fact not one foreign country has relied so exclusively on these three instruments, partly because the general absence of developed money and capital markets has precluded the effective use of open market operations, and because many foreign central banks have lacked the authority to establish and to vary commercial bank reserve requirements.

As a result of the various institutional obstacles they face, most foreign countries have resorted to selective and direct credit controls of one kind or another, but the mixture of individual credit controls has varied greatly from country to country. In a number of the financially more advanced countries, open-market operations and a few selective and direct credit controls have served in a subordinate manner to reinforce discount policy and, in some, discount policy and reserve requirement changes. In others, discount rate changes have been combined with direct restrictions on access to the central bank's "discount window" and with special reserve requirements, often called minimum liquidity ratios, which in addition to cash include government securities among the reserve eligible assets. Among the financially less developed countries, variations in reserve requirements have sometime been buttressed by ceilings on commercial bank borrowing at the central bank or by differential discount rates; in a few cases, the impact of reserve requirement changes on bank reserves has at times been supplemented by transfers of Treasury deposits between the central bank and the commercial banks. Elsewhere, discount policy in all its ramifications has been used in conjunction with special devices, such as import-predeposit requirements and bank-portfolio ceilings. The variations have been almost innumerable and have depended not only on a country's economic and financial structure but also on the other economic policies in force and on the kind of difficulties to be overcome.

These differences in techniques notwithstanding, the original postwar shift to monetary policy generally included measures to reduce the excessive liquidity of the commercial banks. (Some European countries also attempted to reduce the liquidity of the whole economy through monetary reforms, which essentially consisted of drastically reducing everybody's cash balances; but generally—Belgium and Germany being the only exceptions—these reforms did not herald a shift to credit control.) Without such measures the central bank of the countries concerned would have been unable to regain control over credit creation. In a number of countries the central bank was able to achieve this critical step by abandoning its rigid supports of the prices of government securities, just as the Federal Reserve System did in 1951. Such pegging had been almost universal in the first postwar years, but by now it persists in only a few of the countries with relatively developed financial markets. In several countries the pegs were reimposed for a time after they were first withdrawn, and sometimes the pegs were removed only gradually. Canada and the United Kingdom, following the opposite pattern from that in the United States, first freed long-term rates and only later the yields on Treasury bills.

Some countries, notably the United Kingdom and the Netherlands, reduced the liquidity of the banking system by the funding of short-term government debt held largely by the commercial banks. A number of other countries, notably Belgium, Italy, and France, turned to a new device—commercial bank minimum-liquidity ratios—to achieve this end. These ratios, discussed further below, locked in the commercial banks' holdings of government securities and forced them to become dependent on central bank credit for any further expansion of loans. By preventing the banks from running off their securities holdings as they matured, the minimum ratios also eased the government's debt management problems, which in a number of these countries were very grave since the commercial banks' government securities holdings had risen to unusually high levels during the war and the capital markets remained disrupted.

The postwar use of central banking techniques abroad has also had in common a gradual increase in the emphasis on some instruments and a corresponding toning down of others. Since the early 1950's a definite movement toward a primary reliance on the general quantitative instruments has been evident among the central banks of the financially more developed countries. In the financially less developed countries, the stress on the same kind of controls is also increasing, even though direct and selective credit controls continue to predominate. The techniques that have most generally fallen into disuse include such administratively cumbersome devices as central bank "screening" of individual bank loans. Commercial bank cash reserve requirements have been the one instrument to which more and more central banks have turned in their efforts to improve the tool kit at their disposal. More emphasis has also been placed on open-market operations, but little concrete progress has been made with this instrument. Open-market policy requires a relatively broad financial market in which to operate, and the development of such markets takes time, since it depends not only on the assistance of the monetary authorities but on economic growth and diversification.

DISCOUNT POLICY, OPEN-MARKET OPERATIONS, AND RESERVE REQUIREMENTS

The discount policies of foreign central banks during the postwar period have differed substantially from the discount policy of the Federal Reserve System, both in their form and in their results.

Foreign discount policies have generally been more complex in structure and, largely because of the smaller scope for open-market operations, have in many countries carried more weight in over-all monetary policies. Much of the difference in form may be traced to the fact that in only a few foreign countries do the commercial banks show the same reluctance to remain indebted to the central bank for long as they do in this country. Since the banking system can offset the central bank's attempts to limit the reserve base by borrowing from it, the absence of a tradition against borrowing at the central bank may create a major problem for credit control.[8] As a result various ways have been devised to strengthen the central bank's control over the amount of its discounts and advances. Some central banks, notably the Bank of England and the Bank of Canada, set their rates high enough to make them "penalty rates" (usually above the rate on the pivotal assets, such as Treasury bills, through which commercial banks adjust their portfolios) in order to discourage borrowers.[9] Other countries have turned to more direct means of limiting commercial bank recourse to central bank credit. At the extreme, a number of central banks (e.g., those of Austria, Belgium, Colombia, France, Germany, and Peru) have imposed specific ceilings on the amount of such commercial bank borrowing, and have at times varied the ceilings in accordance with the requirements of monetary policy.

A number of countries (e.g., Chile, Finland, and Japan) have buttressed such discount quotas limiting commercial bank borrowing at the central bank by progressive discount rates that increase with the amount borrowed. This setting of not just one but of many different discount rates is another feature that differentiates discount policy abroad and here. A few central banks have charged different rates

[8] The opposite problem has existed in a number of countries, particularly in the less developed areas, where commercial banks have operated with such ample reserves that they have found no need to borrow from the central bank, thus robbing discount policy of much of its effectiveness. It should also be noted that while commercial banks in the United Kingdom do not borrow from the Bank of England directly as a matter of tradition, they meet short-term drains on their cash reserves by reducing their call loans to the discount houses, which then borrow from the central bank. As far as the injection of central bank credit into the system is concerned, this arrangement is equivalent to an absence of tradition against borrowing.

[9] In Canada, the discount rate has since November 1951 been set each week at one-fourth of 1 per cent above the average Treasury bill tender rate. However, the Bank of Canada retained control over its discount rate, since it can exercise a decisive influence in the Treasury bill tender because of its large bill holdings.

according to the duration of the borrowing, a number have set rates varying with the type of loan and collateral, and about half of them have imposed different rates based on the purpose of the loan.

The manner in which discount rate changes have been carried out is another major difference between the discount policies of foreign central banks and of the Federal Reserve System. Discount rate changes abroad have frequently led rather than followed the market and at the same time have generally been larger than in the United States, partly because most foreign central banks have put a greater emphasis on discount policy. Discount rate increases of one percentage point, for example, have been quite common, and there have been some as large as two percentage points. The early timing and the relatively large size of discount rate changes abroad has had two effects. First, the psychological influence of discount policy has been enhanced, with the result that the impact of discount rate changes on domestic and foreign expectations has been a major aspect of discount policy in many countries. Second, the pre-World War I practice under which the lending rates of the commercial banks follow the discount rate more or less automatically has been strengthened.[10] Discount rate changes in many foreign countries have thus had a relatively rapid impact not only on market interest rates but also on rates set by the commercial banks.

Open-market operations have only rarely been the primary credit control tool abroad that they have become in the United States. The most serious barrier to the use of open-market operations has been the lack of broad and active money and capital markets, even among the more financially developed countries. Such markets enable the central bank to sell or buy government securities in appropriate amounts to exert the desired effect on commercial bank reserves, and at the same time they absorb these transactions without wide price fluctuations. A number of countries, notably Canada, Belgium, and

[10] This practice seems to have originated because commercial bank loans then mainly took the form of discounts of commercial paper and such paper served as the basis of central bank credit. This is still true in many foreign countries, with almost one-half of foreign central banks (for which such data are available) lending a greater amount in the form of discounts of commercial paper than of advances. The foremost instance of the linking of commercial bank rates to the discount rate is England, even though bank advances there have by now far outdistanced bank discounts of commercial bills. In that country this linking is actually specified in most loan agreements, so that discount rate changes are automatically reflected in the rates not only on new loans but also on those already outstanding.

the Union of South Africa, have since the war made determined efforts to establish and broaden their money markets. So far, however, Canada has been the only one of these countries to have made sufficient progress to make it possible for the central bank to operate effectively in the market.

A few foreign central banks have attempted to use open-market policy as a credit control instrument despite the existence of only thin financial markets. They have, however, done this in a manner substantially different from that used in this country, and have had more limited results. Thus, in the Union of South Africa, the central bank has mainly concerned itself with using open-market operations to influence interest rates. The bank has quoted buying and selling prices for government securities, based on a pattern of yields that it has decided upon from time to time, according to circumstances and monetary policy aims. In the fall of 1955, for example, it announced that it would raise the entire pattern of interest rates at which it operates in the market, and actually did so by amounts ranging from one-fourth to one and one-half percentage points. Similarly, in Germany, the aim of the central bank's open-market policy during 1955-57 was to offset the effect on the liquidity of the banking system of a heavy inflow of foreign exchange. Over this period the central bank succeeded in selling large amounts of short-term government securities. Nevertheless, in the absence of a true market for these securities its operations appear to have been rather passive. It has restricted itself to changing from time to time its published selling and buying rates for the securities it deals in, and the actual transactions have then depended on the decisions of the banks and the public authorities with which the central bank deals.

In some countries where the financial markets are broad enough to permit the carrying out of effective open-market operations, the central bank has been prevented from doing so because it has not had sufficient marketable securities. Thus, in Switzerland, where the commercial banks have been very liquid during most of the postwar years, the central bank's securities portfolio has been too small to allow it to engage in major open-market sales.[11]

[11] Several other countries (e.g., the Netherlands, Germany) have been able to overcome this particular problem by transforming the Treasury's book debt to the central bank (inherited from the war) into marketable securities. In addition, the central bank in Ceylon has issued its own securities when its government securities holdings were exhausted.

In other countries, effective open-market operations have been frustrated by the government's budget and debt management policies, even after the central bank withdrew its rigid support of government securities prices, or even where the central bank had never engaged in such support operations. In Belgium, for example, the central bank acknowledged that open-market sales had been thwarted by the heavy borrowing of the government and its agencies in the market to help meet large deficits. In the United Kingdom, conditions have at times been similar since the war, even though the institutional conditions for effective open-market operations have been present there and despite the fact that the central bank's continuous operations have enabled it to maintain close technical surveillance over the market. However, the Bank of England does not appear to have been able to exert a sufficiently great control over the banking system through its open-market operations during the inflationary periods of recent years in the face of the Treasury's policy of financing its large cash deficits through substantial issues of Treasury bills placed in great part with the banking system.

Canada has been the only foreign country where open-market operations have been the primary instrument of monetary policy since the war. The Bank of Canada's operations, however, have differed from those of the Federal Reserve System in that it has operated in the whole range of the government securities market. The Canadian central bank, just as the Federal Reserve System, has operated in the market in order to minimize the daily or other temporary swings in market liquidity and in order to keep bank reserves at the level appropriate from the point of view of credit control. Its operations, however, have also aimed at influencing the tone of the securities market. The bank has endeavored to help make a market for all government securities and has been a substantial buyer and seller. Nevertheless, as the bank has explained, while it has acted as a stabilizing influence in the market, it has not operated against the market to prevent long-run tendencies based on real changes in supply and demand.

Compared to open-market operations, reserve requirement changes are considered a much blunter instrument for influencing the availability of funds for bank loans and investments. But because the absence of broad financial markets so frequently limits the scope for an effective open-market policy, commercial cash reserve requirements have been established in a great many countries in recent years and changes in minimum ratios have increasingly come to be used as a major credit control tool. Some central banks abroad, notably in Canada and in Germany, it is true, have regarded the varying of reserve requirements in a similar manner as has the Federal Reserve System: as an instrument appropriate mainly for major adjustments in the volume of available bank reserves, made in response to fundamental changes either in the reserve position of the banking system or or in monetary policy. Other central banks, however, have used changes in reserve requirements as a substitute for open-market operations.

The New Zealand practice has been the outstanding instance of such an application of variable reserve requirements. (The central bank in that country has not operated in the government securities market, which is rather thin.) Since 1954, the New Zealand central bank has varied the reserve requirements frequently in such a manner as to produce a pressure on bank reserves needed to keep bank credit at a level desired from the point of view of monetary policy. In mid-1956 it refined its policy by keeping the commercial banks informed of the level of bank loans it regards as appropriate each month, and by adjusting the reserve ratios in such a way as to make the banks borrow from it an amount equal to the amount by which actual bank loans exceed this target level. At that time the New Zealand discount rate (set at 7 per cent in October 1955) exceeded by two percentage points the average rate that the commercial banks were permitted to charge on their loans, which are by far their most important asset since they hold only minor amounts of securities. The banks thus found it to their immediate financial advantage to bring down their loans as required and to maintain them at the prescribed level.

The greater emphasis on changes in reserve requirements abroad has resulted in the development of special techniques to reduce their possible sharp and uneven impact on individual banks. Many of the existing arrangements provide for advance notice of changes in requirements and permit changes to be made only gradually. A number of countries, particularly in Latin America, have in addition turned to the imposition of supplementary reserve requirements against *increases* in deposits after a specified date. These requirements have minimized the problem arising out of an uneven distribution of excess reserves among banks. This device has been particularly useful during periods of sudden but temporary increases in bank reserves, and supplementary requirements as high as 100 per cent have at times been imposed to prevent a secondary deposit expansion on the basis of such reserve additions. However, supplementary requirements of this kind penalize those banks whose deposits are growing most rapidly, and therefore they have rarely been imposed for more than brief periods.

Instead of using cash reserve requirements (and sometimes in addition to them), a number of foreign countries have adopted securities reserve requirements or a variant thereof, often called minimum liquidity ratios. Under these requirements (which are akin to the supplementary securities reserve requirements discussed in the United States in the early postwar years), commercial banks must maintain minimum reserves in the form of prescribed liquid assets such as cash and government securities in specified proportions of their deposits. These requirements are somewhat similar to cash reserve requirements in that they both are an instrument intended to control bank deposits through the regulation of one kind or group of bank assets. There is, however, a crucial difference between the two: under a policy of cash reserve requirements, the volume of the asset in question—bank cash —is within the control of the central bank; but under the policy of required liquidity ratios, the volume of eligible liquid assets—of which government securities are generally the most important one[12] —is not.

The liquidity ratios have been used in two main ways. As a primary anti-inflation instrument (already noted), they have been used to lock in the commercial banks' holdings of all types of government securities, in order to force the banks to become dependent on central bank credit for any further expansion of bank loans. As a supplementary instrument, liquidity ratios have been intended to speed the impact of other monetary restraint policies by preventing the banks from reducing their short-term government securities holdings beyond a certain point.[13] The liquidity ratios of this second kind have been established in only a few countries and only recently (e.g.,

[12] This is so, even though the liquidity ratios are usually applied to the sum of cash plus government securities (and other liquid assets).

[13] It must also be noted that a minimum liquidity ratio has been observed by the clearing banks in England. The observance of this ratio should enable the authorities to regulate the volume of bank deposits by regulating the volume of the banks' liquid assets, since the former would be a multiple of the latter. In practice, however, this has generally not been the experience during the inflationary periods since the war, mainly because the Treasury has not been in a position to limit the banks' holdings of liquid assets, primarily Treasury bills.

in Canada in mid-1956), so that their effectiveness has not as yet been tested. The experience with the first type of ratios, however, has been extensive.

These ratios were first established soon after the war in Belgium, Italy, and France and in the early 1950's in several other countries (e.g., the Netherlands, Sweden). They generally accomplished their purpose and halted the inflationary expansion of credit which was under way when they were established. During subsequent boom periods, however, the liquidity ratios more often than not were worse than useless, since they not only failed to prevent an excessive growth of bank loans to private borrowers but also served as a vehicle to facilitate the financing of government deficits.

DIRECT AND SELECTIVE CREDIT CONTROLS

Foreign central banks have relied on a great variety of direct and selective credit controls during the postwar period. These controls are designed to affect specific economic activities or financing operations directly, unlike the general quantitative instruments, just discussed, which exert their influence on the whole economy in a general manner.

The direct credit controls employed abroad have been both informal and statutory, and have imposed limitations upon the lendings of individual commercial banks as well as of the entire banking system. These controls have included such devices as minimum ratios of capital to total assets, absolute ceilings on the aggregate volume of bank assets, limits on the rate of increase of bank loans, and the official setting of bank interest rates. Generally, however, the reliance on direct credit controls has gradually diminished, except for the use of central bank directives to the commercial banks. The form of these directives has varied widely, from informal expressions of concern over certain credit developments to the laying down of specific targets for credit trends. In essence, they have put the burden of enforcing central bank policy on the commercial banks, making them a direct rather than an indirect agent of the central bank. The application of directives has been simplified by the structure of foreign banking systems, which, as already noted generally consist of a small number of banks with widespread branch networks. Such a system lends itself more readily to this type of control than a unit banking system consisting of a great many independent banks. Central bank directives of one kind or another have been a part of the credit policies of all central banks abroad. During the first postwar years they were often the only credit control instrument. In recent years, in contrast, they have been relied upon primarily in conjunction with general quantitative measures.

The selective credit controls used by foreign central banks during the postwar period have been even more varied than direct controls. Besides a number of specifically selective instruments, even the general credit controls—with the exception of open-market operations—have been applied in a selective manner. Selective credit controls abroad have also differed from those in this country in that they have aimed not only at curbing credit extensions in directions deemed undesirable but also at stimulating lending to sectors regarded as essential.

The selective application of discount policy has been particularly widespread abroad, and has been somewhat similar to the practices which were followed in this country by the Federal Reserve System over the first two decades of its operations. Discount policy has been used both to encourage and discourage bank lending for particular purposes by easing or restricting the access to the central bank's discount window according to the type of paper presented for rediscount or as collateral for borrowing. Thus, aside from a basic discount rate, numerous central banks—mainly in Asia and Latin America— have had a variety of other rates depending on the purpose of the original loan. A further degree of selectivity has been applied through different elegibility requirements intended to promote or to curb various types of credit; some central banks have at times even refused to rediscount at all some types of paper, such as import bills or consumer installment paper. In addition some central banks have favored the preferred types of credit by rediscounting them without limitation outside of the commercial banks' discount ceilings.

Commercial bank reserve requirements have also been used selectively in a number of countries. Some countries (e.g., Mexico) have included among reserve-eligible assets bank loans for preferred purposes, while others (e.g., Israel) have granted exemptions from the requirements to the extent that banks had made such loans. Central bank directives and formal bank-portfolio ceilings have been the other major quantitative instruments applied as selective controls, the former more generally in more financially advanced countries, the latter among the less developed ones.

Of the three specifically selective credit controls that have existed at one time or another in the United States, only regulations over consumer credit terms have been used abroad. The Regulation W type of controls have in recent years been introduced in about a dozen foreign countries, primarily in Western Europe and the British Commonwealth, where consumer credit had increased markedly. Other countries, however, where the postwar expansion of such credit had been equally rapid, have not resorted to this type of control, either because of the absence of any legal authority or because the authorities felt that general quantitative measures were adequate. No foreign country has relied on formal changes in margin requirements on stock market credit and in terms of real estate credit as part of its monetary policy.

In addition, there have been two major kinds of selective credit controls abroad. Some countries have required that all bank loans above a certain amount be first approved by the authorities. Such detailed screening of individual bank loans, which had been in force in several Western European countries in the early postwar years, now mainly exists in Latin America. A number of European as well Asian and Latin American countries have introduced or have continued to use import-predeposit requirements. These requirements, under which importers must deposit with the central bank a part of the value of the import when they apply for an import license, have been introduced to curb the expansion of import credit in order to help reduce balance-of-payments deficits.[14]

GENERAL QUANTITATIVE VERSUS DIRECT AND SELECTIVE CREDIT CONTROLS

Today, most foreign countries relying on monetary policy resort to a mixture of general quantitative and of direct and selective credit controls. Nevertheless, as already noted, there has been a definite trend in recent years away from the latter to the former. Direct and selective controls used alone have generally proved a failure. In a thoroughly regimented economy they would undoubtedly have their place, but in a primarily free-market economy they are bound to

[14] Import-predeposit requirements also tend to have a restraining effect on bank credit in general, since the resulting accumulation of funds at the central bank brings about a pressure on bank reserves.

create more problems than they cure, unless the money supply and all the credit markets are regulated as well.

While there seems to be more general agreement on this point than there used to be in the immediate postwar years, the appropriate place of direct and selective credit controls within a framework of general quantitative measures is far from settled. The mixture clearly will vary from country to country and from time to time, depending on the institutional setting, the degree of economic development, and the urgency and type of problems to be solved. On the basis of the foreign experience it seems clear to the writer that direct and selective controls are best kept to the minimum possible, because both of these kinds of controls have presented such serious administrative problems, and have tended to develop so many loopholes that after a time even the most effective among them have lost much of their usefulness.

Selective controls of the restrictive kind have best accomplished their purpose the closer they impinged on the ultimate spender, since leakages were then least likely to occur. That is, regulating the minimum down payments and maximum maturities of installment credit has tended to be more effective than restricting the rediscounting of installment paper at the central bank. Even then it has not been easy to control the end use of credit. A more important limitation has been the ability of borrowers to obtain larger loans for the "preferred" purposes and to employ their own funds thus freed on nonessential expenditures that are supposedly being restricted. Moreover, some selective policies, such as the screening of bank loans, have frequently been ineffective in the face of the seemingly irrefutable justification that can always be discovered for each loan, even when the resulting aggregate demand will clearly be in excess of the country's physical capabilities.

The administrative problems connected with selective controls have also been formidable. For instance, it has usually been necessary for both the central bank and the commercial banks to distinguish arbitrarily in precise operational terms that can be followed consistently over a considerable period, between essential and nonessential sectors of the economy, between productive and nonproductive investment, and between speculative and nonspeculative borrowing. Furthermore, the authorities have had continuously to concern themselves with frequent and, at times, serious inequities, with possible discrimination as between banks, and with the division of responsibility between the central bank and the commercial banks over the approval of all loan applications.

The problems of administration and enforcement have been large even in credit areas that can be relatively easily delineated, such as the financing of installment buying, of foreign trade, or of home building. Thus, in several countries new consumer credit regulations have periodically had to be issued as more and more loopholes were discovered and new ways found of getting around the existing controls. The problem of policing the official credit terms has likewise not been easy, especially because feelings of being discriminated against have aroused opposition in the regulated areas.

The second kind of selective controls—those designed to benefit a particular type of activity—has encountered additional problems of its own. Such controls have not always been able to create the demand for the type of credit that they have been intended to encourage, but could only satisfy it in preference to other types. Often such a policy has involved an injection of central bank credit which was intended to support this favored credit extension, but in fact also made possible loans for other purposes. The favored loans have frequently expanded so rapidly that either other loans have had to be severely restricted or inflation has developed, or else funds obtained for "preferred" activities have been used to finance other projects. Moreover, once one type of credit or activity has been exempted from monetary restraint or has otherwise been favored, the pressure of public opinion has at times forced other types to be added to the favored list. The least problematical method of channeling credit into preferred directions appears to have been through specialized official financial institutions established to provide credit to the critical areas (and often also technical assistance), since then the leakages have best been controlled.

Of the various direct credit controls, flexible central bank directives have had the best results. But, as with selective controls, to be effective they have had to be supported by general restraint. Moreover, as a rule, they have been maintained only as a temporary expedient, since their effectiveness has tended to wear off with the passage of time.

General quantitative measures, on the other hand, have not encountered these particular problems. The postwar experience abroad has shown that open-market policy can be a most effective instrument for influencing the money supply and credit conditions in general, provided the institutional setting is appropriate and debt management is not given priority over monetary control. The foreign experience also stresses the invaluable importance of cash reserve requirements, even though they have been a blunter tool than open-market operations. First, such requirements have provided a fulcrum on which open-market operations or other measures changing the volume of bank reserves obtained the necessary leverage. And even in the absence of such measures, unchanged reserved requirements have directly transmitted the impact of bank reserve drains, due to influences such as gold and foreign exchange losses on commercial bank assets. Second, actual variations of reserve ratios have been an effective instrument for regulating the volumes of bank deposits.

Discount policy, on the other hand, has only rarely since the war been used to influence bank credit availability directly, and then it has been able to accomplish this through changes in discount quotas rather than changes in discount rates. Nevertheless, it has much to its credit. On the defensive side, discount policy has been used to prevent increases in borrowing at the central bank from offsetting effects of other monetary restraint measures, without an abandonment by the central bank of its duty to act as a lender of last resort. The discount rate has also been a powerful psychological instrument to influence expectations of banks and other lenders and borrowers wherever it has been used in a vigorous, consistent, and timely fashion. When so used, it has tended to bring about equilibrating flows of short-term capital across national boundaries, both through its direct effect and through changing expectations. Finally, the discount rate has had a direct and immediate impact on commercial bank and short-term market interest rates, and a somewhat smaller and slower one on long-term rates.

CONCLUSION

Evaluating the effects of monetary policies is not an easy task. Disentangling the influence of credit controls in each country from that of other economic policies and from other forces is often not possible. The evaluation is likewise made difficult by the absence of any simple criterion of success. Monetary policy abroad must be judged in terms of its contribution to both internal stability and balanced expansion and to external equilibrium—goals which at times may be in conflict. For these reasons and because the subject of monetary policy itself has at times in recent years evoked more heat than light, the judgments of the results of monetary policies abroad have covered a wide range, from complete failure to absolute success.

While space does not permit a full buttressing of the arguments, it is the opinion of the writer that monetary management has been able to contribute importantly to balanced economic growth of many foreign countries, even though its limitations are readily recognized in some underdeveloped countries.

This appears to have been so despite the greater and more numerous obstacles encountered by foreign central banks in comparison with the experience of the Federal Reserve System. An examination of the statistical record shows that in most financially advanced countries during periods of general monetary restraint—and the emphasis has to be on restraint because since 1946 there have as a rule been no serious recessions abroad—most economic series moved in the direction they were intended to do. Interest rates rose, the availability of bank credit came to be restricted, mortgage and consumer installment loans of specialized lenders often declined, money supply trends became less buoyant, and the increase in the velocity of money, which frequently served to temper the effects of monetary restraint, slowed down. At the same time, inflationary strains eased during the later periods of monetary restraint, as investment booms tapered off, inventory accumulation ceased, consumer buying moderated, and excessive imports declined.

These changes rarely came as promptly as might have been desired, it is true, and monetary policy can hardly be claimed to have been responsible by itself. Often other economic policies were at work as well, or the economic changes were in part due to the normal working out of economic forces. But a comparison of periods when general quantitative controls were relied upon with similar periods when such controls were absent points up the role of monetary policy. During each of the three main waves of inflationary pressure from 1946 to 1957 (the late 1940's, the early 1950's, and 1955-57), the countries that relied heavily on monetary restraint fared better than countries that did not. This is true as regards both internal stability and external equilibrium. Similar contrast show up for individual countries that ignored monetary policy in one period and emphasized it in another. All this, of course, does not by itself prove that monetary policy has worked, or that it has earned most of the credit, but it does suggest that the contribution of monetary policy has not been negligible.

The postwar experience, however, likewise shows that central banking cannot carry the burden of needed economic readjustments alone and that credit control measures may well in the long run do more damage than good if they are applied only halfheartedly, since their lack of success under such circumstances is bound to discredit monetary policy. Foreign central bankers have been the first to stress this. The monetary restraint policies of various foreign countries have shown widely divergent results. While some appear to have accomplished the aims of the monetary authorities concerned, others have contributed relatively little to moderating inflationary pressures. The alleged failures of central banking, however, do not seem to have been failures of central banking as such. They have generally resulted from the manner in which monetary measures were applied. Often public opinion delayed the resort to credit restraint or forced the authorities to apply it without sufficient vigor. Moreover, in some countries, monetary policy was doomed to failure from the beginning since it operated in an insufficient institutional framework or received no, or limited, support from budgetary, debt management, and other economic policies, or even had to combat their unfavorable repercussions.

SUGGESTED READINGS

BANK FOR INTERNATIONAL SETTLEMENTS, Annual Reports, Basle.

BECKHART, BENJAMIN H., ed., *Banking Systems,* New York, Columbia University Press, 1954.

BLOOMFIELD, ARTHUR I., "Monetary Policy in Underdeveloped Countries," in *Public Policy, A Year Book of the Graduate School of Public Administration of Harvard University,* Cambridge, Mass., Graduate School of Public Administration, 1956, Vol. VII, pp. 232–74.

CRICK, W. F., *The Practice of Monetary Policy: An International Survey,* London, Institute of Bankers, 1956.

FOUSEK, PETER G., *Foreign Central Banking: The Instruments of Monetary Policy,* New York, Federal Reserve Bank of New York, 1957.

GREGORY, SIR THEODORE, *The Present Position of Central Banks* (The Stamp Memorial Lecture, delivered before the University of London on October 31, 1955), London, University of London, The Athlone Press, 1955.

INTERNATIONAL BANKING SUMMER SCHOOL, GARMISCH-PARTENKIRCHEN, 1957, *Relations Between the Central Banks and Commercial Banks*

(Lectures delivered at the tenth International Banking Summer School), Frankfort on Main, Fritz Knapp Verlag, 1957.

KOCK, M. H. DE, *Central Banking,* 3rd ed., London, Staples Press Limited, 1954.

SAYERS, RICHARD S., *Banking in the British Commonwealth,* Oxford, Clarendon Press, 1952.

————, *Central Banking after Bagehot,* Oxford, Clarendon Press, 1957.

SEN, S. N., *Central Banking in Undeveloped Money Markets,* Calcutta, Bookland, Ltd., 1952.

INDEX